Contested Countryside

Gorsebrook Studies in the Political Economy of the Atlantic Region

General Editors: Ian McKay and L. Anders Sandberg

1. Gary Burrill and Ian McKay, eds., *People, Resources and Power: Critical Perspectives on Underdevelopment and Primary Industries in the Atlantic Region* (1987).

2. Michael Earle, ed., *Workers and the State in Twentieth Century Nova Scotia* (1989).

3. L. Anders Sandberg, ed., *Trouble in the Woods: Forest Policy and Social Conflict in Nova Scotia and New Brunswick* (1992).

4. Daniel Samson, ed., *Contested Countryside: Rural Workers and Modern Society in Atlantic Canada, 1800-1950* (1994).

The Gorsebrook Research Institute for Atlantic Canada Studies was formed in 1982 to encourage and support interdisciplinary research concerned with a variety of socio-economic, political, environmental and policy issues specific to Canada's Atlantic Region. Closely allied to the Atlantic Canada Studies Programme at Saint Mary's University, Halifax, the Gorsebrook Research Institute encourages interdisciplinary cooperation across the Atlantic Region.

Contested Countryside:
Rural Workers and Modern Society
in Atlantic Canada, 1800-1950

Edited by
Daniel Samson

Published for the Gorsebrook Research Institute for
Atlantic Canada Studies
by
Acadiensis Press,
Fredericton, New Brunswick
1994

Canadian Cataloguing in Publication Data

Main entry under title:

Contested Countryside

(Gorsebrook studies in the political economy of the Atlantic region ; 4)
Co-published by: Gorsebrook Research Institute.
Includes bibliographic references.
ISBN 0-919107-49-0

1. Farmers — Atlantic Provinces — Economic conditions — History.
2. Rural industries — Atlantic Provinces — History.
3. Atlantic Provinces — Rural conditions.
I. Samson, Danny, 1960- II. Gorsebrook Research Institute for Atlantic
Canada Studies. III. Series.

HD1476.C32A75 1994 305.5'55'09715 C94-950008-9

Printed in the Maritimes by union labour

Cover design: Cardinal Communications
Cartographer: Carol Randall
Copy Editor: Charles Stuart
Production: Beckey Daniel, Ruth Vallillee

The paper used in this publication meets the minimum requirements of the
American National Standard for Information Sciences — Permanence of
Paper for Printed Library Materials, ANSI Z39,48-1984.

Contested Countryside:
Rural Workers and Modern Society in Atlantic Canada, 1800-1950

Edited by Daniel Samson

Table of Contents

ACKNOWLEDGEMENTS

This collection was conceived as a collective project, and the outcome has remained true to a spirit of mutual enthusiasm and critique. Many people read different versions of particular manuscripts, and these are acknowledged in each paper. Many others made contributions to the whole work which we wish to acknowledge here. This project was conceived initially over a coffee with Ian McKay; he has remained supportive of it throughout the entire process, reading each manuscript in its first and final drafts, and offering much-needed advice when it was needed. Anders Sandberg also gave this project much support; he oversaw the final version of the text and arranged to have the maps made. We are also grateful for the support of the Department of Geography at York University for the maps and the Department of History at Queen's University for computer printing and graphics services. Jim Ellis of York University read part of the manuscript and made helpful comments. In October 1990, six rather presumptuous graduate students invited a number of historians to discuss our work. T.W. Acheson, Michael Cross, Jacques Ferland, Steven Hahn, Raymond Léger, Rosemary Ommer, Bryan Palmer, Jane Parpart, Jonathan Prude and Anders Sandberg attended our workshop and gave generously of their time and energy. We are not so presumptuous as to think that we have lived up to their very high standards, but we benefited greatly by their criticisms and encouragements. St. Mary's University and the Gorsebrook Research Institute hosted the workshop and provided financial and logistical support. Special thanks go out to Jackie Logan and Laurie Alexander at the Gorsebrook for doing most of the organizational work for our gathering. The workshop also was generously supported by a grant from the Social Sciences and Humanities Research Council. Finally, David Frank, the editor at Acadiensis Press, oversaw this project, half of it from their very early beginnings as thesis supervisor, with great patience and much needed encouragement.

Introduction:
Situating the Rural
in Atlantic Canada

Daniel Samson

History looks different from the countryside. Given that until the inter-war period most Atlantic Canadians were classified in the census as living in "rural" communities, it is surprising that historians have paid so little attention to the rural record in their interpretations of the region. On the other hand, many of our best-known poems and novels draw heavily on rural life. From the melancholic romanticism of "Evangeline" and *Anne of Green Gables*, to the hard-edged realism of Alden Nowlan and David Adams Richards, to the fantasy-land "historical reconstruction" at the Upper Clements theme park in Nova Scotia (five parts Disneyland to one part rural outport), most of the region's cultural producers — be they novelists, poets or bureaucrats — have looked to the countryside for something essential within Atlantic Canadians.[1] The essays in this volume aim to reassess aspects of rural reality in our past. Our principal objective is to examine Atlantic Canadian history from the point of view of those who lived rural lives or who came from and continued to live outside the urban industrial experience that has dominated the writing of our social history.

Rural life has not been, and is not now, only farming or agriculture. Few 19th-century chroniclers of rural society could write without pausing to criticize the farmer who spent part of *his* year — and the term was invariably gender specific — cutting lumber or digging coal to the detriment of the farm. Similarly, academic historians have had difficulties finding a meaning for the rural. Farmers, for these historians, were those who produced crops for the market. Part of the problem social historians have had with older emphases in agricultural history is their failure to go beyond measures of agricultural performance,

---

1   See, among many others, David Adams Richards, *The Coming of Winter* (Toronto, 1973); M.T. Dohaney, *The Corrigan Women* (Charlottetown, 1988); George Elliott Clarke, *Whylah Falls* (Winslow, B.C., 1990); and Alistair MacLeod, *The Lost Salt Gift of Blood* (Toronto, 1976). See also Gwendolyn Davies, *Studies in Maritime Literary History, 1760-1930* (Fredericton, 1991), especially pp. 9-22, 141-99; and the essay by Erik Kristiansen in this volume. In the realm of miscellaneous cultural producers see Ian McKay, "Among the Fisherfolk: J.F.B. Livesay and the Invention of Peggy's Cove", *Journal of Canadian Studies*, 23, 1-2 (Spring-Summer 1988), pp. 23-45. Heartfelt thanks to Alison Forrest, Jim Kenny, Ian McKay and the contributors to this volume for criticisms and support.

the growth of markets and technological change. These are very important issues — ones with which rural social historians must grapple — but they need to be placed in context. Vernon Fowke, an economic historian writing in the 1940s, went well beyond the older emphases in describing the myth of the self-sufficient farmer. Pointing out that the farm sector was divided by production capacities and marketing activities, Fowke outlined the role of class divisions in rural society.[2] But few historians followed the path he set, and much "rural" history continues to be the economic history of farming.

Approaches to Rural History

In English-Canadian historiography in particular, most rural studies have come from economic historians whose treatment of agriculture is limited to its role as a staple-exporting sector. H.A. Innis, perhaps Canada's most influential historian and an important proponent of the staples thesis, described Canada as a nation formed by an expanding frontier of primary staples exploitation (principally the fur trade and the cod fishery) which was followed by the development of secondary staples such as timber, mining and agriculture.[3] Innis wrote little on agriculture, but his influence established the dominant framework for Canadian economic history, including the idea that the development of the wheat staple was the key underpinning for industrialization in Ontario.[4] Within

---

2   V.C. Fowke, "The Myth of the Self-Sufficient Canadian Pioneer", *Transactions of the Royal Society of Canada Series III*, LIV (1962), pp. 28-37; and "An Introduction to Canadian Agricultural History", *Agricultural History*, 16, 2 (1942), pp. 79-90; see also his *Canadian Agricultural Policy: The Historical Pattern* (Toronto, 1946).

3   H.A. Innis, *The Fur Trade in Canada: An Introduction to Canadian Economic History* (New Haven, 1930); *The Cod Fisheries: The Study of an International Economy* (Toronto, 1935); A.R.M. Lower and H.A. Innis, *Settlement and the Forest and Mining Frontiers* (Toronto, 1936); and Robert L. Jones, *History of Agriculture in Ontario, 1613-1880* (Toronto, 1946). On Innis's influence see Carl Berger, *The Writing of Canadian History* (Toronto, 1986), pp. 85-111.

4   See John McCallum, *Unequal Beginnings: Agriculture and Economic Development in Ontario until 1870* (Toronto, 1980); Kenneth Norrie and Douglas Owram, *A History of the Canadian Economy* (Toronto, 1991); Anthony Winson, "The Uneven Development of Canadian Agriculture: Farming in the Maritimes and Ontario", *Canadian Journal of Sociology*, 10, 4 (1985), pp. 411-38; and S.A. Saunders, *The Economic History of the Maritime Provinces* (Fredericton, 1984 [1939]). Other recent works have emphasized the importance of internal markets. See Douglas McCalla, "The Internal Economy of Upper Canada: New Evidence on Agricultural Marketing Before 1850", *Agricultural History*, 59, 3 (1985), pp. 397-416; and Marvin McInnis, "Marketable Surpluses in Ontario Farming, 1860", *Social Science History*, 8, 4 (1984), pp. 395-424. Stephen J. Hornsby's recent study also operates within the broader staples framework. See

that framework, there was little examination of the world-views of Upper or Lower Canadian farmers and little questioning of their goals, aspirations or differences. Like their American counterparts, they were presumed to be essentially conservative, market-oriented, individualistic and independent, all fitting subjects of a nascent liberal democracy.[5] Yet, unlike their American counterparts, Canadian historians imagined a countryside with a much less consequential role in the grand narrative of nation-building. While often presuming liberal democracy to be a natural form of government for a people familiar with the ideals of liberty and parliamentary democracy, and at times flirting with the frontier thesis,[6] they never endowed the Canadian countryside with the crucial role of upholding the Jeffersonian ideal of the propertied small producer as the foundation of the republic.[7] Canadian historians occupied themselves instead

---

his *Nineteenth-Century Cape Breton: A Historical Geography* (Kingston and Montreal, 1992). On wider North American development within a staples framework see John J. McCusker and Russell R. Menard, *The Economy of British America, 1607-1789* (Chapel Hill, 1985).

5   Gerald Craig, *Upper Canada: The Formative Years, 1784-1841* (Toronto, 1963); and J.M.S. Careless, *The Union of the Canadas: The Growth of Canadian Institutions, 1841-1857* (Toronto, 1967). A more complex picture emerges in a recent work by Douglas McCalla who argues that Upper-Canadian "farmers were directly involved in the marketplace and responsive to its demands and signals", but he sees the "farm household as essentially a pre-capitalist social unit seeking autonomy". See his *Planting the Province: The Economic History of Upper Canada* (Toronto, 1993), p. 9. See also Jane Errington, *The Lion, the Eagle, and Upper Canada: A Developing Colonial Ideology* (Kingston and Montreal, 1987). An important social historical interpretation which stresses the material and ideological transitions occurring within the early 19th century can be found in Bryan D. Palmer, *Working-Class Experience: Rethinking the History of Canadian Labour, 1800-1991* (Toronto, 1992), pp. 35-80. See also Bryan D. Palmer, "Social Formation and Class Formation in North America, 1800-1900", in David Levine, ed., *Proletarianization and Family History* (Orlando, Fla., 1984); and Allan Greer and Ian Radforth, eds. *Colonial Leviathan: State Formation in Nineteenth Century Canada* (Toronto, 1992).

6   Michael S. Cross, ed., *The Frontier Thesis and the Canadas: The Debate on the Impact of the Canadian Environment* (Toronto, 1970); E.R. Forbes, "In Search of a Post-Confederation Maritime Historiography, 1900-1967", *Acadiensis*, VIII, 1 (Autumn 1978), pp. 3-21; David J. Bercuson, "Labour Radicalism and the Western Industrial Frontier: 1897-1919", *Canadian Historical Review*, LVIII (1977), pp. 154-75.

7   Louis Hartz, *The Liberal Tradition in America* (New York, 1955); Joyce Appleby, "Commercial Farming and the 'Agrarian Myth' in the Early Republic", *Journal of American History*, LXVIII (1982), pp. 833-49; and William N. Parker, *Europe, America, and the Wider World: Essays on the Economic History of Western Capitalism*, vol. 2, *America and the Wider World* (Cambridge, 1991),

with the evolution of responsible government, an emphasis which relegated most rural people to the sidelines and identified agriculture as another column in the table of staple exports. Where the United States created a mythological basis for its polity in the form of the yeoman and the pioneer continually advancing the frontier, Canadian historians, lacking a revolution but with a strong sense of institutional continuity with Great Britain, put forth the Mounties.[8]

Perhaps because of the symbolic marginality of the rural in our nation-building narratives, rural history remains a small subfield in Canada. A brief browse through the tables of contents of *Canadian Papers in Rural History* indicates something of the eclecticism of rural history in Canada. The studies range from class analyses of agricultural marketing to econometric studies and to broad-ranging analyses of agriculture and modernity. While the collections provide a much-needed forum to bring together rural research, the field has yet to produce a new series of important issues by responding to its editor's recognition that rural people "had more to do with shaping the country in its formative years than did their political superiors".[9] This eclecticism, however, also reflects the tremendous number of issues which have been barely scratched in this country. Over the past 20 years, a number of important economic and social histories have appeared, nudging national historiography in some new directions. Exploring such varied issues as land policy and class formation, the role of women and the household, and the various strands of early Canadian politics, migration, ethnicity, demography and local political networks,[10] Canadian rural histories have

pp. 161-80. See also Allan Kulikoff, "The Transition to Capitalism in Rural America", *William and Mary Quarterly*, XLVI (January 1989), pp.141-2; Steven Hahn and Jonathan Prude, "Introduction", in Hahn and Prude, eds., *The Countryside in the Age of Capitalist Transformation: Essays in the Social History of Rural America* (Chapel Hill, 1985), pp. 3-7.

8   See Keith Walden, "The Great March of the Mounted Police in Popular Literature, 1873-1973", *Communications historiques/Historical Papers* (1980), pp. 33-56.

9   See Donald H. Akenson, "Foreword", *Canadian Papers in Rural History*, I (1978), p. 9. Recent works by economic historians such as Kris Inwood and Marvin McInnis apply econometric approaches and take their analyses well beyond the immediate implications. See Janine Roelens and Kris Inwood, "'Labouring at the Loom': A Case Study of Rural Manufacturing in Leeds County, Ontario, 1870", *Canadian Papers in Rural History*, VII (1990), pp. 215-36; Marvin McInnis, "Women, Work and Childbearing: Ontario in the Second Half of the Nineteenth Century", *Histoire sociale/Social History*, XXIV, 48 (1991), pp. 237-62. Several of McInnis' earlier pieces have been brought together in *Canadian Papers in Rural History*, VIII (1992).

10   Among the more important works are Marjorie Griffin Cohen, *Women's Work, Markets, and Economic Development in Nineteenth-Century Ontario* (Toronto, 1988); Donald H. Akenson, *The Irish in Ontario: A Study in Rural History*

exposed some older shibboleths and added more depth to the rural past, but the field has not yet focused on a clear set of historical issues.

An important exception to that lack of focus is the historiography of Quebec, which offers many instructive opportunities for comparisons with the rural history of Atlantic Canada. Rural society has figured prominently in discussions of national development in Quebec. In few national historiographies could a debate over the importance (or even the existence) of a fall in wheat production assume so much importance.[11] Quebec historians, their work almost invariably tied to the national question, have sought to understand their place in early Canada as a cultural and political minority — a nation within — where agriculture was the principal occupation of most of its peoples, and where conservative nationalists saw the essential features of Québécois culture in place. Many of the contours of Quebec historiography are fitted along economic, spatial and ethnic lines — mercantile and agricultural economies, town and the country, English and French — and, unlike English-Canadian historiography, more attention is focused on the period before Confederation.[12] Most works have sought to explain French-Canadian social development by examining the distinctive pre-Conquest social formation of seigneurial agriculture and its later development under English rule. Were the *habitants* docile peasants, lacking ingenuity and slavishly loyal to priest and seigneur, or were they a "racially" subjugated

(Kingston and Montreal, 1985); Chad Gaffield, *Language, Schooling and Cultural Conflict: The Origins of the French-Language Controversy in Canada* (Kingston and Montreal, 1989); David Gagan, *Hopeful Travellers: Families, Land and Social Change in Mid-Victorian Peel County, Canada West* (Toronto, 1980); Leo Johnson, "Land Policy, Population Growth and Social Structure in the Home District, 1793-1851", *Ontario History*, 48 (1971), pp. 41-60; and Gary Teeple, "Land, Labour, and Capital in Pre-Confederation Canada", in Gary Teeple, ed. *Capitalism and the National Question in Canada* (Toronto, 1981).

11 Fernand Ouellet, *Lower Canada, 1791-1840: Social Change and Nationalism* (Toronto, 1980); Maurice Séguin, *La nation 'canadienne' et l'agriculture* (Trois-Rivières, 1970); Gilles Paquet and Jean-Pierre Wallot, "Crise agricole et tensions socio-ethniques dans les Bas-Canada, 1802-1812: éléments pour une réinterprétation", *Revue d'histoire de l'Amérique-Française*, 26 (1972), pp. 185-238; Serge Courville, "La crise agricole du Bas-Canada, éléments d'une réflexion géographique", *Cahiers de Géographie Québécois*, 62 (1980), pp. 193-224 (continued in 63 (1980), pp. 385-428). For a useful, although now somewhat dated, review of the main issues see T.J.A. LeGoff, "The Agricultural Crisis in Lower Canada, 1802-1812", *Canadian Historical Review*, LV (1974), pp. 1-31.

12 See, however, Jean Hamelin and Yves Roby, *Histoire économique du Québec, 1851-1896* (Montreal, 1971). Even scholars who attempted to situate Quebec within broader North American trends or the universal categories of Marxist class analysis, often reverted to an ethnic-class model. See, for example, Denis Monière, *Le développement des idéologies au Québec* (Montreal, 1977).

people, North America's equivalent of downtrodden peoples in Ireland or South Africa? Was the issue cultural, or was it about colonialism? There is, of course, no single answer to the issue. Most important for our concerns is what we might learn from Quebec historians' realization of the complexity of these issues and their integration of the multiple levels of analysis — embracing culture, ideology, production, exchange and relations of power in an ethnically mixed colonial context. Their work suggests that any useful exploration must bring together the different strands of land use, household strategies for production and reproduction, demography and the interplay of politics and economics at various levels.

In Quebec, as in Atlantic Canada, historical analysis has often been directed by the question of explaining relative underdevelopment. From the 1940s to the 1960s, analyses of Quebec were heavily influenced by the "Chicago school" of social scientists.[13] Positing a "normal" process of social development — where societies proceeded through a series of stages before emerging as modern and industrial — Quebec's countryside provided a location where modernization was underway but where progress faced social and cultural obstacles. While some areas of the province were heavily industrialized, much of it, apparently, remained frozen in a rural, pre-industrial past.[14] Situating the traditional in the countryside and outside the modern town, it was easy to by-pass the complexities of rural life and focus on its "essential" features: typically these were the cultural obstacles to the emergence of capitalist modernity.[15] This emphasis

---

13   See E.C. Hughes, *French Canada in Transition* (Chicago, 1943); "Industry and the Rural System in Quebec", *Canadian Journal of Economic and Political Science*, 4, 3 (1938), pp. 341-9; Horace Miner, "The French Canadian Family Cycle", *American Sociological Review*, 3, 5 (October 1938), pp. 700-8; and Robert Redfield, *The Primitive World and its Transformation* (Chicago, 1953); and *Peasant Society and Culture* (Chicago, 1956).

14   Such studies dovetailed with the social scientific ideologies for state-led modernization championed by neo-nationalists during the "Quiet Revolution". The conservative nationalism of the church was to be replaced by a planned secular-nationalist modernization of Quebec society, a plan which would bring the province through the stages of development and insure the place of French Canadians in their own future. See Michael D. Behiels, *Prelude to Quebec's Quiet Revolution: Liberalism versus Neo-Nationalism, 1945-1960* (Kingston and Montreal, 1985), pp. 97-120.

15   The drive to separate the traditional from the modern continues in many Quebec studies. Compare Allan Greer, *Peasant, Lord, and Merchant: Rural Society in Three Quebec Parishes, 1740-1840* (Toronto, 1985) with Fernand Ouellet, "Ruralization, Regional Development, and Industrial Growth Before 1850", in his *Economy, Class, and Nation in Quebec: Interpretive Essays* (Mississauga, 1991), pp. 124-60. Both authors' rich appreciation of differentiation in the countryside might have pushed the debate on Quebec agriculture out of the

on the internal problems to modernization can also be seen in the works of the "Laval school" of historians. Where the "Montreal school" of historians saw something of a golden age shattered by the Conquest and emphasized the English subjugation of Quebec, those associated with the Laval school placed the onus for the colony's past on cultural conservatism and a weak, insular nationalism. Historians influenced by the sociology of modernization risk falling into the same trap as the sociologists who assume that the "traditional" Québécois were long-standing and central figures of rural Quebec society who had only recently come under attack: if they were still present in the 20th century, they must have been still more traditional in the 18th and 19th centuries.

Quebec historians have been at the forefront of trends in international social and economic history. Some recent works have attempted to distance themselves from the national question by placing Quebec more within the social and economic processes of the North Atlantic world, without losing sight of its distinct features.[16] One recent analysis agrees that Quebec farmers did not "modernize" in the early 19th century, but this had little relation to the culture of the *habitant*. Allan Greer argues that restrictions on small-scale capital accumulation brought on by seigneurial exactions, merchant capital's inability to encourage the transformation of production, and the *habitants'* "safety-first" productive and reproductive strategies dominated the constellation of forces which slowed development in Quebec agriculture. Yet, even in this supposedly stagnant environment, we still see the emergence of a "semi-proletariat" of *journaliers*.[17] Seigneurial agriculture and certain cultural differences (themselves

---

focus on cultural conservatism. Yet, rather than exploring what that differentiation meant in terms of small-scale capital accumulation, Ouellet reverts to emphasizing a dynamic, English-led commercial sector and a necessarily passive countryside, while Greer argues that feudal-like exactions and merchant-capital hegemony blocked further development.

16 See, for example, Dale Miquelon, *New France, 1701-1744: "A Supplement to Europe"* (Toronto, 1987); Jean-Marie Fecteau, *Un nouvel ordre des chose: la pauvreté, le crime, l'Etat au Québec, de la fin du XVIIIe siècle à 1840* (Outremont, 1989); Gérald Bernier and Daniel Salée, *The Shaping of Québec Politics and Society: Colonialism, Power, and the Transition to Capitalism in the 19th Century* (Washington, 1992); and Albert Faucher, *Québec en Amérique au XIXe siècle* (Montreal, 1973). Ouellet endeavoured to employ the "objective", social scientific techniques of the Annales school in France, but as the ongoing debate makes clear, he was unable to extricate his work from the debate. See Serge Gagnon, *Quebec and its Historians: The Twentieth Century* (Toronto, 1985), pp. 81-163.

17 Greer, *Peasant, Lord, and Merchant*, pp. 170-6, 184-8. See also the important critique in Catherine DesBarats, "Agriculture within the Seigneurial Regime of Eighteenth-Century Canada: Some Thoughts on the Recent Literature", *Canadian Historical Review*, LXXIII, 1 (1992), pp. 1-29.

materially rooted) imposed their own constraints, but early-19th-century Quebec was not a hermetic peasant society where capitalism and the pressures of markets were unimportant.

Throughout the 19th century, as the influence of North American and local labour and commodity markets grew and demographic pressures increased, Quebec showed itself to be already quite well-adapted to the social technologies of continental industrialization. Rejecting an insular view of farm life, some writers have described the relationship between forest capital and settlement in the 19th-century colonization districts. The social formation that was "l'économie agro-forestière" was characterized less by its insularity from markets and mainstream North American culture than by its integration with outside capital.[18] Local development was also extensive. Throughout the countryside, small commercial or proto-industrial activity was considerable and many villages were becoming important local centres of development. Labourers and farmer-labourers who might later seek work in Montreal or New England found their first experiences of wage labour very close at hand.[19] While the clerical-agrarian myth placed the farm family on the land as an autonomous social force resisting modernity and assimilation into the North American mainstream, few farm households could actually carry that burden. Even relatively successful farmers in the mid-19th century needed to resort to some waged employment in local forest industries or agricultural and factory labour in the United States. Here too, however, the issue of ethnicity remains central. Economic development appears to have occurred in much the same manner in Quebec as elsewhere in North America, but the model remains largely based on external, ethnically articulated domination.

---

18 Normand Séguin, *La Conquête du sol au 19e siècle* (Sillery, 1977), especially pp. 38-70; and Normand Séguin, ed., *Agriculture et colonisation au Québec* (Montréal, 1980). For details on the farmer-woodsworker see René Hardy and Normand Séguin, *Forêt et société en Mauricie* (Montréal, 1984), pp. 152-70.

19 Serge Courville, Jean-Claude Robert and Normand Séguin, "The Spread of Rural Industry in Lower Canada, 1831-1851", *Journal of the Canadian Historical Association*, (1991), pp. 41-70; Serge Courville, "Un monde rural en mutation: le Bas-Canada dans la première moité du XIXe siécle", *Histoire sociale/Social History*, 40 (1987), pp. 237-58; and "Croissance villageoise et industries rurales dans les seigneuries du Québec (1815-1851)", in François Le-Brun and Normand Séguin, eds., *Sociétés villageoises et rapports villes-campagnes au Québec et dans la France de l'Ouest, XVIIe-XXe siècles* (Trois-Rivières, 1987). A number of urban studies look to the countryside for comparative purposes. See Peter Gossage, "Family Formation and Age of Marriage in Saint-Hyacinthe, Quebec, 1854-1891", *Histoire sociale/Social History*, XXIV, 47 (1991), pp. 61-84; and Bettina Bradbury, "Pigs, Cows, and Boarders: Non-Wage Forms of Survival among Montreal Families, 1861-1891", *Labour/Le Travail*, 15 (Spring 1985), pp. 7-22.

Other analyses of 19th-century colonization programmes and French Canadians' utilization of New England labour markets illuminate the dynamics of differentiation in drawing poor farmers and landless labourers out of rural villages. As Bruno Ramirez demonstrates, the emphasis on the "agricultural crisis" and the "traditional" high fertility of rural Quebec as push factors in out-migration glides over the locally constituted "selection mechanisms" which determined who stayed and who left.[20] Similarly, J.I. Little's description of the colonization settlements in the St. Francis District successfully draws these internal and external, cultural and structural forces together. The St. Francis District was a settler society, but Little resists views which stress either the frontier's transformative power or the transfer of tradition from the old world; instead, he adopts elements of both.[21] Rather than emphasizing settlers' "assimilation", he describes the nature of the collective responses made by the French-Canadian and Scottish settlers. The similarities of the two groups' responses do not warrant a focus on "culture"; conversely, the differences limit the utility of a modernization approach which would smooth the bumpy road of culture and practice. Both groups sought independence in circumstances circumscribed by roughly the same parameters, but they did so in slightly different ways. As the forest economy declined, the responses of the crofters and *habitants* also varied, but they were conditioned by the historical patterns developed in the agro-forest social formation. Little's close analysis of agriculture and dependency — which attends to culture and economy without reducing one to the other — reminds us that it is not enough to study the "needs of capital"; any such explanation must rest upon a better understanding of the material context of the community which capital exploits.

Quebec historians have long recognized the centrality of rural life to their history. They have begun with some fairly basic observations — most Québécois before the Second World War were rural dwellers — and asked a very simple question: what has rural life meant for the shaping of Quebec society? Where Ontario historians could look to settlement and farming as a stage along the way to industrial society, there remained an important cultural gulf between "progress" in Quebec and its connections to the Québécois. In detailing the interconnectedness of the different sectors of rural and urban society, while still retaining a central place for a material context, historians are developing a picture of a society which was far more dynamic than either cul-

---

20 Bruno Ramirez, *On the Move: French Canadian and Italian Migrants in the North Atlantic Economy, 1860-1914* (Toronto, 1991), especially pp. 22-32, 111-37.

21 J.I. Little, *Crofters and Habitants: Settler Society, Economy, and Culture in a Quebec Township, 1848-1881* (Kingston and Montreal, 1991), pp. 134-55. See also his "Ethnicity, Family Structure, and Seasonal Labor Strategies on Quebec's Appalachian Frontier, 1852-1881", *Journal of Family History*, 17, 3 (1992), pp. 289-302.

tural or economic structural arguments would allow. This was a society constrained by its social distance from the dynamic forces of North American
capitalism but never wholly apart from its influences and tendencies. This view
of rural society as a complex whole, where economies are less differentiated
than we have suggested while communities are more so, is a helpful avenue for
inquiry. Together, such studies emphasize the tremendous depth of rural society
in Quebec. Long before the Quiet Revolution, and even before the industrial
"take-off" in the late 19th century, rural Quebec was a complex and dynamic ad-
mixture of the traditional and the modern. Some, though not all, of the essays
gathered in this collection begin with similar assumptions; indeed, a brief overview of the history and historiography of Atlantic Canada suggests there were a
number of important parallels between rural society in this region and Quebec.

The Two Worlds in Atlantic Canada

It is only since the 1940s that more Atlantic Canadians have lived in towns
and cities than in the countryside. European settlement of the region that eventually became the Atlantic Provinces was largely a late-18th- and
early-19th-century phenomenon. Colonization began in the 16th century with
early exploration, trade with the indigenous peoples[22] and the exploitation of the
region's rich fishery, especially off Newfoundland, but the process was slow to
begin and it was protracted once under way. Colonization was inhibited
throughout the 18th century by the ongoing colonial wars between Britain and
France, while in Newfoundland it was officially prohibited. The French created
Acadia in 1603, but it remained a marginal colony on the edge of empires; its
population was no more than 20,000 people by the 1750s.[23] Large-scale im-

---

22 See Alfred G. Bailey, *The Conflict of European and Eastern Algonkian Cultures*
    (Toronto, 1969 [1937]); and the relevant sections of Bruce Trigger, *Natives and
    Newcomers: Canada's "Heroic Age" Reconsidered* (Kingston and Montreal,
    1985). John G. Reid describes the pragmatic relationship which existed between
    Acadians, Micmacs and New Englanders in his *Acadia, Maine, and New Scot-
    land: Marginal Colonies in the Seventeenth Century* (Toronto, 1981). See also
    Ruth Holmes Whitehead, *The Old Man Told Us: Excerpts From Micmac His-
    tory, 1500-1950* (Halifax, 1988).

23 Andrew Hill Clark, *Acadia: The Geography of Early Nova Scotia to 1760*
    (Madison, Wis., 1968); Shannon Ryan, "Fishery to Colony: A Newfoundland
    Watershed, 1793-1815", *Acadiensis*, XII, 2 (Spring 1983), pp. 34-52. On
    Acadia's isolation see also J.B. Brebner, *New England Outpost: Acadia before
    the Conquest of Canada* (New York, 1927). On Prince Edward Island see
    Andrew Hill Clark, *Three Centuries and the Island: A Historical Geography of
    Settlement and Agriculture in Prince Edward Island* (Toronto, 1959); and J.M.
    Bumsted, "The Patterson Regime and the Impact of the American Revolution on
    the Island of St. John, 1775-1786", *Acadiensis*, XIII, 1 (Autumn 1983), pp. 47-
    67. Helpful overviews can be found in John G. Reid, "The 1780s: Decade of

migration of Europeans began in earnest with the arrival of Loyalists following the American Revolution.[24] Colonial governments, more attuned to running military entrepôts than settler colonies, were hardly prepared for the sudden arrival of 35,000 Anglo-American and African-American refugee-settlers, more than doubling the population.[25] The largest group of settlers in the early 19th century were Scots and Irish, many of them fleeing the social disruptions in their home countries.[26] By mid-century, the colonies' population had grown to more

Migration", in his *Six Crucial Decades: Times of Change in the History of the Maritimes* (Halifax, 1987), pp. 2-26, 61-87; Graeme Wynn, "A Province Too Much Dependent on New England", *Canadian Geographer*, 31, 2 (Summer 1987), pp. 98-113; and "A Region of Scattered Settlements and Bounded Possibilities: Northeastern America, 1775-1800", *Canadian Geographer*, 31, 2 (Winter 1987), pp. 319-38.

24 See, however, some of the recent work on planter settlements before the Revolution. These studies demonstrate the important American influence on Nova Scotia and New Brunswick well before the arrival of the Loyalists. See Margaret Conrad, ed., *They Planted Well: New England Planters in Maritime Canada* (Fredericton, 1988); and Conrad, ed., *Making Adjustments: Change and Continuity in Planter Nova Scotia 1759-1800* (Fredericton, 1991). On Nova Scotia as the fourteenth colony which did not join the revolution because of its isolation from New England see J.B. Brebner, *The Neutral Yankees of Nova Scotia: A Marginal Colony During the Revolutionary Years* (New York, 1937). George Rawlyk plays down isolation, arguing that revolutionary fervour was contained by a spirit of religious revivalism, in his *Nova Scotia's Massachusetts: A Study of Massachusetts-Nova Scotia Relations, 1630-1784* (Kingston and Montreal, 1973).

25 Neil MacKinnon, *This Unfriendly Soil: The Loyalist Experience in Nova Scotia, 1783-1791* (Kingston and Montreal, 1986); James W. St. G. Walker, *The Black Loyalists: The Search for the Promised Land in Nova Scotia and Sierra Leone, 1783-1870* (New York, 1976).

26 James Hunter, *The Making of the Crofting Community* (Edinburgh, 1976); Eric Richards, *A History of the Highland Clearances: Agrarian Transformation and the Evictions* (London, 1982); J.M. Bumsted, *The People's Clearance: Highland Emigration to North America* (Edinburgh, 1982); Hornsby, *Nineteenth-Century Cape Breton*, pp. 30-47; J.J. Mannion, ed., *The Peopling of Newfoundland: Essays in Historical Geography* (St. John's, 1977); *Irish Settlements in Eastern Canada: A Study of Cultural Transfer and Adaptation* (Toronto, 1974); and D. Campbell and R.A. MacLean, *Beyond the Atlantic Roar: A Study of the Nova Scotia Scots* (Toronto, 1974), pp. 7-34. It is remarkable that the only major synthesis of pre-Confederation, Atlantic Canadian history devotes very little attention to settlement and agriculture See W.S. MacNutt, *The Atlantic Provinces: The Emergence of Colonial Society* (Toronto, 1965).

than 600,000 people, quickly filling the better settlement lands and pushing native peoples onto marginal reserves and dependency.[27]

Each colony had its own particular settlement pattern: New Brunswick's peopling by Irish and Scottish farmers, heavily influenced by the possibilities and constraints of the timber trade;[28] Prince Edward Island's land question, rooted in the dominance of absentee landowners and tenant producers;[29] Nova Scotia's more diverse settlement pattern and economy, and its more broadly developed, if not more prosperous, farm sector;[30] and Newfoundland's severely limited agricultural possibilities and a population scattered around hundreds of coastal fishing outports.[31] Scattered along each of these colony's coasts were dozens of town and village ports from which locally-produced staples were exported and foreign goods imported. Here in these communities and to a lesser extent in various farm-based rural centres, were the dispersed enclaves of com-

27   See L.F.S. Upton, *Micmacs and Colonists: White-Indian Relations in the Maritime Provinces, 1712-1867* (Vancouver, 1975); and Ralph T. Pastore, "The Collapse of the Beothuk World", *Acadiensis*, XIX, 1 (Autumn 1989), pp. 52-71.

28   Graeme Wynn, *Timber Colony: A Historical Geography of Early Nineteenth Century New Brunswick* (Toronto, 1980); Béatrice Craig, "Agriculture and the Lumberman's Frontier in the Upper St. John Valley, 1800-1870", *Journal of Forest History*, 32, 3 (July 1988), pp. 125-37; and W.S. MacNutt, *New Brunswick, A History, 1784-1867* (Toronto, 1963).

29   J.M. Bumsted, "The Origins of the Land Question on Prince Edward Island, 1767-1805", *Acadiensis*, XI, 1 (Autumn 1981), pp. 43-56; Rusty Bittermann, "Agrarian Alternatives: The Ideas of the Escheat Movement on Prince Edward Island, 1832-1842", *Acadiensis*, forthcoming; Clark, *Three Centuries and the Island*; Ian Ross Robertson, "Highlanders, Irishmen, and the Land Question in Nineteenth-Century Prince Edward Island", in L.M. Cullen and T.C. Smout, eds., *Comparative Aspects of Scottish and Irish Economic and Social History, 1600-1900* (Edinburgh, 1977).

30   Walker, *The Black Loyalists*; Hornsby, *Nineteenth-Century Cape Breton*, pp. 48-120; Alan R. MacNeil, "Early American Communities on the Fundy: A Case Study of Annapolis and Amherst Townships, 1767-1827", *Agricultural History*, 62, 3 (1989), pp. 101-19; R.L. Gentilcore, "The Agricultural Background of Settlement in Eastern Nova Scotia", *Annals of the Association of American Geographers*, 46, 4 (1956), pp. 378-404; Campbell and MacLean, *Beyond the Atlantic Roar*; Robert MacKinnon and Graeme Wynn, "Nova Scotian Agriculture in the 'Golden Age': A New Look", in Douglas Day, ed., *Geographical Perspectives on the Maritime Provinces* (Halifax, 1988), pp. 33-55.

31   W. Gordon Handcock, *Soe longe as there comes noe women: Origins of English Settlement in Nefoundland* (St. John's, 1989); C. Grant Head, *Eighteenth Century Newfoundland* (Toronto, 1976); Ryan, "Fishery to Colony"; Mannion, *The Peopling of Newfoundland*; Sean Cadigan, "The Staple Model Reconsidered: The Case of Agricultural Policy in Northeast Newfoundland, 1785-1855", *Acadiensis*, XXI, 2 (Spring 1992), pp. 48-71.

merce, shipbuilding, sawmilling and fish-curing: the localized commercial hubs where producers and merchants exchanged with each other and the world of trade beyond.[32]

Out of this structure emerged a formal economy dominated by the export of staples, especially the timber trade and the fisheries. After the mid-19th century, there were some signs of industrial "progress" in the coal industries and the building of railroads (especially the Intercolonial, which linked the Atlantic colonies with the united Canadas), and shipbuilding continued to expand. For the most part, however, large-scale industry was limited until spurred by the import substitution measures of the National Policy in 1879. The National Policy had a dramatic effect on economic and social relations in the Maritime Provinces. Much of the form of industrial activity changed as the combination of favourable tariff structures and freight rates opened new markets, community-based joint stock companies were formed and the increasingly frequent investments by American and Central Canadian capitalists seemed to fulfil the new provinces' ambitious and optimistic aspirations for progress and industrial development. By the late 19th century, coal production was increasing dramatically, iron and steel plants were operating alongside other metals industries and dozens of new industries emerged in glass, cotton, sugar, brewing, shoes and textiles.[33]

def?

The early history of the colonies has been read as the story of two worlds: a world of merchants and politicians who shaped the colonies' political future and dominated its economic life, and a world of settlers carving out a meagre existence, isolated from the larger world of commerce and production. Merchants, especially in the region's major urban centres of Halifax, Saint John and St. John's, traded local staples and British and American manufactured goods throughout the Atlantic world, ostensibly establishing the conditions of the

32 These rural networks of exchange and interaction with the international trade in timber are described in Wynn, *Timber Colony*. See also R.E. Ommer, *From Outpost to Outport: A Structural Analysis of the Jersey-Gaspé Cod Fishery, 1767-1886* (Kingston and Montreal, 1991); T.W. Acheson, *Saint John: The Making of a Colonial Urban Community* (Toronto, 1985); and Hornsby, *Nineteenth-Century Cape Breton*.

33 T.W. Acheson, "The National Policy and the Industrialization of the Maritimes, 1880-1910", *Acadiensis*, I, 2 (Spring 1972), pp. 3-28; and L.D. McCann, "The Mercantile-Industrial Transition in the Metal Towns of Pictou County, 1857-1931", *Acadiensis*, X, 1 (Autumn 1981), pp. 29-64; Donald Macgillivray, "Henry Melville Whitney Comes to Cape Breton: The Saga of a Gilded Age Entrepreneur", *Acadiensis*, IX, 1 (Autumn 1979), pp. 44-70. In Newfoundland, an independent Dominion until 1949, the state also moved toward import substitution policies, although later and to less effect than in New Brunswick and Nova Scotia. See David Alexander, "Newfoundland's Traditional Economy and Development to 1934", *Acadiensis*, V, 2 (Spring 1976), pp. 56-78.

colonies' prosperity. Rural society has conventionally served as a backdrop to their ventures, and few historians have examined its institutions.[34] Only in Newfoundland, where the resident fisherfolk dispersed along the colony's coast were long recognized as central to its single-staple history, was there a strong sense that the two worlds of the town and the country were part of a single larger picture.

If merchants were seen as world-striding entrepreneurs, settlers, on the other hand, were imagined as clearers of the land and founders of autonomous communities. Their only connection to the merchants' world was their unwillingness to devote themselves wholly to the land and their all-too-willing seduction by the easy money available in cutting timber rather than hay and harvesting fish rather than potatoes. This, together with an alleged subsistence orientation and technological backwardness of the Maritime farmer, created a rural society characterized by its "cultural isolation" and "primitive" condition.[35] Writing in the 1970s, D. Campbell and R.A. MacLean saw an essentially homogeneous and undifferentiated Scottish culture in eastern Nova Scotia from the 19th century to the 20th century, which they linked implicitly to the area's weak economic development.[36] Occasional evidence of progressive social behaviour was explained largely in terms of religious and cultural variations, but the general pattern was distinctly un-modern, characterized by the dominance of age-old

---

34   J.S. Martell, "The Achievements of Agricola and the Agricultural Societies, 1818-1825", *Bulletin of the Public Archives of Nova Scotia*, 2, 2 (Halifax, 1940); and "From Central Board to Secretary of Agriculture", *Bulletin of the Public Archives of Nova Scotia*, 2, 2 (1940); L.J. Burpee, "The Golden Age of Nova Scotia", *Queen's Quarterly*, 36 (1929), pp. 380-94; D.C. Harvey, "The Spacious Days of Nova Scotia", *Dalhousie Review*, 19 (1939), pp. 132-42. One recent study situates these rural institutions within a social context which recognizes the stratified structure of rural society. See Graeme Wynn, "Exciting a Spirit of Reform Among the 'Plodholes': Agricultural Reform in Pre-Confederation Nova Scotia", *Acadiensis*, XX, 1 (Autumn 1990), pp. 5-51.

35   This is largely an older view found, for example, in Gentilcore, "The Agricultural Background of Settlement"; Clark, *Three Centuries and the Island*; and Campbell and MacLean, *Beyond the Atlantic Roar*. The quotations, however, are much more recent, drawing these terms from those older studies and suggesting their continued influence. See Michael J. Troughton, "From Nodes to Nodes: The Rise and Fall of Agricultural Activity in the Maritime Provinces", in Day, *Geographical Perspectives on the Maritime Provinces*, pp. 25-46, quotations at p. 29. See also Richard Apostle and Gene Barrett, *Emptying Their Nets: Small Capital and Rural Industrialization in the Nova Scotia Fishing Industry* (Toronto, 1992). Alan MacNeil has effectively criticized aspects of these assumptions in his "Cultural stereotypes and highland farming in Eastern Nova Scotia, 1827-1861", *Histoire sociale/Social History*, 37 (May 1986), pp. 39-56.

36   Campbell and MacLean, *Beyond the Atlantic Roar*.

traditions and culture and maintained by those who resisted the pull of the "Boston states". While not explicitly grounded in any theoretical background, these interpretations bear a strong resemblance to many descriptions of rural society in Quebec. These peasant-farmers operated in what some theorists have labelled a peasant or domestic mode of production where production and consumption was determined by household needs and community expectations.[37] This emphasis on a collective resistance to change, however, avoids discussing both structural constraints to poorer landholders improving their situation and evidence that some households were able to accumulate capital and reinvest it in their holdings. It leaves us with only the story of an apparently contented middle group, ignoring those who fell off the bottom or emerged out of the top.

There has been an uneasy balance in Atlantic Canadian historiography between admiration for the jack-of-all-trades settler who could be found "superintending the cultivation of a farm or building a vessel at the same time...not only able to catch and cure a cargo of fish but to find his way with it to the West Indies or the Mediterranean", and condemnation for the "farmer [who] neglected his farm and went to square timber".[38] Historians have only gradually taken more notice of this oft-noted "occupational pluralism". It was not until the publication of Graeme Wynn's *Timber Colony* in 1980 that historians began to appreciate that off-farm employment was a requirement for 19th-century New Brunswick farmers.[39] Wynn's study of industry before industrialization, while arguing that the timber trade was central to the developing New Brunswick society, stresses the close ties between the timber trade and agriculture and provides an important corrective to a single-staple emphasis. Rosemary Ommer's study of the Gaspé fishery carries this insight to the level of

37 Income in peasant households was minimally maintained by community standards and maximally by decreasing marginal utility benefits above basic household needs. The classic work here, written in Russia in the 1920s, is A.V. Chayanov, *The Theory of the Peasant Economy*, Daniel Thorner, Basile Kerblay and R.E.F. Smith, eds., (Madison, Wis., 1986 [1966]). Teodor Shanin's introduction to the 1986 edition is a useful discussion of the reception to Chayanov's work since the English translation in 1966. See also Teodor Shanin, ed., *Peasants and Peasant Societies* (Harmondsworth, 1971). Allan Greer's *Peasant, Lord, and Merchant* is the best English-Canadian employment of Chayanov's theoretical framework. See also Catherine DesBarats critique which provides a very useful criticism of this literature (including Greer's work), as well as Marxist interpretations, in her "Agriculture within the Seigneurial Regime".

38 Thomas Chandler Haliburton, *The Old Judge, or Life in a Colony* (Ottawa, 1978 [1849]), p. xxi; George Patterson, *A History of the County of Pictou Nova Scotia* (Montreal: 1877; reprint edition, Belleville Ont: 1979), p. 246.

39 Graeme Wynn, *Timber Colony*. See also L.D. McCann, "'Living the Double Life': Town and Country in the Industrialization of the Maritimes", in Day, *Geographical Perspectives on the Maritimes*, pp. 93-113.

the household, highlighting the importance of understanding both the formal and informal economies of the merchant fisheries.[40] Yet few other researchers have followed these insights, and fewer still have carried them beyond the settlement and staples period. Most have contented themselves with a standard "two worlds" approach.

This "two worlds" approach has been maintained in the emphasis on industry and urbanization, especially after 1880. This period has had a dramatic effect on the way our histories have been written in the past 20 years, what Kris Inwood has aptly labelled our "modern scholarly passion for smokestacks".[41] Where an earlier regional historiography was divided largely into two periods — the pre-Confederation "Golden Age" and the post-Confederation decline — we now seem to have three: a reconsidered but still largely golden age of independent commodity producers and "wood, wind and sail" merchants; the period of industrialization (which, in effect, has become the New Golden Age)[42]; and the period of de-industrialization. Rural developments seem part of the era left behind with the onset of industry and progress, an assumption confirmed by that older rural historiography.

The region's "search" for a post-Confederation historiography has been almost singularly concerned with understanding the social, economic and political framework of industrialization, de-industrialization and underdevelopment. While this rejuvenated historiography has in no way answered all the questions we need to ask, it has undoubtedly provided us with a much better understanding of that period — roughly 1870 to 1930 — by detailing an industrially focused history of society and politics which has reinstated the Atlantic Provinces at the centre of Canada's industrial revolution.[43] Heavily influenced by T.W.

---

40   R.E. Ommer, *From Outpost to Outport: A Structural Analysis of the Jersey-Gaspé Fishery* (Kingston and Montreal, 1991).

41   Kris E. Inwood, "Maritime Industrialization from 1870 to 1910: A Review of the Evidence and Its Interpretation", *Acadiensis*, XXI, 1 (Autumn 1991), pp. 132-55.

42   It is noteworthy that among the largest headings in the recently published index to the region's major historical journal are the industrially focused headings of working-class history and economic history. See Eric Swanick and David Frank, comp., *The Acadiensis Index, 1971-1991* (Fredericton, 1992).

43   E.R. Forbes, *The Maritime Rights Movement, 1919-1927: A Study in Canadian Regionalism* (Montreal and Kingston, 1979); *Challenging the Regional Stereotype: Essays on the 20th Century Maritimes* (Fredericton, 1989); Daniel Hickey, ed., *Moncton, 1871-1929: Changements socio-économiques dans une ville ferroviare* (Moncton, 1990); Michael Earle, ed., *Workers and the State in 20th Century Nova Scotia* (Fredericton, 1989); Nolan Reilly, "The General Strike in Amherst, Nova Scotia, 1919", *Acadiensis*, IX, 2 (Spring 1980), pp. 56-77; David Frank, "Class Conflict in the Coal Industry: Cape Breton, 1922", in G.S. Kealey and Peter Warrian, eds., *Essays in Canadian Working Class History*

Acheson's important essay on industrialization and the National Policy, historians have since focused most of their attention on Atlantic Canadian society as seen from its towns and cities. Indeed, it became evident that Atlantic Canada, far from being on the periphery, experienced the great transformations of the Western world in the period from the mid-19th to the mid-20th centuries: a pre-industrial period, the emergence of industry and the consolidation of industrial capitalism.[44]

The essays in this collection do not set out to disprove this periodization. We do, however, wish to suggest the limitations on the conditions which have informed it by highlighting its rural background and scrutinizing the barriers which historians have constructed between the two worlds. Although industry in the region was clearly spurred by import-substitution tariffs, as it was elsewhere in the country, an exclusive emphasis on that moment of change obscures the processes which preceded it and the conditions which continued in its wake.[45]

(Toronto, 1976), pp. 161-84; "Company Town/Labour Town: Local Government in the Cape Breton Coal Towns, 1917-1926", *Histoire sociale/Social History*, 27 (May 1981), pp. 177-96; "Contested Terrain: Workers' Control in the Cape Breton Coal Mines in the 1920s", in Craig Heron and Robert Storey, eds., *On the Job: Confronting the Labour Process in Canada* (Kingston and Montreal, 1986), pp. 102-23; Don Macgillivray, "Military Aid to the Civil Power: The Cape Breton Experience in the 1920s", *Acadiensis*, III, 2 (Spring 1974), pp. 45-64; "Henry Melville Whitney Comes to Cape Breton"; Ian McKay, "Strikes in the Maritimes, 1901-1914", *Acadiensis*, XIII, 1 (Autumn 1983), pp. 3-46; "'By Wisdom Wile or War': The Provincial Workmen's Association and the Struggle for Working-Class Independence in Nova Scotia, 1979-1897", *Labour/Le Travail*, 18 (Fall 1986), pp. 13-62; "The Realm of Uncertainty: The Experience of Work in the Cumberland Coal Mines, 1873-1927", *Acadiensis*, XVI, 1 (Autumn 1986), pp. 3-57; The Craft Transformed: An Essay on the Carpenters of Halifax, 1885-1985 (Halifax, 1985); D.A. Muise, "'The Great Transformation': Changing the Urban Face of Nova Scotia, 1871-1921", *Nova Scotia Historical Review*, 11, 2 (1991), pp. 1-42; "The Industrial Context of Inequality: Female Participation in Nova Scotia's Paid Labour Force, 1871-1921", *Acadiensis*, XX, 2 (Spring 1991), pp. 3-31; and "Iron Men?: Yarmouth's Seagoing Workforce in Transition, 1871-1921", in Colin Howell and Richard Twomey, eds., *Jack Tar in History: Essays in the History of Maritime Life and Labour* (Fredericton, 1991); L.D. McCann, "The Mercantile-Industrial Transition"; "Metropolitanism and Branch Businesses in the Maritimes, 1881-1931", *Acadiensis*, XIII, 1 (Autumn 1983), pp. 112-25.

44 Eric Hobsbawm, *The Age of Capital: 1848-1875* (New York, 1975); and also his *Industry and Empire* (Harmondsworth, 1968). This periodization is also evident in the titles of the Readings in Canadian Social History Series edited by Michael S. Cross and Gregory S. Kealey. See also Palmer, *Working-Class Experience*.

45 Janine Grant and Kris Inwood, for example, have noted the implications which the continued importance the household production of cloth might have had on markets for local cloth manufacturers in the region in the years between 1870

Some recent writers have suggested frameworks which might help us better understand aspects of regional economy and society by drawing together these sectors and assessing their interaction. Works by T.W. Acheson, on Saint John before 1850, and Ian McKay, on the Nova Scotia coal fields in the 1870s, have emphasized the limits placed on industrialization by those areas' domination by merchant capital.[46] Both writers have suggested that merchant-capital hegemony delayed economic diversification before the National Policy and, once the policy was in place, limited its ability to transform the region's economy.

Acheson's description of Saint John merchants and their social, political and economic clout details the manner by which economic diversification was thwarted. Saint John's merchants produced "the dominant economic class, the institutions and myths" which formed the community of Saint John; they also determined the "desirable material goals of the city and the strategies necessary to achieve them", goals and strategies which before mid-century precluded any form of tariff protection which might encourage the economic diversification sought by many farmers and artisanal producers.[47] The politically powerful timber merchants, with their commercial links to the country storekeepers and rural workers who produced that timber, effectively inhibited the possibility of a stronger agricultural sector: "At the very least", Acheson writes, "the *combination* of rewards which the [timber] trade could offer to the rural inhabitants, coupled with the refusal of the provincial legislature to provide any protection for the nascent colonial agriculture, severely retarded the development of a sub-

and 1900. See Janine Grant and Kris Inwood, "Gender and Organization in the Canadian Cloth Industry", *Canadian Papers in Business and Economic History*, 1 (1989), pp. 17-32. Such work also has important implications for understanding the specific gendered components of rural production and exchange, as also developed by Cohen in her *Women's Work*. Larry McCann explores related issues in his "'Living the Double Life'".

46   Ian McKay, "The crisis of dependent development: class conflict in the Nova Scotia coalfields, 1872-1876", in G.S. Kealey, ed., *Class, Gender, and Region: Essays in Canadian Historical Sociology* (St. John's, 1988), pp. 9-48; and T.W. Acheson, "The Great Merchant and Economic Development in Saint John, 1820-1850", *Acadiensis*, VIII, 2 (Spring 1979), pp. 3-27; "The National Policy and the Industrialization of the Maritimes. See also T.W. Acheson, "The Maritimes and 'Empire Canada'", in David J. Bercuson, ed., *Canada and the Burden of Unity* (Toronto, 1979), pp. 87-114; L. Anders Sandberg, "Dependent Development, Labour and the Trenton Steel Works, Nova Scotia, c. 1900-1943", *Labour/Le Travail*, 28 (Fall 1991), pp. 127-62; and Eric Sager, "Dependency, Underdevelopment and the Economic History of the Atlantic Provinces", *Acadiensis*, XVII, 1 (Autumn 1987), pp. 117-37; and Ommer, *From Outpost to Outport*.

47   Acheson, *Saint John*, p. 66.

stantial agriculture".[48] McKay's work, like Acheson's, is primarily directed at processes within merchant capital towns — in this case, those linked to Cape Breton County coal mines — but again suggests broader implications for the countryside. Both point to the doubly bound context for Maritime agriculture by noting that some farmers needed the wages merchant capital provided, while agriculture was denied a stronger home market by the merchant capitalist's preference for imported foodstuffs.

McKay's analysis resists a simplified version of dependency theory which argues that merchant capital was "parasitical" and actively blocked development. He argues that if we look at particular export economies we find significant differences in their ties to the world market and their internal social relations, which, while variable, over time "tended to combine in patterned ways".[49] Merchant capital, though facilitating development in some respects, discouraged local commodity production (by preferring to trade), limited the accumulation of capital (especially among artisans and independent producers) and maintained sufficient influence on state policy-making to block alternative policies (especially with respect to trade and tariffs). It also failed to encourage fully the generation of free labourers (whether viewed in terms of its demand for labour, or in terms of the encouragement of the creation of a supply of wage labourers by the development of commercial agriculture and its concomitant differentiating processes). So long as these conditions were maintained — and it is important to recognize their interrelationship — a more complete development of industrial capitalism would be restrained. In terms of the countryside, the important features were these economies' demand for labour (not only in terms of numbers but also the regularity of that employment) and for agricultural surpluses (for a general economic prosperity would facilitate capital accumulation, reinvestment and improvement by some farmers). The result was a non-agricultural sector which demanded the labour of rural people more than their products. Meanwhile, the farm sector also required that work but was largely unable to choose exclusively one economy or the other.

In Newfoundland, while the particulars are quite different and the issues much more contentious, a similar condition has been described, characterized by merchants' effective abilities to limit economic diversification and stifle the development of capitalist social relations by their stranglehold on both colonial economic policy and the producers themselves.[50] It is important to note the im-

48 Acheson, "The Great Merchant", p. 196 [emphasis added].

49 McKay, "Dependent Development", p. 16. See also Charles Bergquist, *Labor in Latin America: Comparative Essays on Chile, Argentina, Venezuela, and Colombia* (Stanford, 1986); Geoffrey Kay, *Development and Underdevelopment: A Marxist Analysis* (London, 1975); and Christobal Kay, *Latin American Theories of Development and Underdevelopment* (London, 1989).

50 See, for example, Gerald Sider, *Culture and Class in Anthropology and History: A Newfoundland Illustration* (Cambridge and Paris, 1986), and James K. Hiller,

portant distinction here between McKay's approach and one such as Gerald Sider's. In terms of its relation to the countryside, McKay's argument is based on a structural description of merchant-capital's weak linkages with the farm economy (two existing sectors, as opposed to Sider's argument that merchant capital prevented another sector from developing) and does not reduce workers' role to that of victims of that structure. Sean Cadigan, too, has argued that these apparent blockages were never so strong as Sider would suggest. In contrast to Sider's description of fishing people's powerlessness, Cadigan effectively argues for the importance of their resistance against attempts by merchants to undermine well-established expectations, emphasizing the combined effects of "fishermen's desire for independence and merchant's desire for profit".[51]

These works have attempted to move beyond structural descriptions of uneven development, by locating people, not structures, as the agents of history. But, when viewed from the countryside, these analyses still seem only partial. Although the work of Acheson and McKay has pushed the discussion beyond the National Policy and post-1879 industrialization, it has not broken with the focus on urban/industrial change. The countryside, while in many ways central to their argument, has formed only a background to their urban and industrial stories.[52] Given the emphasis regional historians have placed on blockages to development, and their apparent connection to the countryside, it is surprising how little the connections have been explored from a rural perspective. The few studies which have directed their attention to these issues suggest that these impediments in no way fully thwarted independent producers from exploiting markets or the emergence of social stratification in the countryside.[53] In the

"The Newfoundland Credit System: an Interpretation", in Ommer, ed., *Merchant Credit and Labour Strategies*, pp. 86-101.

51   See Sean Cadigan, "Battle Harbour in Transition: Merchants, Fishermen, and the State in the Struggle for Relief in a Labrador Community during the 1930s", *Labour/Le Travail*, 26 (Fall 1990), pp. 125-50. On merchants, fishers and agriculture in Newfoundland see Sean Cadigan, "The Staple Model Reconsidered"; and Ommer, ed., *Merchant Credit and Labour Strategies*. On agriculture in Newfoundland see Robert MacKinnon, "Farming the Rock: The Evolution of Commercial Agriculture around St. John's, Newfoundland to 1945", *Acadiensis*, XX, 2 (Spring 1991), pp. 32-61.

52   See, however, T.W. Acheson, "New Brunswick Agriculture at the End of the Colonial Era: A Reassessment", in Kris Inwood, ed., *Farm, Factory and Fortune: New Studies in the Economic History of the Maritime Provinces* (Fredericton, 1993), pp. 37-60.

53   Bittermann, "The Hierarchy of the Soil"; Craig, "Agriculture and the Lumberman's Frontier"; and Debra McNabb, "The Role of the Land in Settling Horton Township, Nova Scotia, 1766-1830", in Conrad, ed., *They Planted Well*, pp. 151-60.

towns and outports of the region, as well as in the countryside, processes which could be seen as preparatory to industry were well under way by the 1840s.

Eric Sager and Gerald Panting's work on the Atlantic Canadian shipping and shipbuilding industry carries this approach beyond the industrial towns and into hundreds of coastal shipbuilding centres around the region. Effectively erasing the distinction between the town and the country — and in some ways between culture and economy — they view shipbuilding not as a "single industry but a marine complex, with all its social and cultural underpinnings".[54] Moving well beyond a description of the rise and fall of an industry, their work illustrates the potential importance of a household-level understanding of a rural industry which might have transformed, slowly and perhaps incompletely, into industrial capitalism, and which had numerous direct and indirect ties to the countryside. Cash inputs made available by employment in shipping and shipbuilding "helped to stabilize" subsistence farming and petty production and "detracted from any incentive to transform agriculture". Where local merchants accumu-lated capital in their dealings with smallholders and independent producers, many smallholders and independent producers owned schooners and shares in other small ships which "helped to preserve the outport family and the small farm".[55]

Yet here, too, when we redirect our attention toward processes *within* the countryside, there is the problem of situating stratified rural societies within this framework. Sager and Panting, much like Acheson and McKay, suggest how the countryside was reproduced in the merchant capitalist economy but offer little guidance toward an understanding of the dynamic rural processes which others have described. Focusing on a single stable stratum guides history by its con- tinuous elements, ones we should by no means ignore but which must be understood as components of a more complex and dynamic social structure. Capital accumulation and class formation were in progress throughout the 19th century. Some pre-Confederation farmers effectively marketed their surpluses despite the importation of cheaper foodstuffs, and while most rural households continued to produce for use value — combined with local exchange and stints of wage labour — some were specializing their production for markets.[56] Local conditions, specifically the differentially constituted markets for labour and commodities, combined with the structures of the mercantile political economy to produce the general contours of rural production in the region. It is apparent that there was a much more complex relationship between industry and agricul- ture than had been imagined by those who saw them as two distinct worlds. And

54 Eric Sager with Gerald E. Panting, *Maritime Capital: The Shipping Industry in Atlantic Canada, 1820-1914* (Montreal and Kingston, 1990), quotation at p. 18.

55 Sager and Panting, *Maritime Capital*, pp. 173-6, 191-6.

56 See especially Bittermann, "The Hierarchy of the Soil".

it is also clear that historians who assume an unmoving "traditional" countryside may be in for some surprises.

Defining the Rural

Everyday life in the countryside revolved around the social experience of work. It was here that rural people developed relations with each other — which conditioned how labour was exchanged, how family and household structures were reproduced, how resources were allocated, how value was assessed — and it is here that we find a location for observing the structures of meaning and power. Work on farms and in rural industries conditioned much of the life experience of women and men of the region. In more urban or industrial settings, work was often conditioned by rural labour problems as many industrial workers came from and often maintained ties to the countryside. In the 1860s and 1870s in the coal towns of industrial Pictou County, for example, more than half of the young men entering mining were born on farms in the surrounding countryside. Many others continued to live a peripatetic existence tending the fields in the spring and the fall and relying on the household to finish an entire farm season's work.[57] On the other hand, while waged work took place predominantly in industrial settings, it was also common on farms and other non-industrial settings throughout the countryside.

Given this variable terrain, some definitions of what makes an area or society "rural" are in order. Typically, responses to the question of what is rural vary among academic historians, but certain key aspects are common. The definition proposed by Robert Swierenga, an American historian of the countryside, is commonly cited: "The new rural history is the systematic study of human behaviour over time in rural environments". He outlines a four-faceted approach entailing the "economic, social, political, and environmental forces" which affected rural people, and an awareness of time and change. This is sensible and straightforward (and flexible) enough to be useful, and in fact well describes what rural historians do. Less helpful, however, is his definition of rural: "The standard operational definition of rurality includes two criteria — residence in an *area* of low population density and chief livelihood earned in agriculture".[58] The standard figure used in both the U.S. and Canadian census is 2,500, but in 1828 that figure carries very different significance than it does in

---

57   Danny Samson, "Family Formation in Mining and Farming Households: Pictou County, Nova Scotia, 1860-1880", Paper presented at the meeting of the Canadian Historical Association, Charlottetown, June 1992. David Frank has explored the cultural aspects of this movement in his "The Industrial Folk Song in Cape Breton", *Canadian Folklore canadien*, 8, 1-2 (1986), pp. 21-42.

58   Robert P. Swierenga, "Theoretical Perspectives on the New Rural History: From Environmentalism to Modernization", *Agricultural History*, 56 (1982), pp. 495-502, quotations at pp. 495-6 [original emphasis]. These parameters are almost universally applied in rural sociology. One recent work defines its subject as the

1951 or even 1901. In the context of Atlantic Canada, a definition based on population leaves very little urbanity left to study, but it does leave a number of difficulties. It does not require a demographer to realize that Middle River was not Philadelphia. But many instances are less clear-cut. According to the census, the population of the town of Inverness, Nova Scotia, the location of one of the following essays, peaked at just over 2,900 people in 1911, making it urban by some measures and rural by others.[59] "Country village" hardly seems an appropriate label for a town that had a mayor and a council of seven people, a permanent police force, several banks, a municipal water system and an industrial facility that employed almost a thousand men. Yet, for all this, the town was small and situated in a large agricultural county which heavily influenced its character. An arbitrary cut-off figure for defining the rural, while perhaps necessary in a large-scale study, only creates a distinction where one may not exist.

When we move on to the second criterion of "rurality" — that of agriculture — the issue becomes still less clear. In the Atlantic Region, at least, an emphasis on agriculture can be extremely misleading. If, when we study rural society, we focus only on agriculture — as we might focus on industry in urban society — we surely overlook the variety of forms available for provisioning the rural, or non-urban, household. Agriculture does not figure prominently in the essays which follow. The "settlers" described in Bill Parenteau's contribution to this collection did not derive their principal means of support from agriculture, although it was from the land (in the form of timber), and farming often provided a supplement. The situation was similar for the Newfoundland fishers Sean Cadigan describes. Yet both groups were clearly rural. They were independent commodity producers (although the "independent" clearly requires some qualification in this context): people who produced for themselves, either for their own consumption or for exchange with others. Conversely, many of the farm-based wage labourers in Rusty Bittermann's contribution and the farmer-miners described by Daniel Samson produced for themselves but probably

"scientific study of rural people in group relationships" and defines rural as being not urban: "People who live in the country or in towns of less than 2,500 population are said to be *rural*. All others are urban". See Everett M. Rogers, *et al.*, *Social Change in Rural Communities: An Introduction to Rural Sociology* (Englewood Cliffs, N.J., 1988), pp. 17-21, quotation at p. 19 [original emphasis]. See also Olaf F. Larson, "Rural Society", in David Sills, ed., *International Encyclopedia of the Social Sciences* (New York, 1968), vol. 13, pp. 580-7.

59 Hahn and Prude adopt 5,000 as their cut-off, although they recognize that such a figure is highly arbitrary. Rogers employs the figure of 2,500 as used by the United States Census Bureau, which is the same for Canada. See Hahn and Prude, *Countryside in the Age of Capitalist Transformation*, pp. 7-8; and Rogers et al., *Social Change and Rural Sociology*, p. 19.

earned more income off the farm than on it. And those in Steven Maynard's description of late-19th-century Hopewell drew regularly from a wide variety of supplements. Part of the problem here lies in what is meant by agriculture. If we are to be so broad as to include trees and fish within this category, then there is little problem. But the point here is not merely a semantic issue concerning agriculture or what constitutes farming. A useful definition of rural, at least in the context of Atlantic Canada, must employ socially and historically relevant criteria which are broad enough to include these variations and yet still allow us to make some important distinctions.[60]

More problems emerge when we attempt to link agriculture with "an awareness of change", especially when we presume that change to be the modernization of simple rural ways. Modernization has been both a theme and a set of values in writings about the countryside. The topics of "subsistence farming" or "commercial agriculture" have been developed in remarkably teleological ways. We can see this in Swierenga's notion of history — "the more important story" — which is primarily about change, or more specifically about a specific kind of change where rural communities "move through the historical process of establishment, growth, maturity, and decline under the driving forces of modernization".[61] Modernization, as a theory and an assumption, has come under withering criticism for its presuppositions about what should and should not occur in history's march to a pre-determined end and the destruction of everything other than what is modern.[62] Much of what Swierenga points toward — social isolation, extended families, "simplex" social organizations and "an at-

---

60 Compare, for example, Philip Abrams' attempt to break down that rural-urban dichotomy to the extent that it *conceptually* blurs any useful distinctions, with Bryan Palmer's description of the mutual subsumption of town and country under the power of capitalist transformation which *effectively* blurs the distinction. See Philip Abrams, "Towns and Economic Growth: Some Theories and Some Problems", in Philip Abrams and E.A. Wrigley, eds. *Towns in Societies: Essays in Economic History and Historical Sociology* (Cambridge, 1978), pp. 9-33; Bryan D. Palmer, "Town, Port and Country: Speculations on the Capitalist Transformation of Canada", *Acadiensis*, XII, 2 (Spring 1983), pp. 131-9.

61 Swierenga, "Theoretical Perspectives on the New Rural History", p. 497.

62 See, for example, Teodor Shanin, *Russia as a "Developing Society"*, vol. 1, *The Roots of Otherness: Russia's Turn of the Century* (New Haven, 1985), especially pp. 174-95; Jay O'Brien and William Roseberry, eds. *Golden Ages, Dark Ages: Imagining the Past in Anthropology and History* (Berkeley, 1991); Douglas Haynes and Gyan Prakash, eds., *Contesting Power: Resistance and Everyday Social Relations in South Asia* (Berkeley, 1992); and David Warren Sabean, *Property, Production, and Family in Neckarhausen, 1700-1870* (Cambridge, 1990), pp. 24-37, 431-2. David Harrison, *The Sociology of Modernization and Development* (London, 1988), provides a useful and balanced survey of the debate over modernization in development studies. A recent defence of modern-

titude of complacency in the face of nature's forces" — are very much open to question. They are developed as oppositions to what is considered normal in urban society; rurality becomes the necessary historical antecedent and social opposite of what is to come.[63] To be sure, rural society changed in the period under examination here, but its lineage is uncertain.

Rural historians have demonstrated that the countryside was part of the process of change.[64] Yet, as these and other studies illustrate, there were neither normative paths nor necessary outcomes; indeed, some have shown that part of modernization entailed the manufacture of new customs and traditions.[65] Agents of modernity were present throughout the Atlantic Canadian countryside, but

ization theory can be found in Ian Roxborough, "Modernization Theory Revisited", *Comparative Studies in Society and History*, 30, 4 (1988), pp. 753-61.

63 The definitions in the *Oxford English Dictionary* (Oxford, 1989) follow the same pattern. Initially, it notes, there was little distinction between "rural" and "rustic", although the former came to designate a location where in the latter "there is a suggestion of the more primitive qualities or manners naturally attaching to country life". Yet, the definitions offered for rural turns increasingly away from a location (sense 1, "living in the country...engaged in country occupations") and toward rustic (sense 3, "of or pertaining to...peasants or country-folk"; sense 4, "Natural or appropriate to the country or country-people; unpolished, plain, simple"). The rural is explicitly positioned against the urban (sense 5, "characteristic of the country...as opposed to the town") and, as the primitive opposite of the modern town, is seen to move toward the characteristics of the town, as in "rural urbanization" (sense 6, "the investment of the country with an urban character").

64 See, for example, Steven Hahn and Jonathan Prude, "Introduction", in Hahn and Prude, *The Countryside in the Age of Capitalist Transformation*, especially pp. 10-15; Lou Ferleger, ed., *Agriculture and National Development: Views on the Nineteenth Century* (Ames, 1990); Parker, *America and the Wider World*; Mary Beth Pudup, "Social Class and Economic Development in Southeast Kentucky, 1820-1880", in Robert D. Mitchell, ed. *Appalachian Frontiers: Settlement, Society, and Development in the Preindustrial Era* (Lexington, 1991); and Robert Brenner, "Agrarian Class Structure and Economic Development in Pre-Industrial Europe", in T.H. Aston and C.H.E. Philpin, eds., *The Brenner Debate: Agrarian Class Structure and Economic Development in Pre-Industrial Europe* (Cambridge, 1985), pp. 10-63.

65 On modern traditions see Eric Hobsbawm and Terence Ranger, eds., *The Invention of Tradition* (Cambridge, 1983). Ian McKay's cautionary observation that all traditions are historical inventions is a useful reminder for academics keen on debunking the past. See his "Tartanism Triumphant: The Construction of Scottishness in Nova Scotia, 1933-1954", *Acadiensis*, XXI, 2 (Spring 1992), pp. 5-47. See also McKay, "Twilight at Peggy's Cove: Towards a Genealogy of Maritimicity", *Border/Lines*, 12 (Summer 1988), pp. 28-37; and James Overton, "Coming Home: Nostalgia and Tourism in Newfoundland", *Acadiensis*, XIV, 1 (Autumn 1984), pp. 84-97.

many others showed much less enthusiasm for its innovations. The development of "modernity" was not just an abstract, undifferentiated process — of movement from simple to complex, of traditional versus modern, of "modernization" — but a contested ideological and cultural field peopled by women and men with varying ideas about progress and civilization. Grant Marshall, the central character in Charles Bruce's *The Channel Shore*, represents a life not only pushed by the possibilities of progress and "venture" but also pulled by the tug of established ways and a community's older expectations. Like many real lives, his life occupies an ambiguous position, one which neither wholly shelters him from modernity nor prevents him from seeking his own form of improvement. As Erik Kristiansen argues in this volume, Bruce's nostalgic view was not so coloured that he misunderstood the complexity of rural people's lives. In the uneven social terrain of Atlantic Canada, we can locate any number of examples of what must then be labelled backward, conservative and (presumably) premodern. But is this how we should define the rural?

Our hope here is simply to push the boundaries of agriculture-centred definitions toward something which could encompass the vitality of the countryside without reducing it to homespun-dressed industrial society. Any definition must be provisional. It would include fairly standard issues such as low population. The figure for communities used in the Canadian census, 2,500, seems appropriate for the region in the time periods under consideration here, but we need to be mindful of what that figure means at different periods. Nor should we arbitrarily cut off small towns which we can demonstrate to be strongly influenced by the countryside. As the example of Inverness illustrates, the distinctly urban appearance of the town seems less important in light of the nature of the provincial coal industry and its labour recruitment strategies. Moreover, any definition must rest less specifically on agriculture than on various means of provisioning through household labour, only part of which includes abstract exchange. What marked life for country people — and defined it as "rural" life — was their ability to exploit the land or the sea, to produce for themselves a major part of their subsistence either directly (as food, shelter and clothing) or indirectly through exchange, and their ability to obtain some measure of independence — derived from either their own resources or resources from which access was not restricted in this way — at least deferring full dependence on wage labour. Many urban households also worked toward independence, but their capacity for self-reliance usually was much more limited.[66] This is not, it needs to be stressed, about a golden age of independent producers

---

66 Often these practices were carry-overs from rural strategies as workers moved to the city. See Suzanne Morton, "Women on Their Own: Single Mothers in Working-Class Halifax in the 1920s", *Acadiensis*, XXI, 2 (Spring 1992), pp. 90-107; and Sheva Medjuck, "The Importance of Boarding for the Structure of the Household in the 19th Century: Moncton, N.B. and Hamilton, Canada West", *Histoire sociale/Social History*, XIII (May 1980), pp. 207-14. See also Bettina Bradbury, "Cows, Pigs, and Boarders".

or a pre-capitalist utopia. For many, independence was more sought after than achieved; certainly, for most women, it is unlikely that rural patriarchy was fundamentally different than that found in the town.[67] Some found their independence in what we might now call capitalist agriculture — hiring labour, selling specialized production in the market and investing back into the enterprise. Others gave up the Atlantic Region to search for it elsewhere.

An analysis based in work and production could bring some clarity. Access to the resources of the land and the sea shaped variable bundles of practices for provisioning rural lives and strategies for maintaining household security. These practices were strands within a complex package which began with the possibility of households provisioning themselves, of working toward that independence and of living the effects which grew out of such productive relations. We can begin by situating the rural in areas of low population density where households produced directly for themselves and provisioned themselves through various combinations of market and non-market exchange and production. Within both the country and the town, a variety of circumstances prevailed, but rural households lived on and usually owned the means of producing for themselves. Independence, much less self-sufficiency or "subsistence", was seldom achieved, but access to resources allowed rural households the possibility of limiting the holds of dependence. Describing the "rural" (and the "urban") in this manner allows some conceptual space between the ideal types of peasant/country and worker/town. By focusing on specific sets of social relations, rather than ideal types, we can explore across a range of differences and similarities and recognize the diversity within the category "rural". Describing the complexity of rural society broadens our understanding of rurality to mean more than agriculture; moreover, it forces us to reassess the nature of change, the many paths it could have taken and the future courses that are open.

The Rural in Atlantic Canada

The essays which follow were not conceived as elements within a synthesis. They reflect independent work that was in progress in 1989 when the project was conceived. They do, however, draw on similar concerns about the history of rural Atlantic Canada. The two most common themes here are the issues of transition (or transformation) and differences between the town and the country. These essays explore the assumptions which historians bring to the study of the countryside, assumptions which are often too narrow, too urban or too utopian. These studies also urge a reconsideration of our urban and our rural pasts as

---

67 See Shirley Tillotson, "The Operators Along the Coast: A Case Study of the Link Between Gender, Skilled Labour and Social Power, 1900-1930", *Acadiensis*, XX, 1 (Autumn 1990), pp. 72-88; and Palmer, *Working-Class Experience*, pp. 76-8, 98-102.

separate spheres, suggesting, on the one hand, something of their differences, and, on the other, something of their interconnectedness and their relationality. Seldom do these elements find themselves connected as parts of a larger reality. This is not to downplay the differences between urban and rural worlds but to recognize that these differences were alternatively incorporated and reinforced within the broader patterns of social life.

One of the key interpretive issues in the analysis of 19th-century rural studies is how we interpret exchange relations.[68] Few Canadian studies have marked any form of transition from production for use to production for exchange. Combining assumptions that the countryside was largely insulated from urban-based commerce until the effects of the capitalist towns "penetrated" the countryside, most rural studies describe this "pre-capitalist" past as a society outside the influence of the city but which gradually succumbed to its modernizing forces. Thus the presence of both market and non-market activities was, apparently, a reflection of pioneer society. Non-market exchange becomes a problem which the rural society would later overcome, the teething pains of a maturing society.

Two of these assumptions come under question most centrally in the two essays which lead off our collection. Beginning with the myth of the independent yeoman — that self-sufficient figure which many studies presume to have represented the majority during eastern North America's settlement period — Rusty Bittermann explores the prevalence of farm-based wage labourers in the northeastern Maritimes in the first half of the 19th century. In an earlier study of the rural Cape Breton community of Middle River, he found marked differences in the economic positions of households. Relative wealth was less a function of an individual's position in the life-cycle — a factor often put forth to counter interpretations of social differentiation — than of the timing of settlement (especially in an area where good land was limited) and the capital available to individual settlers.[69] If many Middle River farmers engaged in one side or the other of the labour market, how extensive was farm-based waged employment in the region before the era of modern industry? In this essay, he makes a case for the widespread importance of wage labour during a period long believed to be characterized more by independence on the land than dependence on wages. Yet, despite such conditions, the dream of independence on the land continued to

---

68   This is most central in the American literature on the countryside. See Hahn and Prude, *The Countryside in the Age of Capitalist Transformation*; Winnifred B. Rothenberg, *From Market Places to Market Society: The Transformation of Rural Massachusetts, 1750-1850* (Chicago, 1992). For an attempt to reconcile these positions see Kulikoff, "The Transition to Capitalism in Rural America".

69   Bittermann, "The Hierarchy of the Soil"; and "Economic Stratification and Agrarian Settlement: Middle River in the Early Nineteenth Century", in Donovan, *The Island*, pp. 71-87.

exert a strong influence on representations of farm life in both contemporary and more recent accounts.

Bittermann's essay questions both the assumption of an earlier independence that would later be undermined and the view that the impulse for change came from outside rural society. Examining a later period, however, Steven Maynard's contribution emphasizes the continued importance of non-market production and exchange in the rural community of Hopewell, in Pictou County, Nova Scotia. Material needs were met in production centred more on the household than in the market, and there were few people in the village who exercised enough material advantage to dominate social relations. But this is not a description of contented peasants; conflict was very real, both within and between households. Maynard's careful reading of diaries and merchant ledgers argues for an interpretation that emphasizes a transition from a social formation rooted in shared notions of community and familial security toward one centred more on individual accumulation and acquisition. As demographic pressures grew and local industries developed, trade and production became increasingly commercialized, and many of Hopewell's residents were compelled to buy and sell their goods more than they had in the past. Yet few fully embraced all the elements of the steadily growing possibilities of a cash-centred economy. Following suggestions found in the new rural history of the American countryside, Maynard describes how rural people incorporated cash and markets into their older practices, accepting some aspects but also adapting and rejecting them in accordance with their own needs and expectations. These pressures developed, at least in part, not only from the demands of outside merchants and banks but also from conflicts and pressures emanating from within rural households. It is these types of pressures, Maynard argues, that altered social relations in Hopewell when it was "on the market's edge".

Much of the difficulty in interpreting exchange and its apparently changing nature stems from the diversity of forms of exchange we meet in the countryside. Both Maynard's and Bittermann's essays illustrate this, pointing to the interpretive complexity of labour exchange. How *we* interpret these relationships is based on fairly obvious differences: wage labour versus independent commodity production, from working with one's neighbour to exchanging butter for dry goods from a local merchant and to selling produce or one's labour to an industrial firm. Yet, as Maynard's and Bittermann's different emphases suggest, these relations were seldom so clear-cut as the conceptual terms would indicate. Whatever people's reasons for entering the labour market, how do we assess the motivations for their activities or their calculation of the opportunity costs? Did a young woman who entered domestic service do so to help her family or to find independence? Or did both of these considerations, and others, condition her decision? How we sort out these matters is complex. How they were understood by the participants themselves may well have been very different. Clearly, part of that explanation lies in recognizing that rural people's strategies seldom required such distinctions. Their practices combined various motivations — desires, needs, expectations, requirements — in different manners and material circumstances.

In Inverness, Nova Scotia, we find hundreds of those rural workers who made the decision to enter the labour market. Daniel Samson's essay approaches the problem of rural work from the vantage point of a town; here the relationship under examination is more the country's influence on the town than the traditional emphasis of the impact of the town on the country. Coal mines, built by Central Canadian finance capital and serving markets in Montreal, drew a permanent skilled work force to Inverness in the early years of the 20th century. The mines also required a large seasonal work force, most of whom were drawn from the surrounding countryside. Such an adaptable labour market allowed the company the flexibility to produce on demand, while allowing many rural households to find regular but occasional wages nearby. These semipermanent and peripatetic rural workers brought with them different needs and expectations and encouraged new tensions in coal mining labour relations. Straining both their union's ability to protect its craft status and the paternalistic ties which existed between the company's management and its skilled workers, these tensions culminated in a representation strike in 1909-10. During the massive expansion of the provincial coal industry between 1890 and 1914, these conditions were common throughout Nova Scotia, suggesting the crucial role rural workers played in the "industrial" history of the region.

Rural workers were seldom able to join together effectively to protect their own interests. Their effects, generally, were more cumulative than collective.[70] In New Brunswick during the 1920s, rural males applied pressures through local clientele networks to obtain and protect their hold on farm settlement lots — where they cut timber more often than they farmed — which were drawn from the leaseholds of large lumber and pulp companies. As Bill Parenteau's contribution illustrates, rural workers obtained land in order to cut wood legally and illegally as was required of them to compete with the leaseholders for access to the forest. These struggles between the state's administrative apparatus, foresters, businessmen and the settlers were small localized affairs, effectively consuming the time and patience of those who sought to monopolize their hold on the province's forest resources.[71] While this was not class struggle on a grand scale as in the Winnipeg or Amherst general strikes of 1919 or industrial

---

70 See, however, Rusty Bittermann, "Agrarian Protest and Cultural Transfer: Irish Immigrants and the Escheat Movement on Prince Edward Island", in Thomas P. Power, ed., *The Irish in Atlantic Canada* (Fredericton, 1991), pp. 96-106.

71 See also Raymond Léger, "L'impact de l'industrie du bois sur le térritoire et la main-d'oeuvre de la Péninsule acadienne, Nouveau-Brunswick, 1875-1900", in L. Anders Sandberg, ed., *Trouble in the Woods: Forest Policy and Social Conflict in Nova Scotia and New Brunswick* (Fredericton, 1992), pp. 22-42.

Cape Breton in the 1920s, the effects were considerable. As the province emerged out of the period of timber colony toward its industrial future in pulp and paper manufacture,[72] many rural New Brunswickers escaped being drawn into proletarianization, drawing instead on older practices and their own abilities to compete for timber. State policy was directed toward curbing this "evil". Yet, in terms of its administration, the pressures exerted on community-based, political-clientele networks meant that many small battles were won not by capital and the state but by poor independent wood producers.[73]

The Newfoundland case is quite different from that of the Maritimes. Still, there was some common ground, especially in relations between producers, merchants and markets.[74] On the northeastern shore, the fishery operated squarely on the backs of the household. These fishing households were unable to resort to agriculture to supplement their subsistence, although there were some alternatives available in gardening. Sean Cadigan's Newfoundland illustration confronts the debate over the role of merchant capital in thwarting development, in particular its "parasitic" function: exploiting existing productive capacity while actively resisting development which might threaten control of markets. The Newfoundland fishery began its "transition to capitalism" — in the fundamental sense of creating a class of free labourers — early in the 19th century, a condition which in any unilinear understanding of the development of capitalism should have proceeded to the development of a home market.[75] As commodity producers, Newfoundland fishing households could have formed a nascent capitalist class within the fishery, and during periods of high prices and good markets such as the Napoleonic wars differentiation into wage labourers and small capitalists did indeed occur. Exploring the colonial Newfoundland court records, Cadigan asks whether there is evidence that merchants and the courts worked to discourage economic diversification during this crucial period for planters and fishing households. Merchants' power over fishing households

---

72　Bill Parenteau, "The Woods Transformed: The Emergence of the Pulp and Paper Industry in New Brunswick, 1918-1931", *Acadiensis*, XXII, 1 (Autumn 1992), pp. 5-43. See also Serge Côté, "Naissance de l'industrie papetière et mainmise sur la forêt: Le cas de Bathurst", in Sandberg, *Trouble in the Woods*, pp. 43-64.

73　These struggles by independent producers continued well into the 20th century. See Bill Parenteau, "'In Good Faith': The Development of Pulpwood Marketing for Independent Producers in New Brunswick, 1960-1975", and Peter Clancy, "The Politics of Pulpwood Marketing in Nova Scotia, 1960-1985", in Sandberg, *Trouble in the Woods*, pp. 110-41, 142-67.

74　See the important collection of essays in Ommer, *Merchant Credit and Labour Strategies*.

75　See also Sean Cadigan, "The Staple Model Reconsidered: The Case of Agricultural Policy in Northeast Newfoundland, 1785-1855", *Acadiensis*, XXI, 2 (Spring 1992), pp. 48-71.

was undoubtedly significant, but it is much less clear that they actively worked against alternatives or reduced fishing households to a state of powerlessness.

Finally, Erik Kristiansen takes us through some of the important literary landscapes of the Nova Scotia countryside. Charles Bruce and Ernest Buckler, two of the province's most important novelists, focus on the changing countryside in their major novels. Both authors, writing in the middle of this century, describe rural communities set apart from the worlds of cities and industries but where long-held values and virtues were under attack. Again we see in these fictional accounts the two dominant assumptions that have underpinned most historical writing on the countryside: a vision of an achieved independence on the land and of the penetration of this world of independence by modernity. These authors describe communities which were being undercut by urban values and the dynamic of capitalism; these were communities born in experience and maintained in memory, both crumbling and reforming under the pressures of a changing world. Much like Neil MacNeil's memories of his simpler childhood in *The Highland Heart in Nova Scotia*, we can see how these authors selectively remembered their pre-modern pasts, either filtering out or romanticizing the harsher aspects that did not quite fit the dream and thus making their contributions to the myth of the region's rural "Golden Age". But Kristiansen's reading of these novels questions their transparency and brings out more than a romantic longing for a world we have lost. The "history" represented in these novels maintains a consistently critical distance. Bruce and Buckler, Kristiansen maintains, set a past against an uncertain future. While they are in some ways romantic, they should be interpreted as anti-modern writers — critics of their present more than myth-makers of the past.[76]

The images which emerge in fiction, history and myth have some basis in the past; they are, indeed, historical. However disfigured they may be, they appear not only in recent writings but also in contemporary descriptions. Our task must be to locate and critique the sources of those representations, to delineate what lies in their shadows and to plot their genealogies into the present. Together, these essays demonstrate that there were many paths to be taken in the region; how people understood their worlds was very much dependent upon

---

76 The term "anti-modern" is borrowed from T.J. Jackson Lears, *No Place of Grace: Antimodernism and the Transformation of American Culture, 1880-1920* (New York, 1981), where he characterizes it as an ambivalent reaction against the modern. In some ways, these Maritime writers may have been more in touch with modernism's reaction against the modern, perhaps more so than some of the "great" writers and artists of the English countryside. See Raymond Williams, *The Country and the City* (London, 1975); Brian Short, ed., *The English Rural Community: Image and Analysis* (Cambridge, 1992). More critical of these writers, but I believe seriously underestimating their contributions, is Janice Kulyk Keefer, *Under Eastern Eyes: A Critical Reading of Maritime Fiction* (Toronto, 1987).

which paths they trod. In Atlantic Canada, the countryside was at least as important as the city well into the 20th century. The conditions which produced the region's rural-centred myth of the "Golden Age" were not so golden, nor did they end after Confederation or the National Policy. A reassessment of rural history in Atlantic Canada has been long overdue. In the pages that follow we have begun to demonstrate not only the complexity of the rural experience itself but also the importance it holds for understanding the modern history of the region as a whole.

Farm Households and Wage Labour in the Northeastern Maritimes in the Early 19th Century

Rusty Bittermann

One of the most enduring mythologies of rural life in the temperate regions of North America has centred on the freedom resulting from easy access to land. In the New World unlike the Old, the story goes, land was plentiful, free from the encumbrances of a feudal past, and common folk might gain unimpeded access to its abundance and carve an independent niche for themselves. In the 18th and 19th centuries, the mythology was fostered by the effusions of travel accounts and emigrant manuals as well as by the writings of immigrants themselves. Since then it has been broadly sustained in North American historiography.

In keeping with the larger trend, the myth of the independent yeoman has held a prominent place in Maritime literature. It can be found in the works of such Gaelic bards as Allan the Ridge of Mabou, himself one of the many immigrants who arrived in the region from Scotland early in the 19th century. In the New World, he lyricized, "free land" gave rise to "riches and herds of cattle" for common folk: "Now that you have come across the sea / to this fair land, / you will want for nothing the rest of your life; / everything prospers for us".[1] It figures in Joseph Howe's "Western Rambles". With "a wife and an axe", Howe maintained, an industrious man might carve out a handsome competence and become "truly rich and independent".[2] Thomas McCulloch's Mephibosheth Stepsure, too, sustains the contention that in the Nova Scotia countryside a natural abundance ensured that those with frugal and industrious habits would

---

1   Margaret MacDonell, *The Emigrant Experience: Songs of Highland Emigrants in North America* (Toronto, 1982), pp. 90-2. The author wishes to gratefully acknowledge the assistance received from the Social Sciences and Humanities Research Council of Canada, whose financial support aided this research. I am also grateful to Carmen Bickerton, Michael Cross, Margaret McCallum, Danny Samson and the participants in the Atlantic Canada Workshop (Lunenburg, September 1990) and the Rural Workers in Atlantic Canada Conference (Saint Mary's University, October 1990) for their comments on an earlier version of this paper. By "northeastern Maritimes" I mean Prince Edward Island, Cape Breton Island and the northernmost section of peninsular Nova Scotia. I take some liberties with the time frame indicated, occasionally drawing evidence from the late 18th century and beyond 1850. Nonetheless, this essay is primarily about farm-based wage work in the first half of the 19th century.

2   Joseph Howe, "Western Rambles", in M.G. Parks, ed., *Travel Sketches of Nova Scotia* (Toronto, 1973), pp. 95-6.

be rewarded with economic security and independence.[3] The theme of yeomanly independence emerges as well in the writings of these men's descendants: "Every man in Washabuckt", wrote Neil MacNeil, recalling his experiences in a turn-of-the-century Cape Breton rural community, "was his own boss, for he got his livelihood from nature and did not have to work for any other man or thank any one but God for it".[4] And so it is still told to younger generations by older folk in Cape Breton: there was a time before the dependence of the contemporary era when those willing to work might combine their labour with an abundant land to derive a livelihood and secure an independence for themselves. In contemporary regional historiography it re-emerges in the works of those who emphasize the insularity and self-sufficiency of rural households in the early 19th century and conceptualize the history of the countryside over subsequent decades in terms of the loss of an earlier independence rooted in the direct fulfilment of needs through access to the land.[5]

That the image of the independent yeoman was to a certain degree a reflection of a reality experienced by some rural residents in the Maritimes is indisputable. The opportunities for acquiring an independent rural livelihood were relatively greater in British North America than they were in the Old World. Many transformed these possibilities into reality and achieved a "propertied independence".[6] Those who enjoyed such circumstances, however, were but one component of a larger farming population. And many who came to enjoy a modicum of yeomanly independence only experienced this condition during a fraction of their lives. Like any powerful and pervasive mythology, the image of the independent yeoman is partly rooted in a reality. Problems arise, though, when a fragment of the rural experience becomes a characterization of the whole. It is not my intention here to consider how this mythology developed or to unravel the various strands of peasant dream, liberal ideology and social criti-

3   Thomas McCulloch, *The Stepsure Letters* (Toronto, 1960).

4   Neil MacNeil, *The Highland Heart in Nova Scotia* (Antigonish, 1980, [1948]).

5   Charles W. Dunn, *Highland Settler: A Portrait of the Scottish Gael in Nova Scotia* (Toronto, 1953); D. Campbell and R.A. MacLean, *Beyond the Atlantic Roar: A Study of the Nova Scotia Scots* (Toronto, 1974); John Warkentin, "The Atlantic Region", in R. Cole Harris and John Warkentin, eds., *Canada Before Confederation: A Study of Historical Geography* (Toronto, 1977), pp. 169-231; Peter Sinclair, "From Peasants to Corporations: The Development of Capitalist Agriculture in the Maritime Provinces", in John A. Fry, ed., *Contradictions in Canadian Society: Readings in Introductory Sociology* (Toronto, 1984), pp. 276-93.

6   The phrase is drawn from Daniel Vickers' superb analysis of the ideal and some of its implications. Daniel Vickers, "Competency and Competition: Economic Culture in Early America," *William and Mary Quarterly*, 3rd Series, 47, 1 (1990), pp. 3-29.

que that have sustained it. Rather, I want to examine what it has obscured, indeed tends to deny: the importance of wage labour to farmfolk in the northeastern Maritimes in the first half of the 19th century.[7] The survey which follows underlines the significance of wages to the farm population and highlights the profile of farm dwellers within the larger labour force.

Much of the rural population of the Maritimes began farm-making in the New World by spending part of their time as employees. In his study of rural life in Ontario, Robert Leslie Jones suggested a three-tier typology of new agricultural settlers: those with the capital (or credit) to hire others to speed construction and land clearing, those with the means to support themselves during the start-up period of farm-making, and, lastly, those who found it necessary to engage in off-farm work in order to sustain themselves while farm-making.[8] Given what we know of the economic circumstances of many of those who settled in the northeastern Maritimes in the late 18th and early 19th centuries, it is clear that thousands in Atlantic Canada fell in the latter category.[9] Rev. George Patterson's description of the adaptive strategies employed by the passengers who arrived on the *Hector* reflects the difficulties and possibilities available to other emigrants who came to the region under similar circumstances. Initially lacking the means to establish themselves on the land, Patterson noted, they spread out to places distant from Pictou where they could find work: "Not only men, but mothers of families, hired out, and their children, male and female, they bound out for service, till they should come of age".[10] As John Cambridge, a Prince Edward Island landlord, observed in the first years of the 19th century, those who arrived with little or no capital "generally work for others till they have acquired a little stock" and in the years that follow they "get

---

7   The mythology is often incongruously juxtaposed with another reality. Neil MacNeil, for instance, even as he extols the independence Washabuckters achieved on the land, tells of the regular flow of labour southward and of his grandfather's difficult experiences commuting on foot between Washabuckt and a job many miles north in industrial Cape Breton.

8   Robert Leslie Jones, *History of Agriculture in Ontario 1613-1880* (Toronto, 1946), p. 60.

9   J.S. Martell, *Immigration to and Emigration From Nova Scotia, 1815-1838* (Halifax, 1942); R.G. Flewwelling, "Immigration to and Emigration from Nova Scotia", *Nova Scotia Historical Society Collections*, 28 (1949), pp. 75-105; D.C. Harvey, "Scottish Immigration to Cape Breton", *Dalhousie Review*, 21, 1 (April 1941), pp. 313-24; Barbara Kincaid, "Scottish Immigration to Cape Breton, 1758-1838", M.A. thesis, Dalhousie University, 1964; Campbell and MacLean, *Beyond the Atlantic Roar*, pp. 7-75; Helen I. Cowan, *British Emigration to British North America: The First Hundred Years* (Toronto, 1961), pp. 172-227.

10   Rev. George Patterson, *A History of the County of Pictou Nova Scotia* (Montreal, 1877; rept. ed. Belleville, Ont., 1972), p. 86.

assistance by working for the neighbouring farmers, till they have brought their own farms gradually forward".[11]

A good account of the settlement process in Pictou County in the early 19th century is provided by Lord Selkirk. Describing the farm-making labours of a household from Perthshire, he noted that the man of the house was "obliged to work for hire" to feed his family and sustain the credit necessary for purchasing the articles needed for capitalizing his farm. This particular household had the advantage of being settled on good land adjacent to West River, and its occupants had the potential, one would imagine, of escaping from the necessity of wage dependence, but in the early years of establishment, Selkirk estimated that the Perthshire man spent "full half his time employed at wages off the farm".[12]

The ledger book of the Cape Breton merchant Lawrence Kavanaugh provides insights into the process as well. In 1818, Kavanaugh recorded the influx of a number of settlers from Prince Edward Island who took up lands along the eastern shoreline of Bras d'Or Lake. Several opened accounts in St. Peters with Kavanaugh shortly after their arrival. James Corbit began his dealings with Kavanaugh by depositing £5 in cash and selling him a saddle for £2 10s.[13] In return Kavanaugh provided Corbit with provisions and supplies — flour, meal, codfish, tea, vinegar, rum, tobacco, a pipe, salt, cod line, shoes and calico — as well as the financing necessary to buy out a previous occupant of the lot he had occupied. Corbit's account with Kavanaugh was a relatively modest £33 (provisions plus interest) over the next six years, suggesting — particularly given the quantities of goods and the absence of building materials and tools on

---

11 [John Cambridge], *A Description of Prince Edward Island in the Gulf of St. Lawrence, North America with a Map of the Island and a Few Cursory Observations Respecting the Climate, Natural Productions and Advantages of its Situation in Regard to Agriculture and Commerce; Together with Some Remarks, as Instructions to New Settlers* (London, 1805), p. 8. See also John Lewellin, *Emigration. Prince Edward Island: A Brief But Faithful Account of this Fine Colony* (1832), reprinted in D.C. Harvey, ed., *Journeys to the Island of St. John* (Toronto, 1955), p. 199. Captain Moorsom provides evidence on the process as well, though in this case viewed from the vantage point of the agricultural employer. Moorsom notes that in the Windsor region agricultural labourers were primarily recruited from among new settlers who had not become established and from the younger members of poorer farm households who worked away in the summer and returned in the winter. Captain W. Moorsom, *Letters From Nova Scotia; Comprising Sketches of a Young Country* (London, 1830), pp. 207-8.

12 Patrick C. White, ed., *Lord Selkirk's Diary, 1803-1804: A Journal of his Travels in British North America and the Northeastern United States* (Toronto, 1958), p. 51.

13 For Corbit's account see the Kavanaugh Account Book, 1818-24, MG 3, vol. 301, p. 212, Public Archives of Nova Scotia [PANS].

the account — that he was dealing with others as well to obtain his household supplies. To meet these particular debts, Corbit worked for Kavanaugh two and a half days in 1819, 33 days repairing and building a boat in 1821, one day sawing planks in 1822, 24 days sawing the following year, and half a day sawing in 1824. A credit to his account by a man named McAdam for 29 shillings in 1820 probably represents yet another 12 days work, performed in this case for McAdam. The survival strategies of many countryfolk, as the landlord John Hill noted in the case of Prince Edward Island, commonly included temporary work for anyone who might give them "an order on the shopkeepers for cloathing and tools".[14] As well, Corbit sold Kavanaugh a couple of chickens in 1820, an ox and a small amount of fresh mackerel and chickens in 1823, and six shillings worth of butter in 1824, leaving him still in debt to the St. Peter's merchant for £8 at the end of the year. Lacking knowledge of Corbit's dealings with others, it is impossible to gauge how much off-farm work he in fact engaged in during these years or to calculate his progress in farm-making, though the nature and scale of farm produce suggest a rudimentary holding, perhaps of only a single cow. The evidence from Corbit's account and from the other new arrivals from Prince Edward Island who appear on Kavanaugh's books reinforce, though, Cambridge's, Selkirk's, Hill's and Patterson's observations concerning the importance of wage work to new settlers in the early stages of farm-making.

How long might immigrants such as those appearing in Kavanaugh's ledgers or observed by Selkirk and Cambridge spend at wage work before they could sustain themselves and their households with the returns of their farms? The answer would vary, of course, depending upon their circumstances at the time of arrival, the natural resources of their farm properties, the annual returns that could be made from wage work, and the level of their commitment to acquire a self-sustaining operation. Peter Russell's calculation of an average clearing rate in Upper Canada during the early 19th century of 1.5 acres per year per adult male probably is a reasonable estimate for the Maritimes as well.[15] At such a

---

14   John Hill, Memo on Quit Rents, 1802, Colonial Office Papers [CO] 226/18, p. 230.

15   Peter A. Russell, "Forest into Farmland: Upper Canadian Clearing Rates, 1822-1839", *Agricultural History*, 57, 3 (July 1983), pp. 326-39. A listing of squatters on Indian lands in Middle River indicating length of settlement and the extent of their fields gives some indication of the clearing rates of Highlanders in Cape Breton. For the 11 households for which there was adequate data, the average rate of clearing was just under two acres per year. On average these households had been located on their lands for six years and had just under 11 acres of land cleared. If anything these particular rates could be somewhat inflated as the cleared acreages may include lands that natives had cleared and/or those improved by other squatters who were driven off prior to the settlement of these individuals. Nova Scotia, *Journals of the House of Assembly [JHA]* (1862), app. 30, Report of Indian Committee, p. 7.

rate, a minimal 25 acres of fields would, when additional labour could not be hired, typically be realized only after a decade of work. Often, it would seem, this took longer. The itinerant shoemaker and missionary, Walter Johnstone, estimated that on average the first generation of settlers on Prince Edward Island would "not clear more than 20 or 30 acres all their life".[16] Another observer noted that there were "many who have been 20 years in the colony" and "have no more than 5 acres cleared".[17] To the cost of sustaining a household while preparing the land base necessary for household subsistence were added the costs of stocking and equipping such a farm. S.S. Hill, the son of John Hill, one of Prince Edward's Island's largest landlords, advised would-be immigrants to expect costs of roughly £200 for the livestock, tools and supplies necessary for establishing a farm of 30 cleared acres.[18] Though it was not in his interest to exaggerate the costs of farm-making on the Island, Hill's figure seems high.[19] What is beyond doubt is that with wages typically averaging around 2s 6d per day, with work sporadic and seasonal, and with the needs of daily subsistence having first claim on income, raising the monies necessary for equipping a farm was, typically, the product of years of labour.

The cost of land, of course, had to be factored into the farm-making process as well. On Prince Edward Island there was little Crown land, and most immigrants found it necessary to obtain land from landlords. In the 1820s and 1830s, an unimproved freehold would, typically, cost somewhere from ten shillings to one pound per acre.[20] By leasing land a new settler might defer these start-up costs, but in time would incur a rental cost of around £5 per year for 100

---

16 Walter Johnstone, *A Series of Letters, Descriptive of Prince Edward Island* (1822) reprinted in Harvey, *Journeys to the Island of St. John*, p. 126.

17 "Rusticus" to the editor, *Prince Edward Island Register* (Charlottetown), 29 November 1825, p. 1.

18 [S.S. Hill], *A Short Account of Prince Edward Island Designed Chiefly for the Information of Agriculturalists and other Emigrants of Small Capital* (London, 1839), p. 66.

19 Graeme Wynn's estimate of a minimal outlay of £30 to £40 is admittedly a very conservative estimate of simple start-up costs. Working farms of 100 acres with 20 acres cleared would, he notes, have fetched from £100 to £300 in New Brunswick in the 1830s. Graeme Wynn, *Timber Colony: A Historical Geography of Early Nineteenth Century New Brunswick* (Toronto, 1981), p. 80.

20 George Seymour to T.H. Haviland, 5 February 1837, 114 A/508/3, Warwick County Record Office [WCRO]; Robert Stewart to John Pendergast, 23 April 1834, Robert Stewart Letterbooks, Ms. 2989/1, Public Archives of Prince Edward Island [PAPEI]; State of Sales of Land by Sir James Montgomery, Baronet and Brothers, GD1/409/15/C14568, Scottish Record Office [SRO].

acres of land.[21] In Nova Scotia, the costs of acquiring "free" Crown land probably ran around £20 for a typical 200-acre lot.[22] With the termination of a "free" Crown land policy in the late 1820s, these costs increased as lands were sold at public auction with a base price established at 2s 3d to 2s 6d per acre.[23]

Given the costs of land, stock and equipment, and the labour required for preparing fields, even when a household managed to acquire good lands — and many in the region did not — years and probably decades elapsed between beginning the tasks of clearing and planting and arriving at a condition where, as Neil MacNeil phrased it, one did not have to "thank anyone but God" for their living.[24] We can multiply, then, the experiences of Corbit and his fellow Prince Edward Islanders newly arrived in Cape Breton whose wage work appears in Kavanaugh's books, the Perthshire man who Selkirk observed, or those who took passage aboard the *Hector* described by Rev. Patterson, by the thousands of emigrants of modest means who took up farms in the northeastern Maritimes in the late 18th and early 19th centuries — people who of necessity had to follow similar work strategies for many years. The ongoing process of settlement and farm-making was intimately linked with the maintenance of a vast pool of farm-based labourers in pursuit of work opportunities.

Weather conditions and the presence or absence of crop and animal diseases played a substantial part in expediting the progress of household independence or, alternatively, in dashing hopes of agricultural security. A household which enjoyed a margin of independence in a favourable year could be plunged into debt and dependence in another. The extraordinary frosts of 1816 and the 1830s, and the repeated failure of the potato crops due to blight in the 1840s in particular, forced large numbers of farm households into an increased reliance on purchased foodstuffs. Particularly vulnerable were the newer and poorer farm households with limited inventories of livestock and reliant almost exclusively on their harvest of their potato and grain crops. Such natural disasters swelled

21   Selkirk Papers, MG 19, E1, 73/19302-13, National Archives of Canada [NAC]; Rental of the Property of Sir James Montgomery, Baronet and Brothers, GD1/409/16/C14568, SRO.

22   Donald Campbell to [a relative in Lewis], 7 October 1830, reprinted in the *Stornaway Gazette*, 30 September 1972, MG 100, vol. 115, no. 33, PANS.

23   S.J. Hornsby, "Scottish Emigration and Settlement in Early Nineteenth Century Cape Breton", in Kenneth Donovan, ed., *The Island: New Perspectives on Cape Breton History 1713-1975* (Sydney and Fredericton, 1990), p. 58.

24   Graeme Wynn's commentary on J.E. Woolford's 1817 watercolour, *View on the Road from Windsor to Horton by Avon Bridge at Gaspreaux River,* that behind the security portrayed in this image of a farm household which had achieved a comfortable competency there lay a "half-century of unremitting work", is acute. Graeme Wynn, "On the Margins of Empire, 1760-1840", in Craig Brown, ed., *The Illustrated History of Canada* (Toronto, 1987), p. 256.

the numbers in pursuit of work and expanded the commitments many households found it necessary to make to off-farm labour. Employment was needed to pay for provisions and to meet the costs and debts incurred during years of crisis.[25]

For many, the quality of land resources available — particularly when coupled with a poverty that diverted labour and capital away from farm improvements and toward the needs of basic sustenance — precluded ever escaping the necessity of engaging in extensive wage work.[26] As the Crown surveyor in Baddeck, D.B. McNab, noted in 1857, there were "hundreds" of farms in this region of Cape Breton where years after initial settlement their occupants remained heavily reliant on off-farm employment in order to "eke out the means of a scanty subsistence".[27] In general, he contended, such settlers occupied the difficult hill lands, the backlands, of the Island and tended to be squatters rather than freeholders. The Land Commissioners taking evidence on Prince Edward Island in 1860 heard similar testimony concerning areas of Prince Edward Island, often predominantly occupied by squatters, where few settlers successfully managed to derive the bulk of their livelihood from the soil.[28]

While some households made ends meet by combining wage work with the sale of selected farm "surpluses", often enough exchanging costly foods like butter and meat for cheaper breadstuffs and fish, there were others which appear

---

25 On the frosts of 1816, a year that became known as "eighteen hundred and froze to death", see Patterson, *A History of the County of Pictou*, p. 286; Howard Russell, *A Long Deep Furrow: Three Centuries of Farming in New England* (Hanover, N.H. 1976), pp. 136, 147-8. For discussions of those of the 1830s and government initiatives to ban exports of foodstuffs and provide relief see the *Royal Gazette* (Charlottetown), 12 August 1834, p. 3; 9 December 1834, p. 3; 26 July 1836, p. 3; 13 September 1836, p. 3; 14 February 1837, p. 3; 28 February 1837, p. 3; 7 March 1837, pp. 1-2; 11 April 1837, p. 3. The impact the potato blight of the 1840s had on Cape Breton is dealt with in Robert Morgan, "'Poverty, wretchedness, and misery': The Great Famine in Cape Breton, 1845-1851", *Nova Scotia Historical Review*, 6, 1 (1986), pp. 88-104; and S.J. Hornsby, *Nineteenth-Century Cape Breton: A Historical Geography* (Kingston and Montreal, 1992), pp. 111-20. For discussion of the impact of the potato failures of the late 1840s on Prince Edward Island see the *Islander* (Charlottetown), 26 November 1847, p. 2; 24 December 1847, p. 3; 7 April 1848, p. 3; 14 April 1848, p. 3; 3 November 1848, p. 2; 12 January 1848, p. 3.

26 In his study of farm-making in Upper Canada in this period, Norman Ball notes the presence of immigrants trapped by similar cycles of poverty there. Norman Rodger Ball, "The Technology of Settlement and Land Clearing in Upper Canada Prior to 1840", Ph.D. thesis, University of Toronto, 1979, pp. 30-2.

27 D.B. McNab to Uniacke, 3 January 1857, Nova Scotia, *JHA* (1857), app. 71, pp. 421.

28 Ian Ross Robertson, ed., *The Prince Edward Island Land Commission of 1860* (Fredericton, 1988), p. 136.

to have been exclusively, or almost exclusively, reliant on the sale of labour to meet the costs of household goods and food and to procure seed and animal provisions. The ledger books of the North Sydney trader, John Beamish Moore,[29] for instance, reveal a number of backland households who had nothing but labour to sell during the years of their dealings with him.[30] During the period 1853 to 1860, Angus Link's household paid for their supplies of oatmeal, barley flour and oats through a combination of Angus' own labour and that of his wife and daughter.[31] So, too, did the Angus McDonald household pay its debts through Angus' own labour and that of his sons and daughter. The debts of the Murdoch Ferguson household as well were repaid entirely by Murdoch's labour and that of a female member of the household. Moore's account book reveals something of the seasonality of the pressures on these backland households as well. Between 1853 and 1861, the accounts of those identified as backlanders in his books reveal recurrent debts for hay, barley flour and oat meal needed in April and May to replenish exhausted winter supplies, and seed grain (barley and oats) needed in May and June to permit planting another season's crop.[32] Merchant ledgers only reveal a fragment of these patterns. Wealthier members of rural communities as well often took on the role, and assumed the benefits, of acting as provisioners and sources of credit for poorer households through the months of greatest scarcity. It appears to have been particularly common for those acting as road commissioners to sell provisions on credit over the winter and to retain the road-work returns due to these households the following summer.[33]

Backlanders such as these, though possessing or occupying considerable acreages, were yet compelled by necessity to participate extensively in labour markets near and far in order to make up for the great inadequacies of their farm returns. They were, as the Crown surveyor in Baddeck, D.B. McNab, noted, the

---

29   A number of John Moores lived in and about North Sydney in the mid-19th century. Stephen Hornsby treats this account book as being that of John Belcher Moore. The Public Archives of Nova Scotia, though, stand by their description of it as being that of John Beamish Moore. Hornsby, *Nineteenth-Century Cape Breton,* pp. 72, 138-9; private correspondence with J.B. Cahill, 26 October 1992.

30   These backlanders may have been selling farm products elsewhere, perhaps closer at hand, but the fact that they routinely purchased bulky items, such as half barrels of flour and bushels of grain from Moore, without ever selling farm goods seems to suggest that they had little or nothing to sell.

31   John Beamish Moore Account Book, 1848-67, p. 14, Micro Biography, PANS.

32   John Beamish Moore Account Book, 1848-67, pp. 22-3, Micro Biography, PANS.

33   *Spirit of the Times* (Sydney), 19 July 1842, p. 347; Captain W. Moorsom, *Letters From Nova Scotia,* p. 288.

New World equivalent of Great Britain's day labourers; they "represent[ed] this class".[34] Quantitative analysis of census data from Middle River in Cape Breton and from Hardwood Hill in Pictou County suggests that in the third quarter of the 19th century, somewhere between a quarter and a third of the households in these agricultural districts of northeastern Nova Scotia needed to earn $100 or more in off-farm income in order to secure a minimal livelihood.[35] At the common agricultural wage rate of roughly 80 cents per day, this would be the equivalent of 125 or more working days.[36] Viewed in another fashion, given an average family food requirement of roughly $200, these farms at best probably derived only half their food needs from their own resources.[37] Data from Middle River confirm as well D.B. McNab's assertion that reliance on off-farm sources of income most often occurred among those who occupied rough hill lands: 84 per cent of the households with negative net farm incomes estimated to be greater than $100 in 1860-61 were those of backlanders.[38] Physical constraints necessitated much of the pattern of adaptation that McNab and others described.

Besides new settlers requiring an income during the years of farm establishment and backlanders grappling with chronic resource problems, analysis of the census returns from Middle River indicates yet another stream of rural peoples being propelled into participation in the work force in the mid-19th century and beyond. Estimates of the relationship between farm resources and household needs reveal three basic household categories. At one end of the spectrum there were households, primarily those of backlanders, where farm returns were chronically and substantially short of household subsistence needs — households that of necessity had to look for income beyond the farm across the full course of the family life cycle. On the other extreme there was a sig-

---

34 Nova Scotia, *JHA*, 1857, app. 72, p. 421.

35 Rusty Bittermann, Robert H. MacKinnon and Graeme Wynn, "Of Inequality and Interdependence in the Nova Scotian Countryside, 1850-1870", *Canadian Historical Review*, LXXIV, 1 (March 1993), pp. 1-43.

36 The estimate of an average agricultural wage for Nova Scotia is drawn from Julian Gwyn, "Golden Age or Bronze Moment? Wealth and Poverty in Nova Scotia: The 1850s and 1860s", *Canadian Papers in Rural History*, 8 (1992), pp. 195-230.

37 Charles H. Farnham, "Cape Breton Folk", *Harpers New Monthly Magazine*, (1886), reprinted in *Acadiensis*, VIII, 2 (Spring 1979), p. 100. These estimates are considered in detail in Bittermann, MacKinnon and Wynn, "Of Inequality and Interdependence in the Nova Scotian Countryside", and Rusty Bittermann, "Middle River: The Social Structure of Agriculture in a Nineteenth-Century Cape Breton Community", M.A. thesis, University of New Brunswick, 1987, app. IV.

38 Rusty Bittermann, "Economic Stratification and Agrarian Settlement: Middle River in the Early Nineteenth Century", in Donovan, *The Island,* pp. 86-7.

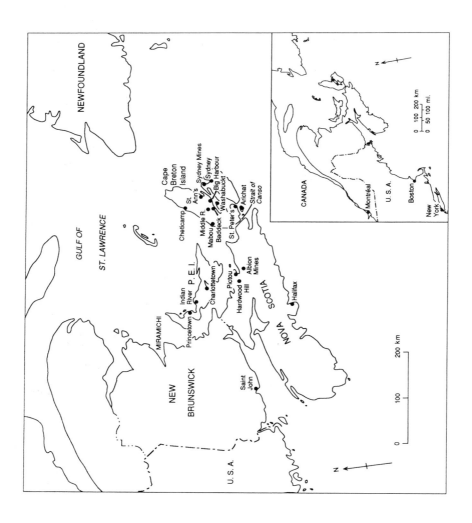

nificant minority of households, the commercial core of the valley's agricultural economy, where farm production was well in excess of household subsistence needs and the returns from farm-product sales were sufficient to permit substantial reinvestments in agriculture and in other pursuits. Members of such households had the option of working for themselves with their own resources or working for others. Wedged between these two strata were families whose condition more closely approximated the image of household self-sufficiency permeating so much of the literature on the rural Maritimes — farms on which the value of production roughly matched current needs. Although they possessed sufficient resources to derive a livelihood from the land, it is clear though, from the census and probate returns, that the resources of many of these households were not expanding at a rate sufficient to permit all their offspring to begin life in similar circumstances. Demographic growth was forcing, and would force, many individuals from an emerging generation within these middle strata households into participation in the labour force.[39]

Throughout the early 19th century, then, substantial numbers of the members of farm households situated in the northeastern Maritimes — new settlers, backlanders (along with others whose farm resources were chronically insufficient for household needs), and some of the offspring of middle-strata households — necessarily had to maintain a significant and regular involvement in the labour force despite their access to extensive tracts of land. Added to the ranks of these workers of necessity were many who were drawn for one reason or another by the opportunities afforded by off-farm work, people who might move in and out of the work force at will, alternately deriving a living from farm resources or choosing to participate in the labour force.

Those seeking employment might work in many different facets of the regional economy. Some of the Prince Edward Islanders who settled along Cape Breton's Bras d'Or Lake in the second decade of the 19th century found jobs with Lawrence Kavanaugh, the merchant from whom they obtained provisions. John Corbit made ends meet in part by sawing lumber and doing boat-carpentry work for Kavanaugh. During the period 1818 to 1824, others worked for this St. Peters merchant building fences, mowing hay, planting potatoes, looking after livestock, driving cattle that he had purchased, rafting timber and working in his fishing operations. Daily wages ranged from 1s 4d to the more common 2s 6d. Some jobs, such as mowing, were arranged by piece work, five shillings per acre, while yet other workers were hired on a monthly basis. Women appear sporadically in Kavanaugh's ledger, "knitting" twine at a fixed price per length and doing washing of some sort, again being paid by the piece.

The variety of tasks for which Kavanaugh hired labour, the different rates and means of payment, and the diverse composition of his work force — both in

---

39 Bittermann, "Economic Stratification and Agrarian Settlement", pp. 86-7; and Bittermann, "Middle River", pp. 157-9.

terms of age and gender — help suggest the complexity of the labour market in this period. The different areas of economic activity noted in his ledger — agriculture, the timber trade, vessel construction, the fishery, and general tasks associated with operating a mercantile establishment — capture much of the array of work available for the farm-based labourer of the northeastern Maritimes in the first quarter of the 19th century. Timber, ships, fishing and trade — the listing of occupations sounds so close to T.C. Haliburton's description of the typical Nova Scotian, who could be "found superintending the cultivation of a farm and building a vessel at the same time; and is not only able to catch and cure a cargo of fish, but to find his way to the West Indies or the Mediterranean" with it, that it is necessary to underline an important distinction between Haliburton's figure and those whose lives are under discussion here.[40] The occupational pluralist figuring in the *Old Judge* is an extension of the independent yeoman of other regional literature; his life is grounded in his control over a material abundance. The goods with which he loads his vessel are the "surplus" remaining from the produce of his farm, and though Haliburton does not address productive relationships, the thrust of this passage is that woods work and shipbuilding are both rooted in family labour which is being applied to resources over which this Nova Scotian exercises ownership or control. Certainly there were such people scattered about the Maritime countryside, although as I have argued elsewhere and will argue below, family labour alone did not typically sustain this sort of productivity.[41] I am focusing here, though, on the property-poor farm dweller whose labour sustained the entrepreneurial pluralism of others. The capital barriers which prevented acquiring an independence in agricultural production tended to be similarly limiting in other sectors of the economy. Whereas, for instance, the household with an agricultural abundance might be in a position to send their oxen to the woods and equip a cutting crew, ultimately selling the end product in the timber market, the participation of the capital-poor in this trade was more likely to be for the wages gained from handling an axe.[42]

---

40   Thomas Chandler Haliburton, *The Old Judge; or, Life in a Colony*, ed. with an introduction and notes by M.G. Parks (Ottawa, 1978), p. xxi.

41   Rusty Bittermann, "The Hierarchy of the Soil: Land and Labour in a 19th-Century Cape Breton Community", *Acadiensis*, XVIII, 1 (Autumn 1988), pp. 33-55.

42   There were, of course, other ways by which impecunious farmfolk might participate in these economies including share systems and the acquisition of outfits on credit. In some regions, though, even the more prosperous farm households increasingly found it difficult to maintain an independent foothold in the logging business in the Maritimes. See Béatrice Craig, "Agriculture and the Lumberman's Frontier in the Upper St. John Valley, 1800-70", *Journal of Forest History*, 32, 3 (July 1988), pp. 125-37.

Although other facets of the regional economy probably rivalled it in terms of the amount of wage employment offered, during the first half of the 19th century agriculture may well have been the pre-eminent type of wage work when measured in terms of sheer numbers of participants, even if the extreme seasonality of demand meant that few worked as farm hands for extensive periods. The labour requirements of agriculture in the Maritimes in the era before the mechanization of harvesting and planting were such that not only big farms with scores of acres in hay and crops, but even many relatively small operations found it necessary to hire seasonal help. Harvesting operations in particular required the assistance of many hands. A small operation might hire an extra worker or two for a few days or weeks to assist with getting in the crops, while a larger operation might add many daily labourers to its more permanent work force. Timber operators also sometimes employed large crews to gather hay for their woods operations.[43]

Peter MacNutt, for instance, a merchant and farmer living near Princetown, Prince Edward Island, harvested his crops in the summer and fall of 1837 with the aid of his "own men" — household members and long-term employees — augmented by the daily labour of 30 workers drawn from neighbouring farms. During that autumn, some worked for only a day, while others worked for MacNutt for ten or 11 days, though never in a continuous stretch. The patterns point to the varied nature of MacNutt's labour needs even during the harvest. There were some tasks that required few or no additional hands and others for which he would hire nine additional workers on a daily basis to complement household members and servants. The composition of his crews varied in accordance with the farm calender and the progress of harvesting operations. For certain tasks, such as raking hay, bundling grain and digging potatoes, MacNutt employed the cheaper labour of women, girls and boys. A few men might, for instance, begin mowing at the beginning of the week and be joined by a growing and more heterogeneous work force later in the week as the mowed hay began to dry and required raking, hauling and stacking.[44]

The patterns of wage work recorded in MacNutt's diary also reflect, one can be sure, the needs of the rural folk recruited to work on his farm. Having to attend to crops of their own, they moved back and forth first between hay-making on their own farms and MacNutt's, and later between the harvesting of their own grain and root crops and those of MacNutt. Records from the 1830s con-

---

43 James Yeo, for example, appears to have recruited large hay-harvesting crews drawing extensively from among the Acadian and Native populations of Prince Edward Island. See George Seymour, Journal of Tour of Canada and the United States (1840), entry for 7 September, CR 114A/1380, WCRO; Robert Stewart to John Lawson, 7 October 1835, Robert Stewart Letterbooks, Ms. 2989/2, PAPEI.

44 Diary of Honourable Peter MacNutt, Sr., Ms. 3552, 7 August 1837, 4 November 1837, PAPEI.

cerning the nearby David Ross farm show Donald MacLean, a casual labourer on the farm, alternately working on his own holding and that of the Rosses, at times spending half a day harvesting MacLean crops and the other working with David Ross. On other occasions he would work at the Ross farm in the evenings, though in general he, like the workers on Peter MacNutt's farm, spent an entire day or a cluster of days working for wages before returning, one assumes, to the demands of the home harvest.[45] The degree of flexibility workers might have in moving between their own farm operations and that of their employer(s) varied, of course, as a function of proximity. Donald MacLean lived close to the Ross farm and might, if he could negotiate it, work on his own *and* his neighbour's farm in the course of a day. Many of the labourers appearing on the payroll of those harvesting the hay on William MacKenzie's fields in Middle River later in the century, however, travelled greater distances to the farm. Workers such as these found it necessary to take up residence at the work site for the duration of the harvest.[46]

In the era before the mechanization of harvest operations, the demand for agricultural labourers during the late summer and autumn was extensive. Analysis of the crop returns and household composition of farm households in Middle River between 1850 and 1875 suggest that roughly one-quarter of the farms there required some help from beyond the household in order to harvest their crops.[47] The labour demands for harvesting the crops on Middle River's farms were typical of those found elsewhere in the agricultural districts of Nova Scotia and Prince Edward Island. There was, as a Nova Scotia report on labour conditions noted at mid-century, "always a great cry for field labour" at harvest time.[48] Certainly the employment of wage labour in the agricultural sector was concentrated in these late summer and autumn months. The difficulty for the worker who was also a member of a farm household was that this was the busiest period on the home farm. Such conflicts of interest could be solved, as Donald MacLean did, by moving back and forth between the work demands of the home farm and wage labour on the harvest of an adjacent holding or, as it would appear that some of those working for Peter MacNutt did , by dividing

---

45   David Ross Diary, pp. 3-5, Prince Edward Island Collection, University of Prince Edward Island [UPEI].

46   William MacLean versus William MacKenzie, RG 39, Series "C", no. 645, PANS.

47   Bittermann, "Middle River", p. 63.

48   Nova Scotia, *JHA*, (1867), Immigration Report, app. 7. See also Captain W. Moorsom, *Letters from Nova Scotia*, pp. 206-7; *Abstract of the Proceedings of the Land Commissioners' Court Held During the Summer of 1860 to Inquire into the Differences Relative to the Rights of Landowners and Tenants in Prince Edward Island (Charlottetown, 1862)*, pp. 101, 141.

the total household work force between the limited requirements of home-farm crops and the wage opportunities on more prosperous farms.

Although the bulk of wage labour was drawn into agriculture during the harvest season, some daily employment was available for men, women and children throughout the year. The David Ross farm hired help for fencing, ploughing, harrowing, sowing, quarrying stones, cutting and sawing firewood and slaughtering livestock as well as for harvest operations. The record books of Alex McLellan at Indian River, Prince Edward Island, and Joseph Dingwell at Little River in the same colony show both purchasing labour not only for the harvest but for threshing in the winter, ploughing in the spring, and fence work and building construction at other times of the year.[49] Labourers also were hired for land clearing.[50] As well, some farmers found it expedient to maintain year-round servants. As with much daily work, the wage rates associated with these long-term contracts varied depending on age and gender. John Lewellin noted in 1832 that while "farming men-servants" were retained at 30 to 40 shillings per month, girls received 12 to 15 shillings.[51]

The use of agricultural machinery that sharply reduced the critical demands for harvest labour was not widespread until well into the second half of the 19th century. Thus the demands for agricultural labour grew at roughly the same pace as the expansion of agricultural output in the first half of the 19th century. Mechanical threshers which permitted grain to be readied quickly for market began to be used in the 1830s, but these reduced a labour demand that could, if necessary, be spread across late fall and winter. The mowers, rakes, reapers and binders that would, when in place, reduce the enormous demands for labour during harvest season by as much as 80 per cent were not a significant presence in the region until the 1860s and afterward.[52]

For many of the Maritime-born, agricultural work probably was their first taste of wage employment. There was demand for the labour of both girls and boys in the harvest fields, and the scale and nature of the work, coupled with the manner in which it was organized, made it a relatively small step from working on the home farm. Those engaged in agricultural employment might work as

49 Alex McLellan Account Book, Ms. 2802/1, PAPEI; Joseph Dingwell, Ledger, Ms. 3554/1, PAPEI.

50 *Royal Gazette* (Charlottetown), 15 March 1836, p. 2.

51 John Lewellin, *Emigration, Prince Edward Island*, p. 196. In 1851 John Lawson reported wages of £24 to £30 per year for farm servants. John Lawson, *Letters on Prince Edward Island* (Charlottetown, 1851), p. 20.

52 *Royal Gazette* (Charlottetown), 18 April 1837, p. 3; James Robb, *Agricultural Progress: An Outline of the Course of Improvement in Agriculture Considered as a Business, an Art, and a Science with Special Reference to New Brunswick* (Fredericton, 1856), p. 18; Bittermann, "Middle River", pp. 150-2.

lone additions to another family's work force, or they might be part of a crew of a dozen or more working the harvest fields. In either case, though, they were likely to be working for someone they already knew in a familiar setting among familiar faces, with a heterogeneous work force — both in terms of age and gender — and to be performing tasks that were the common stuff of agricultural life. The work contract was likely to be informal, struck on a daily basis, and to demand a transportation commitment no more onerous than a walk.

Wage work with the timber trade and the shipbuilding industry — agriculture's great rivals for labour in the first half of the 19th century — was, in general, quite different from that in agriculture. This was male employment, and much of the work in these industries was concentrated at sites at some distance from the farms from which many came. Such employment was often for extended periods of time, as woods work was available from late fall until spring, and shipbuilding, when the market dictated, might be conducted on a year-round basis.[53] There were, of course, considerable variations in the nature of the work experience in woods work and shipbuilding. Some of the employment available within these industries was local and organized in small, perhaps primarily family-based, crews. Hired hands might be added to a cluster of brothers cutting logs for the winter or be employed casually in one of the many lesser shipyards turning out modest numbers of smaller vessels. Employment with small local operations where one might return home on a daily basis aided the integration of wage work with farm work. The Irish who settled on the backlands of Lot 29 in southwestern Queens County, Prince Edward Island, for instance, and who worked in W.W. Lord's timber and shipbuilding operations, were said to have been able to clear their lands and hoe their crops "in spare time".[54] Looking back on his Cape Breton childhood, Aeneas McCharles recalled that his father combined working on his farm in the Baddeck Valley with carpentry work at the shipyards four miles away in the port of Baddeck.[55] Labour in these pursuits, however, was also being organized by capitalists operating on a much larger

53   A.R.M. Lower, *The North American Assault on the Canadian Forest: A History of the Lumber Trade Between Canada and the United States* (Toronto, 1938), pp. 32-3; Wynn, *Timber Colony*, p. 54; Richard Rice, "Shipbuilding in British America, 1787-1890: An Introductory Study", Ph.D. thesis, University of Liverpool, 1977, pp. 178-81.

54   Mary Brehaut, ed., *Pioneers on the Island* (Charlottetown, 1959), p. 58. On the local organization of farm-based labour for Prince Edward Island's shipyards see also Basil Greenhill and Ann Giffard, *Westcountrymen in Prince Edward's Isle* (Toronto, 1967), pp. 56-76; Malcolm MacQueen, *Skye Pioneers and "The Island"* (Winnipeg, 1929), p. 26.

55   Aeneas McCharles, *Bemocked of Destiny: The Actual Struggles and Experiences of a Canadian Pioneer and the Recollections of a Lifetime* (Toronto, 1908), pp. 10-11.

scale, who relied upon recruiting labourers from beyond the immediate locality of their operations. Entrepreneurs such as the Archibalds in Cape Breton and the Popes, Macdonalds and Cambridges on Prince Edward Island hired scores of men to work at their shipyards, sawmills and woods operations. So too did their counterparts elsewhere in the region who, even before steam vessels and rail transportation eased the burdens of travel, were drawing labourers from the farms of northern Nova Scotia and Prince Edward Island to work in their operations. By the 1820s and 1830s, farmers in significant numbers were travelling back and forth between the timber camps and shipyards of the Miramichi and their homes in northern Nova Scotia and Prince Edward Island.[56]

Many of those working in these operations were likely to spend part of their lives as bunkhouse men, living at the worksite and labouring on a regular schedule for extended periods of time.[57] In both logging and boatbuilding, wages might be paid partly in kind — shipyards tended to be organized around a truck store — and differentially paid in accordance with a division of labour along skill lines.[58] Farmers and farmers' sons working in the large shipyards

---

56 *Prince Edward Island Register*, 20 October 1825, p. 3; John MacGregor, *Historical and Descriptive Sketches of the Maritime Colonies of British America* (London, 1828), p. 168; David Stewart's Journal, 3209/28, p. 31, PAPEI; *Royal Gazette*, 30 May 1837, p. 3. See also the *Royal Gazette*, 26 June 1838, p. 3, on the theft of £35 — a season's wages — from a lumberman returning from the Miramichi woods to his residence in West River, Pictou County.

57 Abraham Gesner, *The Industrial Resources of Nova Scotia* (Halifax, 1849), pp. 215-17; Wynn, *Timber Colony*, p. 62; A. R.M. Lower, *Great Britain's Woodyard: British America and the Timber Trade, 1763-1867* (Montreal, 1973), pp. 189-96. On shipyard/bunkhouse deaths due to drunkenness and violence see the *Prince Edward Island Register*, 25 September 1824, p. 3; *Prince Edward Island Register*, 27 February 1827, p. 3.

58 Rice, "Shipbuilding in British America", pp. 171, 186-92. The labour contracts from the 1840s entered in Joseph Dingwell's ledger indicate that he paid most of his labourers half in cash and half in "trade". Joseph Dingwell Ledger, Ms. 3554/1, PAPEI. Capt. Moorsom's account of labour relations on the waterfront in Liverpool in the summer of 1828 suggests the reasons for Dingwell's clear indications of the mode of payment in his contracts. There were, he noted, "two scales of value", the "cash price" and the "goods price", and "the various gradations thereof distinctly marked in all transactions between employers and labourers". Moorsom reported a rate of exchange in favour of cash at a ratio of three to four. Captain W. Moorsom, *Letters From Nova Scotia*, p. 292. For information on Joseph Pope's shipyard and truck store see John Mollison, "Prince County", in D.A. Mackinnon and A.B. Warburton, eds., *Past and Present of Prince Edward Island* (Charlottetown, 1906), p. 86. Lemuel and Artemas Cambridge offered their ship carpenters the choice of employment by the month or payment "by the seam". *Prince Edward Island Register*, 23 May 1826, p. 3.

shared their workspace with greater numbers than did those in woods camps and were engaged in work that required more complex forms of organization.[59] The experience of work in the shipbuilding yards that produced large vessels was, as Richard Rice has argued, that of a large, complexly orchestrated manufactory.

In 1824 it was estimated that perhaps 1,000 men, drawn from a total Island population of roughly 20,000, worked in Prince Edward Island's shipyards to produce some 10,000 tons of shipping.[60] This figure excludes those working in the woods to supply materials for the shipyards and those working in the woods to produce timber for export. If a similar worker/tonnage ratio held in Nova Scotia, the numbers employed at shipbuilding there would be roughly double those of Prince Edward Island. In both cases, the expansion of shipbuilding during the pre-Confederation decades took place at roughly the same pace as the growth of population in these provinces.[61] As a consequence, the percentage of those engaged in shipbuilding in relation to the larger population probably remained more or less the same on average across these decades, while varying sharply, of course, from year to year as the tonnage under construction responded to external demand.

Despite a number of efforts, a commercial fishery based in Prince Edward Island developed slowly. Prior to 1850, the fishery conducted by Island merchants provided few job opportunities.[62] In Cape Breton, on the other hand, fishing was an enterprise of greater significance. Of particular importance were the Channel Island firms that conducted an extensive industry from their bases in Arichat and Cheticamp. Although the scale of operations was large, and the work labour-intensive, it does not appear that these firms drew substantial amounts of wage labour from among the farm population of the interior. Stephen Hornsby suggests instead that their operations were conducted by com-

---

59   According to Dougald Henry (born in 1817) the modest shipbuilding operation run by the Bells of Stanley River, Prince Edward Island, employed 30 or more men in the yards. Working days, he relates, began at six with a break for breakfast at eight. For Dougald Henry's account of shipyard life as compiled by Dr. Hedley Ross, see Brehaut, *Pioneers on the Island*, p. 47.

60   *Prince Edward Island Register*, 27 March 1824, p. 3. Shipbuilding declined precipitously after the depression of the mid-1820s. It would be more than a decade before output on Prince Edward Island would surpass these figures. Evidence compiled by Richard Rice from three Quebec shipyards suggest reasonably similar man/ton labour-force ratios there in the mid-1850s varying from 8.6 to 16.3 tons per man. Rice, "Shipbuilding in British America", p. 179.

61   Rice, "Shipbuilding in British America", pp. 15-16; Warkentin, "The Atlantic Region", p. 180.

62   MacGregor, *Historical and Descriptive Sketches of the Maritime Colonies of British America*, p. 63; *Prince Edward Island Register*, 24 March 1829, p. 3.

bining the independent commodity production of fisherfolk clustered in coastal communities, linked to the firms by ties of credit, with the work of a seasonal wage-labour force drawn from the Channel Islands rather than Cape Breton.[63]

The opportunities available for wage work with the American fishing fleet as it worked in Maritime waters may well have been of greater significance. Vessels working out of New England ports came by the hundreds to the small harbours of the Atlantic coast and the Gulf of St. Lawrence, where they picked up supplies of food and water, profited by smuggling, and often engaged additional hands both for fishing in Maritime waters and for pursuing the fishery off Labrador and Newfoundland.[64] At mid-century, it was estimated that perhaps 4,000 Nova Scotians were working with the American fishing fleet, typically labouring aboard vessels crewed by a dozen or so fishermen. Although the majority would have been drawn from fishing communities about the coast, some of these hands travelled from interior regions to join the fleet as it moved through the Strait of Canso region. Others travelled south to the fishing ports of Maine and Massachusetts to sign on.[65] While the labour of women was a significant component of the family-based inshore fishery, recruitment for the American fishing fleet — as for the timber industry and the shipyards, and unlike wage labour in agriculture — almost exclusively tapped the male members of farm households.[66] Workers were paid, it would appear, either on a monthly

63 Stephen J. Hornsby, "Staple Trades, Subsistence Agriculture, and Nineteenth-Century Cape Breton Island", *Annals of the Association of American Geographers*, 79, 3 (1989), p. 415. Rosemary Ommer also notes the significance of wage workers drawn from Jersey in the Gulf fishery. Rosemary Ommer, "'All the Fish of the Post': Property Resource Rights and Development in a Nineteenth-Century Inshore Fishery", *Acadiensis*, X, 2 (Spring 1981), p. 113. Father Anselme Chiasson, though, notes the exploitation of Acadian wage workers in the early 19th century by the Robin Company in Cheticamp. Father Anselme Chiasson, *Chéticamp: History and Acadian Traditions*, trans. by Jean Doris LeBlanc (St. John's, 1986), pp. 66-7. Certainly too resident fish merchants such as Laurence Kavanaugh made use of local wage labour.

64 MacDougall, *History of Inverness County*, p. 17; Gesner, *The Industrial Resources of Nova Scotia*, pp. 104-110; *Colonial Herald* (Charlottetown), 17 October, 1838, p. 3; *Colonial Herald* (Charlottetown), 5 June 1839, p. 4.

65 For the general patterns of recruitment see Paul Crowell to James Uniacke, 10 February 1852, Nova Scotia, *JHA*, (1852), app. 25 and the statements of David Bears, Nova Scotia, *JHA* (1852), app. 13. On some of the folklore arising from the involvement of Cape Bretoners in these patterns of work see John P. Parker, *Cape Breton Ships and Men* (Toronto, 1967), pp. 130-1; and MacDougall, *History of Inverness County*, pp. 123-4.

66 Marilyn Porter, "'She was Skipper of the Shore Crew': Notes on the History of the Sexual Division of Labour in Newfoundland", *Labour/Le Travail*, 15 (Spring 1985), pp. 105-24.

basis or by a share in the value of the catch and were signed on for periods ranging from weeks to months.[67] Islanders working on American vessels in the late
1830s were reportedly paid at a rate of £6 per month.[68]

Beyond the labour required for the tasks associated with the production of
commodities from fields, forests and fisheries, the merchants and others involved in these trades required workers for the multitude of tasks associated
with assembling, transporting and managing these goods. The ledgers of merchants such as Lawrence Kavanaugh, John Munro, Joseph Dingwell, Peter
MacNutt, Peter Smyth, Robert Elmsley and John Beamish Moore show wages
paid for delivering messages, rounding up and driving livestock, hauling hay,
"looking after timber", sorting fish, stacking deal, loading vessels, tending stock,
both onshore and on voyages to market, and a host of other irregularly necessary
tasks generated by the uneven rhythms of mercantile activity. Work might also
be obtained aboard the vessels moving these goods between ports.[69]

Grist mills, sawmills and other processing industries scattered about the
coast and waterways provided work opportunities for farm-based labourers too.
While most of those employed were men, women and boys as well sometimes
found work in these enterprises. In 1871, nearly 20 per cent of those working in
the carding and fulling mills of the seven northeastern counties of Nova Scotia
were women.[70] Many enterprises, either because they were reliant upon
seasonally fluctuating water supplies for their power or because demand was irregular, were part-time operations requiring labour for limited periods. The
ledger books of John Munro of St. Ann's, Cape Breton, for instance, indicate
that the labourers he obtained for his grist and carding mill in 1851 and 1852
were hired on a daily basis, putting in from 25 to 58 days of work over the
course of the year.[71] Some coming from a distance to work for Munro, such as
Alex McKenzie of Big Harbour, surely must have stayed in St. Ann's during
the period when the mill was running. A similar pattern of part-time employ-

67   Harold Innis, *The Cod Fisheries: The History of an International Economy*
     (Washington, D.C., 1940; rpt. ed. Toronto, 1978), pp. 325, 326-7, 333-4.

68   Prince Edward Island House of Assembly, *Journals*, 1837, pp. 81-2.

69   Lawrence Kavanaugh Account Book, 1817-24, MG 3, vol. 301-2, PANS; John
     Munro Daybook, 1851-55, Micro Biography, PANS; Joseph Dingwell Ledger,
     Ms. 3554/1, PAPEI; Diary of Honourable Peter MacNutt, Sr., Ms. 3552, PAPEI;
     Peter Smyth Ledger, 1833-36, MG 3, vol. 284, PANS; Robert Elmsley Diary,
     1855-89, Micro Biography, PANS; John Beamish Moore Account Book, 1848-
     67, Micro Biography, PANS; Eric Sager, *Seafaring Labour: The Merchant
     Marine of Atlantic Canada, 1820-1914* (Kingston and Montreal, 1989), pp.
     136-63.

70   *Census of Canada, 1870-71* (Ottawa, 1875), vol. 3, p. 316.

71   John Munro Daybook, 1851-55, Micro Biography, PANS.

ment was followed as well by those whom Lawrence Kavanaugh hired for his sawmill operations in St. Peters earlier in the century, and in Middle River too.[72] In 1870, one of the sawmills in the community worked for two months, the other for four. The three grist mills in Middle River operated for seven months of the year on average.[73]

In the first half of the 19th century, farm-based labourers found wages in building construction and work on roads, wharfs, canals and the first of the region's railways. State expenditures on public buildings — such as the construction of Government House and county court houses and jails in Prince Edward Island in the 1830s — played a significant, though often short-lived, role in generating demand for construction workers. So too did projects such as the Shubenacadie Canal and the Albion Mines Railway — portents of the demand for labour that bigger transportation projects would engender in the third quarter of the 19th century. On a more regular and local basis, annual state appropriations for road, bridge and wharf improvements created a substantial amount of wage employment. Such state-generated work was, as Murray Beck has noted, central to the household economies of many of the rural poor, and its interruption could be the cause of considerable deprivation in the countryside.[74] Privately funded rural and urban construction work also provided employment for farm-based workers. Most of this work, like the construction work associated with transportation systems, tended to be seasonal employment for males.[75] When the work was close to home, the remuneration to be gained at road work or on construction jobs might, for those who possessed draft animals, be broadened by bringing horses or oxen to the job. Many, though, took their skills further afield. By the 1840s, if not sooner, labourers from the farms of the northeastern Maritimes were moving seasonally to construction sites in Boston and to other distant centres. Although he was apparently an urban Cape

72 Lawrence Kavanaugh Account Book, 1817-24, MG 3, vol. 301, PANS.

73 *Census of Canada, 1870-71*, Schedule 6.

74 Beck perceptively notes the differential impact of the blockage of appropriations in the revenue dispute of 1830: wealthier farmers suffered because of the deteriorating condition of the roads and bridges they used to move their goods; the rural poor suffered because of the loss of wages gained from working on the roads. J. Murray Beck, *Joseph Howe*, vol. 1, *Conservative Reformer, 1804-1848* (Kingston and Montreal, 1982), p. 72.

75 Those working on road crews gained income both directly from the state through the disbursement of government monies in wages (albeit through the often-sticky hands of local road commissioners) and indirectly through the performance of statutory labour requirements for wealthier rural residents. For examples of the latter see the David Ross Diary, p. 2, Prince Edward Island Collection, UPEI; and Lawrence Kavanaugh Account Book, 1817-24, MG 3, vol. 302, p. 99, PANS.

Bretoner, George Musgrave's description of employment with a crew of nine in Roxbury, Massachusetts — beginning work at dawn with breaks at six for breakfast, noon for dinner, and supper after dark at the end of the day — probably captures the experience of many farm-based workers as well. Working and lodging with other single young men, he set the relatively high wages he was earning, and the expectation that he would soon accumulate enough to enable him to quit, against the discomforts of his long days.[76]

The coal-mining industry also provided work for farm-based labourers, even as it increasingly came to rely upon a skilled work force for the actual mining. In the first decades of the 19th century, few of those working the coal seams of Cape Breton or Pictou were skilled colliers. Men more accustomed to finding their way about fish flakes or over cutover ground might yet find work in the pit, signing on for a few months or a year. The experience of work in the Cape Breton coal fields in this period paralleled in some ways the work in the timber and shipbuilding industries: bunkhouse life, an entirely male work force, the truck store.[77] With the arrival of the General Mining Association in the 1820s and the massive injections of capital that came with it, coal mining became technologically more sophisticated and corporate policy favoured reliance upon a professional core of miners imported from the British coal fields. There remained, however, much demand for less-skilled casual workers in and about the mines. Of the 335 employees on the payroll at the Albion mines in the mid-1830s, only 66 were actually colliers. Scores of others were involved in construction and transportation tasks.[78] To meet this demand, the General Mining Association drew from the surrounding countryside about their mines and farther afield.[79] As Abraham Gesner noted, the labour force employed at the mines was divided. There was a well-housed and well-paid professional core and then there were the others, the "labouring farmers", who received less-generous treatment and were paid at roughly half the rate of the skilled miners.[80] Over time both the General Mining Association and subsequent operators in the

---

76   George Musgrave to Ann, 7 August 1842, Micro Biography Moore, no. 10, PANS.

77   Richard Brown, *The Coal Fields and Coal Trade of the Island of Cape Breton* (London, 1871), pp. 70-2; J.S. Martell, "Early Coal Mining in Nova Scotia", in Don Macgillivray and Brian Tennyson, eds., *Cape Breton Historical Essays* (Sydney, 1980), pp. 41-53.

78   James M. Cameron, *The Pictonian Colliers* (Halifax, 1974), p. 27.

79   The Albion Mines ran ads for "seasonal" labourers in Prince Edward Island in the 1830s. See the *Colonial Herald* (Charlottetown), 4 May 1839, p. 4. See also Joseph Howe, "Eastern Rambles", in *Travel Sketches of Nova Scotia*, p. 163; Cameron, *The Pictonian Colliers*, p. 102.

80   Gesner, *The Industrial Resources of Nova Scotia*, p. 273.

Nova Scotia coal fields would increasingly turn to the countryside for the recruitment of miners as well as general labourers.[81]

Around 1,500 men found employment in and about Nova Scotia's coal mines in the 1830s. Thousands more would be recruited in the coal boom of the third quarter of the 19th century.[82] Some of these workers were young men from the farm communities of the region who were in the process of severing their ties to the soil. Some would ultimately return to the countryside with their savings.[83] Yet others continued to farm even as they worked for mining companies. In the 1860s it was reported in Cape Breton that surface workers by the hundreds "leave their work, at certain seasons, to attend to their crops".[84]

A more heterogeneous work force found wages in employment as domestic servants and in textile work and factory work. With increasing urbanization and the growth of middle-class demand for domestic servants, both within the region and in more distant centres, many young farm men and women were drawn out of the countryside and into domestic service for at least part of their working lives.[85] Wanted "An active LAD from 14 to 16 years of age to be indented as a

81 D.A. Muise, "The Making of an Industrial Community: Cape Breton Coal Towns, 1867-1900", in *Cape Breton Historical Essays*, p. 80.

82 Ian McKay, "The Crisis of Dependent Development: Class Conflict in the Nova Scotia Coalfields, 1872-1876", in Gregory S. Kealey, ed., *Class, Gender, and Region: Essays in Canadian Historical Sociology* (St. John's, 1988), pp. 21, 30-4; Brown, *The Coal Fields and Coal Trade*, pp. 98, 111-39.

83 There were obviously other variations here as well. Some floated back and forth for years at a time between wage work in the mines and life on the land.

84 Nova Scotia, *JHA*, (1864), app. 4, p. 3. On the continuing linkages some mine workers maintained between country home and mine and the significance of these to social relations in the working-class communities about the mines in the late 19th and early 20th centuries see David Frank, "The Industrial Folk Song in Cape Breton", *Canadian Folklore canadien*, 8, 1-2 (1986), pp. 21-42; Danny Samson, "The Making of a Cape Breton Coal Town: Dependent Development in Inverness, Nova Scotia, 1899-1915", M.A. thesis, University of New Brunswick, 1988.

85 Faye E. Dudden, *Serving Women: Household Service in Nineteenth-Century America* (Middletown, Conn., 1983). Claudette Lacelle's study of domestic servants in Montreal and Quebec City in the second decade of the 19th century and Toronto, Quebec City and Halifax in the 1870s suggests a reasonably equal split between men and women domestics early in the century. Over the next half-century, though, the numbers of women in domestic service grew and rural recruitment became increasingly important. Claudette Lacelle, *Urban Domestic Servants in 19th-Century Canada* (Ottawa, 1987), pp. 18-20, 78. John Lawson reported that women servants were receiving £9 to £12 per year in Prince Edward Island at mid-century. Lawson, *Letters on Prince Edward Island*, p. 20. For

house servant. One from the country would be preferred", ran an ad in the Charlottetown paper.[86] By 1851, roughly 20 per cent of Saint John households
employed a servant, or servants, and one out of seven Haligonian households
employed at least one servant.[87] Other farmfolk found employment as domestic
servants in wealthier rural homes. Though putting-out work does not appear to
have been conducted on a large scale in the northeastern Maritimes, some men
and women were hired by merchants to weave homespun by the yard. Women
were hired as well to knit and perform other hand work.[88] More significantly, by
the 1840s women were being recruited from the southern Maritimes to work in
the factories of New England. In July of 1849, the Saint John *Courier* reported
the departure aboard the "Fairy Queen" of "upwards of 100 young women who
had been engaged to work in a factory at Salmon Falls near Portland".[89]

Clearly, as the nature of off-farm work varied, so too the ways in which it
was integrated into the household economy differed. Daily work close at hand,
such as on a neighbouring farm or for a local merchant, permitted, at least in
theory, a good deal of flexibility. That farmers and merchants alike required
casual labour and employed adults and children, both males and females, meant
that various household members might move back and forth between work on
the home farm and wage employment. John Beamish Moore's ledger from
North Sydney in the 1850s, for instance, shows that the backlander Archy
McDonald's household earned wages alternately from Archy's work, that of "his
boys" and that of "the girl".[90] The accounts of other backlanders on Moore's
ledger show a similar heterogeneity in the composition of household labour
made available to the merchant for wages. The same pattern of varying daily
movement of different members of the same household in and out of the local
agricultural labour force is apparent in the MacNutt farm ledger as men and
children, male and female, appear in varying numbers from day to day. One day

an insightful early-20th-century account of a country woman's experience as a
domestic servant in Charlottetown see Bertha MacDonald, *Diary of a
Housemaid* (n.p., 1986)

86   *Prince Edward Island Register*, 23 May 1826, p. 3. See also *Prince Edward Island Register*, 20 January 1825, p. 3; 21 August 1827, p. 3.

87   T.W. Acheson, *Saint John: The Making of a Colonial Urban Community* (Toronto, 1985), pp. 233-4; Lacelle, *Urban Domestic Servants*, p. 81.

88   For examples, see John Munro Daybook, 1851-55, Ann McLeod's account, 2
November 1852, Micro Biography, PANS; John Beamish Moore Account Book,
1848-67, pp. 11, 13, 16, 23, and 30, Micro Biography, PANS; Lawrence
Kavanaugh Account Book, 1818-24, MG 3, vol. 302, p. 193, PANS; Lawrence
Kavanaugh Account Book, 1817-24, MG 3, vol. 301, p. 228, PANS.

89   *Courier* (Saint John), 21 July 1849, p. 2.

90   John Beamish Moore Account Book, 1848-67, p. 22, Micro Biography, PANS.

a father and a couple of sons might be on the payroll, another day perhaps only the sons or only the daughters would be employed. There is no way to know whether the pattern was set by demand or by supply or to discern how in fact those who momentarily disappear from the day book deployed their labour, but clearly local work afforded the possibility of a varied and shifting household response to the needs of the home farm. Local contract work and putting-out work offered similar flexibility. A man who had been hired to mow a field, dig a cellar or clear land might, particularly if the work was close at hand, exercise some discretion in choosing his hours of employment and integrating such work into other tasks concerning his own resources. As well, he might flexibly use the labour of other members of his household to complete the task. Such would also be the case with the farmer/tailors contracted to sew trousers or make shirts or the farm women employed by the piece for spinning, weaving or knitting.

Other employments permitted less flexibility. Some types of work — such as that in shipbuilding, the timber industry, employment with the American fishing fleet, or the construction trades — provided employment almost exclusively for adult males and often entailed working at a considerable distance from one's residence. In homes where the male head engaged in such work, women often were left to manage household and farm for extended periods. Seeking lodgings at a farm house on the Cape Breton side of the Strait of Canso in the summer of 1831, David Stewart, a Prince Edward Island landlord, and his travelling companion, Richard Smith of the General Mining Association, discovered that the man of the farm "was gone to Miramichi to cut lumber".[91] Only Mrs. Mac-Pherson and her two children were home. At mid-century the Crown surveyor in Baddeck, D.B. McNab, reported that there were "hundreds" of farms located on poorer lands in his region of the Island where the men of the household travelled to "distant parts of the province or to the United States" each summer and left the maintenance of the farm to "their wives and children".[92] With the boom in railway construction and coal mining in the third quarter of the 19th century, a local observer noted that Cape Breton farmers and their sons "by hundreds, nay, thousands, [were] leaving their farms to the women, and seeking employment at the collieries and railways".[93] Some, such as a Highlander born on Lewis and residing in Middle River, who planted his crop of oats and potatoes and then travelled on foot to Halifax to work on the railway each year, appear to have regularized their patterns of distant wage work so that they synchronized with the seasonal rounds of farming. Come harvest time, the Lewis man would be back in Middle River.[94] In other households the distant wage work of males was

---

91   David Stewart's Journal, p. 31, 3209/28, PAPEI.

92   Nova Scotia, *JHA*, (1857), app. 72, p. 421.

93   *Journal of Agriculture for Nova Scotia* (July 1871), p. 652.

94   Francis MacGregor, "Days that I Remember", January 1962, MG 12, vol. 71, p. 31, Beaton Institute, Sydney, Nova Scotia.

made possible because females and children assumed a full array of farm tasks.[95]

The types of employment possibilities available to farm-based labourers varied across place — though the mobility of labour minimized the significance of some of this — and across time as the economies of timber, ships, fish and agriculture waxed or waned and as decisions of the state and the private sector shaped the demand side of the labour market. The possibilities for the integration of wage employment into the economies of farm households also varied across the cyclical passages of family time. In some households a wage supplement was only obtainable if the male household head worked off the farm on a daily or more extended basis. In others further along in the family life cycle, younger members of the household, male and female, might take on the role of subsidizing the farm with wage work. As the Prince Edward Island Land Commissioners learned when they inquired into the survival strategies of the rural poor there, household budgets were balanced because "the boys hire out", the family had put their "children out to service", or wages were sent home by family members who had moved away.[96] Such possibilities were available to households only at certain points in the family life cycle. The Strait of Canso household David Stewart and Richard Smith visited — finding a woman and two children at home and the husband in the Miramichi woods — probably was a young family with limited options, but a household with older children might be sustained, in part, by the remittance of money from the earnings of children working at distant locales.[97]

Earnings gained by a younger generation working away for prolonged periods might be sent to support a home farm but might as well be saved to

---

95 These different patterns of domestic life in poorer households no doubt under-wrote the perception that backland women were particularly able workers. Back-land girls, notes Margaret MacPhail's character John Campbell, made the best marriage partners as "they can work outside and in and keeps a fellow warm in bed. What else would you want!" Margaret MacPhail, *Loch Bras d'Or* (Windsor, N.S., 1970), pp. 84, 65.

96 Robertson, *The Prince Edward Island Land Commission of 1860*, pp. 116-19.

97 Alan Brookes, "The Exodus: Migration From the Maritime Provinces to Boston During the Second Half of the Nineteenth Century", Ph.D. thesis, University of New Brunswick, 1978, p. 88; Betsy Beattie, "Going Up to Lynn: Single, Maritime-Born Women in Lynn, Massachusetts, 1870-1930", *Acadiensis*, XXII, 1 (Autumn 1992), pp. 72-3. In her insightful evocation of life in mid-19th-century rural Cape Breton, Margaret MacPhail relates how the MacKiels, a backland family, survived in part because an older daughter working as a domestic in Arichat sent money home as did a son working with the Grand Banks fishing fleet. MacPhail, *Loch Bras d'Or*, p. 7.

finance a new household.[98] For many, prolonged and often distant wage work was an early phase in lives that ultimately would be lived out on the land. Young men or women might work away for years to accumulate the cash necessary to permit them to acquire the things needed to establish a household of their own. "Tell Mary MacDonald", wrote Thomas Murchison from Boston to his cousin on Prince Edward Island, "not to engage with any in marriage until my return".[99] Cousin Malcolm was instructed to look after Murchison's Island property in his absence as well. Further afield, Walter McDonald wrote home to Pictou from Melbourne, Australia, concerning his impending return and his travelling companion's interest in marrying sister Marion, who had remained in Nova Scotia.[100] Such requests must surely have been repeated again and again as young rural Maritimers sought to combine distant earnings with local ambitions. For many others, of course, off-farm work was the first step in lives that would ultimately be lived out elsewhere.

Although remote worksites could be attractive because of the wages being offered (and perhaps the fact that in most cases they were being offered in cash), the ability to gain continuous work was a drawing card for many as well. "It would surprise you", wrote Thomas Murchison on his arrival in Boston in January 1846, "to see all the work there is going on here. As far as I travelled I could not see an idle man that wished to work". He was, he reported, "in very good employment and making money fast" and intended to be back by spring.[101] George Musgrave wrote in a similar vein from Roxbury in August of 1842. Work had been easy to obtain, and though the hours were long he was making five dollars per week plus board and would not be returning to Cape Breton until the fall.[102] Such returns compared favourably to the wages offered in Prince Edward Island and Cape Breton, and the ability to obtain steady employment at cash wages meant that the migrant worker might return with substantial savings. The unusual opportunities for big wages drew others able to afford the passage monies yet further afield. A Yarmouth man working in the California gold fields wrote home in July of 1849 that labourers were receiving from eight to sixteen

---

98 These were not, of course, mutually exclusive endeavours. Labouring to support the home farm could affect one's inheritance and thus ultimately contribute to the ability to become established on one's own at a later date.

99 Thomas Murchison to Malcolm Murchison, 15 January 1846, Ms. 3084/1, PAPEI.

100 Walter McDonald to Mother, 25 December 1862, MG 100, vol. 184, p. 13, PANS.

101 Thomas Murchison to Malcolm Murchison, 15 January 1846, Ms. 3084/1, PAPEI.

102 George Musgrave to Ann, 7 August 1842, Micro Biography Moore, no. 10, PANS.

dollars per day. Though the cost of board was extraordinarily high and life precarious and violent, he would not, he thought, start making his way homeward until the fall for the opportunities for amassing a vast savings were unrivalled.[103]

One of the most striking things revealed by a survey of the waged work of farm-based labourers during this era is its multiformity. Employment might be on a daily basis or for extended periods of time. It might entail working with a small family unit or with a large, complexly organized, stratified work force composed exclusively of wage labourers. It might involve working with those of the same age, gender and class background or with a more heterogeneous grouping. And it might be found in staples production, construction, manufacturing, transportation, or in aid of the "self-sufficient" activities of other farm households. Remuneration might be in cash, in kind, as a positive ledger entry, or in a mixture of these forms.

Insofar as the terms of contract between employer and employee were concerned, working circumstances varied across a broad spectrum of personal and impersonal relationships. Wage work might be found locally with a relative or neighbour or with a previously unknown employer in a distant locale. In the case of a local employer who was a friend or relative, mutually advantageous terms may have been negotiable. Employee choices concerning the timing and terms of work — and employer — may have been more sharply constrained, though, in other localized working circumstances when the resident elite — particularly those possessing the power of a ledger or rent book, or perhaps holding a mortgage — sought extra hands. Did those working for merchants such as Lawrence Kavanaugh, John Beamish Moore and Peter Smyth — whose wages were set against ledger debts already incurred — come seeking employment or were they summoned? And if they lacked the cash or commodities to clear their debts, did they have the freedom to say "no"? The same question clearly applies to the many tenants on Prince Edward Island employed by landlords and land agents for road work, land clearing, construction and shipbuilding whose wages were directly set against their arrears on rent rolls.[104] Although in theory they were working for wages, in practice many of these tenants came to be under a labour obligation to their landlords. At the other extreme were the farm-based labourers earning wages from strangers in distant worksites. The Cape Bretoner George Musgrave was initially put off by the long hours he was expected to

---

103 *Novascotian* (Halifax), 30 July 1849, p. 243.

104 The practice was widespread. Lord Selkirk's agent William Douse, for instance, had at least 80 men working off their rents at a rate of 3s 6d for a 6:00 a.m. to 7:00 p.m. working day in the summer of 1838. Selkirk Papers, MG 19, E1, vol. 73, p. 19207, NAC. See also Robert and David Stewart's notice to tenants in *Royal Gazette,* 30 September 1834, p. 1, and the Worrell rent books, RG 15, PAPEI.

work in Roxbury and in consequence quit his job. But, he wrote home, "on consideration of my employer adding a dollar per week to my wages I returned to work again".[105] Clearly, a cash nexus was at the heart of this work relationship and many others like it.

These variations in the labouring experiences of farm-based workers raise questions about the extent to which paternal or "personal" relations can be said to be broadly characteristic of the working experiences of British North Americans in this period. No doubt paternalism informed the relationship between employers and employees in many instances and quite possibly most. This model, however, with its emphasis on local power structures and non-economic forms of labour recruitment and control, does not effectively capture the labouring experiences of temporary workers, often originating in the countryside, who moved in and out of the work force. As Clare Pentland admitted in his exploration of the concept, their circumstances do not fit the model.[106] The issue of numbers is, of course, important here. If workers such as these represent a relatively insignificant part of the total labouring population, perhaps there is some justification for viewing the nature of their circumstances as marginal to the broader picture. Existing research does not provide a clear answer to the numbers question. It is perhaps significant, though, that seasonal employees equalled or outnumbered permanent workers at the St. Maurice forges and at D.D. Calvin's lumber operations at Garden Island, supposedly classic examples of paternalistic labour practices in action. These enterprises in fact employed more workers who fell outside the model than within it.[107] The pattern was repeated in the Maritimes. The General Mining Association in Nova Scotia, too, had its well-paid and well-housed skilled work force operating within locally sustained, paternalistic structures, and a numerous body of differently treated "labouring farmers" who moved in and out of the mining towns. Such, to varying degrees, appears to have been the case with other Maritime industries as well. Perhaps the circumstances of a skilled fraction of the work force have assumed too great a profile in our conceptualization of labour relations, and worker consciousness, during the first half of the 19th century. Greater attention

---

105 George Musgrave to Ann, 7 August 1842, Micro Biography Moore, no. 10, PANS.

106 H. Clare Pentland, *Labour and Capital in Canada, 1650-1860* (Toronto, 1981), pp. 45-6.

107 The majority of the work force at the forges appear to have been temporary. The division between permanent and temporary workers at D.D. Calvin's operations was roughly equal. Pentland, *Labour and Capital in Canada*, pp. 42-5; Bryan D. Palmer, *Working-Class Experience: The Rise and Reconstitution of Canadian Labour, 1800-1980* (Toronto, 1983), p. 15.

to the lives of farm-based workers is likely to force some reassessment in our understanding of the contours of the experience of work during this period.[108]

The issue of numbers emerges again with the broader argument being presented here. While it is relatively easy to assemble data pointing to the involvement of farm-based workers in a wide variety of wage labour, establishing the breadth of this phenomenon is another matter. One way to approach the issue is from the supply side, from the perspective of the household. Where data — such as census returns — permit, it is possible to estimate farm production and consumption and to calculate the numbers of farms requiring an income supplement. Applying this sort of analysis to the census returns from Middle River and Hardwood Hill suggested that roughly one-quarter to one-third of households fell into this category. Though the ratios would vary, similar analysis of data from farming communities elsewhere in the northeast Maritimes would almost certainly reveal roughly comparable patterns. Perusal of the census returns from the region indicates the recurring presence of farms with insufficient resources to maintain their occupants. It does not require the application of a complex algorithm to discern that, given the climate and soils of this region, a family of eight would not have been able to make ends meet with five cleared acres and a single cow. But since wage work was not the only strategy for augmenting deficiencies in farm income, it is not safe to equate all farm deficits with a comparable involvement in wage labour. Moreover, there were inducements to wage work other than that of immediate necessity. Wage labourers were drawn from across the spectrum of farm types, not just from operations with annual deficits. Likely these numbers more than compensate for those who may have successfully managed to supplement insufficiencies of farm income without recourse to wages, judging from a reading of a variety of sources. What needs to be emphasized is that the analysis of farm deficits ultimately rests on a series of assumptions concerning patterns of production and consumption. No matter how carefully done, the resultant figures are estimates. Shave down the calculations for household consumption levels or increase the coefficients for livestock productivity and we arrive at new estimates for the numbers of farm households requiring income supplements. To test the accuracy of such estimates, we need close analysis of the economic behaviour of specific households.

The problems of quantifying workforce participation do not get any easier when approached from the demand side. Existing evidence concerning employee numbers, length of work and origins is fragmentary, although there are some sectors for which we have contemporary estimates of the numbers of workers. Shipbuilding, according to the editor of the *Prince Edward Island*

---

108 For a consideration of this issue in a European context see Jean H. Quataert, "A New Look at Working-Class Formation: Reflections on the Historical Perspective", *International Labor and Working Class History*, 27 (Spring 1985), pp. 72-6.

Register, employed 1,000 Islanders in 1824. The Island was a relatively small place and the editor took a keen interest in developments in the shipbuilding industry. His figure is probably well-grounded. Assuming that perhaps one-quarter of the total Island population of 20,000 comprised adult males, this would mean that one-fifth of them were working at the shipyards for some period of the year. In adjacent New Brunswick two decades later, it was estimated that roughly 20,000 were employed in the timber industry.[109] Figures such as these can be set against production tallies to provide a starting point for compiling estimates of the labour force in other years and other locales. So, too, fragmentary evidence concerning the numbers of labourers employed on specific farms and in particular enterprises can permit, by extrapolation, the creation of rough estimates of the labour demands of the industry as a whole. Unfortunately, little such work has been done. The fragments of evidence concerning employment, however, suggest that a composite picture would reveal substantial numbers of farm dwellers participating in near and distant labour markets. It needs to be emphasized, though, that for many participation was brief. The percentage of farm dwellers engaging in the wage economy does not reveal the proportion of wage labour performed by farm-based workers, nor does it tell us the extent to which farm people spent their time engaged in wage labour. Which is the more important figure depends, of course, on the questions we ask.

The problem of attempting to quantify the extent of farm-based wage labour in the first half of the 19th century is a difficult one. With more research into the behaviour of particular households and the circumstances of specific communities or industries for which there are good records, it will be possible to obtain a better sense of the scale of the phenomenon. At best, though, the figures will be very rough estimates, reasonable guesses based on limited evidence. What is clear, however, even given the limits of the existing state of our understanding, is that wage work needs to be carefully factored into our understandings of rural life.[110] Though an oft-noted reality, it has not always assumed the profile that it should. Too often the appealing vision of rural autonomy and insularity has nudged it aside. Drawn in by the image of the independent yeoman, we seek to explain his decline. Influenced by the mythology of the autonomous household, or by its more recent derivative, the autonomous community in which households achieved independence by equitable sharing,

---

109 Report from the New Brunswick *Royal Gazette* cited in the *Islander* (Charlottetown), 20 November 1846, p. 2.

110 Certainly, as Larry McCann has noted, these patterns have implications for urban development in the Maritimes as well. Larry McCann, "'Living the Double Life': Town and Country in the Industrialization of the Maritimes," in Douglas Day, ed., *Geographical Perspectives on the Maritime Provinces* (Halifax, 1988), pp. 93-113.

we examine rural life in terms of narrowly defined geographical communities. None of this is entirely wrong-headed, but we need to recognize more explicitly that the presuppositions that are guiding these questions and approaches originate in a powerful mythology that is only partly rooted in the rural reality of the early-19th-century Maritimes.

I am reminded of the discrepancies in the assumptions the scholar Bernard Pares brought to his study of the Russian countryside and the reality that he encountered when he actually moved among rural folk on the eve of the Revolution of 1905. Arriving at a peasant meeting in Tver, miles from the nearest train station, he expected to find rural folk with but a dim perception of the world that lay beyond their village. He discovered instead that more than 40 per cent had worked in either Petersburg or Moscow.[111] The rural world that he found was not the insular one he had expected. Charles Farnham had a similar experience in Cape Breton in the 1880s. Travelling across the remote northernmost highlands, he encountered a young woman along the road and gave her a lift. When she asked to be put down at an intersecting cart trail, Farnham, who had come to Cape Breton to experience life in its primitive purity, inquired as to the direction she was taking. "Where does that road go to Maggie?" "It goes to the Strait of Canso, sir, and on to Montana".[112] Twenty years earlier, perhaps the answer would have been Boston and half a century before, as David Stewart and Richard Smith discovered when they wandered the island, the trails led to Chatham and the Miramichi. The paths, roads and waterways of the northeast Maritimes took countryfolk in many directions. And they brought many of them back again, weeks, months and years later. Work in a neighbour's field or house or mill provided training for, and gave way to, work in more distant settings. With their movements, farm-based labourers continuously integrated a host of near and distant economies and experiences into the fabric of rural life. In Margaree, Marshy Hope and Bear River, life was shaped not just by local crop returns and the relations between neighbours but by wages remitted from away and by the experiences and ideas of those who worked elsewhere.[113] Externalities visited on familiar feet.

From a rural perspective, from the hearths of these workers, there is a central commonality in many of these work experiences: their function, their in-

111 Bernard Pares, *A Wandering Student: The Story of a Purpose* (Syracuse, N.Y., 1948), p. 127.

112 Farnham, "Cape Breton Folk", p. 97.

113 For a splendid example of how a focus on migratory labour can deepen our understanding of change in agrarian and urban and industrial society, see Bruno Ramirez, *On the Move: French-Canadian and Italian Migrants in the North Atlantic Economy, 1860-1914* (Toronto, 1991).

tegration into the economies of households that maintained a commitment to (or reliance upon) a soil-based livelihood.[114] Many worked so that they might farm. For the new settlers that Lord Selkirk and John Cambridge observed, wage work was undertaken as a temporary means by which sufficient capital might be acquired to permit an escape from the necessity of working for others. So too for the young men and women labouring to acquire a nest egg, wage work was a necessary phase in a life that it was hoped might be lived primarily outside of it. The contemporary language of praise underscores the importance of the objective. Describing the agricultural prosperity that a cousin had come to enjoy on Prince Edward Island, John McRa indicated the extent of his accomplishments by reporting that he had become "very independent".[115] Joseph Howe spoke to the same goal and perhaps beyond when he argued that the industrious Nova Scotia yeoman might with "a wife and an axe" become "truly rich and independent". The Rev. John MacLennan, on tour in the 1820s from his parish in Belfast, Prince Edward Island, lauded the condition of some of Middle River's farm households by noting that they were in "very independent circumstances".[116] Donald Campbell indicated the extent of the good fortune he had obtained in Cape Breton by saying that he was free from the impositions of factor and laird and "any toilsome work but what I do myself".[117]

These people had to some extent gained what many sought. The dream of achieving control over one's labour and its product and of acquiring "independence" was, of course, a widely shared aspiration of rural and urban dwellers alike. The language and arguments used to articulate these ideals in the Escheat struggle on Prince Edward Island in the 1830s were not dissimilar to those employed by many urban workers in this period.[118] The belief that such goals of autonomy and independence might best be achieved by securing a land-based livelihood was both widespread and persistent even among those deeply imbedded in an industrial labour force. The Ohio labour commissioners who

---

114 For Russian peasants, the perceived importance of the functional commonality of all such off-farm work is reflected in its designation by a single word, *promysly*, meaning all those activities necessary to round out the insufficient returns gained from the soil. Teodor Shanin, *Russia as a Developing Society*, vol. 1, *The Roots of Otherness: Russia's Turn of Century* (New Haven, Conn., 1985), p. 68.

115 John McRa to Archibald McRa, 1 January 1817, Ms. 3363/2, PAPEI.

116 Letter of Rev. John MacLennan, 1827, Glasgow Colonial Society Correspondence, M-1352, p. 129, NAC.

117 Donald Campbell to [a relative in Lewis], 7 October 1830, reprinted in the *Stornaway Gazette*, 30 September 1972, MG 100, vol. 115, no. 33, PANS.

118 Rusty Bittermann, "Agrarian Alternatives: The Ideas of the Escheat Movement on Prince Edward Island, 1832-42", *Acadiensis* (forthcoming).

assembled the state's first annual labour report in 1877 estimated that roughly one-half of the mechanics and labourers in Ohio's urban centres were working to accumulate the savings necessary so that they might acquire a farm.[119] Similarly, as Ewa Morawska has argued, the majority of East and Central European peasants who travelled to American industrial centres at the turn of the 20th century engaged in wage labour thousands of miles from home so that they and their families might become more securely established on the soil; they did so with the intention of returning to their rural communities.[120] Such was the case as well, Theodore von Laue has argued, with much of the industrial work force in late-19th- and early-20th-century Russia.[121] For centuries peasants in the Friuli and Saxony have "consciously" chosen, Douglas Holmes and Jean Quataert contend, to integrate wage work with agrarian pursuits on their rural holdings as a way of resisting a "propertyless working-class existence".[122]

Other farm-based workers in the northeast Maritimes, of course, may have resigned themselves to the necessity of perpetually maintaining the dual commitments of self-employment and working for others, or may indeed have embraced wage work never seeking to attain a degree of choice over their involvement in the labour market.[123] Given the sporadic and uneven nature of the

---

119 Cited in Peter H. Argersinger and Jo Ann Argersinger, "The Machine Breakers: Farmworkers and Social Change in the Rural Mid West of the 1870s", *Agricultural History*, 58 (July 1983), p. 401.

120 Ewa Morawska, "'For Bread with Butter': Life-Worlds of Peasant Immigrants from East Central Europe, 1880-1914", *Journal of Social History*, 17, 3 (Spring 1984), p. 392.

121 Theodore von Laue, "Russian Peasants in the Factory, 1892-1904", *Journal of Economic History*, 21 (1961), p. 80.

122 Douglas R. Holmes and Jean H. Quataert, "An Approach to Modern Labor: Worker Peasantries in Historic Saxony and the Friuli Region over Three Centuries", *Comparative Studies in Society and History* 28, 2 (April 1986), p. 202.

123 Many emigrants had experience with similar work patterns before they migrated. See Barbara M. Kerr, "Irish Seasonal Migration to Great Britain, 1800-38", *Irish Historical Studies*, 3 (1942-3), pp. 365-80; Anne O'Dowd, *Spalpeens and Tattle Hokers: History and Folklore of the Irish Migratory Worker in Ireland and Britain* (Dublin, 1991); A.J. Youngson, *After the Forty-Five: The Economic Impact on the Scottish Highlands* (Edinburgh, 1973), pp. 182-4; T.M. Devine, "Temporary Migration and the Scottish Highlands in the Nineteenth Century", *Economic History Review*, 32 (1979), pp. 344-59; William Howatson, "The Scottish Hairst and Seasonal Labour 1600-1870", *Scottish Studies*, 26 (1982), pp. 13-36; E.J.T. Collins, "Migrant Labour in British Agriculture in the Nineteenth Century", *Economic History Review*, 29 (1976), pp. 38-59. As Maritimers moved on, some carried these patterns of work to new locales. See McCharles, *Bemocked of Destiny*, p. 28; Neil Robinson, *Lion of Scotland* (Auckland, 1952, 1974), pp. 28, 80, 99.

demand for labour in the region in the early 19th century, life without the fall-back of an agricultural holding could be precarious.[124] Rather than working so that they might farm, some, no doubt, farmed so that they might live to work. For many, however, access to the soil held out the hope of achieving control over their time and their labour, and persistence in straddling two worlds constituted a way of resisting the imperatives and dependence of wage work.[125]

We need to look more closely at the transformation of these dreams, which had been closely associated with the myth of the independent yeoman, and at changes in the strategies adopted by working people. Few still maintain that true independence is to be gained by eschewing wage work for agricultural pursuits and by struggling to gain a toehold on the soil. The goal of a "propertied independence" that was embedded in the mythology and once held such an important position in the aspirations of working people of the North Atlantic world has long since lost its lustre. And though many rural residents in the region continue to engage in seasonal work at near and distant job sites, fewer and fewer rely on farming as a means to survive periods when they are not engaged in wage work.[126] Surely these will be key themes for those who would write the environmental history of the region. The decline of the belief that the labourer's salvation was to be found on the land and the decline of agriculture as a safety net have profoundly affected our perception of the significance of arable soil, and of land more generally. For increasing numbers, even of rural residents, it is no longer a matter of importance.

---

124 Judith Fingard, "A Winter's Tale: The Seasonal Contours of Pre-Industrial Poverty in British North America, 1815-1860", *Communications historique/Historical Papers* (1974), pp. 65-94; D.B. MacNab to Uniacke, 3 January 1857, Nova Scotia, *JHA* (1857), app. 71, p. 421.

125 On the significance of agrarian strategies to working-class struggles in Great Britain and the United States in this period see Malcolm Chase, *"The People's Farm": English Radical Agrarianism, 1775-1840* (Oxford, 1988); Sean Wilentz, *Chants Democratic: New York City and the Rise of the American Working Class, 1788-1850* (New York, 1984), pp. 164-216, 335-43; Paul Conkin, *Prophets of Prosperity: America's First Political Economists* (Bloomington, Ind., 1980), pp. 222-58.

126 The terms of eligibility for unemployment benefits have played a role here in forcing some to choose between a state-based or land-based safety net and/or to define themselves as workers rather than farmers.

Between Farm and Factory:
The Productive Household and the Capitalist Transformation of the Maritime Countryside, Hopewell, Nova Scotia, 1869-1890

Steven Maynard

His name was James Barry. Born in 1820, he lived all his life in rural Pictou County, Nova Scotia. He married Isabella McLellan and together they had two children. A miller by trade, he built himself a modest grist and shingle mill on the Six Mile Brook. Barry left behind a detailed diary which provides a wealth of information on the daily activity of his family, household and mill. From the diary it is clear that the Barry family attempted to produce most of their material needs through the combined labour of husband, wife and children. Isabella supplemented the household economy by boarding mill labourers or by taking in a school teacher. What was not produced in the home (whether by choice or necessity) was obtained by exchanging goods and services with neighbours. In return for his milling services, Barry variously accepted sundry goods, stints of labour and sometimes cash, but most often he would obtain a portion of the ground grain. Barry, in turn, used his portion of the ground grain as an exchange product in the local economy or for feed and food in his own household.[1]

All this may sound quite unspectacular, but the picture emerging from Barry's diary of the rural Maritime economy in 1871 holds little place in recent historical writing on the region. This is so for at least two reasons. First, much of the existing literature focuses on the region's urban centres and demonstrates that factory production, commodity exchange and the making of a working class were already well under way by the 1870s.[2] While this investigation has

1   Diary of James Barry, Public Archives of Nova Scotia [PANS], MG 1, vols. 1216-21 [hereafter cited as Barry, Diary, 1871]. This article began as a B.A. honours thesis at Mount Allison University in 1985. I thank Larry D. McCann not only for introducing me to the history of Pictou County and James Barry, but also for teaching me to think critically. While working on my M.A. thesis at Queen's University in 1987, I benefited from working with Bryan D. Palmer, particularly in strengthening my grasp of theory. More recently, I presented a version of this paper to the conference "Rural Workers in Atlantic Canada", held in Halifax in October 1990. I thank the conference participants for their comments. I owe a special debt to Jonathan Prude for his encouragement and thoroughgoing critique. Finally, I would like to thank the anonymous readers of *Acadiensis* for some very helpful suggestions.

2   T.W. Acheson, "The National Policy and the Industrialization of the Maritimes, 1880-1910", *Acadiensis*, I, 2 (Spring 1972), pp. 3-28; David Frank, "The Cape

revealed much about class and social formation in places such as Sydney, Amherst, the Pictou metal towns, Halifax and Saint John, we still know little about how the capitalist transformation unfolded across the region's countryside. Second, while a reconsideration of the Maritime countryside is beginning to emerge,[3] the historiography has remained largely untouched by the lively debates in other countries, particularly in the United States, over the "transition to capitalism" in the countryside.[4] This is curious given the rural character of the

Breton Coal Industry and the Rise and Fall of the British Empire Steel Corporation", *Acadiensis*, VII, 1 (Autumn 1977), pp. 3-34; Ian McKay, "Capital and Labour in the Halifax Baking and Confectionery Industry During the Last Half of the Nineteenth Century", *Labour/Le Travailleur*, 3 (1978), pp. 63-108; Peter DeLottinville, "Trouble in the Hives of Industry: The Cotton Industry Comes to Milltown, New Brunswick, 1879-1892", *Communications historiques/Historical Papers* (1980), pp. 100-15; L.D. McCann, "The Mercantile-Industrial Transition in the Metal Towns of Pictou County, 1857-1931", *Acadiensis*, X, 2 (Spring 1981), pp. 29-64; L. Anders Sandberg, "Dependent Development, Labour, and the Trenton Steel Works, Nova Scotia, 1900-1943", *Labour/Le Travail*, 27 (Spring 1991), pp. 127-62; Ian McKay, "'By Wisdom, Wile or War': The Provincial Workmen's Association and the Struggle for Working-Class Independence in Nova Scotia, 1879-97", *Labour/Le Travail*, 18 (Fall 1986), pp. 13-62; Ian McKay, "The Realm of Uncertainty: The Experience of Work in the Cumberland Coal Mines, 1873-1927", *Acadiensis*, XVI, 1 (Autumn 1986), pp. 3-57; Ian McKay, "The Crisis of Dependent Development: Class Conflict in the Nova Scotia Coalfields, 1872-76", in G.S. Kealey, ed., *Class, Gender, and Region: Essays in Canadian Historical Sociology* (St. John's, 1988), pp. 9-48.

3   See, for example, Alan R. MacNeil, "Cultural Stereotypes and Highland Farming in Eastern Nova Scotia, 1827-1861", *Histoire sociale/Social History*, XIX, 37 (May 1986), pp. 39-56; Robert MacKinnon and Graeme Wynn, "Nova Scotian Agriculture in the 'Golden Age': A New Look", in Douglas Day, ed., *Geographical Perspectives on the Maritime Provinces* (Halifax, 1988), pp. 47-59; Debra McNabb, "The Role of the Land in the Development of Horton Township, 1760-1775", in Margaret Conrad, ed., *They Planted Well: New England Planters in Maritime Canada* (Fredericton, 1988); Rusty Bittermann, "The Hierarchy of the Soil: Land and Labour in a 19th Century Cape Breton Community", *Acadiensis*, XVIII, 1 (Autumn 1988), pp. 33-55. Future debate on the 19th century countryside will have to engage seriously with Bittermann's work in a way that this paper does only implicitly. In an earlier version of this paper presented to the "Rural Workers in Atlantic Canada" conference, I provided some initial critical comments on "The Hierarchy of the Soil". For a review of recent work in Maritime rural history see C.A. Wilson, "'Outstanding in the Field': Recent Rural History in Canada", *Acadiensis*, XX, 2 (Spring 1990), pp. 177-89.

4   A now dated but still useful overview of these debates is E.G. Burrows, "The Transition Question in Early American History", *Radical History Review*, 18 (Fall 1979), pp. 173-90. For a more recent overview see Allan Kulikoff, "The

Maritime Region and also because (as Barry's diary so clearly reveals) the 19th-century Maritime countryside was caught in the throes of transformation. The diary reveals a rural economy turning on traditional routines and rhythms but in which there are signs of coming change.

To begin to pin down more precisely the nature of the economic and social transformations of the Maritime countryside, I want to look at the people who lived in and around Hopewell, Pictou County, Nova Scotia, during the late 19th century.[5] Drawing upon the work of American rural historians,[6] I want to focus attention on the rural productive household. I will begin by focusing on household production and exchange networks in the local economy; for much of

---

Transition to Capitalism in Rural America", *William and Mary Quarterly*, XLVI (January 1989), pp. 120-44. Graeme Wynn has recently called for historians of the rural Maritimes to engage with this literature in "Exciting a Spirit of Emulation Among the 'Plodholes': Agricultural Reform in Pre-Confederation Nova Scotia", *Acadiensis*, XX, 1 (Autumn 1990), p. 51.

5   While this study focuses primarily on the people who lived in and around Hopewell, it will draw heavily on the story of James Barry. As the narrative weaves back and forth between Hopewell and Barry, it should be kept in mind that Barry was not a resident of Hopewell; he lived in the district of Six Mile Brook, Pictou County, approximately 15 kilometres to the west of Hopewell. He is given a central role in this story by virtue of the existence of his diary, which allows for a detailed look at economic and social relations in a neighbouring and similar rural district.

6   See Michael Merrill "Cash Is Good To Eat: Self-Sufficiency and Exchange in the Rural Economy of the United States", *Radical History Review*, 3 (Winter 1977), pp. 42-71; James Henretta, "Families and Farms: *Mentalité* in Pre-Industrial America", *William and Mary Quarterly*, XL (1978), pp. 3-32; Christopher Clark, "Household Economy, Market Exchange and the Rise of Capitalism in the Connecticut Valley, 1800-1860", *Journal of Social History*, 13 (Winter 1979), pp. 169-89; Jonathan Prude, *The Coming of Industrial Order: Town and Factory Life in Rural Massachusetts, 1810-1860* (Cambridge, 1983); Steven Hahn, *The Roots of Southern Populism: Yeoman Farmers and the Transformation of the Georgia Upcountry, 1850-1890* (Cambridge, 1983); Gary Kulik, "Dams, Fish, and Farmers: Defense of Public Rights in Eighteenth-Century Rhode Island", in Steven Hahn and Jonathan Prude, eds., *The Countryside in the Age of Capitalist Transformation: Essays in the Social History of Rural America* (Chapel Hill, 1985), pp. 25-50; Jonathan Prude, "Town-Factory Conflicts in Antebellum Rural Massachusetts", in Hahn and Prude, *The Countryside*, pp. 71-102; Steven Hahn, "The 'Unmaking' of the Southern Yeomanry: The Transformation of the Georgia Upcountry, 1860-1890", in Hahn and Prude, *The Countryside*, pp. 179-203; and most recently, Christopher Clark, *The Roots of Rural Capitalism: Western Massachusetts, 1780-1860* (Ithaca, N.Y., 1990). Much of the original inspiration for my work on Hopewell came from reading the work of those listed here. The influence of their powerful interpretations of the countryside and the many debts I owe them will be obvious on the following pages.

this period production remained centred in the rural household and based on the labour of family members. Local exchange networks turned primarily on the needs of household and community. I want to then look at how the productive household shaped social relations both within the household and in the broader community, in particular, at the ways in which gender hierarchies operated in and alongside the household system. Finally, because the productive household also embraced wage labour and market relations, I will retain my focus on the household to explore the subsequent transformation of economic and social relations in the countryside.

On the Market's Edge

The shift to factory production and commodity exchange was already under way by the 1870s in many parts of the Maritime Region. In Pictou County, coal mining and the manufacture of steel gave a decidedly industrial character to the towns of New Glasgow, Stellarton and Westville; and, as a port, Pictou town had long been a busy commercial centre.[7] But within the protracted and uneven transformations of the 19th century, the Maritime Region nourished a variety of productive and social forms. As Ian McKay noted some time ago, the late 19th century was a "complex period of concurrent modes of production". In the towns, craft and manufactory production continued to exist alongside the emerging factory system; and in the countryside, the "production of use-values within households remained an important feature of many nineteenth-century communities".[8] Hopewell was one such community.

Hopewell was established in the early 19th century, part of the general Scottish settlement of Pictou County after 1800. Originally called Milltown, the name of the village was changed to Hopewell when, so the story goes, residents met in Duncan Falconer's tavern and all agreed to the change suggested by Neil McKenna, who had seen the name "Hopewell" on a store sign in Halifax. Between 1810 and 1815, Donald Gray and Simon Fraser erected a grist mill in Hopewell which, because of the scarcity of such crucial enterprises in the county, attracted settlers to the area. Hector McLean opened the first store in 1829, followed by another six years later.[9] Hopewell was situated in Nova Scotia's central farming region where, according to Graeme Wynn's work on the agricultural patterns of Pictou County in 1851, improved land averaged about 25 to 35

---

7   McCann, "Mercantile-Industrial Transition".

8   McKay, "Capital and Labour", pp. 64-5.

9   *Colonial Standard* (Pictou), 28 March 1882.

10   Wynn, "Exciting a Spirit of Emulation", p. 18.

acres per farm family.[10] By mid-century, Hopewell was a small but important service centre for the surrounding agricultural district.

Whether in the village or on the farm, the household stood at the centre of economic life in Hopewell. It was a system of production in which family members worked together as a unit. Much in the manner of rural people in other areas, families in Hopewell supplied many of their basic requirements by producing a wide variety of goods in their own households. In 1871 the majority of household heads in the Hopewell area worked in agriculture. The census rolls reveal that most farm households raised a variety of field crops and had cows for milk, butter and cheese, as well as cattle and pigs for meat. In addition, sheep provided wool to make into cloth.[11] This did not mean, of course, that all residents owned land. According to the census of 1871, almost one-half of the families located in the village lacked title to property. Yet it would be misleading to insist on a simple division between landowners and landless, for even those who owned no land, such as the stationmaster James McDonald, might grow a bushel each of beets and carrots in their yards. Although owning no land, storekeeper Enon McDonald's family still raised one cow and two pigs on their village lot and churned 40 pounds of butter.[12]

Artisan-headed households were equally integrated into the household organization of production. Most often owning no land, the majority of artisan households still raised cows and pigs. Hector McLean and Daniel Munro, both shoemakers, owned a cow, and Daniel's family raised seven sheep on a village lot.[13] James Barry was typical when noting in his diary, "killed my little pig today for domestic use", an entry echoed on many other occasions.[14] Also common were backyard gardens for vegetables: potatoes, carrots, beets and peas were important crops. In addition, none of the artisans listed in the village directory of 1869 identified a place of work that was clearly detached from their place of residence, further evidence of the close connection between production and household.[15] In addition to farmers and artisans, roughly 25 households in the surrounding Hopewell countryside were headed by coal miners. Again, the

---

11 Data on land ownership, crops, livestock and household production in Hopewell are generated from the nominal census returns for 1871. See "Hopewell Division I", RG 31, vol. 1229, 1871, 200 (Pictou County), M-1 (Hopewell-I), National Archives of Canada (Ottawa). Further reference to this data will be listed as "Census of Pictou County, 1871".

12 Census of Pictou County, 1871.

13 Census of Pictou County, 1871.

14 Barry, Diary, 28 December 1871.

15 Census of Pictou County, 1871. *McAlpine's Nova Scotia Directory*, 1868-69, p. 622.

16 Census of Pictou County, 1871.

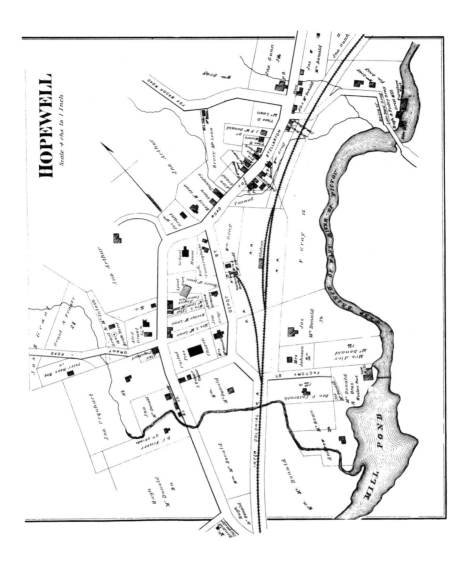

census reveals that miners and their families employed many of the strategies associated with the productive household.[16] While these colliers were engaged in industrial pursuits, finding work in the nearby coal towns of Pictou County, they also kept one foot on the land. During the summer months when coal production was slack, these rural-based miners worked on their small farms. In this way they were able, at least for a time, to avoid complete dependence on wage labour.[17]

The productive household did not turn solely on the work of farmer, artisan or miner, but demanded the labour of all family members. This did not mean, however, that work was divided in an equal manner. In fact, as Marjorie Cohen has found in her study of farm households in 19th-century Ontario, household production rested on the dominant sexual division of labour. "The division of labour by gender", Cohen writes, "was of a fairly traditional nature.... Women's work was rarely the same as men's.... Female labour's primary responsibility was to meet the immediate needs of the family by producing clothing, food, household articles, and services for the maintenance of individuals in the family". In the Maritime context, Marilyn Porter has explored the sexual division of labour in Newfoundland outports, while others writing about the 19th-century productive household in other places have documented a similar division of labour.[18]

In Hopewell, men's varied work, the household and the village economy more generally were all underpinned by the domestic, most often unpaid, work performed by women in the home. While the census most often failed to record the work specifically done by women, it is possible from a number of sources to

17 For more on Pictou County's rural-based miners see L.D. McCann, "'Living a Double Life': Town and Country in the Industrialization of the Maritimes", in Day, *Geographical Perspectives*, pp. 93-113.

18 Marjorie Cohen, *Women's Work, Markets, and Economic Development in Nineteenth-Century Ontario* (Toronto, 1988), p. 67; Marilyn Porter, "She Was Skipper of the Shore-Crew: Notes on the History of the Sexual Division of Labour in Newfoundland", *Labour/Le Travail*, 15 (Spring 1985), pp. 105-23. In the Georgia upcountry, Steven Hahn found that the "household economy had its own division of labor, one based chiefly on sex and age. Husbands, older sons and perhaps the few slaves did most of the field work. Wives and older daughters by and large attended to spinning, weaving, cooking and other domestic chores. Younger children filled in when able and called upon": Steven Hahn, "The 'Unmaking' of the Southern Yeomanry", in Hahn and Prude, *The Countryside*, p. 181; Christopher Clark documented a similar division of labour in the Connecticut Valley where there was a "fairly complex division of labor...between male and female tasks within the household", Christopher Clark, "Household Economy", p. 173; Julie Matthaei has also traced the gendered division of labour in the colonial family economy in *An Economic History of Women in America: Women's Work, the Sexual Division of Labor, and the Development of Capitalism* (New York, 1982), pp. 15-65.

piece together some of their contributions to the household economy. A focus on women's productive role opens up numerous issues, and some of these will be examined in the following section. For now, a brief examination clearly reveals how production in the rural Maritime social formation remained thoroughly embedded in the household and work was divided by gender and age.

The census reveals that most households in Hopewell made butter and cheese and spun and wove wool into cloth. Recent studies of farm women's labour in the 18th and 19th centuries demonstrate that the bulk of this production was the work of women.[19] That such was the case in Hopewell is seen, for example, by the fact that in the village's only female-headed household, Jane McBain and her daughter Annie raised two cows and five sheep, made 80 pounds of butter and 20 pounds of cheese, and produced 22 pounds of wool and 48 yards of homespun.[20] In addition to meeting household needs, women could use the products of their domestic labour for exchange in the local economy. Barry, for example, who also ran a small store in Six Mile Brook, often purchased butter from local women. "I also sent...31/3 to David Conner's wife to pay for 31¼ lb. butter".[21] But, as Cohen found in her study of women's household production, as long as markets remained underdeveloped, the bulk of women's production and exchanges remained geared to meeting household needs. It is also important to recognize that the label "domestic labour" belies the fact that women's work also extended beyond the household and into fields and gardens. In the summer months, for example, Barry's wife Isabella and daughter Josephine often went berry-picking: "the folks are away up to Roger's Hill on a raspberry excursion", and a few days later, "all the household folks were away all day at the Blueberries".[22]

Finally, women could supplement the household economy by taking in boarders. On different occasions Barry noted in his diary, "the school mistress commenced boarding with us on Monday" or the "schoolman boarding here these times".[23] While many households were based on a simple nuclear family, they could at times be quite complex arrangements. Isabella Barry, for one, ran a household that included not only her husband and two daughters, but at times

---

19 See, for example, Rosemary Ball, "A Perfect Farmer's Wife: Women in 19th Century Rural Ontario", *Canada: An Historical Magazine*, 3, 2 (1975), pp. 2-21; Cohen, *Women's Work*, pp. 59-92; see also Joan Jensen, *Loosening the Bonds: Mid-Atlantic Farm Women, 1750-1850* (New Haven, 1986), pp. 3-129.

20 Census of Pictou County, 1871.

21 Barry, Diary, 3 February 1871. See Joan Jensen, "Cloth, Butter and Boarders: Women's Household Production for the Market", *Review of Radical Political Economics*, 12, 2 (Summer 1980), pp. 14-24.

22 Cohen, *Women's Work*, p. 68; Barry, Diary, 17, 22 August 1871.

23 Barry, Diary, 5, 21 December 1871.

also a live-in labourer from the mill, a boarder and sometimes day labourers. So Isabella, occasionally with the help of a domestic servant, cooked and cleaned for her family as well as usually for two or three others. And while she often had to leave the house to help with field work, the same reciprocity of labour was not true of her husband. Barry, who kept so detailed a record of his work, never once mentioned doing anything in the house. After housework was finished for the day, many women shouldered additional responsibilities — such as child care — which almost certainly made their working day longer than a man's. A woman often played no small part in the success of household production; Hans Medick has argued that "it was often her activity that assured the vital margin of subsistence in the family economy".[24]

Children also contributed their labour to sustain the household economy. After school age, children were expected to contribute directly to the family's subsistence.[25] Most helped around the home. Norman Grant worked as a clerk in his father's store and Alex Urqhart apprenticed in his father's shoe shop. In farm families there was usually enough work to keep at least one son busy on the farm; Thomas Fraser, Colin Gunn and Hugh Gray each helped with the farm labour.[26] Other sons on the family farm had to look for work in other places. Although cases in Hopewell were admittedly few, some young men worked as agricultural labourers while waiting for a possible inheritance or for some other kind of more permanent work.[27] Still others found work in the village. John and Alex Gray supplemented the farm household by working as a tanner and a har-

24   Hans Medick, "The Proto-Industrial Family Economy", in Peter Kriedte, Hans Medick and Jurgen Schlumbohm, eds., *Industrialization before Industrialization: Rural Industry in the Genesis of Capitalism* (Cambridge, 1981), p. 62.

25   Historical investigation of child labour within the household economy is well developed. Mary Ryan, for example, has argued that in the 'corporate family economy' in Oneida County, New York, between the years 1790 and 1820, children "were taught even as infants to conceive of themselves as workers as well as children". See her *Cradle of the Middle Class: The Family in Oneida County, New York, 1790-1865* (New York, 1981), p. 26. In the Canadian context, Joy Parr has argued that in rural Ontario "families functioned like firms. Children took from the enterprise in supervision, clothing and food and were expected to repay their debts through their labour". See her *Labouring Children: British Immigrant Apprentices to Canada, 1869-1924* (Montreal, 1980), p. 83.

26   Census of Pictou County, 1871.

27   While cases in Hopewell were few, historically the experience of agricultural labour has been the lot of some men, at least for a portion of their working lives. The case is made for Ontario men by Joy Parr, "Hired Men: Ontario Agricultural Wage Labour in Historical Perspective", *Labour/Le Travail*, 15 (Spring 1985), pp. 91-103. Parr stresses that in the minds of most men, agricultural wage labour "should be undertaken only for a short time and as a route towards some other way of earning a living", p. 103.

nessmaker. The range of such work open to daughters was narrow, and most young women were listed in the census, like their mothers, as having no occupation. Many, such as Josephine Barry and Annie McBain, had little choice but to remain in the home to help their mothers. For a few young women, such as Matilda McBain, the only opportunity to work outside the home was usually to work in someone else's house as a domestic servant.[28]

Divided by gender and age, residents of village and countryside nevertheless shared similar routines of work and a common experience of time. In communities such as Hopewell and Six Mile Brook that were so heavily tied to agriculture, the passing of seasons left a decisive imprint on rhythms of work. Looking at his diary entries over the course of the year 1871, it is possible to capture the seasonal nature of Barry's work. In general, Barry was busy grinding in September and October after the autumn harvest. Activity picked up again in January, February and March as farmers brought in stored grain for grinding to feed animals kept inside during the winter. When work was slow in the grist mill, Barry had his own field crops to tend and a small store to run. When not occupied by mill, farm or store, he could turn to sawing shingles, mending fences, hunting game or collecting spruce gum, each according to the season. Clearly, Barry's work time was not regulated by a factory bell or time clock, but followed the more "natural" work rhythms integral to an agrarian-based economy. In addition, he paid the occasional labourer at the mill not by the hour, but by the day, half-day or the task. Similarly, the Hopewell Woollen Mill rarely paid labourers by less than a "half-day".[29] Labourers were not yet paid on the basis of a capitalist market in labour power, but on more customary notions of work and time. Like men's work, women's domestic labour probably followed natural rhythms and was oriented to the successful completion of a task rather than some maximum hourly production. Such a rhythm of work and notation of time have been described as task-orientation. Work was determined not by hours in the day, as is the case in the wage labour system, but by what were considered to be the necessary tasks of rural existence.[30]

Traditional routines underscored the experience of work and time, but they exerted broader influences as well. In 1869, the local economy was only modestly diversified, made up of several stores, one grist mill, two sawmills and a tannery. Crafts were highly traditional, comprising blacksmiths, carpenters, a shoemaker, a tailor, a millwright and a wheelwright.[31] For many, production in

28 Census of Pictou County, 1871.

29 Cashbook of the Hopewell Woollen Company, 1869-79, MG 3, vol. 232, PANS.

30 See E.P. Thompson, "Time, Work-Discipline, and Industrial Capitalism", *Past and Present*, 38 (1967), pp. 56-97; Prude, *Coming of Industrial Order*, pp. 15-17.

31 *McAlpine's Nova Scotia Directory*, 1868-9.

mill and shop remained decidedly pre-industrial. Artisans plied age-old production processes within small, independent shops, few employing more than one or two labourers.[32] In James Barry's mill it was the circular motion and steady rhythm of the mill wheel that supplied the power which turned the millstones and ground the grain. But the miller remained the essential part of the production process. It was the miller who knew how to dress or sharpen the grindstones. With his mill-pick, Barry chipped grooves into the stones, all at precise angles and depths, to make cutting or grinding edges. He had to dress the stones often to ensure a fine ground flour. It was with a careful eye that Barry gauged the distance between the stones. It was crucial that the distance be perfectly set: too far away made a coarse flour, too close might cause a fire.[33] The tools and skills of Barry's trade remained traditional, far removed from the era of full-scale mechanization.

Artisans also continued the practice of custom work — independently soliciting work from their neighbours — rather than exchanging their labour for wages. Barry continued the practice of custom milling. Farmers brought in their various grains to be left at the mill. Barry kept a portion — called "toll wheat" — as payment and then ground the remainder of the grain into flour and meal to be picked up later by the farmer. Barry could use his toll wheat as an exchange product or in his own household economy. The practice of custom work fit nicely into an economy that continued to turn on production for household and local use. In creating articles from grain, wool or animal hides, families allocated only one stage of household production to artisans: the processing rather than the production.

The productive household, combined with Hopewell's stores and shops, allowed families to satisfy many of their material needs. This is not to say that individual households or the village were entirely self-sufficient, but it did mean that, for a period, dependence on an outside market remained limited.[34] Residents resorted to an external market mainly to obtain goods not available in the local economy. At Barry's store, for example, one found sugar, tea and molasses

---

32   Census of Pictou County, 1871.

33   Details of the country milling process are found, in part, in Barry's diary. More about the grist milling process as practised in the Maritimes is set out in "Grist Mills", in David E. Stephens, ed., *Forgotten Trades of Nova Scotia* (Halifax, 1972), pp. 1-9.

34   I want to stress here that I am not arguing that individual households in Hopewell were entirely self-sufficient. Much of the existing discussion about the countryside in the United States (and, I would argue, to a degree in the Maritimes) has been bogged down in a debate over the extent to which early farm households were self-sufficient. As Christopher Clark has made clear, this "debate" has proceeded based on the tendency of some to misread the work of such historians as Michael Merrill and James Henretta. See Clark, *Roots of Rural Capitalism*, p. 12.

brought in from Pictou town. But Hopewell's stores were small and invariably they did a local business. Similarly, the trade generated by sending crops and goods from Hopewell for sale in outside markets remained small. Farms were generally too modest in size to be entirely market-oriented enterprises.[35] Rather than specializing in any one cash crop, Hopewell farmers continued to raise a variety of crops and livestock that could meet the local demand for foodstuffs.[36]

Instead of relying primarily on the market to provide the goods they could not, or chose not to, produce themselves, Hopewell families entered into networks of exchange with neighbours. For Michael Merrill, looking at rural New York over the years 1750 to 1850, such rural exchange networks had several defining characteristics. First, cash did not mediate all exchange relations and was substituted with a variety of goods and manual labour. When used, cash represented only a particular use-value, one of the many products used in exchange as opposed to the ultimate means of payment. Second, exchange networks were informal and governed by local custom. Payment did not always immediately follow exchange, and a vast tangle of debts stemmed form this social reality. Third, in a highly personal and local market, rural people regularly co-operated in their work. These features of exchange in the household system of production differed radically from the capitalist mode in which producers engaged in specialized production for the purposes of sale on an impersonal market.[37]

The nature of exchange in Hopewell bears a close resemblance to the relations described by Merrill. James Barry, for example, stood at the centre of a local economy, and his diary reveals a complex web of transactions extending far out into the countryside. Barry usually kept a portion of the grain as payment for his services, but he also accepted payment in kind. "I sold 13 cwt oatmeal to Ben Brown", wrote Barry on 21 April 1871, and "he is getting the pig tomorrow". The following day Barry recorded, "Ben Brown got my pig this evening — weight 244 lbs.". On another occasion, Barry "sawed some shingles and ground one grist of oatmeal for the pigs" of Joe McLeod. Barry often made his own payments with the products of his mill. In return for butter, Barry "gave John Heughan's wife 4 lb. oatmeal". He also supplemented cash payments with goods from his store: "I paid Donald Gunn 5% — cash and tea".[38]

---

35 A rough estimate derived from farm sizes as indicated on a map of the Hopewell countryside contained in the *Illustrated Historical Atlas of Pictou County, Nova Scotia, 1879* (Halifax, 1879).

36 Census of Pictou County, 1871.

37 The nature, dynamics and importance of rural exchange networks are developed in Merrill, "Cash Is Good To Eat".

38 Barry, Diary, 21, 22 April 1871, 27 July 1871, 25, 28 January 1871.

Storekeepers in Hopewell followed similar practices. It was common for stores to accept payment in kind and labour. Alexander Urqhart, for example, advertised "all kinds of Market produce taken in exchange" for the staple and fancy dry goods at his store as late as 1879.[39] Exchanges in kind and labour better suited an economy in which the household provided a range of goods which could be used for trade. Artisans, for example, could obtain food products from farmers in return for their particular craft skills. One thinks here of the various farm products, from pigs to butter, which James Barry received in return for his milling services. In this way, Barry and people in Hopewell "entered into exchanges with one another...not in order that they might transform their own products into a universal equivalent, but in order that they might obtain with it particular equivalents, specific use-values, directly and without the mediation of money".[40]

Even when the sources suggest the use of cash, one must be careful not to take such indications as clear evidence of commodity relations. Barry recorded transactions in his diary in a number of ways. In some cases the use of cash is clear: "I sold Geo. Ross 676 lbs. oatmeal today...for the cash". More often, however, Barry noted his exchanges in the following manner: "Sold 100 lbs. siftings to McGuire.... Received a little pig from John Horon this afternoon.... Gave Adam McDonald 114 lb. oatmeal".[41] From such entries it is not at all clear that cash changed hands. If it did, why then did Barry specifically distinguish the use of cash in some transactions and not in many others? As Michael Merrill argues, the fact that goods or acts of labour were "equated in the imagination...to the prevailing standards of price was by no means the same thing as exchanging these products for money".[42] Moreover, when Barry clearly did use cash, it tended to be for specific purposes, usually to purchase imported goods. From Pictou, Barry got "a barrel of sugar from Hislop — 240 lbs. costing $25.20"; on another occasion he paid $100 for an iron water-wheel shaft.[43] We may tentatively conclude that beyond its use for such specific purposes, cash was not widely regarded as having value in itself, as the ultimate measure of all worth. More likely, in such rural settings cash was only one of many useful items in exchange networks, readily substituted by oats, manual labour, pigs or butter.[44]

---

39   *Teare's Directory*, 1879-80.

40   Merrill, "Cash Is Good To Eat", p. 56.

41   Barry, Diary, 18 November 1871, 31 July 1871, 13 May 1871, 28 February 1871.

42   Merrill, "Cash Is Good To Eat", p. 56.

43   Barry, Diary, 28 January 1871, 29 March 1871.

44   My analysis of the use of cash draws on the work of Merrill cited above as well as Clark, "Household Economy", pp. 173-4; Prude, "Town-Factory Conflicts", p. 75; and Hahn, "The 'Unmaking' of the Southern Yeomanry", pp. 184-5.

That debts were often allowed to accumulate over time is further evidence that the rural economy was still very much governed by local custom rather than the balance sheet. Again, account books reveal that goods and labour were not always immediately and directly exchanged for some means of payment. For example, Barry made a first payment of $14 on the $25.20 worth of sugar he bought from Hislop six days after the original purchase.[45] Barry treated those who owed him in a similar way. On 22 February 1871, Barry recorded: "I received from Alexander Cameron...$5 in part payment of the notorious River John Cameron's bill, for shingles he received from me some time ago". It was not until the following December that "I got the balance of my money...that was due me".[46] Many times in his diary Barry made entries such as "I received $50 from Ben Brown for oatmeal *some time ago*".[47] These transactions only hint at what must have been an elaborate network of credit arrangements. While some merchants in the Maritime countryside were charging interest at this time, nowhere is there evidence that credit at Barry's mill or store entailed interest payments. Similarly, at the Hopewell Woollen Mill, accounts payable and accounts receivable were carried over for months, sometimes years. Significantly, the woollen mill paid interest on its accounts payable (most often involving non-local firms) but did not charge interest on the accounts of local residents.[48] And, as already noted, when payments finally were made, they were often done so in kind or labour.

Residents were bound together not only by customary credit and debt relations, but also through co-operation in labour. Barry's relations with other producers reveal the extent to which residents were accustomed to co-operative forms of labour. Maintenance of the mills, for example, often required more than one hand, so Barry and Donald Gunn helped each other: "Donald Gunn was helping me to fix the buckets of the great mill wheel, and we repaired the gate of the saw mill". Barry lacked his own means of transportation, yet he could get to town on a borrowed horse: "I went to Pictou today — Johnny McLeod's horse", or on another occasion, "went to Pictou today; Donald Gunn's horse". Sharing horses and wagons was commonplace. In the spring of 1871, Barry recorded that W.G.A. Fulton of Londonderry "came for his wagon he left here the first of the winter" in exchange for the sled he borrowed from William Gunn. Exchange of labour regularly occurred between artisan and farmer, serving to reinforce the already strong links between village and countryside and thereby provide an example of the community-wide division of labour. Occupied with mill and store, Barry most often needed help with his land and

45   Barry, Diary, 2 February 1871.

46   Barry, Diary, 22 February 1871, 1 December 1871.

47   Barry, Diary, 10 April 1871 [emphasis added].

48   Cash book of the Hopewell Woollen Mill Company, 1869-79; MG 3, vol. 232, PANS.

livestock. On 22 May 1871, Alexander Gunn took half a day to spread his manure on Barry's fields and Barry "sent out cow up to A. Gunn's" to graze. Another time Barry noted, "Alexander Gunn cut my hay". Pig-killing was another farm related task for which Barry sought help: "Donald Gunn and David Ritchie killed two of my pigs today"; this was only one of several such entries made by Barry in his diary. Co-operation in labour also took place between artisans. Noting in his diary, "William Grant was here tonight and cut out leather for Donald Gunn and I", was only one example of the co-operation or sharing of skills between artisans.[49] For Michael Merrill, the fact that relations between producers often took the form of exchanges of labour rather than being mediated by money is further evidence that early rural communities were not entirely guided by commodity relations. "Exchange", Merrill writes, "took place as a natural part of the cooperation of the concrete labor of individuals and groups within the community".[50]

None of this, of course, precluded an economic hierarchy in Hopewell. There were visible differences between those who monthly lined up for aid from the "overseer of the poor" or those caught stealing from Hopewell stores and those such as Henry McLean or Alexander McDonald who owned land, operated commercial and craft businesses, had large houses and drove carriages.[51] As already mentioned, however, through most of the 1870s no enterprise in Hopewell required a large, full-time labour force. The more substantial farmers may have hired a few agricultural labourers, some shopkeepers and artisans may have used several employees, and there were those who worked in the coal mines, but many producers in Hopewell still owned their own productive resources; as such, farmers, shoemakers and millers lived their day-to-day lives largely free from the authority of employers. This, along with the customary nature of exchange and debt relations, meant that it was difficult for a few individuals in Hopewell to translate their wealth into coercive economic power over others.[52] As we shall see, however, the power to be

49   Barry, Diary, 10, 25 April 1871, 22 May 1871, 1 July 1871, 7 August 1871, 29 November 1871, 1, 2 December 1871.

50   Merrill, "Cash Is Good To Eat", p. 61. Co-operation in labour and its implications for rural economic relations are also explored in Kulik, "Dams, Fish, and Farmers", pp. 25-50.

51   Account Book, "Poor Section #17, Hopewell, Overseer of the Poor, 1886", MG 1, vol. 2053, Edwin T. Bliss Collection, PANS; Census of Pictou County, 1871. Some clothing was taken in a burglary at Henry McLean's store (*Eastern Chronicle* (New Glasgow), 24 July 1879) and, on another occasion, a small amount of money was stolen from John Fraser's store (*Eastern Chronicle*, 23 August 1877).

52   This paragraph draws heavily on Prude, *Coming of Industrial Order*, pp. 12-13, 30-3; and Prude, "Town-Factory Conflict", p. 76.

derived from the existing hierarchy in Hopewell would be consolidated by those on top, as the productive household and the local economy underwent a substantial transformation in the coming years. But first, more needs to be said about the nature of life in Hopewell in the 1870s, especially concerning how the household system of production shaped the social relations of household and village.

Households and Conflict

Historians have often romanticized rural life in the 19th century. They argue that if within the productive household each family member made essential contributions to production, then family relations must have been relatively egalitarian. James Henretta, for example, assumed that the reciprocal nature of the farm-family economy in pre-industrial America generated equally reciprocal social relations between family members. If it was primarily older men who owned and controlled the land, children's labour was needed to make it work. This forged, in Henretta's terms, a reciprocal intergenerational exchange of youthful labour for an eventual inheritance.[53] There is little sense here that land ownership and inheritance were sources of tension and conflict between generations and were based upon some fundamental gender inequalities. As Allan Kulikoff has explained, "the presumption of household unity precludes the possibility of conflict and tension within households, especially between husbands and wives, over authority, the sexual division of labor, and the distribution of goods produced by members for consumption, exchange, or sale". He correctly points out that "the romantic imagery sometimes found in descriptions of non-commercial economies stems from this failure to understand the internal dynamics of patriarchal families".[54]

Feminist historians have provided helpful direction in this regard. Feminists have been the most consistent in laying bare the ideological assumptions which often underlie the study of the family and particularly the notion of reciprocal family relations. Nancy Folbre, among others, has argued that even though capitalism had yet to work its magic on much of the countryside, any notion of a harmonious rural utopia is still misplaced given the privilege and power men held over women and children. She demonstrates, for example, that while household production in colonial New England required the collective labour of all family members,

it did not necessarily guarantee them [women and children] any significant power within the family. In fact, production within the

53 Henretta, "Families and Farms".

54 Kulikoff, "Transition to Capitalism", pp. 137-8.

55 Nancy Folbre, "Patriarchy in Colonial New England", *Review of Radical Political Economics*, 12, 2 (1980), p. 5.

colonial household took place in the context of patriarchal social relations which gave the male head of household control over his family and power to benefit from their labour.[55]

Indeed, as Folbre maintains, because the transition to capitalism had not yet drawn distinct class lines between families, the shape of patriarchal authority stood out in sharp relief.[56] Similarly, the patriarchal family stood at the centre of social and economic life in Hopewell. Despite the collective nature of work in the home and in the wider community, the household system — based on a division by gender and age — gave prominence to patriarchal notions of hierarchy and authority.

The census manuscripts can be helpful here.[57] As Hugh Gray, Hopewell's census enumerator in 1871, went from door to door, he dutifully listed the occupations of most men in the village, but he failed to record in the occupation column the work specifically performed by women. Even though in his own household it was most likely his mother and three sisters who churned the butter, made the cheese, spun the wool and wove the cloth, Gray listed them in the census with no occupation. This invisibility in the census rolls says much about the value attached to women's domestic work, even when such labour played no small part in sustaining men in their various pursuits and ensuring the successful reproduction of the family unit. Other documents, such as business records, leave us with the equally misleading impression that the rural economy turned solely on the formal trade and exchange carried on predominantly by men.

Women in Hopewell made substantial contributions to the household economy including various kinds of production for both home and exchange use. What is less clear is the power a woman could derive from her productive role. She did exercise control over her own labour process. Most often in the field or shop, husbands did not stand over women through the day telling them how or at what pace to do their work. The key to economic power, however, lay not in work as such, but in the management and control of the products of that work. While we know that women in Hopewell traded "surplus" products they produced in the home it is difficult to know whether they independently controlled the "profit". For example, women often exchanged their household products with James Barry, but Barry often made payment for the goods he received from local women through their husbands. Moreover, even if a woman was directly reimbursed for her labours, we still do not know how much control she had over

---

56   Folbre, "Patriarchy in Colonial New England", p. 11.

57   The nature and limited number of sources for Hopewell, especially those that shed light on the experience of women, prevent a detailed or very sophisticated reconstruction of gender relations. While current feminist history explores many diverse and complex issues, we will have to be content here with providing the general outlines of gender hierarchies in the household and village.

the internal distribution of family resources. More generally, while playing a significant role in household production, women did not — unlike most men in Hopewell — own their own productive resources, except perhaps in the case of a widow. In her analysis of 19th-century Ontario, Marjorie Cohen sums up the meaning of the "patriarchal relations of production" in the farm household: inheritance practices and ownership of productive resources all determined that the family "was not an egalitarian unit and neither custom nor law considered that the family per se owned the means of production". Rather, men's control over women's labour meant that "female labour was not in a position of equality with male labour in the family economy" when "the ownership and control of property were in the hands of the male alone".[58]

Women's unequal position within the productive household extended far out into the village economy. Numerous business directories publicized the gendered inequality in access to employment in the village. In 1871, all crafts and all service occupations (such as storekeepers) were occupied by men.[59] As Hopewell's economy slowly diversified over the 1870s, a woman might find a job outside the home as a weaver or a milliner, but always in a shop owned by a man, never in her own independent enterprise. Even when a woman did own a business it meant very little. When Daniel Gray died in the 1870s, he left his mill to his wife Mary. An 1879 directory confirms this arrangement, advertising "Mrs. Daniel Gray" as the proprietor of the Hopewell Mills. But the same directory also reveals that Daniel left the actual operation of the mill to his cousin and former apprentice Finlay Gray.[60] The transfer of the mill attested to the ties of kinship but also suggests that the dominant notions of gender and work deemed it inappropriate that the craft be wholly turned over to a woman. With most crafts and other businesses closed to her, a woman might use her skills in domestic labour to find work outside the home. But there were few opportunities in the village to work as a domestic servant. In 1871, only Matilda, the daughter of widow Jane McBain, was listed in the census as a servant. Ten years later, three young Hopewell women worked as domestics; one in the home of a widowed shoemaker, the other two in farm households. Within the village economy this placed women in a subordinate position to men as domestic work held little potential for economic autonomy; the low price and value set on domestic labour meant that some men could purchase it in the form of a domestic servant.

Despite the gender hierarchy within the village economy and the fact that women's work was centred largely around the household, women's existence was not one of isolation or confinement to the home. A woman's experience —

58 Cohen, *Women's Work*, p. 44.

59 Census of Pictou County, 1871; *McAlpine's Nova Scotia Directory*, 1868-9.

60 Census of Pictou County, 1871; *McAlpine's Nova Scotia Directory*, 1868-9.

the complex interplay of work, marriage and family or kinship — extended her social identity beyond the home to embrace a community-wide network. In her work on northern colonial New England, Laurel Thatcher Ulrich discovered that by "borrowing tools and commodities, working in other women's kitchens and yards, exchanging products and children, early American housewives were bound to each other through the most intimate needs of every day". For Ulrich, this is more proof that early rural communities were not self-sufficient, but rather were bound together in the common enterprise of subsistence, in this case through the trading, exchanges of labour and resource sharing carried on by women.[61]

As individual households in Hopewell were never entirely self-sufficient, women must also have been drawn together through co-operation in labour and by sharing resources. Certainly, aspects of their daily work had social dimensions which gave women the opportunity to get out of the house and which linked them to the broader village economy. As we have seen, Isabella Barry spent many a summer afternoon picking berries in various fields and meadows around the village. She and her daughter jumped at the chance to get out of the house: "Josephine and the little body", as Barry sometimes referred to Isabella in his diary, "are off with the 'John Gordon' up to Murdoch McKay's for currants". As Ulrich has suggested, "berrying" was a particular activity which "joined work with sociability".[62] Other women in the village, as we have already seen, left their homes to make trips to the mills and stores to exchange their butter and cheese.

In addition to work, ties to family provided women with connections outside their homes. Isabella made frequent trips to her parents' home in nearby Roger's Hill. Sometimes her visit was only for a day: "The little body went up to Roger's Hill this morning and came back in the evening". Other times, Isabella's trips lasted for days. Once in January 1871, Isabella and her daughters left for Roger's Hill on the 1st and did not return until the 7th. Again, on 1 September 1871, Barry noted that "the little body is up at Roger's Hill still", and not until 5 September did he write that "the little body came down this evening".[63] Because the evidence of Isabella's trips to her parents comes from her husband's diary, it is difficult to know why she went. No doubt familial responsibility played a large part. Again, Ulrich has noted that events such as births, illnesses and

---

61 L.T. Ulrich, "A Friendly Neighbor: Social Dimensions of Daily Work in Northern Colonial New England", *Feminist Studies*, 6 (Spring 1980), p. 398; and "Housewife and Gadder: Themes of Self-Sufficiency and Community in Eighteenth-Century New England", in Carol Groneman and Mary B. Norton, eds., *'To Toil the Livelong Day': America's Women at Work, 1780-1980* (Ithaca, N.Y., 1987), pp. 21-34.

62 Barry, Diary, 31 July 1871; Ulrich, "Housewife and Gadder", p. 30.

63 Barry, Diary, 20 July 1871, 1, 7 January 1871, 1, 5 September 1871.

deaths were often the reasons rural women left their own homes to visit those of other women.[64] Whatever the case, having a place to go allowed Isabella the opportunity to escape her household and its confinements, perhaps creating some space for herself beyond her husband's direct authority. Josephine, the eldest daughter, also made frequent trips to help out in her grandparents' home. Like her mother, she sometimes stayed for up to a week.

While Isabella and Josephine seem to have come and gone as they wished, Barry's diary clearly reveals that he was by no means pleased by such arrangements. He most often referred to their destination as "that damned Roger's Hill" and to that side of the family as "the damned tribe that they are". Religion, or "preechings" as Barry called it, also provided women with time outside the home, but again Barry closely monitored the whereabouts of his family, most often expressing displeasure at their absence.[65] Indeed, studies indicate that the relationship between husband and wife was expected to be one of authority and obedience.[66] If Isabella carved out some independence through her frequent trips to Roger's Hill, Barry's comments suggest she no doubt felt his scorn upon her return. Even Isabella's control over household affairs was circumscribed as Barry more than once intervened to exercise his authority by firing domestic servants.[67]

Household and family — and the power relations which characterized them both — shaped much more than the experience of women. It was also in the context of household and family that children matured and struggled with such decisions as marriage and leaving home. Josephine, still living at home at age 20 and with no job outside the home, was typical of young people in Hopewell. In fact, of all children residing at home in 1871, 42 per cent were 18 years of age or older. In 1871, Annie Gray still resided with her parents at age 35, and Alex and Annie McBain, 28 and 26 respectively, still lived with their widowed mother. Ten years later the pattern persisted: Jessie and John Gray were at home at 30 and 28, and Catherine Gunn, 34, could still be found with her parents.[68] This period of extended adolescence when many young people continued to live and work in their parents' home was reflected further by relatively late ages at marriage. During the 1870s, 27 was the average age of marriage for both women

---

64 Ulrich, "Housewife and Gadder", p. 31.

65 Barry, Diary, 13, 15 July 1871.

66 See Nancy Cott, "Eighteenth Century Family and Social Life Revealed in Massachusetts Divorce Records", *Journal of Social History*, 10 (Fall 1976), pp. 20-43; Ulrich, "A Friendly Neighbor", pp. 392-405; Carole Shammas, "The Domestic Environment in Early Modern England and America", *Journal of Social History*, 14 (Fall 1980), pp. 3-24.

67 Barry, Diary, 18 February 1871.

68 Census of Pictou County, 1871, 1881.

and men in Hopewell.[69] What factors explain the experience of youth in Hopewell?

It would be misleading to suggest much similarity in the experience of Hopewell's young women and men. The opportunities and restrictions of work, marriage and leaving home differed for each gender. While the local economy clearly set limits on the options open to young people and the timing of life-course decisions, so too did such factors as gendered inequality in the economy and fathers' control over the land. A number of possibilities existed for young men. For farm boys there was the hope of an inheritance. When Hugh Gray's father died he took over the family farm; John and Thomas Fraser each received a portion of their father's land.[70] But the realities of the long-settled Hopewell countryside were that not every son could count on a place on the farm. The fact that fathers retained ownership of the land while alive meant that many more farm boys continued working on what Nancy Folbre calls "the patriarchal farm". Patriarchal authority, she asserts, grew out of a father's control of the land and often expressed itself in a son's late age at marriage and his inability to establish a separate household.[71] In Hopewell, Colin Gunn, for instance, was unmarried and still working his father's farm at age 36. Sons of shopkeepers and artisans, if they were lucky, found places in Hopewell's modest occupational structure. Hugh and Norman Grant, storekeeper's sons, became a teacher and a clerk.[72] Of those fortunate enough to attain economic independence through land or an occupation, many were able to leave home, marry and settle in Hopewell.

The range of opportunities open to young women was much more restricted. They did not inherit land, nor did their fathers provide them a place in the "family business". Mary and Annie McDonald found work as a seamstress and a milliner, but many more young women in Hopewell lived at home and were listed in the census with no occupation. While at home, daughters no doubt had to do their share of the domestic labour, but such work provided little opportunity for economic autonomy, especially in this rural area where the call for domestic servants was limited. Overall, the few new such niches which emerged in the Hopewell economy over the 1870s were filled predominantly by males, thus reproducing among the ranks of the village's youth the gendered inequality of access to employment prevalent among adults. It seems that a young woman was expected to put her family before her own independence. Many daughters stayed on with a widowed parent; some stayed for other reasons, such as Jane

---

69 Marriage Registers, 1870-9, Pictou County, Nova Scotia Vital Statistics, microfilm #16540, PANS.

70 Census of Pictou County, 1871, 1881.

71 Folbre, "Patriarchy in Colonial New England", pp. 6-8.

72 Census of Pictou County, 1871, 1881.

McDonald, who at age 29 assumed responsibility for raising her two young brothers after the death of her parents.[73]

For most young women, leaving home meant getting married. For those who were able to marry and stay in Hopewell this did not happen until their late twenties. But more women than men had to leave Hopewell to marry. Young women marrying men from outside Hopewell most often had to leave home and family to relocate with new husbands. Those women who followed the latter course usually married a year or two earlier than those who stayed in Hopewell.[74] But even marriage was no guarantee of independence from one's parental home. Mary Gray, for example, married in the early 1870s, and by 1881 her husband had died, leaving her with three children. With no way to support her young family, Mary at age 35 was again living with her parents.[75]

Young people in Hopewell experienced what one historian of family and youth in the Maritimes has called a "protracted period of semi-dependence". Looking at the fishing village of Canning, in southwestern Nova Scotia, Alan Brookes argued that population pressure and declining economic opportunities throughout the 1870s and 1880s forced many young women and men to migrate, particularly to the New England states.[76] While there are some remarkable similarities between the experience of young people in Canning and Hopewell — most notably in the long wait before attaining independence — differences do stand out. Youth in Hopewell were far less mobile than their counterparts in Canning. Of the 65 children in Hopewell listed in the 1871 census, no less than 91 per cent were still in Hopewell in 1881. Of the few who left, most chose nearby destinations such as Middle River and Westville.[77] Perhaps growing up in a fishing outport with ready and long-established connections to New England partly explains the propensity of Canning youth to migrate. In Hopewell, however, patriarchal control of both farms and access to privilege undoubtedly prevented many young people, especially women, from striking out on their own. For some young men, the availability of work in the nearby coal and metal towns at least partially accounted for the relatively high level of youthful persistence. Both in leaving Canning or staying in Hopewell, family

---

73 Census of Pictou County, 1881.

74 Marriage Registers, 1870-9, Pictou County, Nova Scotia Vital Statistics, microfilm #16540, PANS.

75 Census of Pictou County, 1881.

76 Alan Brookes, "Family, Youth and Leaving Home in Late Nineteenth Century Rural Nova Scotia: Canning and the Exodus, 1868-1893", in Joy Parr, ed., *Childhood and Family in Canadian History* (Toronto, 1982), pp. 93-108.

77 Something of the migration patterns of Hopewell's youth can be determined by tracing place of birth (Hopewell) with subsequent place of marriage in the Marriage Registers for Pictou County, 1870-79.

78 Census of Pictou County, 1871, 1881.

and kin remained central to the experience of a young person. In her venture to the "Boston States", a young Canning woman relied on the assistance of family to make the move and find a job. In Hopewell in the 1870s, flexible families adapted to a slowly growing economy by allowing children to remain at home until a late age. Family ties were strong and persistent in Hopewell. Of the families in 1871, 87 per cent were still in Hopewell ten years later.[78]

Finally, the productive household and the power relations that held sway shaped the experience of women, children and men in the home, but they extended further still. They were also the fulcrum on which much of the social, political and cultural life of the village turned. In Hopewell, associational life expressed itself in various forms. Churches — there were two in Hopewell, the Presbyterian and the Church of Scotland — were important institutions. Members took out subscriptions and most paid for them in four instalments, very few families being able to pay the full amount at once. In September 1879, the local chapter of the Masonic Lodge held a bazaar and picnic with reportedly more than a thousand people in attendance.[79] In the same year, the *Eastern Chronicle* declared the Odd Fellows Dominion Day Picnic "a success".[80] Weddings and holidays were also occasions for sprees and frolics. As Barry noted on 31 August 1871, "the late Joseph Elliot's daughter got married today and all hands at some kind of spree tonight". On Christmas Day of 1871, Barry recorded that "there is a ball at Alexander Bell's and one at Robert Creighton's".[81]

But, as Mary Ryan has argued, if village social life was rooted in family and household, "the relations of subordination within the family were the source and standard for a social hierarchy that extended to 'superiors' throughout the community".[82] Much of the associational life in Hopewell, for example, was either exclusive to men — as with the Masonic Lodge — or at least dominated by men. Lists of church lay officials were always men. Farmers, artisans and shop-keepers — all men — filled the positions of school trustees.[83] It should not be forgotten that adult men remained the only enfranchised individuals in the family. Such a system meant that while women played crucial roles in the community, the institutional structures that linked family and household to church and village were established by men and the privilege they possessed.

The overlap and interplay among family, community and work arising from the household system of production is clearly visible in many of the village's

---

79   Information on churches and Masons in Hopewell comes from J.C. Bain, *The History of Hopewell* (n.p., n.d.).

80   *Eastern Chronicle* (New Glasgow), 3 July 1879.

81   Barry, Diary, 31 August 1871, 25 December 1871.

82   Ryan, *Cradle of the Middle Class*, p. 32.

83   Bain, *The History of Hopewell*.

workplaces. The community grist mill provides a telling example. In addition to its economic functions, the grist mill was also an important social centre. Writing about nearby McPherson's Mills, one local historian explained: "the community centre of yesteryear, the old grist mill was for many years the focal point of community life. There within its walls were the local post office, the barber shop and the village store".[84] In Hopewell, the mill was a place for people — especially the men of the village — to gather and discuss the matters of their day. Hopewell residents John Gray and John Grant often talked politics at the grist mill:

> As citizens and neighbours [Mr. Gray and Mr. Grant] lived in peace and harmony, but on politics they never could agree. John Gray was an ardent admirer of [J.W.] Johnston and John Grant fairly idolized [Joseph] Howe. It was said to be very amusing when they met in the village or at the old mill when seated on a log each endeavoured in his bluff way to enlighten the other in order to convince him of the error of his way, each attributing to the other an ignorance of matters political. Both lived to a good old age and died in the political faith received from their fathers.[85]

Even the mill pond had a social importance beyond supplying power to the mill, for it was, according to the season, a swimming hole in the summer and a skating rink in the winter.

As the proprietor of this crucial community space, the miller played a central role in social life. James Barry provides a good illustration. Like Mennochio, the heretical miller in Carlo Ginzburg's *The Cheese and the Worms*, Barry was, according to the census, an "infidel".[86] He often engaged people in debate about God, the Devil and politics. He did not accompany his family to Sunday "preechings" and took a critical view of mainstream politics.[87] In addition to being a miller and storekeeper, Barry was also a printer and a bookbinder, spending many hours in his small shop setting type or fashioning leather bindings by hand. His collection of books parallel his own eclectic radicalism, the Barry library including such titles as *Secular Thoughts*, *The Religion of Charles Darwin* and *Militant Freethought*. On one occasion he noted in his diary: "I was

---

84 Catherine Ross McDonald, "New Grist for an Old Mill", *Atlantic Advocate* (August 1980), pp. 74-5.

85 "Hopewell As It Was Fifty Year Ago", newspaper article from Westville, Nova Scotia, 19 January 1906, in "Scrapbook on Halifax, Pictou, and Cape Breton Counties", MG 9, vol. 44, PANS.

86 Census of Pictou County, 1871; see Carlo Ginzburg, *The Cheese and the Worms: The Cosmos of a Sixteenth Century Miller* (Baltimore, 1980).

87 Barry, Diary, 11 June 1871.

in my shop, setting type in 'Paine's Age of Reason'. It's a very useful book to any person who wants to know what kind of book the Bible is".[88]

But it was Barry's love of the fiddle that turned his mill into a social centre. His diary gives evidence that his mill was visited by many neighbours, and often they came to hear the fiddle. On 17 March 1871, Barry was visited by "the Blair man", a "kind of a fiddler, and peddlar and doctor". Several days later "the Blair man came back here...and is still here. We fiddled a good deal indeed". Again on 31 March 1871 Barry wrote, "Johnny McLeod, fiddler, was here this evening and I put on the fiddle at a great rate indeed".[89] So for Barry, being a miller posed no contradiction to his interest in music, books, religion, politics and sociability. His mill, turning on grinding grain, was able to develop alongside a particular kind of community sociability, his business and community roles blurring into one. It was the nature of production in the countryside — embedded in the household rather than the factory — that allowed Barry to set his own work time, to drop his mill-pick at the chance to "put on the fiddle".

The persistence of family, village networks of neighbours and kin, various forms of community and workplace sociability — these were some of the features of social life in the countryside. As James Henretta has stressed, family values among rural dwellers were at the centre of a pervasive *mentalité* in pre-industrial America. Maximizing profit was not yet elevated to a dominance that challenged "the maintaining of established social relations within the community".[90] Similar values structured much of social and economic life in Hopewell. But the more important question concerns the nature of these social relationships and who was most eager to maintain them. Despite the collective forms of work in the household and the village, social relationships in Hopewell were not egalitarian, but rather were based on patriarchal authority and gender hierarchies. By the end of the 1870s, relations of power shaped by gender, as well as the existing household system of production and exchange in Hopewell, would be complicated by further change.

The Changing Countryside

Went to Pictou today with 5 cwt of oatmeal to Irving and the damned buggar [*sic*] would not take it, and after coaxing me to send it down to him.[91]

So wrote Barry on 28 January 1871. While Barry always noted the activities of his day in his diary, this small incident is nonetheless significant. Here, in the few words of a country miller, are captured the growing tensions in the

---

89 Barry, Diary, 17, 21, 31 March 1871.

90 Henretta, "Families and Farms", p. 16.

91 Barry, Diary, 28 January 1871.

Table One
Businesses and Artisans in Hopewell, 1869-1879/80[95]

	1869	1879-80
Grist Mill	1	1
Sawmill	2	1
Woollen Factory	-	1
Furniture Factory	-	1
Brickyard	-	1
Tannery	1	1
Blacksmiths	4	2
Shoemakers	1	3
Carriagemakers	-	2
Carpenters	3	3
Milliners	-	1
Tailors	1	1
Painters	-	1
Millwrights	1	-
Wheelwrights	1	-
Storekeepers	3	6
Hotelkeepers	-	3
Total	18	28
Farmers	87	72

countryside as it made the transition to capitalism. Barry's traditional practice of custom milling — in which he ground grain for specific customers — was slowly giving way to merchant milling. Merchant millers, generally located in the towns, purchased and ground large quantities of grain to sell on the open market at a profit. Irving, in refusing the oatmeal he had earlier requested from Barry, failed to operate within the accepted rules of custom work. He was no longer dependent on country grist mills for his grains. Located in Pictou, a town with a ready supply of merchant-milled grain, Irving perhaps did not feel compelled to take Barry's product. A small incident, no doubt; yet it throws into relief the increasingly uneasy co-existence of two very different forms of production and economic relations in the countryside. It reveals Barry's increasing involvement with an extra-local market, reflecting more generally the growing interconnection of town and country, and hinting at the growing importance of the merchant in economic relations. Most important, Barry's sense of anger reminds us that the rural transformation was felt at the level of human experience. The household system and custom work were part of an old rural order that was passing. Out of its demise would rise something entirely different as commercialization and industrialization took firmer root in the countryside.

The shifts and tensions captured in Barry's diary were widespread in Hopewell. Farmers in the area — who declined slightly in number over the 1870s — began to turn from mixed farming for local use and put into their fields crops demanded by growing town populations. By 1881, the production of crops such as peas and turnips was down significantly, replaced by much greater specialization in wheat and potatoes.[92] Even more visible was the shift to market production in manufacturing. In 1882, a Pictou newspaper, the *Colonial Standard*, drew attention to the changes at work in the Hopewell economy: "The rare advantages which it [Hopewell] offers in the way of water-power, location...are attracting the attention of Capitalists, and promise to make it an important Manufacturing Centre at no far distant day".[93] By 1879, traditional artisans such as blacksmiths, millwrights and wheelwrights were in decline (see Table One). Crafts new to Hopewell, such as carriage making, were drawing artisans, attesting to the increasing needs of residents to be mobile, perhaps to get to town for their needs. Alongside the old grist and sawmills a brickyard, a woollen factory, a tailor shop and a furniture factory took their place, while the old tannery greatly expanded its operations. By 1886 a newspaper article claimed, "Hopewell industries [were] all doing well", the Woollen Factory "employing many hands", and McLean's Tannery and the McArthur Furniture Factory "equally busy".[94] The presence of farmers working in the nearby coal mines was perhaps the most obvious sign of the changes rippling through the Hopewell countryside, evidence that Hopewell did not stand apart from the industrial world growing up around it. Rather, the very nature of the rural transformation was partly captured by the tension suggested in the census designation "coal miner/farmer".

Alongside the changes in farming and manufacturing, Hopewell's commercial base and activity picked up pace. Storekeepers doubled in number. Though still too small to support its own newspaper, Hopewell merchants did advertise

92 Total number of heads of household listed as farmers in Hopewell in 1871 was 87; by 1881, the number had decreased to 72. Census of Pictou County, 1871, 1881. Production of selected field crops:

	1871	1881
Peas (bu.)	666	157
Turnips (bu.)	3,384	2,493
Wheat (bu.)	2,731	6,694
Potatoes (bu.)	19,262	23,695

93 *Colonial Standard*, 28 March 1882.

94 *Colonial Standard*, 25 November 1886.

in business directories, pointing to a new commercial orientation.[96] The appearance of three hotels in the village reveals again an upsurge in mobility. As an advertisement for "Hopewell House" put it, the hotel was "fitted up for the accommodation of Visitors, Strangers, Commercial men and the travelling public generally".[97] People who came through Hopewell on the Intercolonial Railway, stayed in hotels and then moved on again must have seemed odd to a village so long attached to the household and the persistence of family. This movement reflected the growing fragility of the old order's stability. Finally, that R.G. Dun and Company began to give credit ratings to Hopewell residents reflected a growing commercialism and suggested that, at least to some degree, economic networks were broadening beyond the local area.[98]

These, briefly, were the outlines of the commercialization and industrialization of Hopewell's economy. This transformation of the countryside was not the product of one or two factors such as the role of the land and the timing of settlement or the inexorable growth of markets. Rather, change was a complex process comprised of many forces both internal and external to the rural social formation. As we have seen, the tug of extra-local markets for wage labour was significant as signalled by the number of Hopewell men who went to work in the coal and metal towns. But also central to this transformation, and what I want to briefly focus on in the remaining pages, was the often conflicting roles played by different households *within* Hopewell as it went down the path of early capitalist development.

Households in Hopewell headed by local storekeepers were often responsible for initiating the move toward industrial production and a greater commercial orientation. Henry McLean, for one, owned over 200 acres of land and was one of the village's most prominent merchants. Years later it was remembered that his store "did a large business during his lifetime".[99] Profits reaped from land and trading did not sit idle but were invested in his tannery, which, by 1871, was capitalized at $3,000 and employed at least three men the year round.[100] At the opposite end of the main road from McLean's tannery was

95 *McAlpine's Nova Scotia Directory*, 1868-9, and "Business Directory of Hopewell" in *Teare's Directory*, 1879-80. Total number of heads of household listed as farmers for Hopewell Census Division, Census of Pictou County, 1871, 1881.

96 See, for example, "Business Directory of Hopewell", in *Teare's Directory*, 1879-80, pp. 162-4.

97 *Teare's Directory*, 1879-80, p. 163.

98 R. Dun, Wiman and Company, *Mercantile Agency Reference Books*, 1881, Dalhousie University Archives.

99 Census of Pictou County, 1871; "Hopewell As It Was Fifty Years Ago".

100 Census of Pictou County, 1871.

Alex McDonald's store. Alex was himself a substantial landholder of 152 acres. He, along with his brother James, started the Hopewell Woollen Mill in 1869 as a joint stock company.[101] Already by the 1870s, then, a combination of land ownership and commercial activity allowed a few households in Hopewell to experiment with industrial production, helping to secure their place at the top of the economic hierarchy.

The manufactories opened by local merchants, as well as the brickyard and the furniture factory, were a clear departure from the productive household and the individual artisans' shops. Rather than operating on a seasonal cycle as was the case with the old grist mills and sawmills, the manufactories ran all year round. They also intensified the rate of production. Another tannery opened by John McLean in 1882, for example, became one of the largest manufacturers of harness and upper leather in the province, turning out up to 400 pieces of leather a week.[102] Not only did this increase the workload of tanners employed by McLean, it also clearly signalled a break with the practice of individual custom work. Manufactories, then, by gradually regulating time and intensifying production, brought a certain degree of work-discipline to the village economy. By centralizing and intensifying production in this way, merchants clearly moved production beyond the old goal of satisfying household and local needs.

In addition to starting manufacturing enterprises, Hopewell merchants expanded their business activity beyond the local village, thereby drawing Hopewell into a much wider economy. John McLean's tannery took in hides and hemlock bark from all over the county. Finished leather was transported by walking cart to the railway station and from there shipped to markets as far away as Newfoundland. Also during the 1880s, John McArthur expanded his sawmill into a small furniture factory producing sashes, blinds, windows, chairs and doors.[103] Invoices remaining from his business indicate that by 1895 his operations extended well beyond Hopewell; he sold chairs in Hantsport, Nova Scotia, and he bought supplies in Halifax and Massachusetts.[104] On a more modest scale, we see the same process at work in James Barry's operation. His business increasingly took him beyond his local area to deal with town merchants. By the late 1880s, one writer commenting on commercial activity in Hopewell wrote that "a large trade is carried on in the winter with various lumber camps in Halifax and Guysboro Counties, and the Gold Mines at Fifteen Mile Stream".[105] Over the course of the 1880s, as storekeepers and others forged

---

101 Census of Pictou County, 1871; Bain, *The History of Hopewell*.

102 *Halifax Morning Chronicle*, 31 August 1901; Bain, *The History of Hopewell*.

103 Bain, *The History of Hopewell*.

104 Invoices, John McArthur and Sons, Cabinet Maker, MG 100, vol. 55, nos. 134–6, PANS.

105 *Colonial Standard*, 6 November 1888.

business connections in distant places, primarily local exchange networks were broadened, and Hopewell was drawn into a much larger market. This process was paralleled by changes in local exchange relations. Cash exchange became increasingly frequent. We see this, for example, in the account books of the woollen mill, which more and more noted transactions in the following manner: received payment "by cash from...".[106] Account books also reveal that the tannery paid its workers $1.10 for a day's work, and a full day for the woollen mill put $1.25 in a labourer's pocket.[107] These occurrences marked a shift in the local economy as payments formerly made in kind or in labour were giving way to the more abstract, market-oriented medium of cash.

A focus on the merchant and the manufactories helps to locate the origins of industrial production within local rural society and highlights the growing interplay between the local economy and wider market society, but it does not entirely account for the actual process of capitalist transformation in the countryside. Hopewell merchants lacked the means — advanced mechanization and a large, dependent labour force — to fully refashion production completely along capitalist lines. While the evidence for Hopewell remains only suggestive, it would seem that Hopewell merchants did not entirely reorganize production so much as intensify the exploitation of the prevailing household system.

By 1882, the woollen mill employed over 30 people. This was accomplished by drawing on the productive household, particularly by using the labour of women in the home. As the records of the Hopewell Woollen Mill noted, cash was paid to women specifically for the spinning and weaving of cloth in the home.[108] James Keith hired four men and four women to work in his tailoring business. As neither Hopewell maps nor business directories indicate the existence of an actual tailoring shop, it seems probable that at least some of the women and men who worked for Keith did so out of their own homes.[109] By 1888, John McLean's tannery had hired 15 hands and, again, many of those working for McLean lived outside of Hopewell in the surrounding countryside and mixed their tannery work with the demands of farming.[110] Merchants and

---

106 Cashbook of the Hopewell Woollen Mill Company, 1869-79, MG 3, vol. 232, PANS.

107 Bain, *The History of Hopewell*; Cashbook of the Hopewell Woollen Mill Company, MG 3, vol. 232, PANS.

108 Bain, *The History of Hopewell*; and "Cashbook of the Hopewell Woollen Mill Company", MG 3, vol. 232, PANS. For more on the uses of women's labour see Thomas Dublin, "Women and Outwork in a Nineteenth-Century New England Town, Fitzwilliam, New Hampshire, 1830-1850", in Hahn and Prude, *The Countryside*, pp. 51-69.

109 "Industrial Returns", Census of Pictou County, 1871.

110 Employees of the McLean tannery, listed in Bain, *The History of Hopewell*, were linked to the 1881 census; some tannery workers lived not within the village of Hopewell but in the countryside and reported their occupation as farmer.

others who established industrial enterprises in Hopewell, then, depended at least in part on the participation of the productive household and its family labour system. Those who introduced industrial production and wage labour in Hopewell found families long accustomed to combining a number of economic activities so that work for wages, whether in a manufactory or in the home, complemented the logic of the productive household.[111]

Gradually, however, family involvement with the manufactories undermined the old village economy. Labour previously given to the production of use-values in the home was turned to the benefit of merchants through the manufacture of commodities. Clothes production provides an important example. Cloth production and clothes making in Hopewell had long been household activities. But by the early 1880s the tailoring business, the woollen mill and the village store which retailed dress goods all challenged the household's hold over production. The woollen mill in particular tapped the productive capabilities of the household, and, as we have seen, families responded to this opportunity to augment their household economies. By 1888, the woollen mill produced a vast array of items including yarn, shirting, blankets, even "homespun".[112] By sending workers into the mill and by taking work into the home, families played a key role in this development, but soon found its impact turned against them as the production of cloth and clothing was removed from the home to the mill. In the case of those who worked in the home, actual production might remain within the household, but control of that production was transferred from the home to storekeepers or small-scale capitalists. Though it is difficult to measure, the availability of commodities on the local market, coupled with the introduction of wages, must in turn have served to further diminish the semi-subsistence base of the household and the local market for the products of independent artisans.

This transition had contradictory repercussions for women. On one level, the abandonment of household textile production was one way for rural women to

---

111 I want to stress that I am not suggesting here that merchants and others in Hopewell employed the same elaborate outwork systems found, for example, in the New England countryside. The evidence, at least for Hopewell, is too limited. At the same time, I do not think this prevents one from arguing for an important relationship between the productive household and early rural capitalist development, a relationship that could include people in their homes working for those who introduced industrial production in the countryside. For the importance of the outwork system to rural capitalist development in other places see Jonathan Prude, "Protoindustrialization in the American Context: Response to Jean H. Quataert", *International Labor and Working-Class History*, 33 (Spring 1988), pp. 23-9. More research is needed before we can reach a conclusion about the significance of outwork in the Maritime countryside.

112 Items produced by the Hopewell Woollen Mill Company found in Bain, *The History of Hopewell*.

reduce their work burdens and to take advantage of the lower cost of factory-made, store-bought cloth and clothes.[113] Yet the transfer of production from home to factory transformed use-values into commodities and converted women's labour into men's jobs. As Mary Ryan explains, "small-scale capitalists gradually usurped productive roles from the family economy — often from their own wives".[114] A similar process was at work in the Ontario countryside during the 19th century. Marjorie Cohen shows how, with the growth of markets, women's traditional household production of dairy products became increasingly oriented to the market. But women's lack of ownership and control of production meant that over time "farm women's access to the market through production within the household was usurped by males".[115] The same thing happened in Hopewell: when production was finally transferred from the household to the manufactory, the new positions in Hopewell's manufactories went to men.[116] Although rural capitalist development initially gave some women employment, it could just as easily take it away by transferring jobs from the home to the mill. As capitalism made its twists and turns, changing the shape of the local economy, gender divisions and inequalities were both used and maintained in the process.

The transformation of the countryside was slow and uneven as both old and new tugged at Hopewell. Parts of the old household system survived into the 1880s. In the words of one historian of Pictou County:

> Barter at stores was still for farmers in the 1880s and later a customary thing....The early years practice of farmers sharing their labour was carried over into this period by shared purchase of agricultural implements...The village of Hopewell in the 1870-80s had a tannery, a grist mill, sawmills, blacksmiths, carpenters, two shoe-makers, a tailor...The village tradesmen served the rural populace in a wide area, and this pattern continued until the automobile in the 1920s began to supplant the horse.[117]

---

113 Clark makes the same point in *Roots of Rural Capitalism*, pp. 139-46.

114 Mary Ryan, "Femininity and Capitalism in Antebellum America", in Zillah R. Eisenstein, ed., *Capitalist Patriarchy and the Case for Socialist Feminism* (New York, 1979), p. 154.

115 Cohen, *Women's Work*, p. 157.

116 This is clearly revealed by looking at the gender of the employees in Hopewell manufactories and shops as listed in the "Industrial Returns", Census of Pictou County, 1871.

117 James Cameron, *Pictou County's History* (New Glasgow, N.S., 1972), pp. 224-5.

Older ways persisted because they continued to make sense in their cultural and economic context. Yet, by the end of the 1880s, industrialization had already done much to substantially transform the nature of productive and social relations in Hopewell.

The Hopewell Experience

Hopewell's experience suggests that within the Maritime Region, those who lived in rural communities experienced the great economic and social changes of the late 19th century in ways markedly different from their urban counterparts. In the same decades usually considered the high-water mark of indigenous Maritime capitalist development and the making of a working class, people in Hopewell lived and worked by daily routines which in many ways predated the rise of industrial capitalism. Similarly, we could look to the "pre-capitalist modes of production in the coalfields" of Cape Breton where for a time mineral and coal resources were used as common property or to the persistence of pre-industrial productive and social relations aboard the ships of Atlantic Canada's merchant marine.[118] While we are just beginning to understand the extent and importance of such economic and social relations in the Maritimes, limited evidence points to a region that, within the overall framework of capitalist development, nourished a variety of productive and social forms. Indeed, as Ian McKay has suggested, "the survival of essentially pre-capitalist relations... retarded the full development of capitalism in the crucial period between the fall of the old mercantile system and the formation of the Canadian state, leaving a fragmented and dependent region vulnerable to rapidly expanding central Canadian capital".[119] Eric Sager echoes these thoughts on regional under-development, arguing that "relatively slow capitalist development was deeply rooted...in the relationships between capitalist and pre-capitalist modes of production".[120] If such hypotheses turn out to be true, then an understanding of the persistence and later transformation of productive and social forms in places such as Hopewell may help to throw new light on the process of regional under-development.

Hopewell's experiences also provide some possibilities for a conceptualization of rural history in the Maritimes, the centrepiece of such a conceptualization being the productive household. For much of the 1870s and 1880s, the productive household, a slowly expanding economy and established

---

118 McKay, "The Crisis of Dependent Development", pp. 20-1; see also Eric Sager, *Seafaring Labour: The Merchant Marine of Atlantic Canada, 1820-1914* (Kingston, 1989).

119 McKay, "The Crisis of Dependent Development", p. 16.

120 Eric Sager, "Dependency, Underdevelopment and the Economic History of the Atlantic Provinces", *Acadiensis*, XVII, 1 (Autumn 1987), p. 136.

rhythms of work and village life characterized Hopewell. Material needs were met by production that remained centred in the household and was accomplished by the family's collective labour. What was not produced in the home could usually be found locally by exchanging with neighbours rather than relying on the outside market. These local exchange networks coupled with customary co-operation between farmers and villagers bound local residents together in an economy which set household and local needs before individual gain. The household system of production and exchange in turn shaped much of the social relations of home and community. In fact, household, work and village converged in complex ways, giving rise to a community that expressed itself in co-operation in work and various forms of village social life. Households which retained control of productive resources also allowed people to set their own work time which, as in the grist mill, made for a distinct workplace sociability.

A focus on the productive household also throws into relief the hierarchies and inequalities of gender both within the household and beyond. Despite the collaborative nature of work in the household labour system, tasks were not distributed equally but were divided by gender and age. Although playing a crucial role in the household economy, women could count little on their productive role in terms of concrete power. In addition, the operation of gender and age hierarchies meant, among many things, that women encountered gender segregation and inequality in the local economy and children faced extended periods of semi-dependence given their fathers' control over access to the land.

Looking through the prism of the productive household also brings into view the subsequent transformation of the countryside. The household played a crucial role in the rural transformation, providing much of the initial basis for the shift to both industrial production and commercial/market relations. Merchant-headed households, in particular, were responsible for starting Hopewell down this path by developing manufactories and co-opting the labour power of other households. In doing so they introduced wage labour on a new scale as they connected Hopewell to a wider sphere of market relations.

This process was riddled with tensions and in some rural areas it gave rise to conflict, sometimes even to a critique of capitalism itself. During the mid-19th century, for example, residents of the Connecticut Valley, steeped in the values and reciprocal practices of the household system, cried out against "the monopoly of wealth and income in the hands of the few". For historian Christopher Clark, this activity made it increasingly clear that as the century passed its mid-point:

> The world of the market and of capitalist production was tying up "the many" in lines of exploitation and of class division that created new barriers in rural society. Their misfortune was that the values of household integrity, and of neighborhood co-operation and

reciprocity...had lost their effectiveness....These values had drawn them into a new system, but had no longer the power to get them back out.[121]

There is little evidence of overt conflict in Hopewell, although some, such as James Barry, responded with anger as the ground of customary economic and social relations began to shift beneath him. But in some ways the experience of Hopewell was not entirely dissimilar from that of the Connecticut Valley. Over the 1880s, Hopewell's merchant-manufacturers prospered while many others in Hopewell were pushed toward proletarian status, even if only in part. Living between farm and factory proved anything but a blessing for the majority of people in Hopewell.

Finally, it needs to be stressed again that the history of Hopewell should not be construed as some utopian rural world we have lost. This becomes particularly clear when we look at the unequal relations of power between men and women in Hopewell or the ultimately weak defence the productive household provided against a dynamic capitalism. But the history of Hopewell does demonstrate that some Maritimers once constructed a world in the countryside based at least in part on need and co-operation rather than greed and exploitation. Parts of that vision are still worth remembering.

---

121 Clark, "Household Economy", pp. 184-5.

Dependency and Rural Industry:
Inverness, Nova Scotia, 1899-1910

Daniel Samson

For a century prior to 1895 we had the, alleged, base of prosperity here with us in N.S., but the base itself did not prevent our young men, and fair maidens, leaving the old home and hieing to the new land. For the lack of the population there was no home market, and for the lack of a home market the base became moss covered. We may talk of farming as the basis and the back-bone, but without mining the base is of small value.
Robert Drummond, *Minerals and Mining in Nova Scotia* (Stellarton, N.S., 1918), p. 23.

Farmers, as a rule, have to avail themselves of various other means of adding to their income. Some near the shore combine farming and fishing. Some are farmers and carpenters. Some find work at industrial centres. Some sell railway ties, pit props, timber and firewood. And then by earning a little here and a little there, and by the constant practice of careful economy, they are able to enjoy the necessaries of life, but by no means many of its luxuries.
John L. MacDougall, *History of Inverness County* (Belleville, Ont., 1972 [Truro, N.S., 1922]), pp. 181-2.

Both Robert Drummond and John L. MacDougall knew something of the relationship between agriculture and mining in Nova Scotia around the turn of the century. From their different perspectives, both recognized that agriculture needed mining more than mining needed agriculture. The converse position, however, is that agriculture made labour available for the mines. Mining companies had at their disposal a large force of labour from those farms otherwise unable to meet their subsistence requirements. These workers, together with a steady stream of immigrants from abroad, form something of an anonymous mass in the industrial history of Nova Scotia, and indeed of most industrializing economies. Histories of Nova Scotia coal mining have devoted little attention to the rural background of many of the industry's workers. While they recognize the importance of rural migrants, the cultural background they brought with them and their position within a stratified work force, such histories emphasize how cultural homogeneity becomes a force for working-class unity and a defining element of "class consciousness" in the turn-of-the-century coal towns.[1] Once they take us into the coal towns, there is little sense of the differential pressures on the various sub-groups that made up the Cape Breton working class, as if the employees were all fully proletarianized, urban workers. Such a presumption neglects much of the diversity and unevenness that characterized life in Nova Scotia coal towns before the First World War. Here I wish to argue against the views of a culturally homogeneous work force in one coal town by demonstrating the important differences introduced with the influx of rural workers.

Two suggestive paths of investigation have been established in histories of Cape Breton coal mining and agriculture. Ian McKay, in his work on the relationship between the development of the Sydney coal fields and their social

---

1   See David Frank, "Tradition and Culture in the Cape Breton Mining Community in the Early Twentieth Century", in Ken Donovan, ed., *Cape Breton at 200: Historical Essays in Honour of the Island's Bicentennial*, (Sydney, N.S., 1985); "The Industrial Folk Song in Cape Breton", *Canadian Folklore Canadien*, 8, 1-2 (1986), pp. 21-42; D.A. Muise, "The Making of an Industrial Community: Cape Breton Coal Towns, 1867-1900", in Don Macgillivray and Brian Tennyson, eds., *Cape Breton Historical Essays* (Sydney, N.S., 1980), pp. 76-94; and Ian McKay, "The Realm of Uncertainty: The Experience of Work in the Cumberland Coal Mines, 1873-1927", *Acadiensis*, XVI, 1 (Autumn 1986), pp. 3-57. McKay has also noted urban carpenters' concerns about rural workers entering the city of Halifax; see his *The Craft Transformed: An Essay on the Carpenters of Halifax, 1885-1985* (Halifax, 1985), p. 15. See also Craig Heron, *Working in Steel: The Early Years in Canada, 1883-1935* (Toronto, 1988), pp. 78-87. Examinations of migrant workers in the coal towns have been limited to specific groups who came from easily identifiable, if still somewhat general, locations. An important exception is Ron Crawley, "Off to Sydney: Newfoundlanders Emigrate to Industrial Cape Breton, 1890-1914", *Acadiensis*, XVII, 2 (Spring 1988), pp. 27-51. On "foreign" (that is, non-British) immigrants to industrial Cape Breton, see Michael Owen, "Making Decent Law-Abiding Canadian Citizens: Presbyterian Missions to Cape Breton's Foreigners, 1900-1915", in Kenneth Donovan, ed., *The Island: New Perspectives on Cape Breton History, 1713-1990* (Fredericton, 1990), pp. 113-28. The author gratefully acknowledges the support, at different times in the researching and writing of this piece, of the University of New Brunswick, Queen's University and the Social Sciences and Humanities Research Council. This paper benefited greatly by the criticism, encouragement, and assistance of many people. I would like to thank Ernie Forbes, Jim Kenny, Ian McKay, Bryan Palmer, Gail Pool and especially David Frank for comments on the original version of this paper. The comments of participants at the Rural Workers in Atlantic Canada conference in Halifax in October 1990, and especially those of Jacques Ferland, were helpful. The comments of four anonymous *Acadiensis* readers also proved beneficial. As helpful as all these people were, they could do only so much; thus, of course, what's muddled is solely my own.

history, argues that "essentially pre-capitalist relations and paternalist politics retarded the full development of capitalism in the crucial period between the fall of the old mercantile system and the formation of the Canadian state" when other regions successfully made the transition. McKay's analysis of these developments in staple-exporting, industrial enclaves focuses on the limitations placed on development, especially in terms of socialized labour and the home market.[2] Within these enclaves class formation did not occur as it had where capitalism emerged in a more gradual fashion as primitive accumulation slowly displaced non-market social relations and brought together, often violently, capitalist production, socialized labour and a home market. [3] Instead, mercantile-like monopolies and restricted expansion were maintained, and poorly developed, usually seasonal, labour markets required masses of migrant workers to maintain production. Capitalist enterprises focused on building their export economies. In the areas surrounding the enclave, much of the economy was reorganized in relation to, but not completely transformed by, the development. The result was an economy designed primarily to service its new centrepiece and dependent upon the production of a single export. The present study explores the relationship between one such dependent enclave and the surrounding countryside as it affected work and broader social relations in Inverness Town.

---

2   Ian McKay, "The Crisis of Dependent Development: Class Conflict in the Nova Scotia Coalfields, 1872-1876", *Canadian Journal of Sociology*, 13, 1 (1988), pp. 15-16. See also Anders Sandberg, "Dependent Development, Labour, and the Trenton Steel Works, Nova Scotia, 1900-1943", *Labour/Le Travail*, 27 (Spring 1991), pp. 127-62; and Eric Sager, "Dependency, Underdevelopment and the Economic History of the Atlantic Provinces", *Acadiensis*, XVII, 1 (Autumn 1987), pp. 117-37. The Latin American literature is important here. See Charles Bergquist, *Labor in Latin America: Comparative Essays on Chile, Argentina, Venezuela, and Colombia* (Los Angeles, 1986); Florencia E. Mallon, "Labor Migration, Class Formation, and Class Consciousness among Peruvian Miners: The Central Highlands, 1900-1930", in Michael Hanagan and Charles Stephenson, eds., *Proletarians and Protest: The Roots of Class Formation in an Industrializing World* (New York, 1986); Norman Long and Bryan Roberts, *Miners, Peasants and Entrepreneurs: Regional Development in the Central Highlands of Peru* (Cambridge, 1984); and Adrian DeWind, "From Peasants to Miners: The Background to Strikes in the Mines of Peru", *Science and Society*, 39, 1 (1975), pp. 44-72.

3   See, for example, Michael Hanagan, "Agriculture and Industry in the Nineteenth-Century Stéphanois: Household Employment Patterns and the Rise of a Permanent Proletariat", in Hanagan and Stephenson, *Proletarians and Protest*, pp. 29-50; Donald Reid, *The Miners of Decazeville: A Genealogy of Deindustrialization* (Cambridge, Mass., 1985), pp. 26-36; Maxine Berg, *The Age of Manufactures: Industry, Innovation and Work in Britain, 1700-1820* (London, 1985); Marjorie Griffin Cohen, *Women's Work, Markets, and*

A second theme to be explored is how rural workers came to occupy such a pivotal place in the early history of Inverness. Recent work by Rusty Bittermann and others has described relations between the development of markets for farm goods and farm labour and the process of economic differentiation in Cape Breton in the 19th century.[4] More fundamentally, they have focused attention on the complexity of the relationship between economic development and rural society, noting that traditional staple-based studies have emphasized the demand created by production rather than the "ready supplies of labour originating in the countryside".[5] Some farmers in Middle River found ready markets for surplus production in industrial Cape Breton, just as those farmers who were unable to meet their households' basic requirements found a market for wage labour in the same place.

Between these two approaches, we can formulate a broader, more inclusive way of explaining the interconnected histories of work and economic development during Nova Scotia's "industrial revolution", a history we should label a social history of development. In many ways the coal mine at Inverness was a rural industry. Characterized by its location, its seasonality, its use of farm-based workers and, most important, its capacity to shift part of its costs onto the shoulders of the rural household, it was in many ways similar to the situation we see in the more easily identified forms of rural industry such as shipbuilding, the fishery, tanning and merchant outwork. What marked Inverness in distinction to other rural industries was the scale of the operation, especially the much greater concentration of workers — a condition which facilitated organization and working-class institutions and may mislead us into categorizing these workers as *the* working class.[6] Once we have done this, it is too easy to follow urban-in-

Economic Development in Nineteenth-Century Ontario (Toronto, 1988); and Bruno Ramirez, *On the Move: French-Canadian and Italian Migrants in the North Atlantic Economy, 1860-1914* (Toronto, 1991).

4   Rusty Bittermann, "The Hierarchy of the Soil: Land and Labour in a 19th Century Cape Breton Community", *Acadiensis*, XVIII, 1 (Autumn 1988), pp. 33-55; Rusty Bittermann, Robert MacKinnon and Graeme Wynn, "Of Inequality and Interdependence in the Nova Scotian Countryside, 1851-1870", *Canadian Historical Review*, LXXIV, 1 (March 1993), pp. 1-43; Robert MacKinnon and Graeme Wynn, "Nova Scotian Agriculture in the 'Golden Age': A New Look", in Douglas Day, ed., *Geographical Perspectives on the Maritime Provinces* (Halifax, 1988); Alan R. MacNeil, "Cultural Stereotypes and Highland Farming in Eastern Nova Scotia, 1827-1861", *Histoire sociale/Social History*, 37 (May 1986), pp. 39-56; and from a different perspective L.D. McCann, "Leading the Double Life: Town and Country in the Industrialization of the Maritimes", in Day, *Geographical Perspectives*.

5   Bittermann, "The Hierarchy of the Soil", p. 51.

6   Bergquist, *Labor in Latin America*, pp. 7-14; McKay, "The Crisis of Dependent Development".

dustrial assumptions and emphasize the distinctions between town and country proletarians and countryfolk, and so on. There were differences between the town and the country, and between experienced industrial workers and recent migrants from the countryside, but the differences were not so sharp as these oppositions suggest.

Most of the Inverness Railway and Coal Company's employees can be characterized as having come from one of three backgrounds: permanent proletarians with prior industrial work experience, recently dispossessed farmers and fishers, and peripatetic workers still maintaining a more or less regular footing in a (sub)subsistence rural economy.[7] Although we cannot definitively ground this typology in the data available, Inverness nonetheless suggests that it is a useful tool in describing class formation in the region's industrial enclaves. For a seasonal industrial facility such as Inverness, this form of work force was more than useful or convenient: it was essential. No enterprise whose seasonal labour demands varied so widely (ranging from as low as 100 to as high as 850 workers) could operate with its entire work force dependent on the company for their living. Just as the working-class households of the company's permanent workers lowered the necessary (wage) value of men's labour, households with access to land provided the company with a large reserve of labour, which imposed an even lighter wage burden. Preserving and reproducing the household, "labour power" was in effect subsidized.[8] For most employees of the company, and concomitantly for their families, relative social standing was in large part a measure of their position within the company/mine hierarchy, a factor — especially in the early years of the company — closely related to their positions as skilled or unskilled workers and, ultimately, to their industrial or rural backgrounds. In the writing of social history, rural workers seldom rise above their

7   This is meant only to be a rough characterization. I would not deny the likelihood that some of these rural workers had acquired class experiences outside the implicitly limited and local assumptions which might seem to influence these types. It is, however, to argue for some regularities of context amongst some identifiable groups which would allow some level of generalization, even within a local and particular situation, of what was probably their dominant experience.

8   On the role of urban working class households' attempts to continue these rural strategies in the city, see Bettina Bradbury, "Pigs, Cows, and Boarders: Non-Wage Forms of Survival among Montreal Families, 1861-1891", *Labour/Le Travail*, 14 (Fall 1984), pp. 9-46; on households straddling rural and industrial lives, see Joan Smith, "Non-Wage Labor and Subsistence", in J. Smith *et al.*, eds., *Households in the World Economy* (Beverly Hills, 1984); Gay Gullickson, *Spinners and Weavers of Auffay: Rural Industry and the Sexual Division of Labor in a French Village, 1750-1850* (Cambridge, 1986); and Sharon B. Stichter and Jane L. Parpart, "Towards a Materialist Perspective on African Women", in Stichter and Parpart, eds., *Patriarchy and Class: African Women in the Home and the Workforce* (London, 1988).

positions as problems on the supply side of the labour market. But in Inverness rural workers, experienced in class processes in both the town and the country, pushed the local working class in new directions.

Inverness is illustrative of the rapidly changing character of class struggle in the coal fields of Nova Scotia prior to the First World War. Conflict was an everyday aspect of town life in Inverness, and its diversity of communities made class cohesion difficult. These communities were rooted in their backgrounds but emerged as critical points of differentiation in the workplace. Strikes exposed the boundaries of these communities.[9] We are reminded that the remaining record of industrial disputes leads us only to the culmination of conflict in the workplace and usually misses underlying social conflict. In 1909, roughly half of Nova Scotia's miners struck for the recognition of the United Mine Workers of America (UMW), rejecting the locally based Provincial Workmen's Association (PWA), which had represented most of the province's miners since 1879. There has been a tendency, both within older labour histories and newer social histories, to view the UMW as the natural representative for the more militant needs of the Nova Scotia working class.[10] McKay's interpretation of the PWA has demonstrated the importance of differentiating between the cautious, public pronouncements of its leadership and the highly militant orientation of some of the lodges. He also notes the changed conditions of activity after 1891, partly due to internal struggles but also coinciding with the emergence of monopoly control of the industry following the rise of the Dominion Coal Company.[11] However, conditions had changed to such an extent in the intervening years, that the very core of the PWA's platform — a progressive programme directed at working-class independence, but whose class consciousness was burdened by masculinist and nativist ideas — was simply un-

---

9   Here I am following lines similar to those emphasized in David Smith, "Tonypandy 1910: Definitions of Community", *Past & Present*, 87 (1980), pp. 158-84; and Donald Reid, "Labour Management and Labour Conflict in Rural France: The Aubin Miners' Strike of 1869", *Social History*, 13, 1 (1988), pp. 25-44. See also Dipesh Chakrabarty, *Rethinking Working-Class History: Bengal, 1890-1940* (Princeton, 1989).

10 Harold Logan, *History of Trade Union Organization in Canada* (Chicago, 1928); Eugene Forsey, *Trade Unions in Canada, 1812-1902* (Toronto, 1982); Sharon Reilly, "The Provincial Workmen's Association of Nova Scotia, 1879-1898", M.A. thesis, Dalhousie University, 1979; Ron Crawley, "Class Conflict and the Establishment of the Sydney Steel Industry, 1899-1904", M.A. thesis, Dalhousie University, 1980; and Danny Moore, "The 1909 Strike in the Nova Scotia Coalfields", unpublished paper, Carleton University, 1977.

11 Ian McKay, "'By Wisdom, Wile or War': The Provincial Workmen's Association and the Struggle for Working-Class Independence in Nova Scotia, 1879-97", *Labour/Le Travail*, 18 (Fall 1986), pp. 13-62.

tenable in the expanding Nova Scotia coal industry. The PWA was a craft union in a changing context that was coming to demand an industrial strategy.

Rural workers had always been a central component of the industry's work force, and the PWA had always attempted to protect its membership from the coal companies' desire to dilute the craft through the use of cheaper foreign and rural labour.[12] But the expansion and changes in the industry during the 1890s and 1900s were greater than the union had ever experienced. Class formation continued to be a protracted process — one still structured by the seasonality of production — but it was on a greater scale than ever before. The concentration of production in small locations demanded a large influx of workers and families who came from the farms of the surrounding countryside and the mines and farms of Belgium, Bulgaria and beyond. They composed the elements for a new working class in a new capitalist structure. The Nova Scotia coal industry had grown dramatically in the past decade. Inverness, a product of those changes, suggests the degree of class fragmentation which had to be overcome.

Many, if not most, of the workers who came to Inverness did not fall into the categories of urban artisanal or skilled workers.[13] The town's startlingly quick growth as an industrial enclave highlights its rural context. At the same time, there are no sources for analysing the town's non-permanent proletariat better than in any other of the province's coal towns. There are no company payrolls for the mines[14] or accessible census manuscripts to measure precisely how many workers came from the countryside peripatetically or permanently, or even how many came from previous industrial backgrounds. But many sources — oral history, scattered obituaries in scrapbooks, a Presbyterian minister's brief attempt to record new arrivals in his parish, occasional comments and asides in newspaper reports — continually point to large numbers of rural migrants coming to Inverness to find work in the mines. This study uses many of the standard

12 Donald MacLeod, "Colliers, Colliery Safety and Workplace Control: The Nova Scotia Experience, 1873-1910", *Communications historiques/Historical Papers* (1983), pp. 226-54. On rural coal miners in Nova Scotia in the mid-19th century, see Danny Samson, "Family Formation and Household Reproduction: Mining and Farming Households in Pictou County, Nova Scotia, 1860-1880", paper presented at the meetings of the Canadian Historical Association, Charlottetown, June 1992.

13 The major Canadian studies here are Bryan D. Palmer, *A Culture in Conflict: Skilled Workers and Industrial Capitalism in Hamilton, Ontario, 1860-1914* (Montreal and Kingston, 1979); Gregory S. Kealey, *Toronto Workers Respond to Industrial Capitalism, 1867-1892* (Toronto, 1980); and McKay, *The Craft Transformed*. Bryan D. Palmer's *Working-Class Experience: Rethinking the History of Canadian Labour, 1800-1991* (Toronto, 1992) is the important synthetic assessment of the Canadian working class.

14 There are payrolls available for the railway side of the company, but none for the mines; two sets of books existed for all aspects of the company's record keeping.

sources on working-class life, but with new questions about the context of working-class life in the countryside. This essay proceeds in three sections. First, the emergence of an industrial enclave at Broad Cove (which only in 1901 became known as Inverness Town) is examined and situated in the political economy of the county. In the second section, some of the cultural features of social relations in the town are described, drawing on the different groups' myriad backgrounds, understandings and expectations as seen through social, institutional and workplace activities, as well as the coal company's highly selective paternalist strategies. Finally, the third section describes how these economic and social forces played out in the realm of workplace struggles, focusing on a series of strikes between 1901 and 1909.

The Rural Context of Dependent Development

Coal has been mined at Broad Cove since at least the 1830s. Local settlers mined outcrops at Broad Cove Banks and near the Big River. Some cut the coal in shallow pits while others carried it out in creels along a narrow path cut into the hillside.[15] There were no attempts at commercial mining until 1864 when, following the break-up of the General Mining Association's provincial monopoly on coal, the colony granted a lease to two entrepreneurs, Blackwood and McCully. Coal mined near the Big River was transported by a tramway to the beach, loaded onto scows and transferred to larger vessels offshore. Two companies, one in the late 1860s and the other in the 1890s, attempted to cut a channel through the beach from MacIsaac's Pond to the ocean, but neither was able to keep the channel open without continually dredging the passage.[16] At the end of the 19th century, despite much boosting by speculators and the state,[17] no commercial mining occurred at Broad Cove.

---

15 MacDougall, *History of Inverness County*, p. 112.

16 Robert Drummond, *Minerals and Mining in Nova Scotia*, (Stellarton, N.S., 1918), pp. 279-83; *Canadian Mining Review*, XVI, 12 (December 1897); Nova Scotia, *Journals of the House of Assembly* [*JHA*] (1901), "Mines Report"; and Ned MacDonald, "The Broken Ground: A History of Inverness Town" (Inverness, N.S., n.d., [1978]). On the GMA see D.A. Muise, "The General Mining Association and Nova Scotia's Coal", *Bulletin of Canadian Studies*, 7, 1 (1983), pp. 70-87; Marilyn Gerriets, "The Impact of the General Mining Association on the Nova Scotia Coal Industry, 1826-1850", *Acadiensis*, XXI, 1 (Autumn 1991), pp. 54-84; Richard Brown, *Coal Fields and Coal Trade of the Island of Cape Breton* (London, 1871); and Drummond, *Minerals and Mining*, pp. 172-91.

17 P.K. Hyndman, "Report on the Inverness Railway and Broad Cove Coal Mines" (Ottawa, 1890). The report was commissioned by Henry Paint of the Inverness and Richmond. Hyndman was an engineer and also a shareholder in the company. See also *JHA* (1891), "Report on Subsidized Railways".

This brief background sets up much of the story of how Inverness came to be developed as it was. First, it points to the central place of the state in determining who would be able to develop the mines. If the mines were to be developed to serve the export market, any developer faced major transportation problems. Confronted with no harbour — indeed, the coast was a two-mile-long, white-sand beach — any coal operation required a railway to get the coal to market. Railways meant politics. The province granted charters to several local groups in the 1880s and 1890s, but no roads were built. These groups, aligned with various political parties and economic factions in the province, struggled with various levels of the state, with each other and with local interests in an effort to reap the possible rewards. There were two inextricably linked prizes to be won, but aligning the two would be difficult. The first was the coal reserves of the county, particularly those at Broad Cove. The second was the subsidies available for railway construction from all levels of government; these could amount to over $12,000 per mile of line built. Both were potential money-making opportunities, but only if combined. If the mines were developed, they would be profitable to operate only if a railway was there to ship the product. With the subsidies, there were profits in building the railway but unless there was freight to carry, the line would be unprofitable to operate. The problem then was getting railway rights, mineral leases and capital all in one package.

The election of the Laurier Liberals in 1896 brought about a political alignment between Ottawa, Halifax and the men behind the Inverness and Richmond Railway. They arranged almost $700,000 in subsidies, payable upon completion of the line. They needed contractors with capital. With the politics in place, Premier George Murray, one of the original stockholders in the company, "invited" the famous railway promoters William Mackenzie and Donald Mann to build the line.[18] Mackenzie and Mann built the road in exchange for stock; thus, upon completion of the line in 1901, they owned it. The Inverness and Richmond was reorganized in 1902 as the Inverness Railway & Coal Company (IR&C) with $7.5 million in fully subscribed and paid-up stock. The list of company directors read like a who's who of Canadian finance.[19] Following the completion of the railway, Mackenzie and Mann sold additional bonds to

---

18 Donald Mann to Wilfrid Laurier, 4 August 1906, Sir Wilfrid Laurier Papers, Micro C825-100358, National Archives of Canada [NAC], For more on Mackenzie and Mann see T.D. Regehr, *The Canadian Northern Railway: Pioneer Road of the Northern Prairies, 1895-1918* (Toronto, 1976).

19 Returns of the Inverness Railway and Coal Company for 1902, 1907 and 1909; NAC, RG 46, vol. 943, NAC. Other than Mackenzie and Mann, the board consisted of: R.M. Horne Payne, of the British Empire Trust Company; James L. Brass, General Manager, Canadian Northern Railways; L.W. Mitchell, Secretary, Canadian Northern; Zebulon A. Lash, Mackenzie's friend and solicitor, as well as Vice-President of the Bank of Commerce; and D.B. Hanna, Vice-President of the Canadian Northern; see also Nova Scotia, *Statutes*, 1902 (chapter 162).

finance the opening of the mines. This brought their total bonded debt up to $2,115,000 at five per cent.[20] Thus their first debt payment required $105,000 every year as interest on their bonds. The repayment schedule, however, elevated that to more than $200,000.[21] By 1908, the IR&C seemed to be a healthy operation. The company's value was growing as its owners' retained earnings increased each year. Despite the recession of 1907-8, the mine was also doing well with both production and sales at all-time highs. The mines now employed almost 600 men, with the railway employing another 250.[22]

The Eastern Canadian coal market was dominated by two large companies, the Dominion Coal Company and the Cumberland Railway and Coal Company; by 1910, that would be reduced to one, as Dominion bought Cumberland. Dominion Coal officials viewed the smaller companies as "a disturbing factor in the market". They were especially concerned about whether the smaller companies, in particular Inverness, were "maintaining prices" — that is, not trying to undersell Dominion.[23] Yet Inverness was not simply a small-scale operation. It was far too large to operate in a catch-as-catch-can market. The company's extensive investments — the railway, housing, mining equipment, the shipping pier at Port Hastings and especially the bonded debt — required that the company have steady and reliable markets. Inverness was no match for Dominion Coal. But with its own market and its own transportation system, and as long as its prices were competitive, the IR&C was more immune from Dominion than were other companies. The "financial wizardry" of Mackenzie and Mann had created a delicate monstrosity, balanced on a stable coal market and increasing prices and production. It had also, of course, created a town and introduced an important new force into the county's political economy.

Nothing even close to the scale of the industrial developments at Inverness had ever existed in Inverness County. A pre-industrial economy centred on

20 Canada, *Sessional Papers*, No. 20 (1903), Volume 37, Table 1: "Summary statement of capital of subsidised railways". See also the annual reports in *Poor's Manual of Railroads*. For information on these convoluted dealings see Danny Samson, "The Making of a Cape Breton Coal Town: Dependent Development in Inverness, Nova Scotia, 1899-1915", M.A. thesis, University of New Brunswick, 1988, chapter 1.

21 *Halifax Herald*, 20 February 1912.

22 *Halifax Herald*, 27 September 1906. The article notes that $20,000 "was paid out at the pay office last week", but the article does not note that this pay was biweekly and distributed among at least 500 men. Shipments on the railway were up 86 per cent between 1906 and 1908, and the net profit on the railway alone — that is, not including the mines — was $95,546.

23 Alexander Dick (Dominion Coal) to M.R. Morrow, 29 June 1906; correspondence tabled in Rex vs. Cowans and Dick (Exhibit H/26), RG 21, series "A", vol. 328, PANS.

agriculture, the fishery and a rural merchant elite structured the county's late-19th-century social formation. The 1890s were a period of decline. Agriculture was stagnating with inadequate markets, and the merchant capitalist-dominated fishery was also in decline.[24] Out-migration was extremely heavy. About 4,000 people left Inverness County between 1891 and 1901; the population of the county actually declined by 1,426.[25] Manufacturing was limited to local artisans serving local needs, tanneries, shipbuilding and a few mills. Coal mining, while occasionally attracting some investment, was typically utilized only locally by farmers digging outcrops for fuel. Only at Port Hood and Mabou was there any settlement directly related to mining.

Parts of the economy were still largely outside a market dominated by money. As late as 1880, cash constituted only 18 per cent of one local merchant's business, while a woollen mill conducted most of its business in exchange and long-term credit.[26] Families' involvement with the market depended on their particular circumstances. Household production remained a critical component of the family economy. For some products it was essential: in 1890, for example, there were no commercial creameries on Cape Breton Island, only two small woollen mills and a tiny cheese factory. Yet, in 1901, in the two census districts that covered what would include Inverness Town, 373 households produced 82,588 pounds of butter, 42,077 pounds of cheese and about 7 tons of wool. Many families, however, especially the roughly 70 per cent of households living on the backlands, were unable to meet their minimum needs through their own production. They usually needed to exchange their labour for access to these basics. Their sons and daughters often earned much-needed cash in wage labour. Sons worked other families' farms or went further afield to the mines or

---

24 A very helpful overview can be found in Stephen Hornsby, *Nineteenth-Century Cape Breton: A Historical Geography* (Montreal and Kingston, 1992); see also M.C. MacLean, "Cape Breton A Half Century Ago", in Macgillivray and Tennyson, *Cape Breton Historical Essays*. For more on the merchant economy of the Jersey fishing companies which operated at Cheticamp and at Canso, see Rosemary Ommer, "'All the Fish of the Post': Property Resource Rights and Development in a Nineteenth-Century Inshore Fishery", *Acadiensis*, X, 2 (Spring 1981), pp. 107-23; David Lee, *The Robins in Gaspé, 1766 to 1825* (Markham, Ont, 1984); and Anselme Chiasson, *History and Acadian Traditions of Cheticamp* (St. John's, 1986).

25 Canada, *Census of 1891*, vol. I, table II, 6; Patricia A. Thornton, "The Problem of Out-Migration from Atlantic Canada, 1871-1921: A New Look", *Acadiensis*, XV, 1 (Autumn 1985): pp. 3-34, quoted figures in Appendix 1.

26 Stephen J. Hornsby, "An Historical Geography of Cape Breton Island in the Nineteenth Century", Ph.D. thesis, University of British Columbia, 1986, p. 124; James Mariner Smith Papers, MG 12, 1 (76-98), Beaton Institute. The proprietor, W. MacDonald, often seemed relatively unconcerned about two-year-old debts. See, for example, the entry for 8 April 1909.

industries of other parts of the province or New England. Daughters typically worked in domestic employment, sometimes locally, more often in Boston.[27]

Construction of the railway brought numerous benefits to the county. While most of the money left the county to purchase rails and rolling stock, construction gave a substantial and immediate boost to the local economy. The railway created a large demand for rail ties, temporary trestles, fences and even train stations. Most of this lumber was purchased locally, and local merchants saw more cash than usual.[28] Construction also provided a number of short-term jobs. During the two years of construction, from June through December, there were on average 1,000 men employed daily as labourers clearing the road and laying the tracks. Most were locals, farmers and the sons of farmers along the route, although some came from as far away as Sydney to find work. The use of immigrant workers was not extensive, a situation often enforced by locals.[29]

Port Hood was the first community to benefit from the railway's presence. The mines at Port Hood had operated only irregularly for the previous 20 years. In 1900, the mine was able to maintain production throughout the winter for the first time, and the company was able to employ 250 men for the entire year.[30] Interest in the area was growing wider. To the north of Broad Cove, an "English syndicate" had purchased the small mines at the Chimney Corner fields, while other developments were reported at Mabou, Cheticamp and Lake Ainslie.[31] Most of this was only more speculation; the actual benefits were significantly less. The IR&C was clearly the dominant factor. They dealt ruthlessly with the smaller companies which were dependent on their larger rival's railway. The Port Hood Coal Company complained bitterly to the premier in early 1907 that

27 Bittermann, "Hierarchy of the Soil"; figure of 70 per cent backlanders from Hornsby, "An Historical Geography", p. 164; on one woman's experiences in the "Boston states", see "With Katie Margaret Gillis, Mabou Coal Mines", *Cape Breton's Magazine*, No. 38 (1985), pp. 1-15.

28 *JHA* (1901); "Engineer's Report", pp. 2-3; MacBean, *The Inverness and Richmond*, p. 43; "Annual Report of Superintendent of Education" [John McKinnon], Inverness and Victoria counties, 1901, as cited in D. Campbell and R.A. MacLean, *Beyond the Atlantic Roar: A Study of the Nova Scotia Scots* (Toronto, 1974), p. 154. The James Mariner Smith Papers (MG 12, 1 [76-98], Beaton Institute) contain much commentary on the building of the railroad.

29 *Amherst Daily News*, 15 May 1901; my thanks to Ian McKay for drawing this article to my attention.

30 *Maritime Mining Record*, 11 September 1900; *Halifax Morning Chronicle*, 8 June 1901; *Halifax Herald*, 31 December 1901.

31 *Monetary Times* (Toronto), 17 March 1899, 25 August 1899, 3 November 1899, 15 September 1900, 12 June 1903; *Halifax Herald*, 28 July 1906; *Mining Record*, 11 July 1900, 5 September 1900, 19 September 1900.

the IR&C would never supply them with enough cars to ship their coal. They also pointed to the excessive rates — the same charge as IR&C coal but over half the distance.[32] Fishers also complained that the "rates [were] so high that they cannot ship their fish".[33]

The other side of the railway was that it brought the larger market to Inverness. The proprietors of a woollen mill at nearby Glendyer were thrilled when they learned the railway would pass directly by their mill — so much so that they modernized it in anticipation of improved access to markets. The reasons for the company's failure in 1912 are not clear. What we do know, though, is that the company was having trouble paying its debts and that its products were less competitive in Sydney than in past years. It seems likely these problems were linked to the importation of cheaper woollen goods from outside.[34] Neither the railway or the town appeared to aid agriculture, and it continued to stagnate between 1900 and 1920. Farmers found only a small market in Inverness Town. Fruit and vegetable production increased, reflecting some response to a market, but this was small and improved acreage actually declined by almost 20 per cent.[35] The long-promised boon to industry and agriculture in Inverness County was something of a boondoggle outside the town. But at Broad Cove, now named Inverness, a town was emerging, a town whose promise for the future everyone seemed sure of.

Conflict emerged between the town and other parts of the county as the town and the company grew. County officials often complained about the poor service provided by the railway and were especially angry about the company's single-minded attention to its own needs. Of particular contention was the uncompleted portion of the line. The railway was supposed to continue north another 40 miles to serve Cheticamp and the Margaree Valley. But the company refused to lay any more tracks and, as J.L. MacDougall wryly noted, "got away with it on the *ethical* ground that 'half a loaf is better than no bread'".[36] Others were concerned about the town's effect on older ways of life, noting with some alarm that the town was "spreading money...[and] enticing many away from farming and

---

32 Port Hood Coal Company to the Provincial Secretary, March 1907. The letter detailed more than 20 other complaints; this situation may also explain the Port Hood mine's inability to hold the contracts it obtained, such as the Nova Scotia Sugar Refinery noted in the testimony of Thomas Cutler, in Rex vs. Cowans and Dick (Exhibit H/26), RG 21, series "A", vol. 328, pp. 644-5, PANS.

33 James MacDonald to George Murray, 13 December 1901, RG 7, vol. 131, PANS.

34 W. MacDonald to James M. Smith, 8 October 1890, 12 December 1899, 27 March 1909; James Mariner Smith Papers, MG 12, 1 (76-98), Beaton Institute.

35 All agricultural figures are county figures from Canada, *Census of 1901*, vol. III, table VII; and 1911, vol. V, table III.

36 MacDougall, *History of Inverness County*, p. 118 [original emphasis].

fishing".[37] Many feared the urban problems the town brought with it. Residents of Port Hawkesbury complained that "foreigners", drawn to the area's developing industries, brought with them "contagious and infectious diseases". While the area around the town of Inverness "benefitted very materially by the works carried on there", their 1906 petition complained, the taxpayers of Port Hawkesbury had to pay "large sums of money" to contain the diseases they believed the foreigners brought with them.[38]

While the county was concerned about the town attracting contagions to the country, some in the town were trying to keep out what they considered rural contagions. Inverness was built on farmland and farms were still in operation a few hundred yards away from the bankhead. Livestock roaming the streets was common, as were reminders that they may have passed through recently. Town council, regularly concerned about health standards in the town, tried to keep farm animals out of the town.[39] But their concerns were not only with health. A conscious programme was set in many minds to rid the town of its rural character and make it "look as much like a big town as possible", as one sceptical commentator remarked.[40] Central Avenue was always the focus of these concerns. For merchants, through their Inverness Association, and the newspaper, the emphasis was on how the town's main street looked to outsiders: "The promenade must be put in through [*sic*] repair...and other public buildings must, in their location, accommodation and architecture be such as shall worthily maintain the credit of the town".[41] The company, too, sought to symbolize its importance through grand public works. In 1910, the company donated land for a new town hall, but backed down when the manager decided council's plans were not grand enough.[42] It took months of haggling before the two could agree on just how grand the building would be.

Politics in the county, both formal and informal, continued to be played out in a context of town/country conflict into the 1920s. Politics was dominated by the Grit and Tory machines, but often wrapped in assorted labourist and socialist colours. Socialist activity had been noted in the town as early as 1906. "A Clergyman" writing to the *Halifax Herald* noted that "a numerous colony of

37 *MacTalla*, April 1904 [English translations from the original Gaelic in the Beaton Institute]. See also Frank, "The Industrial Folk Song in Cape Breton", pp. 23-5.

38 "Petitions", RG 5, series "P", 1906, vol. 38, no. 41, PANS.

39 Inverness Town Council Minutes, microfilm copy in PANS, 31 May 1905, 7 May 1906, 19 February 1910; fumigating, 18 January 1909.

40 *MacTalla*, April 1904.

41 See the *Inverness News*, 25 August 1904 (reprinted excerpts published by the Inverness Historical Society).

42 Inverness Town Council Minutes, 26 June, 23 August, 8, 26 October 1910.

Belgians and others at Inverness are pioneers of the co-operative common-wealth". The town could claim the largest per capita readership in Eastern Canada of the socialist newspaper *Cotton's Weekly*. And while socialists did not fare well in provincial or federal elections, a number were consistently elected to leadership roles in the union or as checkweighmen at the mines.[43] The dominant thrust in working-class politics, however, was a reform tendency best identified as labourism. PWA leaders such as A.B. MacIsaac and Thomas Keating led efforts within the PWA Grand Council for stronger lobbying and encouraged support for "a true labour representative" in federal politics:

> There should be no grit or tory; it should be working men all through. For this reason the whole kite that we fly should be sent into the air by our own efforts. Let us form committees, let us organize, let us agitate, above all, let us progress and march on in the line of united workmen, and make our influence felt.[44]

MacIsaac was elected to town council on the heels of the union's success in the strike of 1906. Three more miners were elected over the next six years, including Rod MacNeil, a supporter of the UMW. Minutes of the town council reveal few significant differences between the elected miners and their fellow councillors; their difference lay in their constituency, their significance more symbolic than political or ideological.

Candidates running in the town and the county had to address issues important to miners in order to expect support from the town's mining population. Inverness Town usually voted differently than the other parts of the county. In 1911, in the great reciprocity election, Inverness County stayed Liberal, resisting the tide to Borden's anti-reciprocity Tories. But the mining centres of Inverness and Port Hood voted to protect their home markets, and supported Tory Thomas Gallant almost two to one.[45] C.E. MacMillan, the county's Tory member in the Provincial Legislature, buttressed his attack on the Liberal government's speech from the throne with extensive quotations from the labour newspaper, *Industrial Banner*. He described proposed legislation as "class legislation" and asked, "was the government to have different definitions of fair for capital and labour?"[46]

---

43 *Halifax Herald*, 22 December 1906; *Cotton's Weekly*, 24 October 1912, lists 188 subscribers to the paper in the electoral district of Inverness, the county. My estimate of 100 for the town assumes, based on all the other figures, that it was the industrial centres which attracted subscribers. The estimate is probably low.

44 PWA, *Grand Council*, Minutes, October 1907 (IV, 615-16); on labourism in Canada see Craig Heron, "Labourism and the Canadian Working Class", *Labour/Le Travail*, 13 (Spring 1984), pp. 45-76.

45 *Halifax Herald*, 22 September 1911.

46 Nova Scotia, *Debates and Proceedings of the House of Assembly*, 1910, pp. 25-6.

MacMillan was defeated in the 1911 election but easily won the Inverness town polls. The mining vote was not enough to obtain victory. The industrial centre and the rural county seldom found common ground, at least not in politics. Outside the town, pragmatic politics meant that labourist concerns had to be integrated into the political mainstream. Still, these differences found expression inside the town as well.

Communities of Labour

The people who came to live and work in Inverness came from a variety of backgrounds and circumstances which affected both what they experienced in Inverness and how they interpreted and understood those experiences. Not only did they come from different social and economic backgrounds, but within the town each employee of the company was marked by his wage relationship with the company. Thus an experienced collier from the Pictou County coal fields and a young man off the farm from Broad Cove Marsh might have little in common despite both now being working-class Scots Catholics. Such diversity meant the town was not simply one community, but several communities whose boundaries were highly uncertain. This section describes the cultural and institutional features of town life and the backgrounds of the people who followed the railway to Inverness. I wish to outline the factors which divided them and those which brought them together.

What these people brought to the town significantly affected their standing within the company hierarchy, the work force and the town. It was from these backgrounds that workers and other townspeople interpreted and evaluated their experiences. Yet their experiences in Inverness also allowed them the opportunity to reinterpret their world. Working within the ideas of Pierre Bourdieu, we may conceptualize these varied communities as each having its own *habitus*. Bourdieu's concept can be understood in terms of socially structured tendencies within individuals and groups which form the context in which meaning derived from experience is evaluated; conversely, experience subjects the *habitus* to revaluation. Perhaps the best one-word analogy would be "disposition", which suggests a background for practice but lacks an absolute determination of outcome.[47] Bourdieu's work, like that of many social theorists, is directed toward understanding what mediates between social structures and human agency; the critical difference here is Bourdieu's attempt to historicize practice by emphasizing people's capacity to (re)evaluate their understandings through experience. The experience of class can promote common tendencies but only while filter-

---

47 Pierre Bourdieu, *Outline of a Theory of Practice* (Cambridge, 1977), pp. 72-87; *Logic of Practice* (London, 1990), pp. 23-141; Donna Young and Danny Samson, "The Theory of Practice and the Practice of Theory: Pierre Bourdieu and the Labour Process", paper presented at Critical Anthropology Conference, York University, May 1989.

ing through and re-evaluating older understandings. Class formation, understood as class in itself, was structured in the context of this particular dependent political economy; but, understood as class for itself, it was understood and acted upon through the backgrounds and expectations these people brought with them.

The building of the railroad and the promised opening of the mines at Broad Cove and Port Hood did not end out-migration, but these activities did have a significant effect on the local population. Most of the town's residents arrived between 1901 and 1904. Dramatic as the local growth was, it was not enough to outweigh that overall out-migration from the county. Nevertheless, for the first time, the county had a population centre which could act as a draw for some of its population, allowing them to stay a little closer to home and in some cases drawing some out-migrants back to the area.[48] Attention was quickly drawn to the opportunities awaiting those willing to relocate in the new community forming at Broad Cove Mines. "A Traveller" who corresponded with the Gaelic Sydney newspaper *MacTalla* reported the movement, even observing the sexual division of labour: "They are building a railroad in Inverness County and a great number of people from the county are going there; there are almost as many boys there as there are girls in Boston."[49] Most of this work was unskilled, heavy manual labour. As for men experienced in mining, the 1891 census informs us that there were only two men in the county who called themselves miners. While it is difficult to assess the extent of mine work, we know that Inverness County men did sojourn to the mines of Cumberland, Pictou and Cape Breton counties, and some may have worked in the smaller mines which had been worked over the past 30 years. Indeed, many were probably the products of families who had lived the "double life" for generations.[50] At the same time, it

---

48 "Record of the Congregation, Strathlorne Presbyterian Church, 1894-1906", MG 13/144, Beaton Institute. These records list the names of all family members, their addresses, usually the head of the household's occupation, and very often a comment noting where the family had come from; obituaries often note the movement of people, see Scrapbook #19, Beaton Institute; and interviews with Charlie MacMaster by the author. Census reports cannot tell us where migrants came from with the specificity we desire let alone inform us of the backgrounds of individuals' desires to relocate. Many local sources at the time, however, comment on the draw created by the town on their local populations, and most of these comments come in the form of a suggestion that this was a welcome opportunity for many. See also W. MacDonald [Glendyer Mills] to James M. Smith, 15 May 1900 and 12 July 1900, James Mariner Smith Papers, MG 12, 1 (76-98). Beaton Institute; *MacTalla*, 15 January 1898, and 27 October 1899; "Petition of Residents of Port Hawkesbury", RG 5, series "P", vol. 38, no. 30, PANS.

49 *MacTalla*, 27 October 1899.

50 McCann,"'Living the Double Life'", pp. 98-100. In this essay I do not wish to try to explain why people led this peripatetic existence, but I find McCann's play

seems clear that Inverness County was not what might be labelled a mining society. The building of the railway and the creation of the town changed all that.

We can get an overall view of the town from the 1911 census. The portrait of Inverness suggested by the census suggests significant homogeneity. The coal towns of Cape Breton County averaged about 45 per cent Scots and 54 per cent Catholic.[51] In Inverness, 2,100 of 2,700 (77 per cent) people in the town claimed Scottish ancestry. The other significant groups were French (Acadians from the Cheticamp area) at 10.3 per cent, Irish at 4.3 per cent and Belgians at 3.0 per cent.[52] Religious denominations were dominated by two groups: Roman Catholics (64.1 per cent) and Presbyterians (28.7 per cent) composed more than 90 per cent of the town; only 7.2 per cent of the residents claimed any other affiliation.[53] Labourers, including miners, constituted more than 85 per cent of the town's adult male population. The vast majority of the men were wage labourers employed by the IR&C.[54] Certainly, if class position and ethnicity were significant forces in the development of a mining culture, then Inverness would seem to have provided a strong cultural pool from which to draw.

There are difficulties in applying this portrait to particular social and economic positions; that is, we may not have described the typical miner or merchant or manager, just a mythical average citizen. Indeed, despite the apparent homogeneity, we can see that many of these people's backgrounds differed widely. It is impossible to quantify even from where these various people came, but we can make some careful generalizations. We know that many of the skilled miners were recruited from the existing mining centres of the province, especially Cape Breton County, but also Westville and Stellarton in Pictou

with both necessity (an economic explanation) and choice (a "cultural" explanation) unsatisfactory. While it is obvious that any individual's choices were materially structured, McCann regards these choices as part of a culture of occupational pluralism, a Maritime way of life.

51 Frank, "Tradition and Culture", p. 205.

52 Canada, *Census of 1911*, vol. II, table VII, pp. 196-9.

53 Canada, *Census of 1911*, vol. I, p. 36; these figures correspond very closely with the county figures — Roman Catholic, 66.6 per cent; Presbyterian 26.3 per cent; and others, 7.1 per cent.

54 This number is based primarily on a survey of the names in the 1908 *McAlpine's Directory of the Town of Inverness* which lists heads of households and boarders, usually with their occupation. This was compared with the company's reported number of employees as listed in the provincial "Mines Report" for the same year. While this method does not yield an exact figure, it provides a reasonable estimate for the company. It is impossible to verify in any way the accuracy of the other figures, but there is no reason to presume that the figure for clerks, school teachers, merchants, farmers and all those who composed the other groups are under-represented.

County and a few from Cumberland County.[55] The company sometimes recruited foreign workers, complaining that it often "found much difficulty in getting loaders and labourers".[56] They were able to attract a group of experienced Belgian miners who had recently immigrated. Most of these men were miners who, whether recruited or simply transient, were experienced and skilled workers who had already been introduced to the new regimes of industrial production.[57] The largest group, however, were the hundreds from the surrounding countryside, drawn from as far north as Margaree and Cheticamp and as far south as Judique and Port Hastings.

Contemporary accounts noted with alarm the abandonment of farms and the loss of so many of the young people. The Broad Cove correspondent to *MacTalla* noted the effect coal mining had had on the area, and particularly the disruption of the older economy: "This work is enticing many away from farming and fishing, those two types of work in which most people in the county made their living until now".[58] Residents of Port Hawkesbury, 90 kilometres to the south, complained that their community had "suffered a diminution of its population, by so many of its residents removing" to Inverness.[59] The local labour pool was predictably large but few were skilled in mining. Most were the sons of farmers who, whether by choice or by necessity, did not continue farming. Of 47 miners who married between 1901 and 1908, 27 (57.4 per cent) identified their fathers' occupations as farmers; 23 of these were from Inverness County. Only 13 (27.7 per cent) identified their fathers as miners. More than three-quarters of the women who married miners identified their fathers as farmers; all but two of these were from Inverness County.[60] This is a small sample and it is biased toward the young unmarried men and women. But Inverness had a young work force, and these data suggest that most recent arrivals

55 *Halifax Herald*, 16 March 1904; "Record of the Congregation, Strathlorne Presbyterian Church, 1894-1906", MG 13/144, Beaton Institute.

56 *Labour Gazette*, June 1906, p. 1300. In late 1906, the company had contracted with the Salvation Army to bring 22 English workers, but they did not arrive until the winter and the company refused them and any responsibility for their welfare. See *Halifax Herald*, 18, 21, 30 March 1907.

57 *Halifax Herald*, 16 March 1904; interview with Joseph Vandenbroeck, Provincial Archives of New Brunswick. Vandenbroeck, together with a number of other Belgians, left Inverness after the First World War moving first to Springhill then finally settling in the coal-mining town of Minto, New Brunswick. See Marjorie Taylor-Morell, *Of Mines and Men* (Minto, 1981); author's interview with Pauline Vandenbroeck.

58 *MacTalla*, April 1904.

59 "Petitions", RG 5, series "P", 1906, vol. 38, no. 41, PANS.

60 Nova Scotia, Vital Statistics, RG 32, vols. 120-2, PANS; the sample is a 100 per cent survey of marriages where the male identified his occupation as miner.

came from the countryside. While some of these men probably had worked in mines elsewhere in the province, it is reasonable to presume these people made up most of the unskilled sector of the mining community. Many had migrated once already — to Westville, to Sydney, to the Prairies and, of course, to the "Boston States" — but returned with the industrial boom in the county.[61] Also, there was at least a third "type". Many workers left their farms only seasonally, or daily. Some mine workers were farmers who, when the work force increased in the summer, worked seasonally. These men boarded in the town or travelled daily, depending on where they lived.[62] Although the census data suggest remarkable homogeneity, marked differences existed in the experiences and cultural backgrounds of those drawn to the new town.

Not surprisingly, this social structure was closely related to the labour requirements of the company. The company needed enough skilled miners to establish levels of productivity and safety (a factor not unrelated to productivity) necessary for such a large investment. These workers formed the core of the company's work force: they worked on a contract basis (based on output) and earned certain perquisites, socially, in terms of leadership and position within the mine hierarchy, and materially, in terms of higher pay and more regular employment. Employment levels at the mines fluctuated seasonally. In 1908, more than 800 men were employed in the summer, whereas the figure was only about 200 in the winter.[63] But this seasonality was not strictly synchronous with the rhythms of farm labour requirements. Indeed, autumn was the peak period for both the mines and the farms, and neither required so much labour in the winter. Nevertheless, many farm families successfully met their requirements by combining work on the farm with work in the mines. Such employment allowed some families to hang on to their farms. With so much labour available and with immigrants and rural migrants competing for the lowest paid jobs, the company usually had cheap labour available whenever it was needed.

---

61   This information is gleaned from scattered sources including: obituaries found in Scrapbook #19, Beaton Institute, and interviews by the author with Charlie McMaster, and John Eddy McKay. An age profile shows only 6 of 351 men over the age of 40. See *Labour Gazette*, August 1909.

62   Interviews with Frank Chisholm and Charlie MacMaster; *Halifax Morning Chronicle*, 28 October 1909, mentions mine workers coming in from as far as Margaree.

63   Each year, the provincial "Mines Report" (published in the *JHA*) lists employment figures, broken down by whether they were surface workers or underground employees, and by skill designations; it also breaks down coal sales by market (where it was sold), how it was transported, and by calendar quarters. Winter slowdowns were noted in many sources, especially the monthly district reports in the *Labour Gazette*. Even that winter figure could be high, as often the mines were reduced to a few maintenance workers.

The division of the town along Central Avenue provides a dramatic symbol of the separate spheres dominated by different groups in the town. The company owned most of the land west of Central Avenue, while the old landowners retained ownership of the lands to the east. We can label the two as the "town side" and the "company side", as did the townspeople of the time.[64] The IR&C purchased about 700 acres of land between MacIsaac's Pond and the Big River.[65] By the end of 1903 the company had utilized most of this land in building the bankhead of No. 2 slope, an expanded terminal rail yard and about 80 double-row houses. On the town side, some of the older landowners turned their holdings into real estate. James MacIsaac, grandson of one of the settlement's original landowners, sold part of his land for $5,300, received $5,100 for railway damages and continued to sell off smaller parcels as building lots over the next few years.[66] Owning more than half of the land that would be developed proved lucrative to MacIsaac and ensured his status as a leading citizen in the town. Together, the company and such leading citizens initiated the push to incorporate as a town. Incorporation was organized at a meeting chaired by the company's general manager, James L. Brass.[67] And the town's first council was composed of six landowners, including James MacIsaac and a company official.[68] Both groups looked to municipal government to underwrite the costs of improving their investments. By the summer of 1906, the town had a water system running from a reservoir behind the town and was preparing to build two schools. Such ambitious expansion had managed to put the townspeople in debt by $55,000.[69] The town councillors optimistically expected returns on the

64 Inverness Town Council Minutes, 16 May 1905, numerous other instances; the reference also came up in interviews, see John Edward McKay.

65 See the transfers in RG 47, PANS (listed alphabetically by year); the precise locations are difficult to determine primarily because so many of the references are to roads or markers which do not exist any more, but it is clear that the four major boundaries are on the north, the Big River; on the west, the shore; on the south, MacIsaac's Pond; and on the east, Central Avenue. The prices varied between the $100 per acre to Mrs. Isabella MacIsaac, to the $17,000 paid to a Donald McKay of Boston, who may have been an associate of Hussey's.

66 The sale values are from RG 47, PANS; the railway damages were reported in the Port Hood *Greetings*, 26 May 1904.

67 MacDonald, "The Broken Ground", p. 16; *Proceedings of the Council of Nova Scotia Municipalities* (1915) records the vote for incorporation.

68 Inverness Town Council Minutes, May 1904. The identification of the names and their "occupations" is from a combination of *McAlpine's Directory* for 1908, the provincial land grant maps and transfers in RG 47, PANS (to identify them with particular parcels of land on the townsite) and the genealogical description in MacDougall, *History of Inverness County, passim.*

69 *JHA* (1907), Appendix 14, p. 6.

town's investment in the form of continued growth. Meanwhile, they had improved their properties and the company had avoided a major expense.

A strong middle class emerged within this framework. Composed primarily of merchants and professionals, this intermediate group provided a bridge between the working class and the company management. Ideologically congruent with the manager class, they were structurally tied to the working class by the rhythms of the mining economy. Like so much of the community, the middle class had been transplanted into the town with built-in class differences. A number were marked by their possession of (or access to) capital in the form of land, which they were able to translate into cash and political power. They were unable to maintain that political strength, although their influence in the community continued.[70] If we add to this group the predetermined management class, we find a completely built-in ruling elite operating in the town. This relatively autonomous middle class provided another strong element of moral regulation through its access to the forces of order: the law, the church, and even (when required) the military. It is here that we see most clearly the interdependent relationship between the company and the town, although it is equally clear that power was heavily weighted toward the company.

Central Avenue's division also structured the pattern of housing (see Map One). The company laid out streets and row houses immediately beside the bankhead, redirecting settlement which had been concentrated about one kilometre to the south on the intervale behind MacIsaac's Pond.[71] These were well-built structures — most still stand today — but the area, situated adjacent to the bankhead and rail yard, could be filthy. Prone to insects and disease, some of the company houses had to be fumigated on at least three different occasions between 1906 and 1910, and there were frequent outbreaks of smallpox, diphtheria and tuberculosis.[72] The conditions, however, were by no means uniformly bad, and in other ways there was even a certain privilege associated with living in the company houses. For all their problems, the company houses could be better places to live than the housing on the town side. The company-owned managers' houses, located on Railway Street, perpendicular to Mackenzie and Mann avenues, were attractive single-row houses with fences and gardens, and they set something of a standard for domestic respectability. An important consideration was that the company houses were employed as rewards for better employees, typically the skilled colliers. It is next to impossible for us to locate

70   Interviews with John Angus MacNeil and John Eddy MacKay, Beaton Institute; these interviews often bring up the names of landowners as prominent people in the town.

71   See the photograph in C.W. Vernon, *Cape Breton, Canada at the Beginning of the Twentieth Century* (Toronto, 1903), p. 224.

72   Inverness Town Council Minutes, 31 May 1905, 7 May 1906, 18 January 1909, 19 February 1910.

many employees in particular areas,[73] but for those we can identify there emerges an interesting pattern of differentiation. Access to company housing seems to have been restricted to full-time employees. In almost all cases, that meant the skilled workers: colliers, overmen, superintendents, engineers, smiths and managers.[74] Not surprisingly, we find most of the leadership of the PWA, all colliers, living in the company houses.

On the other side of Central Avenue the pattern was different, and we begin to see the tendency toward a town residentially segregated on the basis of skill in the workplace. Landowners on the town side sold much of their land as lots. By 1909, 40 per cent of the town's taxpayers owned real property.[75] The town's middle class was not nearly large enough to account for all these property owners. Of residents identifiable as working for the company in the mines, about 60 per cent lived on the town side;[76] thus, many miners must have owned their own homes, although many were tiny two-room shacks. Recent migrants and most of the seasonal employees, especially those coming in from farms in the countryside, usually boarded either with relatives in the town, with families in the company houses or at one of the several boarding houses.[77] Foreign immigrants, notably Belgians and Germans, formed distinct ethnic quarters (one

---

73 Without access to census manuscripts or company records, the best source for identification of individuals is *McAlpine's Directory*; that source makes no workplace distinctions, listing everyone who worked underground as simply "miner".

74 This is the same pattern Michael Hanagan found in the mines of the Stéphanois; see his *Nascent Proletarians*, pp. 11-21.

75 *JHA* (1910), Appendix 14, pp. 6-7. If we compare this with other coal towns we find that Inverness (40.4 per cent) had a slightly higher percentage of real property owners than Springhill (38.8 per cent) and a much higher percentage than Glace Bay (29.9 per cent), although it trailed Port Hood (56.3 per cent).

76 These figures are based on identifications made from *McAlpine's Directory* for 1908. The directory lists 242 names which it identifies as miners and for whom an address is given. Of these 95 are listed as living on Mackenzie Avenue, Mann Avenue, Central Avenue or Railway Street. Two things must be noted. First, the company also provided housing for some of its railway, office and ancillary employees who numbered about 200 [*JHA* (1914), Appendix 6, Table 4]. Thus, any apparent discrepancy between the number of company houses and the numbers occupying them can be explained. Second, this number may actually overestimate because Railway Street ran across Central Avenue (see map). Thus, a miner living on Railway Street may actually have lived in a private home. Similarly, on Central Avenue only the west side of the street was company housing.

77 The oral history frequently points to people beginning their years in Inverness in such a fashion; author's interviews with Pauline Vandenbroeck and Frank Chisholm.

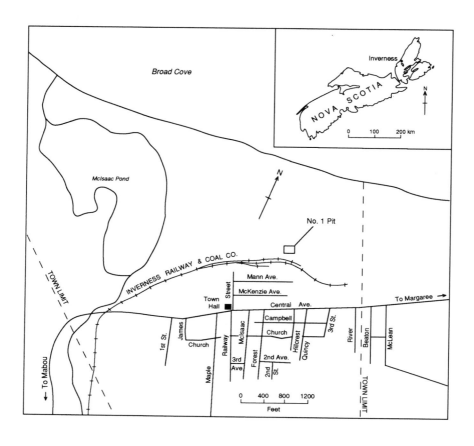

such area is still referred to as "Belgian Town"). Private housing, while small and often poor, afforded miners on the town side an element of independence denied their co-workers in the "Red Rows". In the 1909 strike, those on the company side who supported the strike found themselves, and their families, thrown out on the street.

These boundaries of skill and ethnicity were never fixed. It would be wildly inaccurate to suggest that these categories situated everyone. That there were evictions from the company houses in 1909 indicates that the Red Rows were not the exclusive domain of the PWA. Many Belgians were skilled miners, yet most remained in their homes on Forest Street. There was little incentive to leave a solidly grounded ethnic community for a truly foreign one a few blocks away. Activities among the immigrant communities, while insulated, were occasionally reported, with a suitable ethnographic distance.[78] Together with the Acadian townspeople, some Belgians formed a mutual benefit society, "La Fraternelle", specifically designed to meet the fraternal needs of a separate community.[79] Differences intensified with social and — not unrelated, as we have seen — spatial distance. The son of the station manager, who lived on the company side of Railway Street, remembered that he would simply not go near Belgian Town, while another noted that his friends seldom ventured that way.[80] Nativist ideas made the "foreign element" the scapegoats for violence in the 1909 strike. Over the years these ethnic boundaries began to collapse with intermarriage; similarly, labourers moved through the apprenticeship system and became skilled workers. Nevertheless, in the early years of the town, these segregations effected very real points of conflict.

Social and cultural activities drew on a number of rural and urban influences. Entertainment in the town ranged from debates at the union hall[81] to touring vaudeville-style entertainment troupes, or from a ball put on by the Catholic Mutual Benefit Association (one of the strongest temperance groups in the town) to drinking and gambling at a number of local hotels or even the fire hall. One CMBA ball ended at the respectable hour of ten o'clock, but many of the 200 present moved "up and to the dance hall, where the 'mazy whirl' was kept up till the 'wee sma' hours".[82] The oral history is rich with tales of dances that lasted all night. A two-day picnic at Southwest Margaree, a few miles north of town, saw more than 1,200 people come together for a country "frolic":

78 *Halifax Herald*, 15 February 1903, notes an "unusual" Belgian wedding.

79 Nova Scotia, *Acts* (1910), chap. 149; see the interview with Joseph Vandenbroeck, pp. 5-6, PANB.

80 Author's interviews with Pauline Vandenbroeck, Allister MacBean and Frank Chisholm.

81 *Inverness News*, 5 April 1906.

82 *Port Hood Greetings*, 29 June 1904.

Inverness County is noted for its musicians, so therefore we had no scarcity of pipers and fiddlers. The music was excellent. There were five platforms in the field, and they were kept busy. There was Highland dancing and Lowland dancing, smooth and rough, good and bad. The young people got enough music and dancing anyway, and I should think they wouldn't want another "frolic" for at least a few weeks.[83]

Such after-hours activity reflected the survival of more spontaneous forms of social activity more associated with a pre-industrial popular culture. These stories stress the role of fiddlers and dancers, of older, usually Scottish, forms of entertainment, not of the more North American-style, controlled entertainment promoted by the town's middle class: the summer tea parties and the invitation-only balls. Here the music was smooth and rough, good and bad; while in the "improving" towns, local papers kept progress reports on their brass bands and whether they measured up with those of other towns.[84]

All-night parties in the countryside and the time demands of industrial production did not mix. Absenteeism was always a concern to management, and problems often arose when an event took place during the work week. Sometimes the scale of these celebrations introduced wholly new dimensions to absenteeism, such as this event recorded in the *Mining Record* in 1906:

Down Inverness way they believe in feast days, fast days, holy days, and holidays. Indeed, as at some C.B. collieries any old day will do for an excuse for cessation from labor. The Inverness people, having overwrought themselves on Hallowe'en, made up for it by resting the day after, and made the pretext that they were idle in honor of All Saints Day.[85]

The rationale probably fooled no one, but it was a respectable reason for their absence and adaptable to their needs — a joining of the official and the popular in religion and culture. Clearly their actions were not acceptable to the managers, as they displayed an indifference to the time restraints and work-discipline demanded of workers in production situations.[86]

The company attempted to offset these activities by playing the role of guardian and provider for its employees. Through an unsophisticated and unevenly

---

83 *MacTalla*, 24 September 1897; *Port Hood Greetings*, 29 June 1904.

84 *Port Hood Greetings*, 29 June 1904; author's interview with John Angus MacNeil. I am not trying to suggest brass bands were an unusual feature of mining towns, only that the music of the country, and indeed many features of social life in the country, occurred in a much less formalized context than in towns.

85 *Mining Record*, 14 November 1906.

86 E.P. Thompson, "Time, Work-Discipline, and Industrial Capitalism", *Past and Present*, 38 (1967), pp. 56-97.

applied programme of industrial paternalism, the company moved to control facets of life inside and outside the mine. The IR&C developed a paternalist programme which attempted to create something of a company community by organizing more activities around the company's daily and seasonal production schedules. It worked in a highly selective manner; there were, for example, no company stores. The programme worked on two levels. The first was a general endeavour to weaken workers' self-fashioned activities by providing company-sanctioned ones felt to be less disruptive of production. Second, and more important, a much more specifically directed programme attempted to create a more desirable, and thus somewhat privileged, living arrangement for its valuable core of skilled workers. Company housing was the central feature of the programme. Families living in the "Red Rows" had better housing, with improved services and a few perks such as access to small plots of land for growing vegetables. This part of the programme was directly aimed at one section of the work force and represented one aspect of the larger field of privilege for the families of the skilled workers.

The company also sponsored many activities as well as distributing gifts to the town and its people. Sports were always well funded. Teams and tournaments, ranging from baseball and hockey to quoits, were often sponsored by the company. As in most mining towns, the company recruited athletes from all over the province. These recruits would be given "cushy" jobs around the mines, usually on the railway.[87] While a reluctant provider of services, the company enthusiastically contributed to visible and symbolic largesse. The town was the recipient of land grants to build its town hall and, following the 1909 strike, street lighting.[88] Most notable were the annual Dominion Day celebrations, in which many groups in the town — the union, the churches, the fraternal organizations — participated. With the mines shut down, the company set up a grandstand and picnic tables on its fields below the train station, which was decorated with festively coloured garlands and festoonery. A dozen or so coal cars would be cleaned out and decorated with bunting, and many could enjoy free excursions to Lake Ainslie or Cape Mabou for the day. The event is recollected in the oral history as a community event of great importance, although the central role of the company is unmistakable. It seems evident that the one-day coming together of the various segments of the town created a strong, if fleeting, sense of community.

But associational life was not completely dominated by the company. Church groups and fraternal organizations were unifying vehicles, especially for social movements such as temperance. Here, in any one of several temperance groups, differences in class, ethnicity or religion could be at least temporarily

---

87   See *Halifax Herald*, 6 September 1906 and 15 July 1909; author's interview with Frank Chisholm.

88   Inverness Town Council Minutes, 3 February 1911.

reconciled. Nevertheless, the positions of these groups were very much a product of their visibility as formal organizations, and appearances of unity were often misleading. Some of these groups, such as the CMBA, were strong temperance advocates. So, officially, was the town. The local temperance committee, ominously referred to as the Committee of Ten, regularly appeared before council demanding that more stringent efforts be made to enforce the Canada Temperance Act. But the council did little more than claim their sympathy and promise to urge their prosecutors to more diligent efforts.[89]   At the same time, there also existed an unorganized, popular opposition to temperance which was visible only as a diffuse yet prevalent resistance: many people drank.[90]

While the temperance movement seemed cross-class and non-sectarian, there was an apparent imbalance in its leadership. This was most clear in the Presbyterian dominance of non-sectarian community organizations, as well as of the company's management.[91]   The strongest advocacy of temperance other than the churches came from the company's management and from Starr Lodge, the Inverness local of the PWA. The PWA's official position was in support of temperance, and Starr Lodge's first president was a temperance advocate.[92]   For

---

89   Inverness Town Council Minutes, 12 December 1906, 2 January 1907, 5 June 1909.

90   Inverness Town Council Minutes, 10 October 1910; for a popular account, see MacDonald, "The Broken Ground", pp. 15-16. A press account notes the availability of that "poisonous spirit", see the *Halifax Morning Chronicle*, 8 August 1903. Dun's, *Mercantile Reference Book and Key* (1908) lists five liquor dealers; one of the five was Mrs. W.L. Blair, wife of the chief of the company police. Interviews with Dan MacDonald (Beaton Institute) and Pauline Vandenbroeck and John Angus MacNeil (author's).

91   "Record of the Congregation, Strathlorne Presbyterian Church, 1894-1906", MG 13/144, Beaton Institute. There is little indication that religious sectarianism was an important point of division within the work force or that it became so during the struggles of 1909. A newspaper article during the strike noted that an Orangemen's picnic at nearby Lake Ainslie drew 40 PWA supporters from the pits that day (thus removing only about 20 per cent of the roughly 200 men still working). See *Halifax Morning Chronicle*, 13 July 1909. The records of the Strathlorne Presbyterian church indicate that a number of PWA supporters were Presbyterian (Allan McInnis, D.H. Holland and Ben Roy) as were many of the managers (including James L. Brass and Robert Campbell). On the other hand, A.B. MacIssaac, perhaps the most respected of all the PWA supporters, was Catholic (he was the godfather of the author's uncle; my thanks to Allister MacInnis for this point). It seems much more likely that any favouritism toward Presbyterians or other Protestants was limited to management positions, a point consistent with Mackenzie and Mann's practices elsewhere. See Regehr, *The Canadian Northern Railway*.

92   "Petitions", RG 5, series "P", vol. 38, no. 30, PANS.

the company, temperance fought an industrial evil, one which reduced productivity. For the PWA, the temperance issue was part of their agenda for moral and material self-improvement. While not identical, these positions were complementary, and it is easy to see how the PWA's support for temperance could be construed as being less a moral issue than a "company policy".

There were many communities in Inverness, but the two created by the division along Central Avenue, with its attendant effects, generated a formidable associational framework, one built on conflict. Both sides were strongly influenced by the power of the company, but for those living on the company side that power was experienced at work, in the home, in the family, or in just walking down the company-owned streets. For no one were the ties of dependency stronger than for those living in the company houses below Central Avenue. Few miners could afford to risk falling from the company's good graces when their landlords also were their bosses. As provider and guardian, the company wielded a two-edged sword; it was one thing to benefit from what the company was willing to provide, but another to rely on it. Such was the company's hegemonic presence in the community constructed out of paternalism and dependency. The result was a "company community". It was a world made for its inhabitants; it was a world where their position as employees was more than a work arrangement. Meanwhile, the remainder of the town lived community lives more based in ethnic and workplace identities which, while themselves fractured, were united by their difference from those in the company community. Those living on the town side lacked the stability of the company side, working less regularly and for less pay. And although they were more subject to the vicissitudes of the capitalist economy, the company's grasp on their lives weakened when they returned home at night.

The Workplace in Class Formation

Work was at the centre of social relations in Inverness. Just as ethnic and religious continuity may mislead us into a view of cultural homogeneity, so too would an examination of the workplace which treated all miners alike. In this section, we will examine the hierarchical structure of work and explore its relationship to associational life. The differences we saw in the previous section were largely a product of distinctions emanating from the mines. These distinctions were institutionalized by the PWA as it sought to preserve control over the workplace. Over the first ten years of the town's existence, the union became the source of great conflict, culminating in a major representation strike in 1909 and the most dramatic display of the tensions present in the town. Our purpose here is not so much to describe that strike as to try to understand something of its context.

Skill was a critical point of differentiation. Cutting coal was a skill whose material reality was evident both to producers and those who organized production from above. Working in cramped quarters, often on their knees, while encountering smoke, dust, gas, rats and pools of water, miners toiled in near darkness to fuel the industrial expansion of Canada and make a living for their families. Not only was mining uncomfortable and dangerous, but it was also skilled work that called upon the judgement and ability of the miner to maximize production while not killing himself or his fellow workers. Inverness mine, like most of the mines in Nova Scotia until the 1920s,[93] operated essentially as mines had operated for decades in what was known as "the hand-loading era".[94] Mechanization was largely limited to surface and haulage equipment;[95] underground, where the coal was produced, hand tools and shot-powder prevailed.

Each miner worked his own "face" and employed his own loader. At the face, the miner undercut the coal by lying on his side using only a handpick. Undercutting was a skilled operation which had an economic value for both the miner and his employer in determining how much coal was obtained by the next step: the blasting. Blasting was important and dangerous: too much powder could pulverize the coal or, much worse, bring down the roof. The miner's life depended on the safe use of dangerous powder. Most of these skills were obtained in an unofficial apprenticeship with a collier. A miner's helper watched and learned, and the careful judgement was passed on. It was these skills, and their economic and safety values, that gave the miner's craft a particular importance to any mining operation. David Frank has compared the various workplaces of a mine to "the scattered settlements of a rough, primitive, and often pre-industrial countryside".[96] Coal miners worked independently, away from each other and from their supervisors, and they were paid on their own

93 On the Maritimes, see MacLeod, "Colliers, Colliery Safety and Workplace Control"; David Frank, "Contested Terrain: Workers' Control in the Cape Breton Coal Mines in the 1920s", in Craig Heron and Robert Storey, eds., *On the Job: Confronting the Labour Process in Canada* (Montreal, 1986); and McKay, "The Realm of Uncertainty". Interviews with wives of miners bring out the daily fears, rooted in both concerns for their husbands' well-being and their families' material well-being. See the interviews with Mrs. Joseph LeFort, Mrs. Bella MacIsaac, John Edward MacKay, tape 235, Beaton Institute; Pauline Vandenbroeck, by the author.

94 See Alan Campbell, "Skill, Independence, and Trade Unionism in the Coalfields of Nineteenth-Century Britain, with Particular References to Scotland", *Communications historiques/Historical Papers* (1981), pp. 155-74; Carter Goodrich, *The Miners' Freedom: Study of the Working Life in a Changing Industry* (Salem, N.H., 1977 [1925]); for a short but valuable examination see Keith Dix, "Work Relations in the Coal Industry: The Handloading Era, 1880-1930", in Andrew Zimbalist, ed., *Case Studies in the Labor Process* (New York, 1979), pp. 156-69.

95 "Mines Report", *JHA* (1908 and 1909), have detailed accounts of equipment at the mines.

96 Frank, "Contested Terrain", p. 104.

output. At the same time, they also shared similar experiences from day to day. This combination of individualism and shared experiences and circumstances resulted in an exclusivism which we associate with the notion of the "independent collier".[97]

As with most skills, there was also a socially constructed component to its reality.[98] Lacking a formal apprenticeship system, colliers were largely responsible for maintaining these distinctions on their own through workplace struggles and the reproduction of the colliers' belief system. For the PWA, this struggle formed the heart of its programme. Only by maintaining that distinction could the union maintain the social and material worlds of Nova Scotia colliers. In a coal field flooded with unskilled mine labourers, maintaining those notions of the independent collier gave miners' unions a new tension. In the PWA Grand Council meetings, miners regularly addressed fears of being overrun by the unskilled, usually focusing on the safety issue.[99] While we could read these texts as rooted in both class and craft, the language was largely one of craft. Their concerns were both proactive, in trying to situate their respectability largely by adopting a bourgeois discourse of respectability, sobriety and probity, and reactive, in contrasting their respectability with the untamed variety of foreigners and migrants.[100] This language was employed, albeit unevenly, by the miners themselves, their union, and even the mine management. In a mining town, it underpinned many people's understanding of work and proletarian social relations in and out of work.

---

97 See McKay, "The Realm of Uncertainty"; and Royden Harrison, ed., *The Independent Collier: The Coal Miner as Archetypal Proletarian Reconsidered* (Essex, 1978), esp. Alan Campbell and Fred Reid, "The Independent Collier in Scotland".

98 The literature here is large; two useful pieces are Jane Gaskell, "Conceptions of Skill and the Work of Women: Some Historical and Political Issues", *Atlantis*, 8, 2 (Spring 1983), pp. 11-25; and Steven Maynard, "Rough Work and Rugged Men: The Social Construction of Masculinity in Working-Class History", *Labour/Le Travail*, 23 (Spring 1989), pp. 159-69.

99 MacLeod, "Colliers, Colliery Safety and Workplace Control", pp. 235-48.

100 We should also note the heavily masculine notions which inform most of the extant record of miners' speech and writings. Such gendered notions framed the discursive strategies employed on all sides of these debates, a point which will become more apparent below. Here, however, I wish only to note the class-based oppositions which framed this discussion on skill, without suggesting that class distinctions were all that informed these discussions. For more on the gendered discourse of trade unions see Joan Wallach Scott, *Gender and the Politics of History* (New York, 1988); Ava Baron, ed., *Work Engendered: Toward a New History of American Labor* (Ithaca, N.Y., 1991); and Joy Parr, *The Gender of Breadwinners: Women, Men, and Change in Two Industrial Towns, 1880-1950* (Toronto, 1990), pp. 140-64, 206-28.

The leadership of the PWA emphasized craft and the lingering notions of the independent collier. When the leaders of the Starr Lodge spoke, they did so with pride and a recognition of the importance their craft held to the mine and to the community that surrounded it. When questioned about health risks in mining by the Royal Commission on Pensions in 1907, Malcolm Beaton, the general manager, dismissed the implication of the question: "I don't consider the occupation of mining more dangerous to health than any other".[101] Murdoch MacLean, the first president of Starr Lodge, responding on the same issue, identified his authority first, and then answered the question: "I am a miner. I consider that working below ground is more injurious to health than any other occupation; working continuously in what you might call bad air all the time, that undoubtedly must have its effect on the system".[102] Similarly, Thomas Keating rebuked his boss' ignorance and spoke from his own experience, more forcefully identifying his authority: "I think the miner's trade and occupation is the most dangerous to health, life and limb. I have been in the mine 42 years and I think I know what I am talking about".[103] Yet managers were cognizant of the respectability and value of the collier. Manager Beaton, addressing the same commission, was sure that colliers did not need a retirement pension as they were capable of providing for their own futures, whereas for labourers and surface workers, "a little more aid or encouragement should be given them".[104] Such a statement extended that craft respectability out of the workplace and into everyday life. It noted the status of the collier's position: he was a better man than the simple labourer. We also see the reciprocal side of the relationship between master and miner. Structurally, the miners were subordinated. Yet their superiors' awareness of the colliers' worth allowed them an independence in and out of the workplace not available to an unskilled labourer.

Like skilled workers in many places threatened by the degradation of skill, the Inverness miners were most concerned about protecting their status as privileged workers. The provincial government's system of licensing miners, for which the PWA had lobbied, was completely inadequate and open to corruption. Thomas Keating, well aware of the Inverness colliers' concerns about the flooded labour market, complained that their "board" was "a market gardener...who seemed to have the faculty of making farmers into miners at a rate

101 "Evidence given to the Royal Commission on Pensions" [October 1907], *JHA* (1908), Appendix 24, p. 107.

102 "Evidence given to the Royal Commission on Pensions", *JHA* (1908), Appendix 24, pp. 111-12.

103 "Evidence given to the Royal Commission on Pensions", *JHA* (1908), Appendix 24, p. 110.

104 "Evidence given to the Royal Commission on Pensions", *JHA* (1908), Appendix 24, p. 107.

very profitable to himself but not to the benefit of the miners of Inverness".[105]
The other problem was with immigrants: "The most trouble met with by [our]
board is that of the foreign element coming into our country. These men sometimes state that they have worked two or three years in a coal mine, and it is
afterwards discovered that they were never down in a coal mine *much less being
a miner*".[106] These statements reflect a number of concerns, not the least of
which was safety. But clearly central among these concerns was control of the
workplace, control which in some ways was no longer in the miners' hands.

There was a real sense of difference between the miners and the labourers.
When Starr Lodge obtained the closed shop, they extended their protection to
the unskilled. But their adoption of these men was in the context of a paternalist
protection of inferiors. Again we hear Thomas Keating:

> The loader reminds me of Burns' "Man's Inhumanity." We should do all
> we could to help the labourer. I consider him in the light of the weak
> brother, unskilled, [and] requiring all our aid. We should make that an
> argument to help the loader. I believe that the loader should not only have
> some of the liberty, benefits, and remuneration enjoyed by the skilled
> artisans, but that he should receive a fair days wage for a fair days
> work.[107]

Again we see the tension in the Starr Lodge position. They wanted the closed
shop, but they were also concerned to protect their craft. Swamped with farmers
and immigrants, and having lost control of the certification process to the
provincial government, all they could do was complain. The ideology of the independent collier was not transferable simply on the basis of getting a new job.
It was a traditional myth, reproduced through the belief system of mining culture. Thus, not only was it difficult for the influx of labourers to readily assume
its attendant ideology, but the older colliers were often unwilling to accept the
new men as true colliers. But the structures which supported the myth, particularly the informal apprenticeship system, were nearly impossible to sustain
under the influx of new workers. And the alternative, the provincial licensing
system, was proving to be riddled with corruption and prepared to send un-
trained men into a dangerous workplace.

Two strikes, in 1901 and 1906, illustrated the dominance of craft issues in
the workplace in the early years of the town's history. Both strikes were led by
Starr Lodge, although both took place on the terrain of informally understood
and negotiated, reciprocal relations between master and men. In the first few

---

105 PWA, Grand Council Minutes, September 1907, III, p. 638.

106 PWA, Grand Council Minutes, September 1911, IV, p. 693 [John Chisholm, emphasis added].

107 PWA, Grand Council Minutes, September 1907, III, p. 611.

years of the IR&C, this informal context conditioned workplace relations in Inverness, although in an uneven and often tenuous manner. The 1901 strike centred on a wage cut and craft issues, in particular the inadequate numbers of loaders, haulers, timbermen and track-layers. As colliers, these men had expectations of how a mine was to be run. Such duties not only took away from the time available to cut coal, but also contradicted the colliers' understanding of relations between skilled workers and labourers. The strike shut down the mine for 12 days in December. The miners returned to work until February, when they went out again for ten days. In the final settlement, they recovered only a part of the wage reduction, but on the workplace issues they won concessions on such procedures as the allocation of work places, safety issues related to timbering and the storing and handling of blasting powder, and the hiring of more men, especially for non-collier jobs. Such trade-offs were a necessary part of all bargaining, and they illustrated a mutual understanding and knowledge shared by managers and miners. Manager Fergie, the *Mining Record* observed, knew "how to kill the foxes that spoiled the tender vines".[108]

That informally negotiated understanding broke down again in the late winter of 1906. A slowdown in sales saw work cut to half- time in the fall of 1905, and that winter the mine was completely shut down for several weeks.[109] "Management have been running things pretty close", observed the *Halifax Herald* correspondent as the company began introducing changes to improve efficiency.[110] When the miners descended into the pit on Monday morning, 9 March 1906, they found posted notices informing them that effective the 16th a dockage system was to be introduced. One hundred pounds of stone would see a one ton box docked; more than 100 pounds "and the miner was liable for discharge".[111] Starr Lodge, which since the events of 1902 had been unable to sustain its membership at more than 65 in a work force of over 600, called an emergency meeting, drawing more than 200 miners. They produced their own proclamation calling for a return to the rates and conditions which had prevailed the year before. These grievances, they announced, had been dragging out for

---

108 *Labour Gazette*, February 1902; *Halifax Herald*, 22 January 1902; and *Mining Record*, 4 December 1901; *Halifax Herald*, 13 December 1901; *Mining Record*, 5 February 1902; *Labour Gazette*, February 1902. "Manager Fergie" was Charles Fergie; James M. Cameron notes that Fergie was an English mining engineer who had worked at the Drummond colliery in Pictou County since 1888 and would later become the president of the Intercolonial Company. See his *The Pictonian Colliers* (Halifax, 1974), pp. 37-40.

109 *Sydney Daily Post*, 11 January 1906; *Halifax Herald*, 17 March 1906; *Labour Gazette*, February 1906, p. 827.

110 *Halifax Herald*, 19, 20 March 1906. Donald Mann, in his only visit to Inverness, commented on the need for "new mining techniques" at the Inverness mine.

111 *Labour Gazette*, April 1906, pp. 1154-5.

months, but the imposition of the dockage system, and particularly the method by which it was proclaimed, was "the last straw". If their demands for restoration were not met by the 16th they would strike — as they did.[112]

The 1906 strike was a remarkable success. For one week, the union withheld all but "a half dozen trapper-boys".[113] The terms of the settlement, though immediately unclear, favoured the union and particularly the skilled miners. The dockage system, the main grievance, was dropped, giving some protection to those on contract rates. The reduced datal rates to the loaders and variation between shotfirers remained in place, however.[114] The biggest prize went to Starr Lodge; they were given the checkoff. Only members of the lodge would be given employment by the IR&C. At the same time, the agreement failed to prevent craft dilution. The contract, the first for the Inverness miners, did little to enforce the miners' abilities to control the workplace, and a number of issues, including designation of workplaces and pay assessment, were left "a matter for the management alone to deal with".[115] The lodge had given up its ability to act independently in return for contractual legality and financial solvency. With its enforced inclusion of all mine workers, the contract signalled an emerging recognition of the new industrial conditions and the beginnings of a movement away from the unwritten reciprocity between masters and miners.

While the committee members of Starr Lodge seemed to view their efforts as successful, the contract also was a victory for the company. The company's employees had demonstrated their unwillingness to work in an autocratically ruled workplace. Whether in workplace struggles such as we have just examined or in taking a mass holiday following an "overwrought" Hallowe'en celebration, the Inverness miners had demonstrated their ability to effectively govern aspects of their own working conditions through independent action. But in the union-enforced contract, the company found another way to contain the existing pattern of workers' control. Within two weeks of the settlement and the resumption of work, the company again suspended production, and work remained sporadic until late spring.[116] Company labourers quickly discovered that belonging to a trade union and paying union dues did not guarantee work. By February 1907, the Inverness miners were "working under protest" of the same issues on

---

112 *Halifax Herald*, 16, 17 March 1906; the reply of the mines superintendent, Rod Campbell, dismissing all claims by the miners, is reprinted in *Labour Gazette*, April 1906.

113 *Halifax Herald*, 20 March 1906.

114 *Halifax Herald*, 28 March 1906; *Labour Gazette*, April 1906, p. 1154.

115 *Labour Gazette*, April 1906, p. 1155.

116 *Inverness News*, 5 April 1906.

which they had struck less than a year earlier.[117] This time, however, the contract obliged the men to stay at work — that is, at least for those fortunate enough to have been called in.

Prior to March 1906, Starr Lodge had played a visible but marginal role in the town. Its membership figures indicated that it had a core of supporters, but they were unable to hold more than 15 per cent of the work force until they got the closed shop. Whether this was due to a formal exclusivism on the part of the leadership or apathy on the part of many miners is not clear, although later events would certainly suggest that many men felt the lodge was not worthy of their support. Yet many of the union's leadership held places of respect and prominence beyond their activities in Starr Lodge. The leadership was continually made up of the same people. These men were more than union activists: they led other community groups and projects. It was these men who testified before the provincial Royal Commission on Pensions in October 1907, and several provided working-class voices in town politics. A.B. MacIsaac was elected to town council in 1907 and re-elected along with other miners in 1909 and 1911. MacIsaac was the most notable community leader. In 1904, he was instrumental in setting up the Miners' Relief Society and served as its government trustee for several years.[118] When the lodge was allowed to put forward their own checkweighman, an important position of honour and trust, they elected A.B. MacIsaac. Alan MacInnis, another delegate to Grand Council meetings, was elected to town council for the same years.

So where does Starr Lodge fit in all this? It seems that its leadership and the core of its membership lived on the company side. So too, it seems, did its ideology. With its membership tied to the company community, it was inevitable that the lodge would be equally constrained. It seems useful to label the lodge's leadership a "labour aristocracy". Their position as skilled miners who were better paid and who occupied leadership roles in the workplace and in the town certainly suggests such a role. The package of workplace concessions negotiated in 1906 was designed to preserve what they considered the proper order within their domain. The closed shop ensured that the lodge had some control over job classification, but it granted many prerogatives to the managers.

Starr Lodge emerged from the events of 1906 stronger as an institution but limited in its ability to control workplace conditions. For the unskilled workers,

---

117 *Halifax Herald*, 23 March 1906, 12 February 1907. The later article notes the current protest had been going on for "several weeks". See also the PWA Grand Council Minutes, October 1907, III, p. 650.

118 Testimony of Hugh P. McKinnon, Royal Commission on Pensions, 1907, reprinted in *JHA* (1908), Appendix 24. David Holland was still attending Grand Council meetings ten years after his first appearance in 1902. A.B. MacIsaac, one of John Moffatt's lieutenants as Associate Grand Master from 1908, was on the PWA executive until 1912; and others such as Ben Roy, Alonzo Cassidy and M.L. McLean appeared repeatedly until the lodge was dissolved.

that meant two things. First, the union posed less of an obstacle to their mobility in the workplace hierarchy, that role now lying more with the state and the company. Second, the company still needed the skilled workers much more than it needed labourers. The relations between miners and masters had only shifted; they had not changed altogether. These relations were still reciprocal, but the balance had shifted more to the company's advantage. The privileges accorded the colliers remained in place. The ideological tension continued. The lodge could assert independence and respectability but could not mediate the gulfs in its own ranks. While some lodges around the province were showing signs of adopting the methods of "the new unionism", in Inverness the PWA seemed unable to break decidedly from the language of craft to a language of class. Thus, more work slowdowns in February 1907 and the winter of 1908-09 revealed how little conditions had improved for labourers and how the union seemed to protect some workers more effectively than others.[119]

All this was occurring in the midst of a province-wide debate within the PWA over reform and its direction and tactics for the future. A range of positions vied for dominance; most were represented in Inverness. A.B. MacIsaac was certainly a conservative PWA supporter. Not only did he lead the lodge all through the early years, but he was also PWA leader John Moffatt's right-hand man all through the troubles of 1908-10. Thomas Keating, on the other hand, had come out in support of many reform issues, although without calling for radical change.[120] The other extreme was represented by strong UMW supporters. Here there was an odd mixture of farmer-miners from out of town such as Francis Morien, colliers such as A.C. MacInnis, and the Inverness UMW local's first president, Alex Chisholm, who had arrived in Inverness from a farm near Judique a few years earlier via the mines at Springhill.[121] There were also a number of Belgians, several of whom were socialists and had previous experience with more militant mining unions in Belgium.[122] By the spring of 1909,

---

119 *Labour Gazette*, May 1909, pp. 1171-2; *Herald*, 12 February 1907; and PWA, Grand Council Minutes, October 1907, p. 650.

120 *Halifax Herald*, 14 September 1908. Keating joined Dan McDougall and William Watkins, both UMW supporters, on a committee to recommend improvements for the September 1908 meeting; he also called for the repeal of the IDIA (Grand Council, Minutes III, p. 592), supported reforming the docket and voting procedures (III, pp. 596-7), and hiring an organizer (III, p. 623). We should note also that reform did not die after 1909-10. See Inverness delegate, Dan O'Connor, speaking out in favour of direct election of the executive in September 1912 (V, p. 3).

121 United Mine Workers of America, International Executive Board Meetings, UMW Archives [copies in possession of David Frank; my thanks to him for allowing me access to these copies]; author's interview with Frank Chisholm.

122 See *Halifax Herald*, 22 December 1906; on Belgian trade unionism, see the interview with Joseph Vandenbroeck, PANB.

several lodges around the province were in open revolt and a number had dissolved. The UMW appeared poised to supplant the PWA. But in the provincial vote of 1908, Starr Lodge was one of the few lodges in the province lacking clear support for the UMW. Indeed, little seemed to be going on until Peter Patterson, a UMW organizer, visited the town.

Patterson drew several hundred to a meeting in February 1909. He did not speak of colliers' pride and industrial peace. His message revolved around the equality of workers and resisting the impositions of the coal companies. He did not appeal to the Scots' Highland pride but to the shared concerns of workers, all workers. Indeed, he went so far as to say that even visible foreigners must be treated with respect and as equals: "We must take the Chinamen, the Hindoo, Slavs, and negroes and lift them up to our own level, and give them the same rights and privileges that we enjoy ourselves". His speeches caused quite a reaction, not all of it favourable. Writing to the *Halifax Herald*, "Miner" in Inverness criticized Patterson and the UMW for suggesting that "this unwelcome class of people" should have the same rights as "people who are descendants of our forefathers".[123] But the response was also favourable, and when Patterson returned in April to organize a local of the UMW, he signed on 131 men. More joined the new local over the next few weeks, and by the end of April, Inverness Local 1300 UMW had more than 400 men.

On a Saturday afternoon in May, about 200 men marched down Central Avenue led by a banner proclaiming the emergence of the UMW in the town, and accompanied by a brass band and drums. Along the street, the parade of disaffected miners was cheered on by hundreds more, most probably the families of the miners, while children ran alongside trying to keep up. As a public demonstration, the parade was a dramatic act of defiance. When the UMW committee requested that the company stop collecting PWA dues from those who had joined the rival union, the company announced that anyone who wished to do so could sign a specially prepared form which instructed the company to stop the checkoff. Ten men came forward and signed the form. All were immediately fired. Manager Beaton claimed he "did not know how otherwise he could keep faith with the Provincial Workmen's Association".[124]

The parade, and the response it drew, revealed where much of the tension in the town existed and suggested where much of the discursive terrain for the battle lay. The *Inverness News* came out solidly behind the PWA. The *News* was delighted that there were "only" 200 men in the parade, and that "with the exception of a few Belgians", the parade was made up of "mostly boys and

123 *Halifax Herald*, 19 June 1909; Patterson's rhetoric was very much in keeping with that of UMW organizers across North America; see David Montgomery, *The Fall of the House of Labor: The Workplace, the State, and American Labor Activism, 1865-1925* (Cambridge, 1987), pp. 333-47.

124 *Report of Deputy Minister*, p. 26.

shiftmen". These were not real miners: "Ben Roy, Allan McInnis, Norman Ferguson and the Cassidy boys were not to be seen in the ranks of the U.M.W.".[125] The attack emerged from an understanding of mining culture very similar to the PWA's. The paper's editor, R.C. Hamilton, was not a miner, but he appreciated the respectability of the collier. The article, entitled "Too Many Bad Debts", had a simple message: the agitation in the town was coming from malcontents, lacking the stuff of colliers. The headline suggested more than an accountant's measurement, also serving to individualize their plight, insinuating that it was their debts — a clear mark of their unworthiness — which explained their discontent.[126] We are reminded of manager Beaton's statement to the Royal Commission: real miners could take care of themselves. To both men, low pay plus irregular work did not equal "poor but trying": it meant "unworthy". We also see the prevalence in Inverness of that nativist, particularly Scottish, element to which the PWA appealed. Thus, even those skilled colliers who did attend the parade could be dismissed as "a few Belgians".

Hamilton's comments, like those of "A Miner", betray the importance of racial and gendered notions of masculinity in the maintenance of the union's position. What marked men's worth here was as much tied up with their manhood (they were not "boys") and their Anglo-Celtic heritage (they were not Belgians) as it was by their "natural" position as leaders. At the same time, these rules were seldom absolute; thus, for example, a Belgian who did not support the UMW might show himself to be manly.[127] Masculinity tied together many ideological strands in the mining community. The male-centred wage form and the patriarchal family, the paternal relations between colliers and labourers, the self-regulated hierarchy of the apprenticeship system, and the central place of masculinity in the definition of the collier were clearly related in their common usage of a paternal hierarchy. Without wishing to idealize the rural household, it is possible to speculate that the expectations and understandings of miners coming from rural families differed relatively, not absolutely, from those who had lived with the male-centred, capitalist wage form for most of their lives. While most males from the countryside undoubtedly had firmly entrenched patriarchal notions of how the family worked, how that influenced their understandings of other social institutions — the apprenticeship system, the union — and how the

---

125 *Inverness News*, as cited in *Halifax Herald*, 11 May 1909.

126 An anonymous account book from the period reveals the prevalence of extended debt in the town, as well as many households' inability to keep ahead of their debts. Payments were irregular, especially in the winter months, and usually partial. This is clearly indicative of many workers' inability to obtain full-time work and of at least some merchants' limited leverage over their customers. See "Anonymous Ledger from Inverness Town, 1910-1926", MG 14/126, Beaton Institute.

127 See also McKay, "The Realm of Uncertainty", pp. 23-9.

family as an organizing metaphor influenced their understandings of social relations beyond the family was probably developed differently. The definition of the collier was constructed in opposition to an implicit but clearly defined "other". This other — the rural worker, the immigrant and, equally clearly, the woman — was what the collier was not. These distinctions, while neither clear nor fixed, lay under the surface of many social tensions in the town and in the workplace.

By the spring of 1909, the lines were clearly drawn. For those whose circumstances directed them to support the UMW, the view was one of exclusivism and conflict. One UMW supporter saw quite clearly that the lines of the industrial conflict were within the community. He sent the *Halifax Herald* the following summation of the view from the other side of town: "If every miner in the pit had the same show as those favored ones and a few others with them, there would have been no agitation, no split in the ranks[,] for every one would be satisfied and there would be less bad debts in town".[128] The split was social and it was economic; it was centred in the workplace, and those "favored ones" were the ones holding the PWA line. This writer clearly understood the effect irregular production was having on those whose positions at the mines were precarious, and for whom the PWA was ineffective. The letter ended with a reminder to the *News* and to others who saw only folly in the move to the UMW. They should not be dismissive of these men, or, paraphrasing the biblical turnabout, "the sins of the servants may be visited upon the masters".[129]

On Thursday, 9 July, fewer than 200 men went into the pits. In the next few months, tension prevailed in the town as the two sides fought bitter battles with the company, the town police, the militia and each other. Each day hundreds of men, women and children hurled insults and often stones at the non-striking miners, until the company was able to cordon off the area with barbed wire and electrified fences, more than 100 militiamen, and a Gatling gun mounted on a flatcar. Town council, which then included two PWA leaders, signed on another 30 special constables, while the company supplemented its own police force.[130] With the miners effectively split and troops guarding the mine, the company could simply continue production knowing it could hold out much longer under these conditions. The troops established themselves on the playing fields where only two weeks earlier the annual Dominion Day picnic had been the featured attraction. They were stationed at strategic points around the pithead and also at various points along the railway, especially near trestles. Their presence on the

128 *Halifax Herald*, 11 May 1909, letter signed "UMW, Inverness".

129 *Halifax Herald*, 11 May 1909.

130 *Halifax Herald*, 12 July 1909, more constables were added later; Inverness Town Council Minutes, January 1910; on the fences, see *Halifax Morning Chronicle*, 28 October 1909. There are, rather mysteriously, no minutes for any town council meetings in July 1909.

company side severely limited the strikers' capacity to tie up production. Moreover, it dampened the spirit of the more militant agitators; by Tuesday the 13th, the *Sydney Post* could note, smugly, that "the presence of the soldiers armed with rifle and bayonet [was] having a decidedly cooling effect on the ardor of the strikers".[131]

Press reports portrayed a town in chaos. In almost every article the focus is on the "Belgians and other foreigners" who "compris[ed] a majority of the membership of the U.M.W.", a point belied by the lists of names of black-listed and arrested workers.[132] The newspapers described women (especially Belgian women) rioting, scab houses being firebombed, revolvers being pulled on non-striking workmen, attempts to derail trains or even blow up trestles, and generally a peaceful town "in terror" of a dangerous minority element.[133] These stories undoubtedly were exaggerated, but this should not allow us to underplay the depths of the conflict in the town. For all the reporters' embellishments and xenophobia, there was very clearly a great schism in the town, one which now brought into play the full powers of the state and the united factions of capital. By September, the company claimed production was almost back to normal, and the troops had been recalled. Many of the striking miners had been forced to leave town and several had been evicted from company housing, while many others found refuge in "safe" houses in the countryside.[134] But for many, the strike was not yet lost. On 26 October 1909, strikers attempted to raid the company works. More than 100 men assembled near the mine at about four in the morning; many had journeyed from as far as Margaree, 30 kilometres to the north.[135] The men, equipped with wire cutters and rubber gloves, attempted to

131 *Sydney Daily Post*, 13 July 1909.

132 *Halifax Herald*, 12, 14 July 1909; *Halifax Morning Chronicle*, 28 October 1909; *Amherst Daily News*, 4 August 1909. Inverness Town Council Minutes also show a number of Belgians were hired as special police; see 26 January 1910. See also Canada, Department of Labour, *Labour Organizations in Canada* (Ottawa, 1908-12), which shows very few "foreigners" amongst the leadership of the Inverness local.

133 See especially *Halifax Morning Chronicle*, 12, 14 July 1909; and *Halifax Herald*, 12, 14 July 1909.

134 *United Mine Workers Journal*, 28 October 1909 [reprinted article from *The Casket* (Antigonish)]; *Amherst Daily News*, 4 August 1909. Many were undoubtedly trapped with no farms to flee to or work to be had in the town; some in fact became strikebreakers at other collieries; on Inverness strikebreakers, see an unidentified newspaper clipping entitled "Glace Bay Strikers Fire at Train", in RG 27, vol. 296, file 3163, NAC. A number of Belgians went to Springhill, but when they discovered they were to be strikebreakers they refused to work and the company sued them for the train passage from Inverness to Springhill; see *Eastern Law Reporter*, IX (1910), pp. 210-13.

135 *Halifax Morning Chronicle*, 28 October 1909.

get through the electric fences. They might have succeeded but for an apparent informer in their ranks; the company had learned of the planned assault two days before and awaited the saboteurs on their pre-dawn Saturday morning appearance. A full-fledged battle ensued between the strikers and the company and town police. Shots were fired and several people were injured. In the darkness and amid much confusion, the police managed to make only five arrests, including Alex Chisholm, the president of the local. Chisholm was released and not tried on the condition that he leave town; at this point the last thing the company wanted was a popular figure on trial. Officially, the strike continued on into the next summer, but this was the last serious attempt to reinvigorate the strike.[136]

The early strikes at Inverness were successful defences of craft-consciousness. These issues held only partial interest for much of the work force, although directly affecting their livelihoods as well. Moreover, the privileges associated with the skilled work force were not dealt with adequately by the union and may have been exacerbated by its exclusivism. The miners were divided by their differing relations to the coal company through both the workplace hierarchy and the different social formations generated by the company side/town side division. There were other differences — ethnic, religious, political, even ideological — which separated the town. It is unlikely that very many of the UMW supporters were more radical than their craft brothers, but they at least recognized the limitations of the craft union. The UMW represented a broader class-based organization than the craft-based, paternalist ideology of the PWA; its acceptance suggested a growing recognition by these men of their shared circumstances. The rise of the UMW at Inverness was successful because it seemed to provide a workplace-situated response that addressed workplace issues and the social issues at the heart of the town's divisions. The infusion of foreign immigrants and rural migrants created a multifarious culture where divisions into skilled or unskilled, rural or industrial, foreign or native factions

---

136 As late as the summer of 1910, notices in the *United Mine Workers Journal* continued to advise miners not to go to Inverness because there was a strike in progress. On the afternoon following the raid, the town magistrate (and sometime company solicitor) Frank McEachen had the UMW's agent David Neilson arrested under a provision of the IDIA; a copy of the appeal court's decision is reprinted in UMW Executive Board Minutes, 25 January 1911, p. 57; and in "Rex vs. Neilson", *Eastern Law Reporter*, IX (1910), pp. 210-13. This incident is also discussed in Ian McKay, "Strikes in the Maritimes, 1901-1914", *Acadiensis*, XIII, 1 (Autumn 1983), pp. 41-2; and Paul Craven, *"An Impartial Umpire": Industrial Relations and the Canadian State, 1900-1911* (Toronto, 1980), pp. 316-17. As late as January 1910, the company was still demanding that the town provide and pay for special police; Inverness Town Council Minutes, 26 January 1910. See also Kirby Abbott, "The Coal Miners and the Law in Nova Scotia: From the 1864 Combination of Workmen Act to the 1947 Trade Union Act", in Michael Earle, ed., *Workers and the State in Twentieth Century Nova Scotia* (Fredericton, 1989), pp. 24-46.

made "otherness" apparent. At the same time, the conditions were present for a "remaking" of the town's working class. Rural workers and foreign proletarians effectively constituted a new working class, one lacking residual ties to the old unionism and for whom the PWA was increasingly unsuitable. One of these men, Alex Chisholm, the blacklisted president of Local 1300, followed a path common throughout the rural northeast of North America.[137] In the previous ten years, he had given up his parent's farm near Judique, gone to Springhill to work in the mines, and returned to his home county when the opportunity was presented. Now black-listed in every mine in Nova Scotia, he left for British Columbia to find work.

Conclusion

Inverness' history tells us much about the early-20th-century industrial and financial history of Nova Scotia. Coal mining was the principal engine of industrialism in Nova Scotia. The province's efforts to promote the development of coal mines arose from a combination of fiscal dependency — the heavy reliance on coal royalties — and political necessity. Not only was the state prepared to promote these developments, but it was also willing to underwrite the cost of financing them, believing the money would be repaid through royalties. The state's approach was a curious blend of strongly interventionist activities operating within a laissez-faire ideology. It is in this broad context that industrial development occurred in Nova Scotia. And it is in this context that Mackenzie and Mann came to the province. The state's apparent mercantile development strategy resulted in enterprises that were similarly mercantilist in their impact. This was particularly evident in coal mining, where the capital-intensive requirements of the industry favoured outside capital. We are reminded of the similarities between mercantile strategies and finance capitalism. The development in Inverness was industrial in appearance, but it truly represented a new application of old ways. And the state's *rentier* orientation provided an ideal framework in which to operate.

The Inverness Railway and Coal Company was unusually selective in its interventions in town life. Unlike most coal towns, Inverness had no company stores, and company housing seemed a desirable alternative for many mining families. Company stores were not necessary for those who worked regularly. It seems clear that the company's decisions here were based on a realized need to hold onto its vital skilled workers, not that of "carrying" its work force over the inactive winter months. This restricted involvement allowed the emergence of a

---

137 Crawley, "Off to Sydney"; Thornton, "The Problem of Out-Migration in Atlantic Canada"; Alan A. Brookes, "Out-Migration from the Maritime Provinces, 1860-1900: Some Preliminary Considerations", *Acadiensis*, V, 2 (Spring 1976), pp. 33-4; Ramirez, *On the Move*, pp. 111-49; Hal S. Barron, *Those Who Stayed Behind: Rural Society in Nineteenth-Century New England* (New York, 1984).

NB

civic town with a middle class, a high proportion of private housing and a fairly independent-minded local elite. Together, the company, the original landowners and an elite group of merchants divided the town and their responsibilities towards it. Out of this division, a tidy symbiosis developed. The property owners made money developing the town, and they were also in the best position to organize its civic affairs. This arrangement relieved the company of a substantial economic and administrative burden. Not only could a proper town organize people, but it could also do things that towns were expected to do, such as install water services and provide police and fire protection. Such services cost money, as the town would soon find out, and were best left to the public sector. In doing so, the company relinquished some of its ability to control housing and consumer needs but also passed more of the costs of reproducing labour power onto the workers. For rural households, shouldering the reproductive costs of labour was a part of their very existence. It was precisely because farm-based miners returned to the countryside for the winter that the company did not have to carry a large part of its work force through non-productive periods.

Rural migrants and peripatetic workers, like their fellow migrant workers throughout the world, played a central role in the industrial history of Inverness well into the 20th century. While less visible than the town's permanent work force, their presence shifted the character of class relations, not creating but intensifying tensions among miners, straining the framework that coal miners had for some time tried to enforce. These tensions were centred on the workplace but spilled over into the wider community as pressures emanating from the mines compelled mining families to live these relations outside the mines. Inverness, with its more rapid development as an industrial town, could be viewed as anomalous. Yet, because it was a completely new town, Inverness was only a more visible example of an industry-wide phenomenon in the province in the period between the creation of the Dominion Coal Company in 1893 and the First World War. Cape Breton County's industrial work force saw similarly rapid growth, from sources probably roughly similar to those flooding into Inverness. Labour recruitment was a major problem throughout the industry, despite the apparent availability of labour. Mining and farming were not the only positions available to countryfolk; workers were on the move in and out of innumerable labour markets throughout the region and beyond. Fishers from Newfoundland and farmers from the Cape Breton countryside moved in and out of the rural economies quickly and irregularly, forging essential links through a common labour market. Such periodic migrations formed the necessary, if often inadequate, reserves in an otherwise underdeveloped capitalist labour market. These movements, themselves always in flux, responded both to the demand of industry and to shifts in supply brought about within rural markets and class relations, creating a variegated and highly fractious social context for class formation.

The company's situation permitted it to exploit existing rural conditions while allowing some privileging of its vital skilled work force. It also allowed it to play the two off each other. It is thus not surprising that in 1909 the company would provide some shelter for the PWA. The interests of the company in protecting its vital skilled work force, and the interests of the union in maintaining the craft distinctions which made them vital, dovetailed, facilitating unified resistance to an industrial labour strategy. Conversely, those same conditions were the principal bane of the PWA, even if the union's position was facilitated in the short term. For rural workers and immigrants, the situation was very different. Some, still with access to land and some means of subsistence, escaped or at least deferred full dependence upon wage labour. Others, alienated from the land, found only a new form of alienation in the town — one that was exacerbated by their lowly position even within their class. What Inverness suggests is that an adequate social history of industrialization in Nova Scotia, even in the 20th century, needs to look at more than industry. Only by situating class formation in this context of the social relations of town and country can we successfully describe the process of economic and social development in Maritime Canada.

Planters, Households and Merchant Capitalism: Northeast-Coast Newfoundland, 1800-1855

Sean Cadigan

Students of Newfoundland's social and economic history have long been interested in the origins of truck and family-based production in the cod fishery. The focus of much hypothesizing, but little research, has been the supposed rise and decline of the Newfoundland planter in the 19th century. The *Dictionary of Newfoundland English* points out that the meaning of "planter" changed over time. For most of the 17th and 18th centuries a planter was any island settler who practised a resident fishery, as opposed to following the English migratory fishery. By the mid-18th century, this first use of the term merged with that of a merchant-supplied fisherman who engaged servants on shares to crew his boat or small vessel in the fishery. Through the late 19th and the 20th centuries the term became associated with fishermen who migrated to the coast of Labrador from the island of Newfoundland each fishing season.[1] The usual historical question has been whether the defeat of the planter fishery was caused by the rapacity of merchant capital and the use of truck in a fishery based on household production.

This question presumes that tangible differences existed between the planter fishery and the family fishery. Recent works by Steven Antler and Gerald Sider offer sweeping theories about Newfoundland underdevelopment on the weak foundations of such presumptions.[2] The time has come to examine closely the question of whether the fishery was historically divided by the decline of the planters as Antler and Sider suggest. There is little evidence to support a simplistic distinction between the planter fishery and the family fishery; instead, planters appear, except in the unusual conditions of the Napoleonic Wars, to have relied on household, not wage, labour and merchant credit in truck to conduct the fishery on the northeast coast. Sider and Antler have both fundamentally misunderstood the history of the planter fishery because they have grounded their analysis in a faulty theoretical construction about the conservative nature of merchant capital in social transformation.

---

1   G.M. Story, W.J. Kirwin and J.D.A. Widdowson, eds., *Dictionary of Newfoundland English* (Toronto, 1982), pp. 381-3. I would like to thank Gregory S. Kealey, Daniel Vickers, Rosemary E. Ommer and Steven Hahn for their criticisms of earlier drafts of this paper. A Social Sciences and Humanities Research Council doctoral fellowship provided funding for this paper's research.

2   See Steven Antler, "Colonial Exploitation and Economic Stagnation in 19th Century Newfoundland", Ph.D. thesis, University of Connecticut, 1975; and Gerald M. Sider, *Culture and Class in Anthropology and History: A Newfoundland Illustration* (Cambridge, 1986).

Merchant Capital and Newfoundland History

The desire to blame fish merchants for all or most of Newfoundland's developmental problems has deep roots in Newfoundland historiography. D.W. Prowse's 1895 history remains the clearest expression of the liberal view that English West Country merchants dominated Newfoundland, restricting its function to that of a gigantic fishing station designed to serve the English migratory fish trade in a mercantilist fashion, and opposing the local development of agriculture, settlement and settler institutions.[3] Subsequent works rejected the simplistic attribution of Newfoundland's underdevelopment to Prowse's omnivorous fish merchants, grasping and capricious in their desire to protect the profits of their monopoly over the supply of fishing families in exchange, through truck, for fish, fish oil and seal products. H.A. Innis, for example, accepted the historical reality of the fish merchants' desire to profit as much as possible from the fish trade but pointed out, although in an essentially descriptive fashion, that similar acquisitive impulses on the part of fish merchants in the New England economy did not stunt the latter's development. Eager to advance reasons why Newfoundland lagged behind other parts of North America which from an early stage relied on the cod staple, Innis explained its underdevelopment in terms of the lack of economic alternatives to, or even supplements of, the cod fishery. Merchants were quite willing to change and adapt to the improved economic opportunities of a settled fishery, particularly in response to the disruption of the migratory fishery during the wars of the 18th century.[4]

Innis viewed merchants' use of truck in the Newfoundland fishery as a compromise between fishermen's need for credit at the beginning of the season, before merchants knew what prices for fish would be like, and merchants' need to offset debts which could result if prices dropped at the season's end.[5] He felt that there was nothing inherently bad about truck and argued that it persisted in Newfoundland for a number of geographic and technological reasons. Unlike the New England fishery, where closer access to mid-range fishing banks encouraged the growth of a local, capitalist, entrepreneurial schooner fishery that

---

3   D.W. Prowse, *A History of Newfoundland from the English, Colonial and Foreign Records* (Belleville, Ont., 1972 [1895]), pp. 304-45, 496-7. For a more specific historiography of the Prowse school see Peter Neary, "The Writing of Newfoundland History: An Introductory Survey", in James Hiller and Peter Neary, eds., *Newfoundland in the Nineteenth and Twentieth Centuries: Essays in Interpretation* (Toronto, 1980), pp. 3-15. Keith Matthews laid bare the faulty basis of this school in "Historical Fence Building: A Critique of Newfoundland Historiography", *The Newfoundland Quarterly*, 74, 1 (Spring 1979), pp. 21-9.

4   H.A. Innis, *The Cod Fisheries*, 2nd. ed. (Toronto, 1954), pp. 52-69, 95-110, 144-59, 288-322.

5   Innis, *The Cod Fisheries*, pp. 154-5.

expanded into the coastal trade of North America, the Newfoundland fishery was either inshore, increasingly prosecuted by small-boat family units of production, or remained a large-ship bank fishery. Without alternative resources, Newfoundland remained dominated by a mercantile community interested in the fishery only as a short-term credit prospect. Newfoundland's merchant community remained tied to the fishery's weak and impoverished tropical markets where fish prices fluctuated rapidly and to sources of supplies of agricultural and manufactured imports in markets where prices remained high. Newfoundland was "squeezed" between the price structures of external world markets in which the "merchant and the truck system served as buffers" between discrepancies in export and import prices, forcing Newfoundland fishing families to absorb the difference by forcing down the "standard of living".[6]

The image of the fish merchants which emerges from Innis' work is not one of a class opposed to Newfoundland's development but rather a group of entrepreneurs faced with little alternative economic activity with which to trade and little reason to use anything but truck in the fishery. An explicit denial of fish merchants' hostility to Newfoundland's settlement and colonial development comes from Keith Matthews. His history of their role in the Newfoundland fishery denied that they opposed a resident fishery, settlement or diversified economic activity. Matthews departed from Innis by arguing that even the earliest merchants demonstrated no hostility to settlement, only to settlers' attempts to use government regulation to injure the migratory cod fishery by engrossing shore property essential for large-scale proprietary schemes. West Country merchants were usually quite willing to profit from the opportunities to trade with Newfoundland residents, and they actually encouraged settlement by increasing-

---

6   Innis, *The Cod Fisheries*, pp. 173-7, 458-84. The work of Shannon Ryan is a more recent and complex study of the problems of Newfoundland's reliance on the markets of southern Europe, Brazil and the West Indies. Ryan, as had Innis before, suggested that, given Newfoundland's tough climate and impoverishment in alternative resources, the colony was dependent upon markets beyond its control for the sale of saltfish. The low capital requirements of production in an industry dominated by a free-access resource, especially in the inshore fishery, allowed Newfoundland's population to grow much greater proportionately than any increase in saltfish production during the 19th century. Such conditions ensured a continuing tension between stagnant production and population growth. The consequence of such tension was the restriction of Newfoundland's internal market. The growth of a family-based inshore fishery, created by the demise of an outport planter fishery as merchant capital concentrated in St. John's, aggravated the fishery's impoverishment and encouraged producers to make a poorer-quality fish cure. This technological degradation, as well as reliance on Imperial trade policies which served British rather than Newfoundland interests, put the latter in a weak position relative to new, better-organized saltfish suppliers such as Norway through the 1860s, 1870s and 1880s. See Shannon Ryan, *Fish Out of Water: The Newfoundland Saltfish Trade, 1814-1914* (St. John's, 1986), pp. xvii-xxiii, 39-61, 98.

ly relying on a year-round population to guard property and catch fish. Furthermore, merchants seized on new economic activities by residents, particularly in sealing, salmon fishing and fur trapping. Merchants and fishermen alike chafed at Imperial attempts to limit settlement and did not oppose diversified economic activity. Residents relied on truck for merchants' imports because they could not find local alternatives, and cyclical depressions in the fish trade demanded that both merchants and fishermen rely on the leeway afforded by truck's credit and debt manipulations.[7]

C. Grant Head's historical geography of 18th-century Newfoundland reinforces the perspective that merchants did not oppose the development of settlement. Early proprietary colonial schemes failed, he argued, because they were based on policies of commercial economic diversification which Newfoundland's resources could not sustain. Colonists hoped to combine a commercial fishery with commercial agriculture, a fur trade and local timber processing. While these latter activities proved to be useful subsidiary activities, they could not alone support extensive settlement. Landed proprietors withdrew from Newfoundland, leaving fish merchants to deal with resident fishing families as the migratory trade declined later in the 18th century.[8] Resident fishing people, in Head's as well as Matthews' work, built their own communities supported, not hindered, by merchant credit despite official Imperial neglect.

By the late 1970s, Newfoundland historiography had decisively shifted away from viewing merchants as hostile to Newfoundland's early local social and economic development, or even as the prime movers in its historical development. Historians and geographers looked to the interaction between merchants and fishing people to understand Newfoundland's past. W. Gordon Handcock's 1977 "English Migration to Newfoundland" particularly emphasized understanding the interaction of fishing people and merchants within Newfoundland's resource constraints. Handcock's analysis of the island's demographic development demonstrated that West Country merchants facilitated settlement by encouraging diversified production in furs, sealing and shipbuilding, as well as increasingly relying on the profits from trading with residents. Merchants, by supplying servants from the West Country, and later Ireland, also provided the source material for early resident population development.[9]

Handcock found that West Country merchants were, in fact, so important in actually establishing settlement in Newfoundland that, in his later monograph, he described the process as the "mercantile system of settlement". Population

7   Keith Matthews, "History of the West of England-Newfoundland Fishery", Ph.D. thesis, Oxford University, 1968, pp. 4-5, 119-37, 174-9, 207-28, 315-78.

8   C. Grant Head, *Eighteenth Century Newfoundland: A Geographer's Perspective* (Toronto, 1976), pp. 13-35, 184-228.

9   W. Gordon Handcock, "English Migration to Newfoundland", in John J. Mannion, ed., *The Peopling of Newfoundland* (St. John's, 1977), pp. 15-48.

growth proceeded by merchants abandoning control over production to fishing people, withdrawing into supplying and marketing activities. Handcock agreed with Matthews' and Head's earlier assessments of truck as an accommodation which proved to be the only way fishing families could guarantee access to subsistence and capital goods from merchants on a year-to-year basis, given the lack of alternative local supplies.[10]

Despite a large body of work which demanded that historians consider more than the nature of merchant capital in Newfoundland's development, Gerald Sider's work returned to the old historiographic position of merchant-as-villain.[11] He suggested that Newfoundland's development could not be explained by staple resource production in salt cod. It was not the natural attributes, technology and exchange of the commodity which defined the province's social formation, but the relations of salt cod's production. Sider believed that class, not staple commodity, was causative in Newfoundland's history and that the cultural hegemony of merchant capital over all of society was responsible for the province's underdevelopment. The internal and external dynamics of class relations between production and the market gave rise to the merchant-controlled family fishery of the 19th century. Sider asserted that merchants first engineered the impoverishment of petty production through manipulation of the laws governing the fishery. This impoverishment subsequently inhibited domestic

---

10   W. Gordon Handcock, *Soe longe as there comes noe women: Origins of English Settlement in Newfoundland* (St. John's, 1989), pp. 219-42.

11   David Alexander's opposition to emphasizing the staple as the sole determinant in Newfoundland's underdevelopment actually preceded Sider by redefining the question as having its answer specifically in the nature of the characteristics of fish merchants. Alexander suggested that Newfoundland's dominant conservative mercantile and political strategies offered no long-term development alternatives to stagnating production in the family-based fishery. He argued that the 19th century witnessed the growth of a settled fishery, the end of merchant capital's investment in actual production, and the withdrawal of marketing and capital accumulation to St. John's. Merchants left production to fishing families, and looked only to the short-term profits in the fishery's extensive growth. Mercantile refusal to invest fixed capital in the fishery ensured that Newfoundland could not create a developed resource base to secure internal domestic diversification or better external markets for fish. In Alexander's view, Newfoundland's developmental problem was not necessarily under-endowment in resources but rather over-domination by short-sighted merchants and politicians. His work argued that merchants should have invested much more capital in the fishery and that politicians should have encouraged such investment if merchants failed to do so. Alexander's analysis, however, involves little empirical consideration of the first half of the 19th century. See David G. Alexander, "Development and Dependence in Newfoundland, 1880-1970", in his *Atlantic Canada and Confederation* (Toronto, 1983), p. 6; and "Newfoundland's Traditional Economy and Development to 1934", in Hiller and Neary, *Newfoundland*, pp. 19-30.

capital formation through truck by preventing the development of local alternatives to merchant domination, reducing the amount of cash in domestic
circulation, giving merchants no reason to alter the fishery's structure in the late
19th and the 20th centuries and being dialectically reinforced by a
"traditionalism" — an autonomous, village-based producer culture — supplanting capitalism in the outports.[12]

Newfoundland's underdevelopment, Sider argues, is the result of outport
society being restrained by merchant capital. The island saw little industrial
capitalist development because merchants, by dominating the exchange of
saltfish, harnessed household commodity production to a larger global
capitalism. Sider uses "merchant capital", an abstraction employed by Marx to
theorize about how only change in the production, not circulation, of commodities effected revolutionary social transformation,[13] as a surrogate for
"merchants" in order to construct a theory about how they deliberately undermined those economic and social developments which would have allowed
producers greater independence. Although citing Matthews, Handcock and
Head, Sider ignores their findings about merchants' encouragement of diversified production to ensure a return on their credit and suggested that merchants
"imposed specificity of product demand" on fishing families, refusing to take
anything but saltfish. Theoretically, the nature of merchant capital was not in-
novative; therefore, Sider proposed, merchants' unwillingness to inconvenience
themselves by trading in goods other than saltfish "may well be...a key element
in the domination of merchant capital over its producers, and part of the package
of constraining alternatives (to commodity production) in the communities".[14]
Sider returned to the old historiographic argument, long laid to rest by Matthews
and Head, that the state, acting as the merchants' executive, discouraged alternative production by prohibiting agriculture, not recognizing property ownership
and deliberately opposing the formation of a landed gentry.[15]

Part of Sider's argument appears to be that capitalist productive relations can
emerge out of any regional resource base. Newfoundland's 19th-century cod
fishery could have given rise to production dominated by planters' (i.e., independent resident producers') use of wage labour. But aside from opposing
agricultural development, merchant capital apparently engineered the family
fishery's supplanting of the planter fishery by refusing to follow the custom of
guaranteeing the wages of planters' servants through the recognition of servants'

---

12 Gerald M. Sider, *Culture and Class*, pp. 12-33.

13 A short-hand entry into Marxist thinking on merchant capital as a concept is
    John Weeks, "Merchant Capital", in Tom Bottomore, Laurence Harris, V.G.
    Kiernan and Ralph Miliband, eds., *A Dictionary of Marxist Thought*
    (Cambridge, Mass., 1983), pp. 332-3.

14 Sider, *Culture and Class*, p. 37.

15 Sider, *Culture and Class*, pp. 112-18.

liens on catches. Without a guaranteed wage, planters found servants unwilling to hire out their labour; this forced planters down into petty production alongside those who used to be wage labourers. Sider partly based his argument on Antler's largely unsubstantiated proposition that British regulation of the Newfoundland fishery prevented the development of local institutions which might have effectively protected such rights of lien and free-market exchange. By 1840, according to Antler, planters had been prevented from competing with large fish merchants by merchant-oriented court rulings against the wages and supply lien system.[16] This in turn centralized control of the fishery in merchant hands and prevented the creation of wage labour and capitalist relations in the fishery. Merchants exploited the fishery by impoverishing fishing families through the use of barter as their means of purchasing salt cod for resale. Fish merchants never gave families cash, but rather accounts in which supplies were balanced against catches; overall, some families' successes balanced against others' losses so that the pattern was one of continuing debt to the merchants.[17]

Sider's interpretation of fish merchants as active opponents of development comes from conflating the complex motivations of a group of capitalists with a relatively simple Marxist definition of merchant capital as conservative in that it plays the part of a parasite, living off the unequal exchange of surpluses but not contributing to changes in the relations surrounding the production of those surpluses. The historiographic antagonism between trade and production, with its implications for the definition of the concept of merchant capital hegemony used by Sider in particular, emerged from the English-language debates over the transition to capitalism which began with Maurice Dobb's *Studies in the Development of Capitalism.*[18]

Dobb's work forcefully proposed that we should not look to the expanding trade of the late feudal period for the origins of European capitalism. Only a qualitative change in the production of commodities for trade through primitive accumulation and the growing use of wage labour created capitalism. Merchant capital remained conservative in that it only fastened onto the profits made from circulating these commodities, regardless of how they were produced. Dobb did

---

16 Antler, "Colonial Exploitation", pp. 28-78. Antler's view that merchants dismantled nascent industrial capitalist relations in the fishery is echoed in Ellen P. Antler, "Fisherman, Fisherwoman, Rural Proletariat: Capitalist Commodity Production in the Newfoundland Fishery", Ph.D. thesis, University of Connecticut, 1981, pp. 3-35. Ellen Antler defined fishing families as proletarians because they did not fully control the sale of the commodities they produced to fish merchants, even though they controlled the means of production and received no wages.

17 Sider, *Culture and Class,* pp. 22-88.

18 Maurice Dobb, *Studies in the Development of Capitalism* (New York, 1963 [1947]), pp. 17-126.

not suggest that merchant capital conservatism translated into active merchant opposition to capitalist development, but the subsequent controversy over the "prime mover" in capitalist development — trade versus class relations — of the transition debate began to assume such undertones.[19]

More disturbing is the manner in which the "prime mover" debate insinuated itself into disagreements about the development of the colonies of capitalist Europe. Historians of colonial development do not have to debate the ultimate origins of capitalism, and they thus do not have to establish or refute merchant capital's credentials in such a transition in order to study change in colonial social formations. Criticisms of the work of André Gunder Frank and Immanuel Wallerstein by Brenner, Genovese and Fox-Genovese all muddy the waters over the nature of the merchants' role in colonial social formation. While the "world-systems" school of the former assumes an apparent tautology in their view on the role of trade in the transition from feudalism to capitalism, there is little controversy in their insistence that merchant capital played a crucial role in subjugating non-capitalist areas of the world to that capitalism. Brenner, Genovese and Fox-Genovese attack the circulationist qualities of the world-systems approach by insisting that the merchants' conservative nature allowed them no role in the generation of capitalism in colonial settings or in the continuing inability of some societies to mount an effective class-based challenge against their colonial oppressors.[20]

Brenner offers little empirical evidence to back up his attack on the world-systems school. The more extensive work of Genovese and Fox-Genovese, however, illustrates particularly well the problem which students of the New-

---

19 Dobb, *Studies in the Development of Capitalism*, p. 127. For the transition debate see Paul Sweezy, "A Critique", and Maurice Dobb, "A Reply", in Rodney Hilton, ed., *The Transition from Feudalism to Capitalism* (London, 1976), pp. 33-56, 57-67.

20 André Gunder Frank, *World Accumulation, 1492-1789* (New York, 1978), pp. 16-44, 97; and *Dependent Accumulation and Underdevelopment* (New York, 1979), pp. 44, 238-53. Immanuel Wallerstein, *Historical Capitalism* (London, 1983), pp. 13-27; Wallerstein, *The Capitalist World-Economy* (Cambridge, 1979), pp. 5-19, 86; and *The Modern World-System, I: Capitalist Agriculture and the Critique of Origins of the European World Economy in the Sixteenth Century* (London, 1974), pp. 15-24, 102-7. Robert Brenner, "The Origins of Capitalist Development: A Critique of Neo-Smithian Marxism", *New Left Review*, 104 (July-August 1977), pp. 25-92, directly challenges the "world-systems" school and is informed by his own attack on circulationist interpretations of the transition. See T.H. Aston and C.H.E. Philpin, eds., *The Brenner Debate: Agrarian Class Structure and Economic Development in Pre-Industrial Europe* (Cambridge, 1985). For further criticisms of Frank and Wallerstein see Ian Roxborough, *Theories of Underdevelopment* (London, 1979), pp. 59-65. Robert Miles insists that the material or technological conditions of production in places such as the Caribbean, Australia and South Africa have led to the integration of

foundland fishery face in dealing with the notion of merchant capital conservatism. Their analysis of slavery in the Old South is not all that removed from the world-systems perspective in the suggestion that merchants created a slave-based society to generate commodities for exchange in world markets.[21] Instead of pointing to the material conditions which led to the persistence of slave labour in production in the Old South, Fox-Genovese and Genovese attribute that persistence to merchant capital hegemony. Fox-Genovese and Genovese's analysis of the Old South suggests that the use of unfree labour in plantation economies led to stagnation and underdevelopment because merchants encouraged the continued subsistence of the slave population; it prevented the growth of domestic market infrastructure by not facilitating "commodity exchange within a national or regional market; it facilitated exports". In sum, merchant capital encouraged the transfer of capital to the industrial metropoles and prevented the "qualitative development normal to the expansion of capitalist production".[22]

Merchant capital's supposed conservative hegemony explains why the Old South did not make any transition to industrial capitalism. This is peculiar because Fox-Genovese and Genovese wished to support the contention that the circulationist quality of merchant capital renders merchant capital without any causative influence in history. The relations of production, not those of exchange, explain history.[23] In this view, merchant capital again plays no causative role in contributing to changes in the mode of producing surpluses in colonial formations. Yet, instead of looking for the conditions which encouraged slave production to persist in producing the plantation commodities merchants dealt in, Fox-Genovese and Genovese resort to describing the parasite in order to explain the nature of its host. The historiographic antagonism between trade and production as "prime movers" becomes more than one denying merchant capital a role in the creation of capitalist relations; instead, merchants now had a creative role in forming and maintaining non-capitalist ones which served a larger, global capitalism.[24]

Returning, then, to Newfoundland historiography, where does it sit in this wider context? If we are to accept that merchant capital is conservative and has

---

unfree labour into a capitalist world system in a manner very similar to world-systems analysis. See his *Capitalism and Unfree Labour: Anomaly or Necessity?* (London, 1987), pp. 50-70, 196-225.

21   Elizabeth Fox-Genovese and Eugene D. Genovese, *Fruits of Merchant Capital: Slavery and Bourgeois Property in the Rise and Expansion of Capitalism* (New York, 1984), pp. 22-40.

22   Fox-Genovese and Genovese, *Fruits of Merchant Capital*, pp. 40, 50.

23   Fox-Genovese and Genovese, *Fruits of Merchant Capital*, pp. 5-10.

24   Fox-Genovese and Genovese, *Fruits of Merchant Capital*, pp. 5-10.

little role to play in social and economic transitions, then we cannot accept Sider's use of merchant capital as an explanation of the limited development in a society such as the northeast coast of Newfoundland during the 19th century. Merchants theoretically had no unique role to play in the formation of the social relations of production in Newfoundland, including the maintenance of their own hegemony. There is no reason why merchants would not have taken advantage of the mercantile and commercial opportunities of an industrializing economy and society, if such had developed. Those like Antler and Sider, who continue to insist that we look to the active conservatism of merchant capital in the maintenance of its own hegemony, indulge in circular thinking by avoiding the empirical study of the actual productive relations which developed in the Newfoundland fishery. Merchant capital, according to this tautology, continued to dominate Newfoundland society because Newfoundland society was dominated by merchant capital. This perspective allows little room for exploring the historical dynamic of Newfoundland's class relations.

Marxist historians, by accepting the theoretical conservatism of merchant capital, should not look to merchants as actual historical opponents of colonial economic development, but rather see them as capitalists who limited their activity to exchange, readily seizing on opportunities provided by the growth and diversification of colonial industries as well as those which continued on in staple trade. Blaming merchant hegemony for colonial underdevelopment contradicts the theoretical definition of merchant capital as conservative and serves as an *a priori* judgement about developmental phenomena in places such as Newfoundland.[25] A re-evaluation of the fate of the 19th-century planter fishery furthermore suggests that there are more obvious reasons for its decline than unproven assertions that merchants found a fishing industry prone to cyclical disruptions because of variations in cod-stock availability, weather and international market conditions worth preserving in some sort of mid-19th-century status quo. There is no evidence to suggest that merchant capital conservatism can explain the persistence of merchant truck with planters as household producers who relied on family labour in Newfoundland.

The 19th-Century Planter Fishery

Antler suggested that the British laws regulating the Newfoundland fishery, embodied in Palliser's Act of 1775, secured the development of a nascent capitalist planter fishery by creating the wages and lien system. Such planters began to eclipse the household-based fishery, in which boat owners used shares to hire their boats' crews while family members cured the fish. Antler defines planters as those who operated under the provisions of the 1775 act, guarantee-

---

25   Ian McKay, "Historians, Anthropology, and the Concept of Culture", *Labour/Le Travail*, 8/9 (1981/82), pp. 205-11.

ing their servants' wages through a written contract and first lien on the planters' fish. Merchants who extended credit to a planter had the right to expect that planter to return all of his catch to satisfy the debt of supplying the current fishing season.

Antler clearly felt that planters who hired servants under Palliser's Act were distinct from household producers. Unlike producers in the household-based fishery, planters had economic incentives to improve productivity through investment in physical improvements to the fishery. Antler compared planters to factory owners before the days of trade unions; any increases in productivity were translated automatically into increases in profits because labourers had no means by which they could take any part of that increased productivity as their own. On the basis of such profits and wage labour began Newfoundland's capitalist development and, in particular, the development of a local price system, thereby increasingly freeing planters from the need for merchant credit. Merchants, worried about losing their dominant role in the fish trade, used their influence over the courts of Newfoundland from the 1820s to the 1840s to strike down the wages and lien system. Merchants argued that they could no longer recognize servants' wage liens. Without such liens, planters lost the particular credit they needed to hire wage labour, and other fishermen lost the security of payment which was their incentive to offer themselves to planters for hire. Class differentiation in fish production halted. All that remained were small households relying on family labour to catch and cure fish in return for trade in truck to merchants.[26]

Throughout the late 18th century there are indications that some differentiation existed among resident Newfoundland fishermen. Chief Justice Reeves reported that there still existed some migratory fishermen coming from the English West Country each year to fish. These people often owned a number of boats which they deployed in the inshore fishery by hiring crews. They were, in Reeves' opinion,

> a sort of Yeomanry which was once considered as the great force and support of it; but the number of these is of late years much diminished, whether they have gradually crept into the order next above them,

---

26 Antler, "Colonial Exploitation", pp. 28-78. The purpose here is to determine whether evidence exists to suggest that a nascent capitalist fishery emerged and declined in any way which can be logically associated with Palliser's Act, or with some other factor. The nature of the act's actual restraint of social differentiation in the fishery is a related, but different, question which has been addressed elsewhere. See Sean Cadigan, "Seamen, Fishermen and the Law: The Role of the Wages and Lien System in the Decline of Wage Labour in the Newfoundland Fishery", in Colin Howell and Richard J. Twomey, eds., *Jack Tar in History: Essays in the History of Maritime Life and Labour* (Fredericton, 1991), pp. 105-31.

become merchants, or have fallen thro want of success, to a lower stage, I do not pretend to say.[27]

The "lower stage" Reeves spoke of comprised resident fishermen: producers with little property, completely dependent on merchant credit for capital to conduct a fishery and vulnerable to failure from season to season due to extremely variable cod stocks, weather and international market prices.

The experience of the first 20 years of Palliser's Act appears to have been that of planter dependence on merchants within a stagnant cycle of obtaining credit for a fishing voyage, hiring servants, catching enough fish throughout the season to cover the obligations of credit and wages, and perhaps having enough left over to warrant the merchant extending further credit for winter supplies. Yet by 1798, Governor Waldegrave could write about a new type of "Planter who labours for himself without the assistance of the Merchant". Waldegrave suggests that these were few in number; his report to the Colonial Secretary dealt with the problem of the vast majority of planters, who he describes as being still caught in the capital squeeze of merchant credit and servants' wages.[28]

The presence of differentiation among resident planters reflected the larger changes the island experienced during the Napoleonic Wars. From 1793 to 1815, Newfoundland's permanent population increased rapidly as the fisheries made their final transition from a migratory industry to a Newfoundland-based way of life. The early war years proved disruptive to the migratory trade, while impressment and migration to the United States drove up the price of labour, increasing the prospects for servants trying to find employment in Newfoundland. By 1809, Spanish and Portuguese markets opened to the produce of a largely resident fishery. War with the Americans in 1812 saw the withdrawal of American competition in European markets. With peace in 1814, the residents of Newfoundland could find good employment and wages in the fishery, and an unusually good supply of provisions due to the trade's prosperity. Overall, the period was one of great demand for Newfoundland's salt cod. In addition, resident fishermen began to exploit the profitable spring seal fishery. In consequence, large numbers of Irish servants arrived to take advantage of employment opportunities.[29]

---

27 Chief Justice Reeve's Report to Secretary Dundas on the Legislation and Judiciary of Newfoundland, n.d., ca. 1791, vol. 138, Reel B-678, f. 290-92; Colonial Office Records [CO] 194 [available at the Centre for Newfoundland Studies, Memorial University of Newfoundland].

28 Governor William Waldegrave to the Duke of Portland, 30 October 1798, CO 194, B-679, vol. 40, f. 135-37.

29 Shannon Ryan, "Fishery to Colony: A Newfoundland Watershed, 1793-1815", *Acadiensis*, XII, 2 (Spring 1983), pp. 34-52.

The employment of great numbers of servants in the inshore fishery does not in itself mean that the fishery was becoming more capitalist, if by capitalist one means that the social relations of production were becoming over time dominated by a class of property owners utilizing their capital through the employment of members of a separate class of wage labourers. Fishing servants in this period resembled more the rural servants of early modern England examined by Ann Kussmaul. Such servants were the young of England's rural families whose labour could not find employment within the limits of their particular household's production. These youths joined the households of their neighbours, households which, at different points in the family's life cycle, might require more labour than the nuclear family could itself provide. Servants did not then constitute a class in themselves, but were instead the youth of a class of household producers, residing with and as part of the family of their hirers on an annual contract in a transitional period between adolescence and the establishment of their own households.[30]

The latter part of the period studied by Kussmaul, from 1780 to 1820, constitutes, along with the next decade, the period so well described by Gordon Handcock as being the main period of Newfoundland settlement. Handcock suggests that settlement in Newfoundland arose directly from the labour requirements of the cod fishery. Merchants profited from the trade in fishing servants, recruiting servants, first in the West Country alone and later from Ireland, for employment by their planters in Newfoundland. Like their fellow servants who stayed home, fishing servants intended to return to their own households after serving a year or two in the fishery. Yet in joining the households of their employers, servants often married into the planter's family. Through such marriages servants became residents themselves, expecting to eventually establish their own household within the Newfoundland fishery. Continued migration of servants as well as natural increase pushed resident fishing families from the oldest settled and crowded parts of Conception Bay up the northeast coast as far as the islands of Fogo and Twillingate.[31]

The depression of the cod fishery during the early part of the Napoleonic Wars produced opportunities for differentiation between the households of the planters. Cut off from easy return to a war-ridden Europe and without enough earnings from the fishery alone to survive in Newfoundland, many planters turned to sealing, trapping, shipbuilding and logging to supplement the cod fishery. Combining sealing and the cod fishery meant that some planters could obtain enough credit to outfit a schooner with which, in a year or two, they

30 Ann Kussmaul, *Servants in husbandry in early modern England* (Cambridge, 1981), pp. 3-25.

31 W. Gordon Handcock, "An Historical Geography of the Origins of English Settlement in Newfoundland: A Study of the Migration Process", Ph.D. thesis, University of Birmingham, 1979, pp. 69-240.

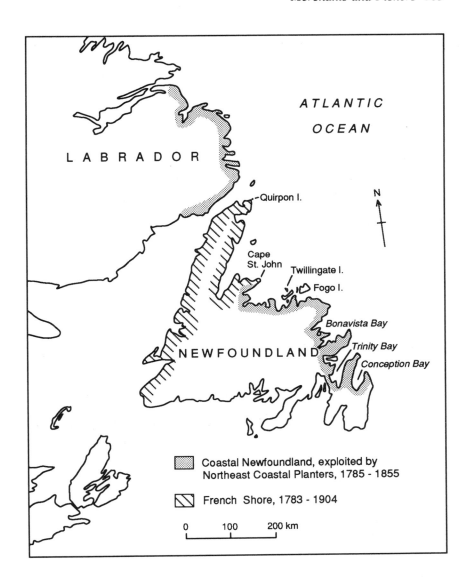

ATLANTIC

OCEAN

L A B R A D O R

Quirpon I.

Cape
St. John

Twillingate I.

Fogo I.

Bonavista Bay

N E W F O U N D L A N D

Trinity Bay

Conception Bay

Coastal Newfoundland, exploited by
Northeast Coastal Planters, 1785 - 1855

French Shore, 1783 - 1904

0   100   200 km

might clear themselves of any credit obligations to particular merchants and trade independently.[32]

The unusual conditions of war, not the wages and lien system embodied in Palliser's Act, allowed this differentiation. Reports from colonial officials at Newfoundland often suggest that this proceeded despite wage guarantees. Lieutenant Governor Barton, in 1801, commented that the great success of that year's seal fishery allowed planters to prosper despite the high wages they were obliged to pay servants at the end of the fishing season.[33] Over the next few years, independent planters could use their schooners to travel to St. John's to buy provisions and equipment at prices cheaper than those made available by their local merchants.[34] But, as Governor Gower observed, while some planters were hiring wage labour and expanding their scale of production, the resident fishery was growing in the hothouse environment of the war and remained an important preserve of family production.[35] The fortunes of war were not kind to many planters, who risked insolvency when they could not obtain sufficient prices for their fish to compensate for high wage rates and high prices for equipment and provisions they had obtained on credit.[36]

Differentiation among planters thrived on the new north shore fishery created by the Napoleonic Wars. Conception Bay fishermen enjoyed unrestricted access to the good fishing grounds of the Newfoundland shore north of Cape St. John, which the French had controlled until war's advent.[37] Governor Gower's description of this fishery indicates that planters involved in the north shore fishery relied for the most part on family-based production, or possibly secured a livelihood as shippers providing a mercantile service to other planters. Planters with schooners transported fishing families to the French Shore, where they established inshore fisheries similar to those at home. Men caught the fish, relying on their female relatives and children to cure it.[38]

---

32   Matthews, "West of England-Newfoundland Fishery", pp. 593-96.

33   "The Report and Remarks made by Robert Barton Esq. Lieutenant Governor of the Island of Newfoundland —1801", CO 194, B-680, vol. 43, f. 26-28.

34   Thomas Tremblett, Chief Justice, *et al.* to Governor Sir Erasmus Gower, 29 August 1804, CO 194, B-680, vol. 44, f. 34-37.

35   Gower to Earl Camden, 24 December 1804, CO 194, B-680, vol. 44, f. 50-53, PANS.

36   Gower to Camden, 18 July 1805, CO 194, B-681, vol. 44, f. 141; Gower to William Windham, 13 February 1806, CO 194, B-681, vol. 45, B-681, f. 15.

37   Shannon Ryan, "The Newfoundland Cod Fishery in the Nineteenth Century", M.A. thesis, Memorial University of Newfoundland, 1971, pp. 48-57.

38   Gower, "Explanatory Observations on the Accompanying Return of the Fishery and Inhabitants of Newfoundland...1804", CO 194, B-681, vol. 45, f. 20.

Gower recognized that, when the war ended, planters would have to return to the less satisfactory Labrador fishery. Deprived of rights to the French-controlled northeast coast, English fishermen had resorted to the Labrador coast to search for better fishing grounds since at least 1762.[39] The earliest evidence of labour being employed in a migratory fishery to either coast by Conception Bay planters is contained in an 1807 dispute in the Harbour Grace Surrogate Court. Richard Palmer sued Henry and James Lilly for £96 damages for allegedly stealing barrels, spreads and masts from his stages at The Needles on the French Shore. Crew members Jonathan Kelly and Joseph Janes of the Lillys' schooner testified for their masters, denying any knowledge of the theft.[40]

That planters used servants to crew a schooner does not necessarily mean that they used servants to actually catch or cure fish. It could well be that the Lillys were shippers and not actually involved in production at all. Another example may illustrate this point. In 1808, Richard Kain sued Francis Pike for £124 damages to fish improperly handled by Pike's schooner crew as they carried it from Kain's room at Goose Cove on the French Shore to Harbour Grace. Kain proved to a jury that Pike's crew allowed 197.5 quintals of fish out of 300 to become wet in shipment, damaging its cure. Pike clearly employed labour in this instance, but not in the fishery itself.[41] Similarly, Michael Kain sued William Peddle for £100 damages for failing to deliver supplies to the former on the

39 Richard Master, Merchant's Hall, Bristol, to the Lord Commissioners of Trade and Plantation, 29 November 1762, CO 194, B-212, vol. 15, f. 45-46.

40 Richard Palmer vs. Henry and James Lilly, 23 November 1807, Surrogate Court Records, Northern Circuit, Harbour Grace, Box 1, Minutes 1878-18, Minutes 1807-10, Charles Garland, Surrogate, GN5\1\B\1, Provincial Archives of Newfoundland and Labrador [PANL]. Questions generally arise about whether the evidence drawn from particular cases can be said to be typical of the entire number of court proceedings. This paper does not rely, for the most part, on the exact nature of court cases, or how they were resolved. In the first instance the records of the Surrogate's Court (1785-24) and the Northern Circuit Court (1825-55) are here used primarily as non-serial sources to put flesh to an interpretative skeleton created from other non-serial sources, such as the Colonial Office Records, merchants' correspondence, newspapers and missionary reports. The interpretation offered in this paper does not depend on the representative and quantitative treatment of the court records. One of the remarkable aspects of researching the 19th-century Newfoundland fishery is that almost no merchant records have survived. Court records offer a wealth of information concerning the fishery, often in ways incidental to the particular disputes that occurred. Evidence offered here is part of a larger study of all the civil proceedings of both courts, not just a sample.

41 Richard Kain vs. Francis Pike, 8 February 1808, Surrogate's Minutes, box 1, GN5/1/B/1, PANL.

French Shore as they had earlier agreed to. Again, Peddle acted as a shipper, not as a producer of salt cod.[42]

The example of Francis Pike is interesting because he was the son of Elizabeth Pike, a rare example of a woman controlling the enterprises of a planter. Elizabeth was the widow of John Pike, a merchant at Harbour Grace. In 1793 she began to assume the conduct of her deceased husband's affairs by going to court over a disputed bill of exchange.[43] By 1808 Elizabeth Pike was involved in a new business: contracting the curing of fish caught on the French Shore by Conception Bay planters. Evidence of this can be found in Robert Ash's suit against Pike for allegedly improperly curing his "trip" of greenfish. Ash used a schooner to catch fish on the French Shore, sending two cargoes of greenfish to Elizabeth Pike's stages during the season of 1807. When the suit first appeared in court, Edward Howard, a shoreman employed by Pike, testified that Ash had salted his fish too lightly and that Pike had plenty of labour employed in curing the fish.[44] After a postponement, the case reappeared before the court. William Howell, a servant of Ash, stated that Ash's fish was well split and salted. David Fitzgerald, another of Ash's servants, stated that he accompanied the fish home from the French Shore on the second trip, and it arrived in excellent condition. H.C. Watts, a Harbour Grace merchant, finally testified that, although Mrs. Pike had just enough servants to properly tend the curing, they spent much of their time doing other garden work to the neglect of the fish. The court awarded the case to Ash.[45]

This case is fascinating in that it reveals that the French Shore extension of the northeast-coast planter fishery was leading to some local market diversification and specialization. Owners of capital — both Ash and Pike — employed servants in a manner that suggests little of a household relationship. There was a regional specialization of labour. Possibly because it was so close, planters concentrated on catching and splitting fish at the French Shore; all the curing was done at the site of marketing in Conception Bay. Schooners could make two trips for extra provisions for a season longer than at Labrador because of its

42 Michael Kain vs. William Peddle, 11 January 1808, Surrogate's Minutes, box 1, GN5/1/B/1, PANL.

43 Henry O'Neil vs. Elizabeth Pike, 20 August 1794; Elizabeth Pike vs. Simon Wells, 23, 27 October 1794; Elizabeth Pike vs. Israel Ryan, 3 March 1795; Elizabeth Pike vs. Israel Hynes, 13 August 1796; Elizabeth Pike vs. William Maher, 13 August 1796; Elizabeth Pike vs. Nicholas Ash, 14 October 1796, Surrogate's Minutes, box 1, GN5/1/B/1, PANL.

44 Robert Ash vs. Elizabeth Pike, Surrogate's Minutes, 1807-10, GN5/1/B/1, PANL.

45 Robert Ash vs. Elizabeth Pike, 2 June 1808, Surrogate's Minutes, 1807-10, GN5/1/B/1, PANL.

latitude, the shorter travelling time and the ability to concentrate labour on catching the fish. That the French Shore fishery was becoming more than one resting on household labour can be seen in the partnership contracts of planters who agreed to supply and carry fishing crews to that shore in exchange for a share of the latters' voyage.[46]

Planters continued to be active in the north shore fishery until at least 1819.[47] But while differentiation might have been making inroads among planters going to the French Shore, the household character of production in the inshore fishery of the northeast coast appears to have changed little as most planters continued to rely on family labour, except at times when their families could not supply enough for cod production.[48] In any event, British peace negotiations with both the French and Americans proved to be the real threat to planters' expanded scale of production through the use of wage labour. Restoring the rights of the Americans to fish at Labrador would undermine Newfoundland planters there, while the French would regain their right to the French Shore. In England, the Committee of the Newfoundland Trade began to call for the exclusion of both nations from rights in the Newfoundland fisheries.[49]

Despite this call, the end of war saw the readmission of both the French and Americans to the Newfoundland fishery. Their competition, along with the loss of preferences for British products on the Iberian Peninsula, witnessed the end of the unusual demand for Newfoundland fish. On the northeast coast this meant the end of any great demand for servants above the requirements of the household fishery. By the winter of 1816-17, widespread unemployment of servants characterized the northeast-coast fishery, forcing many to migrate to St. John's, or to leave Newfoundland altogether.[50] Governor Pickmore observed that the high capital requirements of planters' use of hired labour could no longer be met by the low prices for fish in foreign markets.[51]

The depression of the fish trade, in full swing by 1817, occasioned some interesting commentary on the social relations of production in the Newfoundland

46 Hunt & Co. vs. James Quinlan, 18 December 1809, Surrogate's Minutes, 1807-10; Michael Power vs. James Rafter, 12 May 1814, Surrogate's Minutes, 1813-15, GN5/1/B/1, PANL.

47 Michl. Purcell vs. Wm. Donovan, 22 May 1817, Surrogate's Minutes, box 2, 1816-18; Macfarlane & Scott vs. James Fox, 19 December 1817, Surrogate's Minutes, 1816-18; Colbert and Driscoll vs. Henry Webber & Co., 28 January 1819, Surrogates Minutes, 1818-19, GN5/1/B/1, PANL.

48 Gower, "Observations on certain Parts of His Majesty's Instructions to the Governor of Newfoundland", CO 194, B-681, vol. 45, f. 64.

49 Henry Hunt, chairman of the Committee of the Newfoundland Trade, to Earl Bathurst, 25 April 1814, CO 194, B-685, vol. 55, f. 181.

50 Governor Pickmore to Henry Goulbourn, 20 July 1817, CO 194, B-686, vol. 59, 1817, f. 110-12. Petitions came from the merchants of Bristol, mainly trading to

fishery. J. Newart, who described himself as a long-term resident of New-foundland, suggested that planters were mostly ex-servants, or the descendants of servants, who had managed to acquire enough capital in partnerships (of two or three) to acquire a boat to begin fishing on their own account. Those who caught and dried their own fish were commonly known as boatkeepers. Planters, to be more accurate, were those who dried not only their own fish, but also that of boatkeepers without the flakes, stages or other necessary equipment. This description seems to fit the operations of Elizabeth Pike. These planters' operations were limited by Palliser's Act because it required them to pay wages to any servants they hired regardless of the quality of the servants' work. Even more limiting were the price-fixing manipulations of truck, whereby merchants would not tell planters how much they would be charged for provisions and equipment until the merchants knew how much fish and oil would fetch in the marketplace. Truck normally prevented planters from extending their operations through the employment of servants. But late-war prosperity led some planters and merchants to risk such expansion; the end of war saw the props of such expansion cleared away. Planters with extensive investment in the fishery fell into insolvency, leaving behind only the family fishery. Newart felt that Palliser's Act exacerbated the *decline* of these planters, whose brief rise and fall was directly related to the economic conditions of the war.[52]

Newart's observations were confirmed in the British House of Commons select committee testimony of George Garland, George Kemp, Sr., and George Kemp, Jr., merchants of Poole, and J.H. Attwood, a merchant of St. John's, who stated that the prosperity of wartime was not likely to return and the best thing that resident fishermen could do would be to rely on the labour of their families, not servants, in a combination of fishing and subsistence agriculture if they were to survive the credit restrictions of the post-Napoleonic Wars trade. Again, these merchants advocated shipping Newfoundland's surplus labour from the island.[53]

The residents of the northeast coast did pursue the course laid out in the testimony collected by this select committee. Planters had little choice but to do so

Conception Bay. See Thomas Thorne & Co., William Danson, William Henderson, William Mullowney, and Bartholemew Henderson & Co.; and the merchants of Poole, trading to all parts of the northeast coast: Thomas Colborne, George Garland, Chris Spurrier & Co., Samuel and Jn. Clark, John Slade & Co., Robert Slade, Slade & Cox, Fryer, Gosse & Pack, George & J. Kemp & Co., Sleat and Read, and Joseph Bird; Petitions of the Merchants of Poole and Bristol, 7 and 13 March 1817, CO 194, B-687, vol. 60, f. 185-86, 211-12.

51 Governor Pickmore to Earl Bathurst, 22 December 1817, CO 194, B-686, vol. 59, f. 1 87.

52 J. Newart to Earl Bathurst, 4 March 1817, CO 194, B-687, vol. 60, f. 249-75.

53 "Report from the Select Committee on the Newfoundland Trade, with Minutes of Evidence", 26 June 1817, CO 194, B-687, vol. 60, f. 290-312.

when merchants were not willing to extend enough credit to let them purchase bread, pork or butter as supplies for their families, let alone provision servants at a time when fish fetched low prices.[54] In the most developed parts of Conception Bay around Carbonear and Harbour Grace, families returned to the labour of their households, eating their own fish and potatoes and repairing their own clothing so that they might avoid as much as possible the credit of the merchant.[55] A Wesleyan Missionary Report compiled from the circuit missionaries' observations reported that the northeast-coast inshore fishery had become the preserve of household labour: men and boys went out in small craft to catch fish, bringing it to shore where their female relatives and children split, salted and dried the fish.[56] John Oliver, at Port de Grave, reported that without the labour of their women and children, the families of his area would not be able to earn a living from the fishery.[57]

The years after the Napoleonic Wars were not a good time to be hiring labour in the northeast-coast fishery. In 1820, Captain Nicholas, a naval officer who had served as surrogate judge in Trinity Bay for a number of years, talked about the many problems planters dealt with. In particular, Nicholas felt that the inshore fishery could not support hiring the great number of servants recently brought into the island. By this time planters were simply people who owned boats of their own. Four men crewed the boats, usually from the planter's own family, or servants if the planter did not have enough family members. Increasingly common was the practice of some planters hiring other indigent planters to crew their boats for half the catch instead of wages. Such indigent planters had all their boats and property seized by merchants when their accounts fell in arrears during the post-war depression. The share system proved to be a way in which the insolvent could provide for their families and the solvent could avoid wage obligations. Nicholas felt that planters suffered primarily from truck. Merchants supplied both them and their servants with as much equipment and goods (especially rum) as they were willing to take on credit. Prices were not settled until the end of the season when the fish came to their stores and the merchants knew what it would bring in the market. Planters could not control the nature of credit, but they could control the amount for which they were liable. Minimizing

---

54 John Lewis, 17 December 1816, Wesleyan Methodist Missionary Society, Newfoundland Correspondence, 1808-17, 971.8W1, B-4-4, no. 271, PANL.

55 John Walsh to Joseph Taylor, 10 July 1819, Wesleyan Methodist Missionary Society, Newfoundland Correspondence, 1818-24, 971.8W2, B-4-4, no. 68, PANL.

56 "Observations &c. on the island of Newfoundland", March 1919, Wesleyan Methodist Missionary Society, Newfoundland Correspondence, 1818-24, 971.8W2, B-4-4, no. 137, PANL.

the number of servants hired was one way of doing so.[57] By 1821, Chief Justice Forbes reported that neither planters nor poor fishermen could earn enough to feed their families. The unemployed part of the population left the outports to seek work in St. John's or find a way to leave the island.[58] When they required servants, planters increasingly tended to hire them on shares rather than have servants charge what goods they wanted on their masters' account for a guaranteed wage at the end of the fishing season, regardless of the outcome of the voyage.[60]

Ninian Ball, a Methodist missionary at Bonavista in 1821, reported that planters there could no longer afford to hire servants due to the low prices given for fish and the high wages of £25 per season asked for by servants. If a planter had sons to work his boats then their efforts might pay them a living, but otherwise they would face insolvency. Sharemen — ruined planters — would work for others for one half the catch. This was a common arrangement: "The planter gets the one half of his fish for finding boat &c &c — the shareman gets the other half for his labour. Now supposing he catch 100 qtls. though some have not 70 — at 10/ this is £25 — taking out for bad fish he will not have more than £20 on which he must keep a wife and perhaps 6 or 7 children for the year".[61]

James Stephen of the Colonial Office reported in 1824 that the few planters still paying wages under the provisions of Pallisers' Act could not survive in the Newfoundland fishery. Stephen felt that such planters were not even the true hirers of servants but only *de facto* middlemen of their merchants:

At the commencement of the Fishing Season, the Merchant supplies the planter, with provision, clothing, fishing tackle, and all other things necessary for the conduct of the fishery. The planter hires fishermen, whom he supplies with all the requisites for their labour, out of the stores thus furnished to him by the Merchant. The fish are cured by the planter at his fishing room or station; and the planter also expresses and prepares the Oil. The cured fish and oil are then delivered by the planter to the

57   John Oliver to the Wesleyan Methodist Missionary Committee, 29 October 1829, Wesleyan Methodist Missionary Society, Newfoundland Correspondence, 1822-23, 971.8W4, B-4-4, no. 68-9, PANL.

58   Captain J. Nicholas to Lord Melville, 18 October 1820, CO 194, B-688, vol. 63, f. 250-67.

59   Grand Jury to Forbes, 13 October 1821, CO 194, B-688, vol. 64, f. 139-40.

60   James Dalton to James Butterworth, 4 April 1822, CO 194, B-689. vol. 65, f. 234-35.

61   Ninian Ball to Joseph Taylor, 3 October 1821, Wesleyan Methodist Missionary Society, Newfoundland Correspondence, 1819-22, 971.8W3, B-4-4, no. 2, PANL.

Merchant. The latter pays for them to the planter, at what may be termed the home or Island price; deducting however from the amount of this payment, the price of the Stores supplied at the commencement of the Season. Thus the Planter is a kind of Middle Man between the Merchant and the fishermen, and the planters profits arise from the excess of what he receives from the Merchant for his Stores, and to the fishermen for their labour. The business of the planter therefore is very precarious. He may be said to take upon himself the whole risk of the fishery.

But as the Planters have seldom much capital they rarely can bear up against the consequences of a bad or unsuccessful Season. Hence it has happened that the class of Men are frequently becoming Insolvent.[62]

Long before the demise of the wage lien of Palliser's Act, planters were falling back into the ranks of fishermen below them due to problems in the markets for salt cod.[63]

By 1826, Governor Cochrane reported that the use of labour hired on wages, not shares, had all but disappeared on the northeast coast. Post-war depression had eroded the planters' position, forcing those who had been lucky enough to escape insolvency to retreat from the use of hired labour.[64] "An Avalonian" wrote in 1830 that to continue to hire servants on wages would mean the impoverishment of a planter's family working in the inshore fishery

---

62 J. Stephen, Jr., to Robert Wilmot Horton, 19 March 1824, CO 194, B-691, vol. 68, f. 112-113.

63 A number of documents relate the decline of the wages and lien system none of these have been consulted by Antler. See, for example, Robert Wilmot Horton, "Remarks upon the proposed Newfoundland Acts", CO 194, B-692, vol. 69, f. 76-96; "Pole & Liverpool Copy of the Newfoundland Bill", f. 165; comments by Governor Hamilton on proposed judicial reform for Newfoundland, f. 265; "Report of the proceedings of the Chamber of Commerce", 29 December 1828, CO 194, B-697, vol. 78, f. 17-38; W.A. Clarke to R.W. Hay, 9 March 1829, f. 197-214; R.A. Tucker, A.W. DesBarres, and E.B. Brenton, "Report of our opinion upon the Judicature and Jurisprudence of this Colony", 23 August 1831, CO 194, B-534, vol. 82, f. 24-99; "Report of H.M. Attorney General of Newfoundland on the Judicature Laws of that Colony, February 1832", CO 194, B-535, vol. 84, f. 261-298; "In the Privy Council. In the Matter of the Complaint of the House of Assembly of Newfoundland, against the Honourable H.J. Boulton, Chief Justice of Newfoundland. Case of the Chief Justice", CO 194, B-546, vol. 103, f. 325-424. Almost every issue of the Harbour Grace *Weekly Herald* and the St. John's *Public Ledger* followed debates about the system from 1820 to 1850.

64 Governor Thomas Cochrane to Earl Bathurst, 30 January 1826, CO 194, B-693, vol. 72, Despatches, f. 87-100.

until his sons, progressing towards maturity, if well disposed, at length assist in rendering his life more tolerable, but at the same time, adding a large part of their labour, and in many instances the whole of it, to satisfy the appetite of that Hydra-headed monster, wages, which for ever is swallowing up the fruit of their best exertions, and, like an evil spirit, weighing them down to the dust.

Fishing families were best to hire servants only when their families could not supply the household's labour. If servants must be hired then they should be given a share of the catch.[65]

The Labrador Fishery

Even the Labrador fishery, still resorted to by schooners from Conception Bay, was not a fishery in which planters used many hired servants: "Not an inconsiderable part of the Fishery is carried on to the Northward, on the Labrador coast. In the Spring, vessels go there with whole families, catch the fish & cure it; and in the Autumn return. Carbonear & Harbour Grace, in Conception Bay are particularly engaged in this part of the fishery".[66] In 1824 a Brigus missionary reported that families took their children with them to work the fishery at Labrador.[67]

The Labrador fishery involved the use of schooner crews to ship families to the coast of Labrador in a seasonal round of household activity. Even the sealing voyage in which the schooners were first engaged before they went to Labrador did not much alter the character of the family fishery, although it required large numbers of servants. Such servants were the young sons of fishing families looking to earn money for their families, or perhaps to start up their own households. After the spring seal fishery ended, these young men returned either to go to the Labrador fishery with their families or to stay and fish inshore along the northeast coast in the harbours around their place of residence.[68]

Court records reveal that some planters did use servants to prosecute the Labrador fishery. In a petition to Naval Surrogate Captain Thomas Toker in 1817 asking that William Martin and Martin Murphy be prevented from

65 *Public Ledger* (St. John's), 21 May 1830.

66 "Observations &c. on the island of Newfoundland", March 1919, n.p., Wesleyan Methodist Missionary Society, Newfoundland Correspondence, 1818-24, 971.8W2, B-4-4, no. 173, PANL.

67 W. Knight to the Wesleyan Methodist Missionary Committee, 18 July 1824, Wesleyan Methodist Missionary Committee, Newfoundland Correspondence, 1824-25, 971.8W5, B-4-4, no. 6, PANL.

68 William Wilson to the Wesleyan Methodist Missionary Committee; 6 September 1825, Wesleyan Methodist Missionary Society, Newfoundland Correspondence, 1824-25, 971.8W5, B-4-4, no. 171, PANL.

encroaching on his fishing room at Labrador, William Taylor stated that he used one schooner to employ 13 "hands" in his fishery there. If his room was protected, Taylor planned to use an additional schooner and seven "hands".[69] In another case, George Pippy of Harbour Grace won a suit against Michael Duggan for 40 pounds freight on the shipment of 320 quintals of fish from Labrador to Harbour Grace. Their trial revealed that Pippy agreed to supply Duggan's crew of five men with all the provisions they would need at Labrador. In return, Duggan would pay Pippy to carry home all his fish, oil and salmon at a rate of two shillings per quintal of fish, 20 shillings per ton of oil and two shillings per cwt. of salmon.[70] Thomas Pynn, a planter at Musquetto, Conception Bay, employed crews on two schooners in both the seal and Labrador fisheries in 1825.[71] The sons and son-in-law of Richard Taylor of Harbour Grace employed a number of schooners, and shipped men as servants in the Labrador fishery in 1831.[72]

The schooners of the Labrador fishery were not without their own problems for northeast-coast planters. The problem was that planters who invested in schooners during the Napoleonic Wars did so because of the opportunities of fishing on the French Shore. Since the peace of 1815, the French regained control of that part of the northeast coast, gradually excluding Newfoundlanders from "the very best fishery of Newfoundland, and that our exclusion from thence, has most seriously injured that part of our commerce; the fishery there carried on being now driven to the distant and inclement coasts of Labrador".[73] The St. John's Chamber of Commerce reported that all Newfoundland fishermen who had invested so much in the French Shore fishery "have since the French Possession, been driven to the Labrador, where the catch is more precarious, and the quality and cure generally so inferior that in all foreign markets the British-caught Newfoundland Fish, has already suffer'd a serious depreciation in Value and the high Character which it heretofore sustained, has been brought into disrepute".[73] By 1834, the Newfoundland House of Assembly

69 Petition of William Taylor, 10 June 1817, Surrogate's Minutes, box 2, GN5/1/B/1, PANL.

70 George Pippy vs. Michael Duggan, 20 November 1817, Surrogate's Minutes, box 2, GN5/1/B/1, PANL.

71 The King vs. Thomas Pynn, 22 January 1825, Supreme Court Minutes, box 4, GN5/2/A/1, PANL.

72 Petition of Jonathan Taylor, William Taylor, Richard Taylor, John Taylor, Henry Taylor, Joseph Taylor and John Hinchy to Judge A.W. DesBarres, Northern Circuit Court, 1 June 1831, Harbour Grace Court Records, box 28, file 1, GN5/3/B/19, PANL.

73 Governor Cochrane to Viscount Goderich, 26 September 1827, CO 194, B-695, vol. 74, f. 167-72.

reported a dichotomy in the northeast-coast fishery. Some fishing families stayed the entire summer to fish inshore at their place of residence. Others went to Labrador aboard the schooners owned by planters who had expanded into the seal fishery. Such planters had made their investments counting on the profit of the French Shore fishery, not on the short season, small fish and poor curing conditions of the Labrador. Exclusion from the French Shore, combined with poor fish markets, meant that many fishing families began to leave Newfoundland altogether, emigrating to the greener pastures of the United States.[75]

Servants employed in the Labrador fishery were probably usually hired on shares. Evidence of this can be found in the suit of planters Nicholas Furlong and John Brine to have their supplying merchant, William Bennett, pay the balance of Patrick Rogers' wages. Rogers agreed to serve Furlong and Brine at Labrador for one season "in the capacity of splitter & master of Voyage and for the faithful performance of his duty he is to receive as wages, one half the shareman's catch of fish, by paying Twenty shillings and the freight of his fish home".[76] John Nicholls agreed to serve James Simmons at the Camp Islands in Labrador during the season of 1848 "in the capacity of a Fisherman or anything else in his power for the good of the voyage" in return for "as wages half his catch of fish with the hook and the fifteenth part of the codseine (meaning the fish that might be caught in the codseine)".[77]

The prospects for the development of a capitalist organization of production in the Labrador fishery were dim. This fishery was but part of a delicate balance of fisheries in which too much could go wrong. In 1833, for example, Thomas Danson, a justice of the peace at Harbour Grace, described "the unsuccessful Seal and Cod fisheries the past Season", whose "consequences are their creating so many outstanding Debts, and the whole fish & Oil caught by Planters at Labrador in numerous instances will not nearly pay the Servants Wages the Merchants are in like manner very cautious in advancing their property on credit as their losses are great".[78]

---

74 Petition of the St. John's Chamber of Commerce to Sir George Murray, 1828, CO 194, B-696, vol. 76, f. 324-27.

75 Petition of the House of Assembly to G.C. Stanley, 22 May 1834, CO 194, B-536, vol. 87, f. 174-78.

76 Writ issued in the Northern Circuit Court, 21 November 1827, Harbour Grace Court Records, box 30, file 6, no. 131, GN5/3/B/19, PANL.

77 Plea of John Nicholls, Northern Circuit Court, 1 November 1848, Harbour Grace Court Records, box 21, file 6, GN5/1/B/1, PANL.

78 Thomas Danson to Colonial Secretary James Crowdy, 22 November 1833, Harbour Grace Court Records, box 22, file 5, GN5/3/B/19, PANL.

Failure in the Labrador fishery was a real hazard. Thomas Powell declared in 1827 that, after nine years as a part owner of a schooner in the seal and cod fisheries, he had fallen behind in his account payments to his supply merchants, Gosse, Pack and Fryer, in 1825. Robert Pack attached and had the court sell his share of a schooner, his plantation at Carbonear, and his room and stage at Labrador.[79] The insolvent estate of Denis Thomey, a planter of Musquetto, in 1833 revealed that Thomey owed Thomas Ridley & Co. and Gosse, Pack and Fryer £333 19s 7d in addition to a number of other small debts to the value of £380 12s 8d.The main part of Thomey's assets included his fishing room and plantation at Musquetto (£30), a Labrador fishing room (£10), 40 hogsheads of salt there (£20) and three boats with gear at the Camp Islands at Labrador (£15). £15 worth of gear at Newfoundland rounded this figure to £90.[80]

The insolvency of Edmund Barrett in the same year reveals that wages were an important part of his debt, outweighing the value of Barrett's property and catch. Barrett also had amassed a considerable debt to his supplying merchant. Out of a total of £715, Barrett owed servants £112 and Gosse, Pack and Fryer £582. Against this debt Barrett owned £73 in a fishing room at Spears Harbour on the Labrador, with salt, skiffs, herring nets, part of a caplin seine, cod bags, a cod seine, barrels and utensils. Barrett's catch was only 200 quintals of fish and one hogshead of oil valued at £90 for total assets of £163.[81] The account of planter James Quiddihy with George Forward shows that in 1833 Quiddihy obtained provisions and equipment from January through November to the value of £347 9s 9d. Quiddihy returned against this only £162 17s 5d worth of seals and fish. Added to this the court valued Quiddihy's room and equipment at Battle Harbour, Labrador, at £25.[82] One of the Taylor brothers' Labrador fishery became insolvent in 1834 when John Taylor fell in arrears to the amount of £216 17s 9d to a number of creditors including Gosse, Pack and Fryer, Best and Waterman, and Thomas Chancey and Co.[83] Michael Keefe, a Musquetto planter, ended up in debtor's prison at Harbour Grace at the suit of his supplying mer-

---

79 Petition of Thomas Powell, to Chief Justice R.A. Tucker, 18 May 1827, Harbour Grace Court Records, box 26, file 10, 1827, GN5/3/B/19, PANL.

80 Insolvency of Denis Thomey, 21 November 1833, Harbour Grace Court Records, box 20, file 1, GN5/1/B/1, PANL.

81 "Property belonging to Edmund Barrett", Harbour Grace Court Records, box 20, file 1, 1833, GN5/1/B/1, PANL.

82 Account of James Quiddihy with George Forward, 1833, Harbour Grace Court Records, box 20, file 1, GN5/3/B/19, PANL.

83 Writ of the Northern Circuit Court, William Ash, Jr., and John Taylor to pay two pounds to Robert Pack and William Bennett, trustees of Taylor's estate, 1 July 1834, Harbour Grace Court Records, box 18, file 7, no. 51, GN5/3/B/19, PANL.

chant, J.C. Nuttall, after his Labrador fishery at Battle Harbour failed in the season of 1833.[84]

Edward Shannahan's debt of £470 18s 10d owed to Thorne, Hoope and Co. from 1832 to 1836 led to a petition by the planter which vividly described the problems of using hired servants in the precarious Labrador fishery:

> That your petitioner about Six years ago dealt with Messrs. Thorne & Co. to the amount of £300 and carried on the fishery on Labradore.
>
> That the fishery was very bad that Season and your petr. fell back on his account upwards of £43.
>
> That your petr. dealt the following year with the said Thorne & Co. but could not reduce the balance of the former year although giving him every fish petitioner caught.
>
> That your petr. was refused supplies for his family and was therefore obliged to dispose of what little property he had for which he could not get but very little for.
>
> That your petr. about three years ago dealt with Mr. Wells at the Labrador and that year the fishery almost totally failed and your petitioner did not catch sufficient fish to pay the wages —33 but petr. has since paid him some fish and owe him upwards of twenty eight pounds.
>
> That your petr. has a large helpless family who have no person to trust to but ptrs. labour.

Shannahan pleaded to be declared insolvent so he would not have to face prison.[85] James Glaveen, a Harbour Grace planter, filed a similar petition to be declared insolvent in 1837, reporting that after 32 years of fishing his seal and cod fishery could no longer support the maintenance of his family or pay the expenses of his schooner.[86]

Throughout the 1830s and into the 1850s, such insolvency cases involving planters who fished at Labrador appeared in the Northern Circuit Court. Even when such fishing did not involve the hiring of servants, as in the case of John Day, a Carbonear planter, the risk of the Labrador often proved to be too much:

> Petitioner begs finally to intimate that the nature of his Labrador voyages is such that he seldom realizes sufficient to provide for his family the succeeding winter — that taking his supplies at Labrador at very high

---

84   Petition of Michael Keefe, Planter, to E.B. Brenton, Judge of the Northern Circuit Court, 19 June 1834, Harbour Grace Court Records, box 18, file 18, GN5/3/B/19, PANL.

85   Petition of Edward Shannahan to Judge E.B. Brenton, Northern Circuit Court, May 1836, Harbour Grace Court Records, box 18, file 9, GN5/3/B/19, PANL.

86   Petition of James Glaveen to Judge George Lilly, Northern Circuit Court, May Term 1837, Harbour Grace Court Records, box 18, file 11, GN5/3/B/19, PANL.

prices paying heavily for the removal of his family to and from Labrador and the low price of fish have altogether this year left Petitioner penniless and his family without fuel and without many of the commonest necessaries for the winter.[87]

There are occasional records of the insolvency of planters not involved in the Labrador fishery. They indicate that it was a risky business to be employing servants in the fishery. In the case of John Farrell, for example, his servant James Halfpenny sued Farrell for his wages of £27 at the end of the season in 1855. Farrell could not pay, ended up in debtor's prison, was declared insolvent and eventually signed over his plantation to Halfpenny. Clearly, in such cases, differentiation between servant and planter was tenuous indeed.[88]

The problems faced by planters did not lie in the Labrador fishery alone. The seal fishery was a hit-or-miss industry, characterized by years of poor harvests balancing against good years when schooners could actually find the herds on the pack ice of the North Atlantic. In the long run, heavy capital investment in steamers (to better control access to herds) favoured St. John's merchants, not outport planters.[89] Left with the poor yields of the Labrador fishery and the heavy capital demands of the seal fishery, the planters of Conception Bay often either went under to join the ranks of their fellow household producers or left the province altogether. "Delta", a newspaper correspondent, advised that the remaining planters not hire the labour of people coming into the Bay looking for work on their schooners, but to rely on their own labour:

> By all means, therefore, let the *sharemen* and wealthy exotic planters emigrate. Nearly every article produced by our tradesmen, except perhaps the carpenter and cooper, can be purchased *ready made*, and

---

87 Petition of John Day, Carbonear, 14 November 1848, Harbour Grace Court Records, box 21, file 5, GN5/3/B/19, PANL. See also insolvency of William Thistle, box 18, file 12, 1837; statement of the insolvent estate of Simon Levi, planter, 23 January 1838, box 28, file 10; Maurice Sullivan in account with Joseph Soper, 2 November 1837, box 28, file 5; account of insolvent James Guinea, box 21, file 11; petition of John Delaney, fisherman, 6 November 1850, box 20, file 5; statement of account between John Keilly and Sons and Ridley and Sons, 12 November 1855, box 26, file 3.

88 Writ issued by the Northern Circuit Court on behalf of James Halfpenny against John Farrell, 8 November 1855, box 26, file 4, GN5/3/B/19, PANL.

89 A contemporary account of the seal fishery's problems can be found in the *Weekly Herald* (Harbour Grace), 15 December 1847. For further analyses of the seal fishery see Chesley W. Sanger, "Technological and Spatial Adaptation in the Newfoundland Seal Fishery During the Nineteenth Century", M.A. thesis, Memorial University of Newfoundland, 1973, pp. 12-53; and Ryan, "The Newfoundland Cod Fishery", pp. 17-49.

much cheaper at the shops and stores, and therefore let the tradesmen bid us goodbye. Those who depend on the vicious and stupid for support will, as crime decreases and knowledge extends of course seek support elsewhere. That the ratio between the diminution of the number of fishermen and the proceeds of their voyages will hold, is evidently not founded on experience nor fact. On the sealing voyage if *every crew* were diminished one third, the aggregate catch would scarcely suffer any diminution, at least in ordinary years; and it is notorious that some forty or fifty years ago when twenty boats fished on a given ledge, took *ten* qtls. each, and called it fine fishing, now one hundred craft occupy the same ground, catch two qtls. each, and complain there is not a fish for the kettle! altho' the same quantity is taken as before. Admit, therefore, that single men emigrate — then the sons of the resident planters will obtain berths for Labrador &c; on their return their wages will, of course, find its way to their respective families; the elder branches who remain at home will attend to the ground, and carry on the shore fishery.[90]

"Delta" described a planter fishery at the limit of either intensive or extensive growth on the basis of hired labour. There seems to have been little potential for the growth of any price system or indigenous market diversification and specialization on the basis of such limits.

Households and Merchants

This study supports the findings of recent studies of merchants' roles in the development of colonial American economies which suggest that merchants played a role that was not necessarily hostile to the flourishing of industrial capitalist development within such colonial settings.[91] In the Newfoundland example, Marxist analyses of underdevelopment stumble over a tendency to associate merchant activity with the theoretically conservative circuit of merchant capital in the production of surplus value. But if historians are to accept that merchant capital is inherently conservative, then they will have to stop looking to merchants for explanations as to why a place like Newfoundland did not begin the transition to industrial capitalism in the first half of the 19th century.

Antler and Sider, in particular, have built an unproven conspiracy theory about merchants going to great lengths to use the courts to stymie local capitalist development. Yet there is no evidence to suggest that merchants actually used legal manipulation to undercut capitalist social relations in the planter fishery.

90   *Weekly Herald* (Harbour Grace), 11 April 1849.

91   See the essays in Rosemary E. Ommer, ed., *Merchant Credit and Labour Strategies in Historical Perspective* (Fredericton, 1990), but particularly Ommer's "Introduction", pp. 9-15.

The fishery of the northeast coast of Newfoundland in the first half of the 19th century rested primarily on the labour of families within households, supplemented by servants at times when the family could not supply enough. The offspring of these households sought work as servants in the seal fishery and on the Labrador as a buttress to their families, and perhaps as a transitional stage on the way to the establishment of their own households. What servants were hired on the northeast coast were usually paid by shares, something seen by Antler as having no capitalist potential. The labour of the family proved to be the crucial underpinning of an economy based on household production. Little evidence exists to suggest that a nascent capitalist fishery emerged on the basis of the wages and lien system embedded in Palliser's Act. There is much evidence to support the interpretation that such a fishery struggled to the fore during the boom times of the late Napoleonic Wars despite the actual constraints imposed on planters by the wages and lien system. The end of war saw the end of this development and the reassertion of household production in the northeast-coast fishery.

One could argue that, if merchants did not use unusual legal measures to preserve their hegemony in Newfoundland's fishing society, then there is still the problem of unequal exchange through truck in the credit relationships they shared with fishing families. Elsewhere, however, I have argued that fishing families, with state and merchant encouragement, explored alternatives to complete dependence on fish merchants for their supplies, particularly through the development of local agriculture. Newfoundland's harsh climate and poor soil, however, effectively forestalled fishing families' ability to use agriculture to minimize their reliance on merchant credit, let alone provide an industrial alternative to the economy's domination by mono-staple production.[92] In other colonies, where such limits did not exist anywhere to nearly the same extent, the dynamics of class relations in petty production in agriculture and related manufacturing provided trading opportunities which merchants seized on, aiding in local economic diversification. Surely it is time to focus on the limits to household fishing producers' ability to challenge merchant capital domination through staple trade, rather than start with a predetermined conclusion that only merchants had the power to shape fishing society. We must now focus our attention on the many ecological, economic and political factors which influenced the class relations between fishing people and fish merchants rather than continue to rely on a faulty use of a theoretical abstraction such as merchant capital to understand the persistence of merchant hegemony in Newfoundland's outport society.

---

92 Sean Cadigan, "The Staple Model Reconsidered: The Case of Agricultural Policy in Northeast Newfoundland, 1785-1855", *Acadiensis*, XXI, 2 (Spring 1992), pp. 48-71.

Settlement and the Forest Frontier Revisited: Class Politics and the Administration of the New Brunswick Labor Act, 1919-1929

Bill Parenteau

When Arthur Lower travelled through northern Ontario and Quebec in the 1930s researching his classic *Settlement and the Forest Frontier in Eastern Canada*, he had a chance to observe Crown land settlement first-hand. In the finished study, Lower commented extensively on the failure of settlement programmes in both provinces to achieve their primary intention of developing agriculture-based communities. "This type of person has been active for seventy-five years and has never been eliminated", he wrote disparagingly of the settlers. "He may or may not have some remote intention of making a home, but in the event he always does the same thing, cuts the timber off, having built a shack and perhaps made a little garden, sells it and then moves on".[1] The negative tone of Lower's interpretation stemmed from middle class attitudes regarding the relationship between farming and forest exploitation. His own preconceived notions were reinforced in interviews with "progressive" lumber operators and government foresters, who viewed Crown land settlement as contrary to rational and efficient resource use. What Lower missed in his study was an examination of the goals and aspirations of the settlers themselves. The individuals who pursued such opportunities had very different attitudes toward the Crown forest and farm settlement — attitudes that contradicted and challenged the notions of lumber operators, professional foresters, and state administrators.[2]

---

1   A.R.M. Lower, *Settlement and the Forest Frontier in Eastern Canada* (Toronto, 1936), p. 131. I would like to thank Danny Samson, Rusty Bittermann, David Frank and T.W. Acheson for their helpful comments and suggestions on earlier versions of this essay.

2   For a discussion of the negative relationship between settlers and lumbermen that developed in Ontario and Quebec after Confederation see A.R.M. Lower, *Settlement and the Forest Frontier*; H.V. Nelles, *The Politics of Development: Forests, Mines and Hydro-Electric Development in Ontario, 1849-1941* (Toronto, 1974); R. Peter Gillis and Thomas Roach, *Lost Initiatives: Canada's Forest Industries, Forest Policy and Forest Conservation* (New York, 1986); René Hardy and Normand Séguin, *Forêt et société en Mauricie: la formation de la région de Trois-Rivières, 1830-1930* (Montreal, 1984). Hardy and Séguin argue that the colonization programme in Quebec provided settlers with an opportunity to resist the growing hegemony of lumber operators over the forest resource base. There is a substantial volume of literature on the early settlement in New Brunswick and invariably some comment on the relationship between

Under the Labor Act, a programme similar to those in Ontario and Quebec, Crown land settlement in New Brunswick had for decades been rife with the problems described by Arthur Lower in his 1936 study. The programme was designed to facilitate farm settlement and was open to any New Brunswick male over 18 years of age. Settlers were required to build a home, reside on the lot for three years and clear ten acres of land before they would be given clear title to the grant. By the end of the First World War, however, the New Brunswick Labor Act was more effective in fostering a low-level competition between settlers and leaseholders for control of forest resources than in its intended promotion of agricultural development. Conflict was inherent in the structure of the programme. The provincial government extracted the 100-acre settlement lots from the Crown leases of lumber operators; in turn, the operators were permitted to continue cutting on the lots for one year after they were removed from the licence. The struggles emanating from these conditions were carried on through patron-client political networks and within the administrative apparatus of the state. To combat the pressure that leaseholders exerted on the government to prevent the extension of settlement, applicants for the Labor Act frequently relied on the influence of local politicians to gain approval. Once settlers gained access to the land, the competition for wood began, with each side employing various tactics. As the agency responsible for administering the Labor Act, the Department of Lands and Mines struggled with its own lack of resources, constant criticism from both operators and settlers and its relationship to the evolving political system. After the First World War, the department began making a transition from being a patronage tool of the ruling party to becoming a modern bureaucratic state agency. Although concerted efforts at bureaucratic rationalization of Labor Act settlement were made within the department during the 1920s, they were regularly subordinated to the exigencies of patronage.

An examination of Labor Act settlement illuminates the contradictory pressures of state administration of natural resources. Stewardship of public

---

farming and forestry. Until shown by Graeme Wynn to be a necessary part of successful small-scale farming, historians had long viewed the relationship between lumbering and farming as a barrier to agricultural development in pre-Confederation New Brunswick. In part, Wynn argues, this was a result of historians accepting the moral and religious arguments of middle-class promoters of agriculture. See W.F. Ganong, "A Monograph of the Origins of Settlement in New Brunswick", *Transactions of the Royal Society of Canada* 10 (1904); James Hannay, *History of the Province of New Brunswick* (Saint John, 1909); Lower, *Settlement and the Forest Frontier*; Michael Cross, "The Dark Druidical Groves: The Lumber Community and the Commercial Frontier in British North America", Ph.D. thesis, University of Toronto, 1968; Graeme Wynn, *Timber Colony: A Historical Geography of Nineteenth Century New Brunswick* (Toronto, 1981); "Deplorably Dark and Demoralized Lumberers?: Rhetoric and Reality in Early Nineteenth Century New Brunswick", *Journal of Forest History*, 24 (October 1980), pp. 168-87.

lands endowed the provincial state with the responsibility of deciding who controlled particular resources and, subsequently, of legitimizing and enforcing the divisions that were made. The Crown lands of the province were still very much contested terrain in the 1920s, over which classes of producers and entrepreneurs competed on a number of levels. During the decade, thousands of square miles of Crown land were transferred, with the assistance of the government, from the fledgling lumber industry to the pulp and paper industry; it was a process that not only stimulated a second industrial revolution in the New Brunswick forest industries, but also transformed, at the policy-making level, the relationship between forest capital and the provincial state.[3] Beneath the high-level structural changes of the 1920s, however, were a large set of localized competitions for water, forest, mineral, fish and game resources that continued to unfold as they had for decades. Because it provided a window of opportunity for rural workers to take hold of land from reluctant leaseholders, the Labor Act defied any clear long-term divisions of resources. As a result, the administration of Labor Act settlement involved a considerable degree of conflict management, as the Department of Lands and Mines sought to mediate the many ongoing, localized contests for control of forest resources.[4] Administration was elaborated more through the balance of class forces in specific localities than by a consistent enforcement of statute regulations.

Examination of the Labor Act also demonstrates the extent to which rural class relations could be carried on through clientelist political networks. Patron-

---

3   Bill Parenteau, "The Woods Transformed: The Emergence of the Pulp and Paper Industry in New Brunswick, 1918-1931", *Acadiensis*, XXII, 1 (Autumn 1992), pp. 5-43.

4   A distinction is made in this essay between the *political* apparatus and the *administrative* apparatus of the state. The argument here is that in the modern bureaucratic state the political apparatus (government) enacts laws/regulations, and they are carried out by the administrative apparatus (civil service) employing a set of rules that prevent elected government officials from intervening in the process for their own personal political gain. In the clientelist state, characteristic of Canada in the 19th century, such a separation was much less distinct, as elected officials routinely dispensed jobs and public services and resources to their own advantage. With the introduction of civil service reform and the appointment of a joint government-industry board to oversee its application at the end of the First World War, the New Brunswick Department of Lands and Mines began to make the transition from being a tool of the ruling party to becoming a modern bureaucratic state agency. Although the dispensing of jobs and settlement lots as patronage by politicians continued in the 1920s, these small initial steps toward administrative autonomy had an effect on Labor Act settlement. On the separation of the state into its constituent parts see Ralph Miliband, *The State in Capitalist Society* (London, 1969). On the transition see Reg Whitaker, "From Patronage to Bureaucracy: Democratic Politics in Transition", *Journal of Canadian Studies*, 22, 2 (Summer 1987), pp. 55-71.

client political and economic relationships have been generally regarded by scholars as a barrier to class consciousness, action and organization.[5] Settlers represented a specific class of non-landholders, as defined by the regulations of the Labor Act, and pursued class interests both in the application for lots and in the struggle for forest resources. They were opposed in all their efforts by a specific class of entrepreneurs — Crown land leaseholders. Yet, petty politics in the communities surrounding the Crown land also played an important part in the struggle between leaseholders and settlers. The records of Labor Act administration thus provide a look beyond class organizations to the often hidden texture of rural class politics. It is at the level of community and administrative politics that a clearer picture emerges of how working people in rural New Brunswick conceptualized the political process and used it, albeit in limited ways, to their best advantage.

Settlement and Progressive Reform

The New Brunswick Labor Act was codified in 1869 and survived without formal revision into the 1920s.[6] Any male over the age of 18 years who did not own land in New Brunswick was entitled to apply for 100 acres of Crown land under the act. Upon approval of his application by the Department of Lands and Mines, a lot was drawn out of the timber lease of one of the lumber operators in the province, more often than not in an area designated for settlement. As the Labor Act was intended specifically to promote the development of agriculture, there were guidelines that settlers were required to follow in eventually gaining title to the land. Primary among these were residence on a lot for three consecutive years for at least seven months per year; the erection of a house at least 16 by 20 feet in dimension; and the cultivation of not fewer than ten acres of cleared land. To facilitate farming over forest exploitation, the regulations of the Labor Act allowed settlers to sell only the lumber cut during the process of

---

5   The argument presented in this essay is that while the predominance of clientelism in New Brunswick may have contributed to the underdevelopment of class-based parties, there is a need to look beyond formal organizations in considering class politics. On the influence of clientelism on class action in the province see R.A. Young, "'and the people will sink into despair': Reconstruction in New Brunswick, 1942-52", *Canadian Historical Review*, LXIX, 2 (1988), pp. 127-66. On the responsiveness of the political system in New Brunswick to demands from the producing classes see Allen Seager, "Minto, New Brunswick: A Case Study in Class Relations Between the Wars", *Labour/Le Travailleur*, 5 (Spring 1980), p. 85.

6   The essential elements of the Labour Act were instituted by order-in-council in 1849, but it was not until the later date that it became a legislative act. See P.Z. Caverhill, "Forest Policy in New Brunswick", M.Sc. thesis, University of New Brunswick, 1917, pp. 13-16.

clearing and specifically prohibited cutting outside the ten acres designated for homesteading. The lumber operator from whose lease the lot was drawn was given proprietary rights over all merchantable wood outside the ten acres on which the settler was making a farm for a period of one year after approval was advertised in the *Royal Gazette*.[7]

The survival of the act in its original form was in no way a reflection of satisfaction with its results. As early as 1873, the Surveyor General was condemning the new settlement policy. "Our Labor and Free Grant Acts have proved very largely failures", he claimed in the annual report of the Crown Land Department. "Not only have they to a great extent failed to obtain the end which they were expected to fulfil, but they have frequently been made use of by private individuals for the purpose of obtaining timber land".[8] By the turn of the century, the pattern of failed or bogus settlement had become institutionalized and was causing considerable trouble for the Crown Land Department.[9] Prospective settlers continued to pass over cleared land that had been judged suitable for agriculture, seeking instead well-timbered lots. Once on the land they proceeded to cut at will, with little regard for regulations. Premier and Minister of Lands and Mines George Clarke summed up the cumulative record of settlement in 1915 when he remarked, "I have to repeat what has been said before regarding lands applied for under the Labor Act, and the difficulties in disposing of these applications. I do not think I am far from wrong in stating that not more than one in ten of the applicants succeed in carrying out the terms of the Act".[10] More succinctly, a government forester remarked of the New Brunswick settler: "At heart he is not a farmer but a lumberman".[11]

---

7   "Instructions to Applicants Applying for Crown Lands Under the Labor Act", 1922, in Deputy Ministers Office Records, New Brunswick Department of Lands and Mines [DMOR], RS 106, box 50, Provincial Archives of New Brunswick [PANB].

8   Cited in Raymond Léger, "L'industrie du bois dans la Péninsule acadienne, 1875-1900", *Revue d'histoire de la Société historique Nicolas-Denys*, XVI, 2 (mai-aout 1988), p. 51. The Free Grant Act was passed in 1872 and was quite similar to the Labor Act. It appears to have fallen from use shortly after it was enacted. See Caverhill, "Forest Policy", p. 16.

9   Caverhill, "Forest Policy", pp. 18-20. The correspondence of C.E. Fish, scaling inspector for the Newcastle district, contains numerous interdepartmental letters concerning settlement problems in the first decade of the 20th century. See, for example, W.E. Flewelling, Deputy Surveyor General, to Fish, 11 July 1904, 1 December 1904, 1 February 1905, 27 November 1906, William Fish Collection, MC 156, MS 1, PANB.

10   *Annual Report of the Crown Land Department* (1915), p. xiv.

11   Caverhill, "Forest Policy", p. 18.

In recognition of the failure of the Labor Act, the provincial government initiated new measures to promote agricultural settlement. In 1907, the government bought back 50,000 acres of land that had been granted to the New Brunswick Railway Company in the 1870s. The so-called Blue Bell Tract, located between Plaster Rock and Grand Falls on the Transcontinental Railway in Victoria County, was purchased with the intention of making it the primary focus of settlement. With soil considered excellent for agriculture and easy access to transportation routes, the Department of Lands and Mines, hoping to attract a better class of settlers, promoted the Tract as the finest opportunity for settlement in the province. With the notable exception that applicants were required to pay $1 per acre in four instalments, the regulations of the Blue Bell Tract were the same as for Labor Act settlement.[12] In theory this meant drawing men with some means, who were sincere and had experience in farming; in practice it meant giving preference to settlers from outside the province and anglophone New Brunswickers.

Other attempts were made by the provincial government to enhance agricultural settlement. The most serious of these was the Farm Settlement Board, established in 1912. The three-member board was empowered to purchase, improve and resell real estate in the province that was suitable for farming. The purchase price, which could exceed $1,000, made it necessary that those who settled under this scheme possessed capital and were interested mainly in farming.[13] In 1917, the province passed the Soldier Settlement Act for returning war veterans. More closely regulated than the Labor Act, it provided direct loans to buy stock and equipment and clearly spelled out the procedure for applicants who defaulted on their commitments.[14] Efforts also continued to attract settlers

12 Details on the original land transaction and subsequent purchase of the Blue Tract can be found in "Memo re: New Brunswick Railway Company Lands", [n.d., ca. 1943], Papers of Premier A.A. Dysart, RS 414, file 1.64, PANB; "Schedule Showing Acts of the Legislature of New Brunswick and the Parliament of Canada Relating to the New Brunswick Railway Company". For the regulations of the Blue Bell Tract see G.H. Prince to G.W. Anderson, 7 August 1925, DMOR, box 57, PANB.

13 For the regulations of the Farm Settlement Board see H.P. Webb, "The Development of Forest Law in New Brunswick", M.Sc. thesis, University of New Brunswick, 1923, pp. 156-63. The Farm Settlement Board seems to have had a fairly successful record. By the end of 1922 they had bought and resold more than 400 farms, and 158 of the buyers had already paid off their mortgages in full. See *Annual Report of the Department of Agriculture of New Brunswick, 1922* (Fredericton, 1923), pp. 169-72.

14 Webb, "Forest Law", pp. 263-78. For a discussion of the wider context of soldier settlement in Canada see Desmond Morton and Glenn Wright, *Winning the Second Battle: Canadian Veterans and the Return to Civilian Life, 1915-1930* (Toronto, 1987), pp. 130-49.

from outside Canada. The province participated in federal Empire Settlement schemes and disseminated promotional literature in Great Britain and the United States.[15] Each of these programmes was burdened with its own problems; together they pointed to the continuing commitment of the New Brunswick government to agricultural settlement, and situated the Labor Act as the lowest rung on the settlement ladder.

The general failure of Labor Act settlement was the function of a number of factors related to the resource base, administrative deficiencies and the applicants themselves. By 1900, blocks of Crown land containing soil conditions suitable for agriculture were in short supply. The soil problem was compounded by the absence of any adequate land use classification system to distinguish agricultural from forest lands. When settlers applied for Crown land, the government typically relied on the opinion of a local field agent as to the suitability of the lot. But settlers' considerations were seldom focused on agricultural potential. The determining factors for choosing a particular lot were more often the distance from an established population centre, proximity to kin or friends and, of course, the amount of merchantable wood on the lot.[16]

The lack of soil classification was symptomatic of the administrative deficiencies of the Labor Act programme. For the many inexperienced settlers who moved onto the Crown land, the lack of technical advice made carving out a farm even more difficult.[17] The Labor Act allowed some financial assistance, but the little money spent during the pre-war period was usually earmarked for road construction on the Blue Bell Tract, where the government had made an in-

---

15 Ministers in the Department of Lands and Mines and the Department of Agriculture were enthusiastic about the prospect for settlers from outside of the province after the war. They had representatives to promote immigration in England and occasionally sent men to Boston to interview interested parties. See *Annual Report of the Department of Agriculture* (1908), pp. 157-9. For examples of the promotional literature disseminated in Great Britain and the United States see Canada, Department of Immigration and Colonization, *British Family Settlement in New Brunswick* (Ottawa, 1929); Rev. James Crisp, *Farming as an Occupation: New Brunswick as a Province in Which to Make a Home* (Saint John, 1911); "Homesteading in the Maritime Provinces", *Adventure*, 15 January 1927. For accounts of British settlers who were less than happy with the conditions they found after arrival see William Guy Carr, *High and Dry* (London, 1938); Allistair Cameron, *Aberdeen it Was Not* (Woodstock, 1982).

16 The importance of factors such as proximity to population centres and family were well recognized as a factor in the classification of lands by P.Z. Caverhill, Director of the Forest Survey. See "Classification of the Crown Lands of New Brunswick", in *8th Annual Report of the Commission of Conservation* (1917), pp. 81-91.

17 *Annual Report of the New Brunswick Crown Land Department* (1916), p. 105.

vestment in 1907. Other Labor Act settlers were required to build their own roads in addition to their other considerable responsibilities in meeting the requirements of the act.[18] By the 1920s, the failure of Labor Act settlement had become something of a vicious circle: the legislature was reluctant to put money into a settlement programme with an unsatisfactory record, while the lack of technical and financial aid, in turn, contributed to the programme's continuing failure. Lacking technical and financial assistance, the building of even a subsistence-level farm was beyond the reach of most applicants.

Applicants for land under the Labor Act came overwhelmingly from the rural working class of northern New Brunswick, a condition that was largely determined by the exclusion of landholders and by the better opportunities for aspiring farmers with capital. Coming from the marginal mixed farming areas and the small towns surrounding the Crown lands, most toiled in the lowest occupational level of what historians of Quebec and francophone New Brunswick have called "l'économie agro-forestière".[19] For the rural labourer in the northern half of the province, work was strictly seasonal, alternating between the farm, forest, river drive and sawmill, or occasionally including stints in quarrying, fishing, shipping and construction.[20] Remuneration for common labourers in these industries provided for subsistence at best. Few settlers began with sufficient capital to buy necessary stock and equipment or to carry themselves while establishing a homestead. Labor Act settlement was the domain of the working

18   The legislation allocated $5,000 for aid to settlers; however, expenditures never reached this level before the end of the First World War. Expenditures from 1900 to 1917 are tabled in *Report of the Auditor General on the Public Accounts of the Province of New Brunswick* (1917), p. A19. As well as fulfilling the land-clearing and building requirements, Labour Act applicants were also required to undertake $30 worth of road work or pay $20. There is no indication that the Department of Lands and Mines ever strictly enforced this aspect of the programme, but neither did they provide any assistance in building roads. See Webb, "Development of Forest Law", pp. 251-3.

19   Normand Séguin, *La conquête du sol au 19e siècle: Le cas d'Herbertville* (Montréal, 1977); "L'économie agro-forestière: genèse du développement au Saguenay au XIXe siècle", *Revue d'histoire de l'Amerique française*, 29, 4 (mars 1976), pp. 559-69; Hardy et Séguin, *Forêt et société en Mauricie*; Léger, "L'industrie du bois".

20   See Léger, "L'industrie du bois", pp. 65-79; Patrick H. Burden, "The New Brunswick Farmer-Labour Union, 1937-1941", M.A. thesis, University of New Brunswick, 1983. There is very little published material on the thousands of casual labourers in northern New Brunswick, at least 20,000 of whom worked in the forest. The camp correspondence of the George Burchill and Sons lumber camps are a valuable source for understanding the pattern of labour movement between the mill, farm, docks and woods in the early decades of the 20th century. See George Burchill and Sons Papers, MC 1246, MBU II, PANB.

poor; it involved placing people with little capital and often no farming experience on land with marginal agricultural potential.

Underlying the many failings of Labor Act settlement was the fact that few applicants were committed to building a farm enterprise. Within the Crown Land Department it was simply assumed that most applicants were after a chance to cut wood. T.G. Loggie, who observed settlement from inside the department for more than 50 years, remarked that the principal aim of administration was "to guard the Department against fraudulent applications under the guise of settlement". Loggie understood well that a settler's intention was "to secure a lot sufficiently timbered so as to allow the settler something at the start he can turn into money....The greater number of those applying have no other motive than to cut off the timber and then allow their applications to lapse".[21] New Brunswick applicants were generally well aware of the cumulative record of settlement in their localities and the relative potential for agricultural and forest exploitation.[22] They knew the potential for a viable farm was exceeded by the opportunity to gain access to forest resources and, perhaps, to raise themselves from the level of wage labour to become an independent producer.

The decade after the First World War was decisive in the life and administration of the Labor Act. Labor Act approvals had been fairly constant in the first decades of the 20th century but fell dramatically in the 1920s (see Table One). A number of factors contributed to the progressively strict allotment of settlement lots. The most important were the generally poor prices paid for primary forest products during the decade and the modernization of the administrative apparatus of the state.

The general understanding of critics regarding New Brunswick Crown land settlement was that there was a relationship between the market for forest products and interest in applying for the Labor Act. Lumber operators, at least, often found it "a remarkable coincidence that these people wish to homestead when logs are in good demand, but have no desire to homestead when they are not wanted".[23] It was an opinion shared by Minister of Lands and Mines E.A. Smith. In 1917, with the price of wood high, Smith commented on increased cutting as "far beyond anything ever experienced before in this province", and noted its correlation with trespassing and settlement:

---

21 *Proceedings of the New Brunswick Forestry Convention* (1907), p. 51.

22 Irène Landry came to a similar conclusion in her study of the St. Quentin settlement in Madawaska. See her "Saint Quentin et la retour à la terre: analyse socio-économique, 1910-1960", *Revue de la Société Historique du Madawaska*, XIV, 4 (octobre-decembre, 1986), p. 22.

23 J. Leonard O'Brien to G.H. Prince, 26 March 1923, DMOR, box 34, PANB.

One of the hard problems I found taking over the administration of the affairs of this office was to know how to deal fairly with the settler on Crown Land in disposing of the pulpwood he cuts in making his clearing. If it were a matter of dealing with bona-fide settlers, then the problem would be a simple one, but where the records of the Department show that a very large proportion do not fulfil the requirements of the Settling Act, it will be seen at once the question of dealing out justice is approached with great difficulty.[24]

The number of Labor Act approvals began to drop at the end of 1921 when the post-war recession devastated the New Brunswick lumber trade and ended two decades of expansion in the pulpwood market. Pulpwood exporters dropped the price paid to farmers in York County, for example, from $20 per cord in 1919 to $9 by the end of 1921. In some sections of the province, the demand for pulpwood had been temporarily eliminated.[25] The relatively lower number of Labor Act approvals for the remainder of the decade coincided with an incomplete recovery from the recession of the early 1920s, as the provincial forest industries made a slow and uneven transition from lumber to pulp and paper manufacturing. Throughout the 1920s, the export market for pulpwood continued to suffer from a crisis of overproduction in the North American newsprint industry.[26]

While market forces may have influenced the demand for settlement lots, the decline in Labor Act approvals was more a product of the milieu of progressive reform in the adminstration of Crown lands. In 1918, the province passed the Forest Act and the Forest Fires Act. Touted as the most "progressive and far-sighted" legislation of its kind in Canada, the legislation mirrored the prevailing agenda of conservation organizations in Canada, particularly the Canadian Forestry Association and the federal government's Commission of Conservation.[27] The two acts included a number of conservation measures (such as larger commitments to the classification of Crown land and forest fire prevention), civil service reform to separate the administration of the forest from patronage

24 *Annual Report of the Crown Land Department* (1917), p. 12; on the rise in prices for pulpwood being a stimulus for Crown land settlement in Ontario and Quebec see Sir Clifford Sifton, "Conservation in 1917", in 9th Annual Report of the Commission of Conservation (1918), pp. 1-9.

25 On the decline of the export market for pulpwood see Dominion Forest Service, Transcripts of the Hearings of the Royal Commission on Pulpwood, RG 39, vol. 593, nos. 4, 5, 10, National Archives of Canada [NAC].

26 On the contours of the markets for forest products and the transition from lumber to pulp and paper in the 1920s see Parenteau, "The Woods Transformed".

27 "Committee on Forests of the Commission of Conservation", in *Annual Report of the Crown Land Department* (1919), p. 19.

Table One
Labor Act Approvals, 1899-1929

Decade	Average Number of Approvals
1899-08	320
1909-18	288
1919-29	186

Year	Average Number of Approvals
1919	337
1920	269
1921	293
1922	217
1923	114
1924	148
1925	154
1926	125
1927	115
1928	161
1929	124

Source: Compiled from the *Royal Gazette*, 1899-1929.

politics, and the establishment of the Forest Advisory Commission.[28] Each of these three pillars of progressive reform addressed, in some respect, the problems that conservation-minded foresters and lumber operators saw in Crown land settlement and added to the momentum that had been building against the Labor Act for two decades.

The classification of Crown lands posed a threat to the existing pattern of Labor Act settlement, as one of its primary objectives was to separate the farmer from the forest. With the passage of the Forest Act, the New Brunswick government made a substantial financial commitment to a topographical survey of Crown lands, a programme that had begun in earnest three years earlier.[29] The delineation of agriculture and forest land, conservationists argued, would lead to a more efficient use of resources and reduce forest fires. As New Brunswick

28 *Annual Report of the Crown Land Department* (1918), pp. 8-12, 161-70.

29 Forest classification had been discussed as a measure to control settlement since the turn of the century and was included in the Public Domain Act of 1906. It was delayed by a lack of government finances. See *Annual Report of the Crown Land Department* (1907), p. xx.

Director of the Forest Survey P.Z. Caverhill suggested, revealing the explicit anti-settlement rational of forest classification, "one of the most important features of the survey is...to prevent the denuding of purely timber land under the guise of clearing for agricultural purposes".[30] During the years 1918-21, hundreds of square miles of Crown land were surveyed and classified; however, financial constraints created by the lumber market crash prematurely ended the survey in 1922 after only 40 per cent of the Crown land was classified.[31] While the survey did isolate some likely areas for the opening of new settlement, it had less impact on altering the pattern of settlement than its optimistic promoters envisioned.

Further scrutiny was imposed on Crown land settlement by the development of a modern forest fire protection system. Fire protection emerged as the preeminent conservation issue in Canada after 1900, but was retarded in New Brunswick by financial constraints.[32] When the Forest Fires Act was constructed, its architects were mindful of the prevailing wisdom that the burning of slash from settler land-clearing operations was a primary cause of forest fires. It was an old lumbermen's adage that was embraced by conservationists as an article of faith.[33] The new act set up a permit system that prohibited settlers from burning slash during dry periods and without the supervision of a forest ranger. Its overall impact was to heighten government supervision by sending forest rangers to settlements at more regular intervals and during times of the year when they might otherwise not visit.[34]

---

30 P.Z. Caverhill, Director of Forest Survey, Department of Lands and Mines, New Brunswick, "Classification of Crown Lands in New Brunswick", in *Annual Report of the Commission of Conservation* (1917), p. 84.

31 *Annual Report of the Crown Land Department* (1923), p. xv. The survey was not resumed until the 1940s.

32 As of 1917, the New Brunswick Minister of Crown Lands lamented, the provincial fire service "was more a name than a reality": *Annual Report of the Crown Lands Department* (1917), p. 14.

33 In each of the annual reports of the Committee of Conservation, 1910-21, there was some discussion of the settler as a fire hazard; settlement fires could be numerous, but they were usually small and of short duration. See, for example, the tables in *Annual Report of the Crown Land Department* (1921), p. 78; *Annual Report of the Crown Land Department* (1922), p. 68.

34 On the original inattention to the fire law by settlers see *Annual Report of the Crown Land Department* (1919), p. 88; on the continuing problem of settler slash burning fires see the table on comparative statistics for 1920-25 in *Annual Report of the Department of Lands and Mines* (1925), p. 54. The act also created a new hazard: the intentional lighting of forest fires for employment, especially in the early 1920s when the forest industries went into a recession; the conse-

The appointment of the Forest Advisory Commission also gave lumber operators an opportunity to resist the extension of settlement. Composed of government foresters, industry executives and interested politicians, the advisory commission reflected a particular strain of progressivism that placed great faith in the ability of capital and the state to plan scientifically for the use of resources.[35] Although New Brunswick operators had always exerted a firm hand in shaping forest policy, the Forest Advisory Commission gave some of the most prominent forest industry executives a forum in which to promote their interests with a veneer of rational objectivity and to build a consensus with the ascendent university-trained foresters, with whom they were sometimes at odds.[36]

One of the commission's primary functions was to institute and administer civil service reform in the Department of Lands and Mines. Progressive reformers believed the creation of a non-partisan bureaucracy would lead to more efficient and democratic government. The so-called "patronage evil" played an important role in all facets of Crown land settlement.[37] In theory, the development of a modern civil service would prevent local politicians from pressuring the Department of Lands and Mines into approving unworthy Labor

quent drop in woods jobs prompted some people in the settlement areas to light fires, in order to take advantage of the additional money that had become available under the new act. See Transcript of Dominion-Provincial Forest Fire Conference, 1924, RG 39, Records of the Dominion Forest Service, vol. 597, pp. 45-8, NAC; for New Brunswick see Minutes of the Meeting of the Forest Advisory Board, 13 February 1922, RS 106, DMOR, box 35, PANB; Testimony of G.H. Prince and T.G. Loggie in Transcripts of the Hearings of the Royal Commission on Pulpwood, Fredericton, RG 39, vol. 593, no. 4, pp. 255-7 (Loggie), pp. 278-81 (Prince), NAC.

35 Joint government and industry policy-making commissions were one of the organizational manifestations of this emerging ideology. On this particular aspect of progressive ideology see Robert H. Wiebe, *The Search for Order, 1877-1920* (New York, 1967); James Weinstein, *The Corporate Ideal in the Liberal State, 1900-1918* (Boston, 1969); and Samuel Haber, *Efficiency and Uplift: Scientific Management and the Progressive Era, 1890-1920* (Chicago, 1964).

36 See "Minutes of the Meeting of the Forest Advisory Commission", 13 February 1922, RS 106, DMOR, box 35, PANB. Only sporadic records remain of the meetings of the commission, but they do show that the industry representativeswere adamant in attacking Crown land settlement on the basis of it being a fire hazard. The Liberal-created commission ceased to function shortly after the Conservatives took power in 1925.

37 The phrase "patronage evil" is taken from the Annual Reports of the Commission of Conservation. In each report the commission devoted attention to pointing out which provinces had instituted civil service reform and where it was urgently needed. See, for example, *Ninth Annual Report of the Commission of Conservation* (1918), pp. 162-4.

Act applications. In the 1920s, however, the aspirations of those who would modernize the bureaucracy were not shared by a large number of New Brunswick politicians. Civil service reform did have an effect in reducing Labor Act settlement, but neither field agents nor the ministers in the Department of Lands and Mines were entirely free to exercise their best judgement. In the last instance, county patronage committees and provincial politicians retained the power to dispense with department employees who were perceived to have jeopardized their best interests.

While neither the Forest Act nor the Forest Fires Act was ever fully implemented, the push for reform nurtured the development of a bureaucratic ethic within the Department of Lands and Mines that worked to reducing Labor Act settlement. The person responsible for guiding the progress toward bureaucratic administration was Gilbert H. Prince. As an ardent conservationist, an active member of the growing professional forestry associations in Canada and a strong proponent of civil service reform, Prince was the consummate new-breed forester and would influence forest policy in New Brunswick for the next three decades.[38] He personally wrote the Forest Fires Act, parts of the Forest Act and the "Manual of General Instructions to Forest Rangers". In 1923 Prince replaced the aged T.G. Loggie as Deputy Minister of Lands and Mines.[39]

Prince raised the bureaucratic ethic to the status of a holy mission in his "Manual of General Instructions to Forest Rangers". The forest service was a calling, Prince believed, that required men of "Integrity", "Loyalty", "Humanity" and "Idealism", who were willing to work toward a "Great Ideal". His paean to "Loyalty", in particular, both reflected his progressive missionary zeal and suggested the professional standards that as deputy minister he would demand of the men in the field: "Loyalty is the spirit which puts the organization and its ideals above the man, that recognizes the absolute need of co-operation and discipline, but will not hesitate to incur disfavor if clearly necessary for the good of the Service. It is the chief method of building up an organization and this is a fact that is recognized by all progressive leaders".[40] Less

---

38 On the attitudes of G.H. Prince toward civil service reform, conservation, professionalization of foresters, and fire protection, see "Transcript of the Dominion-Provincial Forest Fire Conference", 7-11 January 1924, pp. 38-48, 198-204, 315-320, RG 39, Records of the Dominion Forest Service, vol. 597, NAC; "Testimony at the Royal Commission on Pulpwood", Fredericton, 20 October 1923, pp. 261-94, RG 39, vol. 593, no. 4, NAC; H.A. Innis Papers, b72-0003, no. 6, "Notes on the Maritime Lumber Industry", pp. 82-85, University of Toronto Archives [UTA].

39 G.H. Prince, "The Forest Service in Relation to Forest Fire Protection", M.Sc. thesis, University of New Brunswick, 1919. The thesis contains an appendix entitled "Manual of General Instructions to Forest Rangers of the New Brunswick Forest Service". Prince was initially appointed Acting Deputy Minister, and the appointment was made permanent in 1924.

40 Prince, "The Forest Service", pp. 49, 55, 56.

desirable character traits defined by Prince included "Indifference" and "Dishonesty", which were, along with the cardinal sin of the forest ranger's creed, "involvement in politics", grounds for suspension or dismissal.[41] By invoking discipline and instilling a sense of professionalism in the ranks, Prince endeavoured, for the duration of his tenure as deputy minister, to bridge the sometimes wide gulf between the statute Crown land regulations and the realities of their implementation in the New Brunswick forest.

The ascension of Gilbert Prince to Deputy Minister of Lands and Mines did not bode well for prospective Crown land settlers. While not categorically opposed to settlement, Prince sought reforms that would make it less contentious and more consistent with the stated intentions of the act. His response to a field agent who accused him of favouring the interests of lumber operators over settlers was instructive in this regard. "I think you are unjustified in stating that the Department is determined to cut and clear lots before settlers go in", he told John Ashworth. "Personally, I have no such desire, but I am much interested in developing such changes as will eliminate the constant strife between the licensee and settlers, as it is apparent that the present system is not encouraging settlement".[42] Nevertheless, from the standpoint of rational use of forest resources, fire protection and the relationship of politics to the administration of the forest, the pattern of Labor Act settlement that existed at the end of the war was antithetical to the deputy minister's progressive philosophy. Prince was more closely aligned with the ideas of New Brunswick lumber operators, which was not coincidental given the central role that the Canadian forest industries played in constructing the conservation reform agenda he so wholeheartedly embraced.[43]

---

41 Prince, "The Forest Service", p. 67.

42 Prince to John Ashworth, 7 February 1927, DMOR, box 57, PANB.

43 Part of the emerging professional revolution of foresters and forest engineers consisted of an effort to create an autonomous administrative niche in which they could expand their power by practising "scientific forestry". In this respect, professionalization was an effort to separate the practice of forestry from the immediate needs of forest capital. However, through agencies such as the Canadian Forestry Association and the Commission on Conservation, forest capital played a vital role in shaping both the ideology of professional forestry and the administrative structures in which the new-breed, university-educated foresters practised their science. G.H. Prince certainly upheld the principles of his profession to the best of his ability, but it was very much within an ideological framework designed by forest capital. The classic statement on the conservation movement in North America is Samuel P. Hays, *Conservation and the Gospel of Efficiency: The Progressive Conservation Movement, 1890-1920* (Cambridge, 1959). On the Canadian conservation movement see Gillis and Roach, *Lost Initiatives*. On the essentially business-driven conservative nature of progressive reform see Gabriel Kolko, *The Triumph of Conservatism: A Reinterpretation of*

Not long after assuming his post, Prince started to initiate policy changes for Labor Act settlement. In January 1926, he began soliciting information and suggestions from New Brunswick Crown land leaseholders and ministers in the Quebec and Ontario forest bureaucracies. The consultations resulted in the appointment of a "special inspector" in 1927, whose responsibility was to ensure that applicants were fulfilling the requirements of the Labor Act and, particularly, that they were not cutting wood outside the ten acres designated for building a homestead.[44] In 1928, the Department of Lands and Mines attempted to relieve direct conflict between settlers and operators by prohibiting operators from cutting wood inside the ten acres in which settlement was to take place.[45] However, these initiatives did not significantly alter either the widespread indifference toward regulations or the conflict between the two competing parties. The only real change to Labor Act settlement in the 1920s was that fewer approvals were issued, a consequence of the progressive administrative efforts of G.H. Prince and, perhaps, the condition of wood product markets, rather than any change in regulations.

Patrons, Clients and Approval

From the inception of these progressive reforms, the Department of Lands and Mines felt the weight of the countervailing pressures for and against settlement. "We very often find this a perplexing and difficult matter to administer", lamented Deputy Minister T.G. Loggie in 1921, "and I might say very unpopular for the person handling it, as he must give offence, no matter how he acts, to one or the other parties interested".[46] Application for a Labor Act lot usually began with a letter to the Department of Lands and Mines or by contacting a field agent. All applicants were required to take an oath before a designated authority that they were 18 years of age, that they did not own land

American History, 1900-1916 (London, 1963). On the co-opting of the engineering sciences by capital see David F. Noble, *America by Design: Science, Technology and the Rise of Corporate Capitalism* (New York, 1977).

44   G.H. Prince to W.E. Anderson, Secretary, New Brunswick Lumbermen's Association, 18 January 1926; Anderson to Prince, 19 January 1926, DMOR, box 25, PANB; Prince to W.C. Cain, Deputy Minister of Lands and Forests, Ontario, 13 February 1926, DMOR, box 51, PANB; Prince to L.A. Richard, Deputy Minister of Colonization, Mines and Fisheries, Quebec, 28 January 1926, 27 January 1926, 11 April 1927; Richard to Prince, 6 April 1927. On the appointment of T.A. MacDonald as inspector of settlement lots see *Annual Report of the Department of Lands and Mines, 1928.*

45   Prince to Fraser Companies Ltd., 10 June 1929, DMOR, box 60, PANB.

46   T.G. Loggie to J.L. O'Brien, 18 February 1921, DMOR, box 34, PANB.

in New Brunswick, that they were interested in the lot for the express purpose of farming and that they had not previously taken out a settlement lot.[47] The remainder of the application was filled out by a local agent of the Crown in charge of the particular settlement or district where the land was located. His duty was to assess the suitability of the land for agriculture and, more important, the sincerity of the applicant and his fitness to fulfil the regulations of the Labor Act. Barring political intervention, the deputy minister usually adhered to the recommendations of the field agents.[48] The autonomy given to field agents was a necessity, but it also meant that the rank and file of the department held a pivotal position in the application process. Quite naturally, this subjected the process to a host of individual opinions, personal relationships, political considerations and community pressures.

To counteract local influences, the ministers attempted to limit the number of men from whom they would accept recommendations. The printed instructions given to applicants specified that Labor Act commissioners were authorized to take oaths from settlers and make recommendations, but in the 1920s few of the more than one hundred commissioners were given this power. Labor Act commissioners were petty patronage appointees of the same type as marriage and game licence vendors.[49] The post of Labor Act commissioner was a strictly part-time position, paid by commission, and not very remunerative unless the holder of the post was conveniently located or able to have a large number of applications approved. Not surprisingly, many Labor Act commissioners were unabashed promoters of settlement and would recommend applications indiscriminately. When Octave King, scaling inspector for Madawaska County, reassured G.H. Prince that "Joe Bourgoine is Labor Act Commissioner [St. Anne] and all his doings are inspected so he can't do much harm if he wanted to", he voiced a prevailing opinion in the higher levels of the department that Labor Act commissioners should be closely monitored and hold few powers.[50] Although it was not always possible, the ministers preferred to have a trusted, salaried employee of the Department who better understood the departmental imperative of maintaining the appearance of detached objectivity, make the recommendations directly or "approve" the application filled out by a Labor Act commissioner. In the areas where applicants were most numerous, a settlement

---

47   "Instructions to Applicants Applying for Crown Land Under the Labor Act", 1922, DMOR, box 50, PANB.

48   G.H. Prince often made this point to field agents; see, for example, Prince to W.R. Davidson, 6 December 1927, DMOR, box 58, PANB.

49   The Labor Act commissioners were almost all replaced after the 1925 election. See RS 9, Records of the New Brunswick Executive Council, August-October 1925, PANB.

50   Octave King to Prince, 25 December 1924, DMOR, box 51, PANB.

"caretaker" could fulfil this role, although most often it was the responsibility of the local forest ranger.

Few senior field agents seemed to have any illusions about the potential for Labor Act settlement, but personal opinions were balanced by an understanding of the countervailing forces surrounding the programme. When asked for their opinions, scalers and forest rangers often returned sceptical comments. In 1926, for instance, Octave King determined that "out of twenty-five applications I don't believe that there is [sic] really two honest to goodness settlers".[51] It was not uncommon for the ministers — whether on their own initiative or at the behest of leaseholders — to ask field agents to investigate an applicant by making inquiries in the community where he lived. The assessments could be quite candid. In 1926, for example, C.V. Pickard reported, "I have made inquiries from good reliable parties, all he wants is to start in and clear some of the wood he could get and leave".[52] More often they were written with an unenthusiastic ambiguity that reflected the pessimistic but resigned attitude of many in the department toward the Labor Act. "These lots are rather favourably situated for settlement", remarked Ranger Michael Fletcher, "that is if the applicants are really sincere... I was talking to a couple of them and they talk as if they are sincere and will settle on the land, but I cannot vouch for them".[53] Some field agents may have promoted settlement in a less overt manner than Labor Act commissioners, or rejected applications with a quiet consistency. But operating in an atmosphere where their actions were closely scrutinized by settlers, leaseholders and the deputy minister, many, like Michael Fletcher, chose to shift responsibility and avoid any decisions that might become controversial.

At the core of leaseholders' resistance to settlement was a desire to retain control over forest resources. In terms of the total holdings of a substantial leaseholder, an individual 100-acre lot or even a group of 10 or 12 lots did not contain a great deal of wood; it was the cumulative gnawing away at the edges of the Crown land and the location of settlements that was significant (see Map One). To ensure applicants a means of travel, settlements tended to be laid off near established roads, rail lines and river banks, which provided considerable irritation to leaseholders. The cost of hauling wood from the stump to the rail or river landing was a major expense in woods operations in the 1920s, especially for lumber operators who were forced by diminishing resources to go deeper into the forest in search of merchantable lumber.[54] Lumber operators often ar-

51   Octave King to Prince, 3 January 1926, DMOR, box 56, PANB.

52   W.E. McMullen to C.V. Pickard, 5 January 1926; Pickard to McMullen, 1 March 1926, DMOR, box 56, PANB.

53   M.J. Fletcher to Prince, 19 June 1926, DMOR, box 50, PANB.

54   It was generally acknowledged by Canadian conservationists that the situation in New Brunswick with regards to forest resource depletion was more critical than in any other province in Canada during the 1920s. See *Report of the Royal Commission on Pulpwood* (Ottawa, 1924).

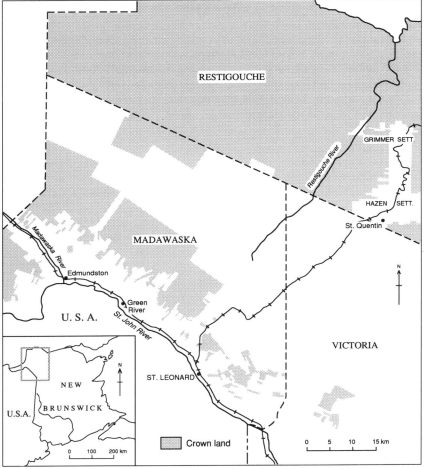

The ragged edges of the Crown lands in Madawaska and Restigouche counties show the progress of Labor Act settlement and the extent to which prospective settlers chose the most accessible forested areas.

gued that settlers were placed — not coincidentally, they surmised — directly in or dangerously near their most accessible stands of lumber. Leaseholders were most irritated by paying ground rent and other government fees on a piece land for decades, only to see it extracted from the lease, sometimes as the forest growth was approaching merchantable size for lumber. "The piece of land taken out was the best Lot that we had on our entire license, containing about 100,000 feet", claimed lumber operator J.H. Irving. "We had been allowing it to stand for some time and had all arrangements made to clear it off this year....we feel we are justified in asking some remuneration".[55]

When lumber operators discovered that lots in their leases were up for application, they often tried to convince the department of the unsuitability of the land for agriculture and the insincerity of the applicants. "I am quite confident that if some of the applicants were investigated, you would find it is largely the timber growth that the applicants are after", insisted A.C. Chapman, manager of the Kent Lumber Company. It would be the same old story: "A log shack, a few years occupied, then vacant".[56] The frustration of leaseholders with the cumulative pattern of settlement was exhibited by Donald Fraser in 1929:

> We are advised by our woodsman, Mr Bowes, that they are laying off lots up along the North West [Branch] in the vicinity of Wayes' Bridge, on both sides of the river [Miramichi], presumably for farming purposes. Our woods foreman is very bitterly opposed to running off this land, as it is very good lumber land, and does not appear to be any good for farming. We suppose this land will be used the same as the land in the so-called Vanderbeck, Morrissy and Curtis Settlements. These lots were abandoned after the lumber was all cleaned off. We do not object to any land being drawn out of our leases, if it is any good for farming, and drawn by men that we know are going to be bona fide settlers, but there have been so many hundreds of lots drawn out of our license by characters that are no good, and replaced in our licenses after the lumber is all stripped off that we are getting rather disgusted. If there is more land required for settlement purposes, why not take up these settlements on the Millstream. We believe this to be very good farming land, and some of the farms are practically cleared now.[57]

---

in any other province in Canada during the 1920s. See *Report of the Royal Commission on Pulpwood* (Ottawa, 1924).

55   J.H. Irving to Prince, 16 February 1924, DMOR, box 51, PANB.

56   A.C. Chapman to Prince, 9 April 1928, 12 April 1928; Prince to Chapman, 10 April 1928, DMOR, box 59, PANB.

57   Donald Fraser to Prince, 23 April 1929, DMOR, box 60, PANB.

Counterbalancing the resistance of lumber operators were the sympathies of northern New Brunswick politicians and the opportunities the Labor Act presented for dispensing patronage. Many of the MLAs from the northern counties, who were not themselves leaseholders, were supporters of Crown land settlement. The most vocal advocates of settlement were the francophone members from Madawaska, Restigouche, Gloucester and Kent, who spoke in the legislature each year on the need to provide more assistance to applicants. Their criticism of the Conservative Baxter government for committing money to the Empire Settlement programme, while thousands emigrated from the province each year due to lack of opportunity, carried a distinct undercurrent of ethnic tension. J. André Doucet, a pulpwood dealer and MLA from Gloucester County, for example, believed that "it would be better to give the same care and encouragement to our own people that is now given to strangers".[58] He and others pointed to Quebec, where settlers were given a bonus for clearing land, as a model to be followed by New Brunswick. The Catholic Church expressed an interest in keeping people on the land as well, although their participation in the 1920s was not nearly as pervasive as it would become during the Depression.[59]

Patronage was a powerful force for the extension of settlement. T.G. Loggie's statement to a disgruntled lumberman that prospective settlers "are clamouring all the time for land in this section of the country and in nearly every case they are strongly represented by representative men in the locality" suggested the pervasive influence of politics in the approval of settlement lots and the popular forces behind the settlement of the countryside.[60] In fact, a majority of the settlers who had their applications approved in the 1920s were aided by a political patron. Supporters of the Labor Act extended whatever political pressure they could muster. Missionary zeal, however, was by no means a necessary precondition for politicians to dispense settlement lots. Satisfying the demands of men "clamouring" for land also could be an effective means of reproducing a

---

58 See *Synoptic Report of the Legislative Assembly of New Brunswick* (1922), p. 13; *Assembly Report* (1924), pp. 18-19; *Assembly Report* (1925), pp. 7, 33-34; *Assembly Report* (1927), pp. 23, 51, 62, 74-5, 79.

59 In the 1930s, Catholic priests assumed the role of brokers for the Department of Lands and Mines in extending settlement throughout northern New Brunswick. They corresponded directly with the department and essentially made the decision as to which applicants were worthy or unworthy of approval. See Jean-Roch Cyr, "The 'Back to the Land Movement' in New Brunswick during the 1930s: Government Policy and the Role of the Catholic Church as an Interest-Group", paper presented at the Atlantic Canada Workshop, Lunenburg, Nova Scotia, September 1990. While not insignificant, the Church did not hold such powers in the 1920s.

60 T.G. Loggie to J.L. O'Brien, 28 October 1920, DMOR, box 34, PANB. The term "representative men" was commonly used in New Brunswick to describe people of political or economic status.

loyal constituency. Members of both the Liberal and Conservative Governments of the 1920s employed the Labor Act as a source of political capital. Any claims to patronage were handled directly by the Minister of Lands and Mines, one of the prime patronage-distributing offices in New Brunswick. As elected officials concerned with the health of the party, ministers had entirely different and sometimes contradictory agendas to Deputy Minister Prince.

Political intervention in the application process could assume a number of forms. In many cases, members of the Legislative Assembly contacted the Minister of Lands and Mines on behalf of an individual or group of men seeking land. The role of political influence in application approval was demonstrated in a letter from Deputy Minister Prince to Forest Ranger Harvey Malcolm in December 1928. Referring to a number of applications for lots in Colebrook Settlement, Restigouche County, he wrote: "it was decided...to accept the applications of Leonard Hachey and one other applicant to the west of that, it being thought that the remaining portion of the range was too hilly for settlement. I might say, however, that the Department has received a letter from Hon. D.A. Stewart urging that we accept Mr Soucie's application". D.A. Stewart was Minister of Public Works, and Mr. Soucie's application was approved.[61] In situations where the government was not represented in a county, the disbursement of settlement lots might be handled by the local patronage committee. Such was the case in 1927, when the Conservative Executive Committee for Gloucester County successfully petitioned Minister of Lands and Mines C.D. Richards to open land on the Big Tracadie River.[62]

Whatever the form, political intervention took precedence over the recommendations of department employees. The extension of Bronson Settlement in Queens County showed the extent to which the decisions of the department could be overridden by political motives. In June 1927, G.H. Prince sent a letter to James Fraser, Forest Ranger, requesting that he meet with a Father Moore of Chipman, who had evidently been agitating for an extension of the Bronson Settlement for some time. Fraser's instructions were to advise Father Moore, as Prince himself had done the previous year, that "there were unoccupied surveyed lots in the settlement itself which were still available, and that it would be desirable that the settlers take up there first before any question of extending the settlement was made". Just the same, applications for the desired land were made, presumably at the urging of Father Moore, and rejected by the department. Prince even sent a letter to the Ranger on July 27, instructing him to reiterate the "attitude of the department regarding applications in Bronson Settlement". The attitude of the department quickly changed, however, when a

61 Prince to Harvey Malcolm, 6 December 1928, DMOR, box 61, PANB; *Royal Gazette*, 1 May 1929, p. 96.

62 A.E. Frenette to C.D. Richards, Minister of Lands and Mines, 3 July 1927; Richards to Frenette, 6 July 1927, DMOR, box 60, PANB.

Queens County MLA intervened. "I have now received recommendation from W.B. Evans, MLA, suggesting that lots be opened between the railway and Bronson Settlement along the highway", the deputy minister informed Fraser in August. By February 1928, despite a survey report that advised "much of this territory is bog and unfit for settlement", the department had received and approved nine applications.[63]

G.H. Prince never acknowledged claims to patronage, and demanded that all department employees follow his example. However, as point men in the field, forest rangers and scalers were not always as well positioned to avoid politics. The correspondence between Donald McBeath, a senior forest ranger in Restigouche County, and Deputy Minister Prince demonstrated the difficult position faced by men in the field, forced to balance the interdepartmental drive for rational administration against the complex machinations of patronage politics in rural New Brunswick:

> I am sorry to say that I had poor success in trying to get Wm. Davidson on scaling for the winter. It seems that the [patronage] Committee up there is comprised of a Mr. Chouinard [pulpwood dealer] and a couple of others and told me that if Wm. Davidson is put back that Mr. Michaud [M.L.A. Madawaska] would be given credit for putting Billy back. Mr. Michaud told them at St. Quentin he was going to see that Davidson would get on again. Mr. Michaud and Mr. Chouinard are at loggerheads. The Committee also told me that Billy Davidson took a part in the election against them but I don't think this is so. Both Mr. Stewart [N.B. Minister of Public Works] and Mr. Culligan [Restigouche County Councillor and Crown leaseholder] was [*sic*] very fair about it and said if the people in St. Quentin and Five Fingers was [*sic*] agreeable they had no objection. So he left it to me to find out and report to him at Fredericton. Would you let Mr. Murchie [Chief Scaler] know the news if he comes home before I telephone[?][64]

Davidson, an employee of the department for seven seasons, was the scaler for the Five Fingers-St. Quentin district in the winter of 1925 and was active in investigating Labor Act violations; it is not clear, however, if these activities or others were responsible for the resistance to his proposed rehiring.[65] What is cer-

---

63   Prince to J.E. Fraser, 28 June 1927, 27 July 1927, 23 July 1927, 6 December 1927, 4 April 1927, DMOR, box 60, PANB.

64   Donald McBeath to Prince, 1 October 1926, DMOR, box 56, PANB.

65   Prince to W.R. Davidson, 31 October 1925; W.R. Davidson to G.H. Prince, 10 November 1925, DMOR, box 54, PANB. J.B. Chouinard was a pulpwood and lumber dealer and general merchant in St. Quentin, whose business revolved around supplying settlers and receiving wood in exchange. His reluctance to

tain is that local politicians, despite the efforts toward civil service reform, were still intimately involved in the administration of Crown lands. In fact, the interests of the Liberal Party, with regard to the activities of specific forest rangers, were openly discussed during some meetings of the Forest Advisory Commission, a condition that was not in keeping with its mandate.[66]

Field agents firmly believed the good will of the ruling party hinged on their co-operation. Fear of reprisal was clearly on the mind of Octave King when he prefaced his report of glaring violations of the Labor Act with the cautionary statement: "I believe I am tredding [sic] on dangerous ground by writing the following letter which is concerning different applications of different partie [sic] through different sections, because if different Members knew that I am against applications (not all) they will think I am bothering them with their campaigns for election personaly [sic]".[67] Indeed, there was something of a purge after the election of 1925. King resigned from his post temporarily to take another position after the election, when he could not get assurances from local Conservative politicians that his job was safe. While he was convinced to stay on, the deputy minister nonetheless confirmed the basis for his concerns: "So many changes have been made in our staff that it makes it rather difficult to get men fully informed as to their duties".[68] For the scaler or forest ranger interested in a long

have William Davidson return to the district may well have had something to do with the scaler's administration of the Labor Act. On Chouinard see RS 39, Transcripts of the Hearings of the Royal Commission on Pulpwood, vol. 593, no. 10, pp. 614-18, NAC.

66 Minutes of Meeting of the Forest Advisory Board, 30 April 1920; 13 February 1922, RS 106, DMOR, box 35, PANB

67 Octave King to Prince, 30 January 1926, DMOR, box 55, PANB.

68 Octave King to Prince, 14 November 1925; Prince to King, 19 November 1925, DMOR, box 55, PANB. Real or contrived, field agents were open to charges of working for the opposition after an election. This seems to be what happened to James Ward, a scaler from Chipman, when W.B. Evans requested that he be removed from office. "I would be very pleased to have James Ward of Chipman removed", the MLA informed Minister of Lands and Mines C.D. Richards. "He has been very active politically...and strong representations have been made to me that he should not remain in office". W.B. Evans to C.D. Richards, 29 October 1925, DMOR, box 54, PANB. Evidently Evans was quite enthusiastic about wielding patronage. In 1925 he got into a dispute with members in neighbouring Sunbury County over the appointment of a police magistrate in Minto. Tellingly, A.D. Taylor, MLA, remarked, "As far as I can see Mr. Evans wants the privilege of naming new appointments but does not want the unpleasantness of removing old officers....Mr. Evans has lots of places for his friends, if he will undergo the criticism of recommending the dismissal of some of the old officials". A.D. Taylor to J.B.M. Baxter, 9 October 1925, Executive Council Cabinet Papers, RS 9, PANB.

career, it was in his best interest to understand the political climate in his district and avoid any actions that might appear defiant toward local politicians.

In the absence of any single controlling force, Labor Act settlement lacked any discernible pattern. Settlements were opened or extended and others shut down, sometimes simultaneously, depending on what pressure could be brought to bear on the Department. The efforts of Prince and others in the Department of Lands and Mines to rationalize the administration of the Labor Act were not insignificant, but they continually ran up against a resistant political culture in rural New Brunswick. Rural people clamoured for officeholders to deliver settlement lots, perhaps in the same way that they had done for the past 50 years. A significant number of officeholders felt obliged to accommodate such demands. The Labor Act thus provided an avenue for landless New Brunswickers to resist the monopoly that lumber and pulp companies exerted over provincial forest resources. Local politicians were often the vehicles which carried the landless to the possession of Crown land.

Class Conflict and Administration

After settlement lots were approved, the Labor Act became even more difficult to administer, for settlement on the New Brunswick forest frontier in the 1920s frequently degenerated into an open struggle for the forest resources. The dispute between a group of settlers in Northumberland County and the D. and J. Ritchie Company illustrated how such a conflict could take shape; it also illustrated something of the difficult, time-consuming and thankless nature of administering the Labor Act, particularly for the field agents. The Curtis Settlement, located outside Newcastle in the 350-square-mile D. and J. Ritchie holdings, was a constant source of irritation to the company. In December 1925, ten lots on the settlement were returned to the lease, after the company convinced the Department of Lands and Mines to investigate applicants who were not meeting the conditions of the Labor Act. Several months later the company learned that one Robert Mullin had applied for a lot in the Curtis Settlement. David Ritchie sent a letter to G.H. Prince, urging that this application be refused, "as the record of the majority of the lots drawn from the Curtis Settlement has been that when the lumber was cut the settler had no further interest in the lot".[69] Prince responded on 7 April, informing Ritchie that a decision had not yet been made on the application but that the department would consider the opinion of the company. Subsequently, on 3 November 1926 the application of Robert Mullin was approved; in addition, his brothers Keith and Ross were approved to

69   D. Ritchie to Prince, 3 April 1926, 24 April 1926; Prince to Ritchie, 7 April 1926, DMOR, box 59, PANB; *Royal Gazette*, 3 November 1926.

settle on two adjacent lots. The brothers were forest workers in the Miramichi region.[70]

Less than a month after approval, the Mullin brothers and the Ritchie Company were at odds. The company had quickly exercised its right to the merchantable timber in the first year of approval, placing a contractor, Joseph Walls, on the Mullin lots. The Mullin brothers responded in late November by informing the department that the Ritchie contractor was cutting undersized lumber (that is, below the 12-inch minimum diameter set down in the Crown land regulations) on the settlement lots. Upon instruction from Deputy Minister Prince, Walls was warned by forest ranger Charles Holohan that he would be penalized for any undersized cutting. The Mullin brothers were not satisfied. E.A. Mullin, probably their father, wrote Holohan on 6 January 1927 demanding that the ranger make a "speedy visit" to stop the undersized cutting which he claimed had continued. He also raised the political spectre, warning Holohan, "I will personally take the matter up with Mr. Baxter who personally issued those lots to Mullin boys, and have a man take your place who will carry out his duties".[71] It is not clear whether Premier Baxter intervened in the application process on behalf of the Mullins, although Ritchie clearly believed the lots were approved with the help of an influential politician.

Deputy Minister Prince sent an urgent telegram to the Ritchie Company on 13 January, instructing it to "see that Joseph Walls operator for you discontinues undersized cutting at once".[72] David Ritchie immediately responded with a letter that revealed his displeasure with the matter and with the activities of Holohan. Commenting on a small number of undersized logs, for which Walls had been penalized, Ritchie remarked, "it looks very much as if [Hollohan] was doing everything possible to prevent Wall from operating on a block of ground that we have been paying renewals on etc...for the last 35-40 years". Ritchie went on to condemn what he conceived as the process by which the lots were approved and portrayed the Mullins in less than flattering terms:

> You are no doubt aware of the circumstances of the drawing of these lots by the Mullin Brothers, as we have already had some correspondence with the Minister, and we repeat again as we did when we wrote him that

---

70 *Royal Gazette*, 3 November 1926. The names Ross and Keith Mullin appear on the list of workers who were unpaid when the William M. Sullivan Company, Ltd. went bankrupt in 1938; Memo, Wage Accounts Payable, Wm. M. Sullivan Ltd., 27 October 1938, DMOR, box 46, PANB.

71 Robert, Keith and Ross Mullin to C.D. Richards, Minister of Lands and Mines, 29 November 1926; Prince to Holohan, 14 December 1926; Holohan to Prince, 22 December 1926; E. A. Mullin to Holohan, 6 January 1927, DMOR, box 59, PANB.

72 Prince to D. and J. Ritchie Company, 13 January 1927, DMOR, box 59, PANB.

the ground is not suitable for agricultural purposes and if your Ranger so reported he was not giving the truth, but it is just possible that he may have been requested to send in a favourable report, and we would not be surprised if this were the case. No sooner were the lots approved than the Mullins were hot-foot for contracts for lath wood cut from this ground, and we submitted the facts to the Minister but of course it was too late for him to cancel the approval, and even if he wanted to someone higher up would frown on any such action...we would like you to know that since he [Walls] has gone on the ground he has been hampered by the Mullins who resented him operating for us very much. As a matter of fact we had to try three different parties before we were able to induce anyone to cut the ground, as they were all afraid of offending the drawees of the lots, and thereby incurring the enmity of the Mullins from now on. It is a nice state of affairs when a condition like this exists, and when the government of a country encourages this kind of thing.[73]

In response to the contradictory information being received and the allegations from both sides against Holohan, the Deputy Minister called in Michael Fletcher, scaling inspector for the district.

Even before Fletcher submitted his report, Prince received a letter from Robert Mullin on 21 January in which he tried to discredit Fletcher, accusing the inspector of "trying to shield Mr. Holohan". Mullin claimed to have confronted Fletcher, calling attention to the size of Joseph Walls' stumps, only to be told that "there was no chance for a kick as they all cut undersized". Holding to his accusation of widespread illegal cutting, Mullin continued that on the day he went to Fredericton to meet with the minister, Walls "put his men to work cutting down lumber without limbing in order to get as much down as possible before you could reach him with orders to stop cutting undersized lumber".[74] When Fletcher's report arrived the next day, it was just as Mullin had predicted. The inspector found "no evidence whatsoever that the Ritchie Company were trying to cut below the 12 inch stump" and, referring to the few undersized trees that were cut during the process of clearing yards and roads, Fletcher "felt sure that he [Holohan] got them all".[75] As the Deputy Minister was satisfied with the report made by Fletcher, and Joseph Walls had finished cutting for the season, the matter was laid to rest, but not before Charles Holohan made his comment on the incident.

In a long letter to Prince, Holohan tried to impress on his boss the impartiality with which he had handled the affair. He reasoned that it "did not seem

---

73   Ritchie to Prince, 13 January 1927, DMOR, box 59, PANB.

74   Robert Mullin to Prince, 21 January 1927, DMOR, box 59, PANB.

75   M.J. Fletcher to Prince, 22 January 1927, DMOR, box 59, PANB.

fair" for the department to "take for granted statements made or written by applicants". He had "favoured no one", wanting "to see both parties follow the regulations". To show to "what extremes they [Mullins] have gone" and to "protect" himself from "threats" and "lies", he enclosed the letter written by E.A. Mullin. Holohan also alleged that Robert Mullin attempted to bribe him in early January, quoting the settler as saying, "I will make it worth your while if you help us".[76] By the time this letter was written, the Mullins seem to have fallen from favour with the department. The favourable report issued by Michael Fletcher, one of the most trusted employees of the department, also helped to restore Holohan's credibility.

It took several months, but the Ritchie Company managed to exact its revenge on the Mullin brothers. The Department of Lands and Mines received a letter from the company in May claiming that its prophesy of bogus settlement had come to pass. The brothers, the company claimed, had cut more than 8,000 logs between them, "at least 200,000 feet of lumber, from which the Government received no revenue". "We know the whole history of the approval of these lots", it continued, "and that they were approved by you with a great deal of reluctance", again insinuating that patronage played a role in the matter. The Ritchie Company had already contacted the Fraser Company, which had obtained the illegally cut wood through one of its many travelling buyers, and informed the department that the Fraser Company was "willing to cooperate".[77] On 21 May, Prince sent a letter to Holohan chastising him for failing to keep a close watch on the lots as he had been instructed some months earlier and ordering him to take the proper action. The deputy minister then contacted the Fraser Company, which agreed to withhold payment from the Mullins pending a settlement on the matter. In total, Holohan reported, the Mullin brothers had sold just over 100,000 feet of lumber to the Fraser Company, cutting over an area of 25 acres. None of the settlers had attempted to clear any land, and only Keith Mullin was occupying his lot when the report was made. The Mullins were charged double stumpage on the illegally cut wood. That undoubtedly reduced the return on the lumber they sold to a figure closer to what they would have received for cutting the equivalent amount in a lumber camp. Finally, Prince recommended to the Minister of Lands and Mines that "these lots remain in the license for at least another year" until the government knew the "intentions of the settlers which appears [sic] very doubtful at this point".[78]

What exactly happened in the dispute between the Mullins and the Ritchie Company? Which of the allegations and counter-allegations were true? There

---

76 Holohan to Prince, 22 January 1927, DMOR, box 59, PANB.

77 Ritchie Company to Prince, 18 May 1927; Prince to Holohan, 21 May 1927; Holohan to Prince, 30 May 1927; Prince to Ritchie Company, 28 July 1927, DMOR, box 59, PANB.

78 Prince to C.D. Richards, 28 July 1927, DMOR, box 59, PANB.

were in all probability some truths, falsehoods and exaggerations coming from both parties. The Ritchie-Mullin dispute makes a worthy reference point for a discussion of the Labor Act in the 1920s, because it brought to the surface many of the conditions surrounding the administration of the act and the strategies used by settlers and lumber companies in fierce struggle over the forest resource. The success of the D. and J. Ritchie Company in thwarting the Mullin brothers demonstrated that, with diligence, operators could enforce some measure of protection on the lands taken out of their lease. In this respect, the company was fortunate enough to know where the wood was being sold and to have the co-operation of the Fraser Company. It was not difficult for the Ritchie Company to convince the Department of ill-intention when it held the scaling slips for 105,000 board feet of lumber which proved to be cut indiscriminately over 25 acres, with no visible effort at clearing land on the part of the settlers. Operators who faced less overt violations of the Labor Act and had little information to give to the Department of Lands and Mines were normally less successful in protecting their leases. In the absence of adequate controls over the cutting done by settlers, lumber operators in the province pursued other strategies.

One of the constants in the Ritchie-Mullins dispute was the company's critical attitude toward the department. At every juncture, the Ritchie Company reminded the Department of Lands and Mines of the contradictions of Labor Act settlement and demanded strict adherence to the regulations. Quite often, as in this instance, the demands made on the department were accompanied by reminders that the leaseholder had been paying ground rent and other fees on the land for decades. Such indignation over losing land to settlement was rooted in a perception among leaseholders that lengthy tenure, in essence, gave them private property rights to the Crown land. Leaseholders went to great pains to point out that when settlers cut wood on the Crown land the government lost revenue because they did not pay stumpage unless they were caught for violations. These constant reminders were a primary means by which operators, large and small, pressured the department into addressing the problem of settlers nibbling away at the wood on their leases.

Leaseholders' tactics could be more personal. As the criticism of Charles Holohan indicated, scalers and forest rangers were targets of personal attacks and intimidation at the hands of operators, who were dissatisfied with their individual handling of settlement matters. The indictment served on Charles McGivney, a forest ranger and scaler in York County, by the frequently vitriolic J.L. O'Brien, demonstrated the pressure that could be put on the men in the field to conform to the conceptions of lumbermen regarding how the Labor Act should be administered. "This man McGivney", O'Brien informed chief scaler A.T. Murchie, "has been acting in such a broad minded and philanthropic manner WITH OUR PROPERTY giving our logs and cutting privileges to others that we cannot believe that we are the first to object to him...The only thing we cannot explain is why he is still retained by the Department". "Boiled down", he concluded, "if some Ranger is put in that district that we can depend on, and one who will not cater to the so called settlers the land may still yield some return. As it is now we are powerless to overcome the local element unless we have help from the Government".[79] Accusation and innuendo, however exaggerated, were effective in keeping the shiny surface of propriety waxed. Any such accusations, especially if they were levelled by a prominent man such as J.L. O'Brien, normally brought about some type of investigation. The investigations could range from requests for a written explanation or the intervention of a senior field agent to a full-scale hearing with witnesses at the Crown land office in Fredericton. Neither the lumber operators nor the settlers ever ran short of illicit tales for the ministers and deputy ministers to consider.

Operators also tried to combat the settlers with methods that relied on the non-enforcement or relaxing of regulations. Each season the Department of Lands and Mines received many reports of operators descending on the settlements and cutting everything that could be sold. "It is terrible to see the devastation of the forest in some places by the lumber companies", reported Hermengilde Boulay, a Labor Act commissioner in Restigouche County. "Along the road in the Grog Brook settlement there is not a standing tree over 5 inches on the stump".[80] A letter from W.H. Coffyn, Conservative MLA for Gloucester County, to Minister of Lands and Mines L.P.D. Tilley shortly after the 1930 election captured both the politicized nature of Labor Act settlement and the efforts of lumber operators to seize the initiative in competing with settlers for forest resources:

> I desire to bring to your notice the fact that there was surveyed in the rear of St. Isidore a parcel of land suitable for settlement, during the election period just passed....Now Sir, what you may not know is: The Gloucester Lumber and Trading Company are quietly, yes very quietly, building camps all over that area and will put in jobbers who will skin that land so that there will not be enough lumber to construct a hut. I asked White's head scaler about this yesterday and he denied all knowledge of it....Now Mr. White is a very good man and a very careful one but he is careful most of all of the interests of himself. He has never thought of anyone else where a bit of land is concerned. He will skin that area beyond description and your government men will permit it because it has always been done.[81]

---

79 O'Brien to Prince, 23 January 1924, DMOR, box 34, PANB [original emphasis].

80 H. Boulay to Prince, 14 January 1928, DMOR, box 58, PANB.

81 Minister's Office Records, Department of Lands and Mines, W.H. Coffyn to L.P.D. Tilley, 11 December 1930, RS 105, box 5, PANB.

Occasionally, through oversight or through less innocent circumstances, the Department of Lands and Mines granted permits for operators to cut undersized lumber on settlement tracts. Lumber operators constantly pressured the department to grant undersized permits in the 1920s, usually arguing that the lumber on a particular lease was slow-growing, insect-damaged or fire-killed. The bottom line was always the same: the operator wanted very much to remove lumber that would otherwise be a total loss to the province, but unless the 12-inch diameter restriction was relaxed it would not be financially feasible.[82] John Ashworth, caretaker on the Blue Bell Tract, was more than a little suspicious of an undersized cutting permit granted to the Fraser Company in late 1926. "Allow me to state that I don't know whatever reason the Department had for issuing this permit, as where they are cutting is the loveliest young growth the eyes of man ever saw", the caretaker observed. "There is [*sic*] no budworm infested areas around here, it is all healthy. I wish you would advise me in the future when anything outside of the ordinary lumber regulations is given to anyone on this tract of land".[83] The undersized cutting permit given to the Fraser Company may have been a mistake, as it was cancelled immediately after John Ashworth's report. However, this was almost certainly not the case with a permit given to George Burchill and Sons in 1923.

In September 1924, Prince corresponded with Percy Burchill, inquiring why his predecessor, T.G. Loggie, had refused to extend the Vanderbeck Settlement, which was in the Burchill lease in Northumberland County. The previous applicants were again agitating for settlement lots, with the backing of two of the county's MLAs. Burchill's response strongly suggested that he had been granted a special favour by the department and also revealed the extent to which settlement could be a community issue. After making the obligatory statement that

---

82   There was a continuous flow of requests for undersized cutting permits coming into the department in the 1920s. While some of them represented legitimate efforts to practise sound forestry, the requests were often made as little more than an attempt to reduce the stumpage on cutting operations. A letter from Angus McLean, President of the Bathurst Company Ltd., was typical in content and tone of the appeals that the ministers received. "You possibly know something about the big storm we had here two weeks ago and the damage that it has done in the woods. The heavy soft snow has broken down the forests and large sections of our forests have been destroyed....With your approval we are prepared to put in small contractors and save as much of the timber as possible and we wish that you would advise us promptly by telephone on receipt of this letter giving us the authority to do so. There is no time to be lost if we are to salvage this timber, and, of course, under the circumstances, we would have to get carte blanche to cut the timber irrespective of size and that there would be no penalty for cutting the undersized stuff". Angus McLean to Prince, 24 October 1925, DMOR, box 49, PANB.

83   John Ashworth to Prince, 15 January 1927, DMOR, box 54, PANB.

the applications were filled out for "some of the best spruce land that we hold", which had "been conserved and preserved by us for a great many years", Burchill explained the situation as it developed:

> This settlement was applied for by some chaps in the town of Newcastle, the great majority of whom had no idea of ever farming it, and your inspector Michael J. Fletcher, made a report to your department in which he took the stand that it was not wise policy to open up this settlement....The report got out, I do not know how, but Fletcher was approached in Newcastle very strenuously by friends of the applicants who knew practically everything that was in Fletcher's report. The Deputy Minister of Lands and Mines at that time, Colonel Loggie, refused to grant the applications although I think one or two of them were approved, and the matter has been hung up ever since. Last year we cleaned the lots off, acting under permit from your department. I do not think it is necessary to add anything or to make any comments. Please keep this confidential.[84]

Aside from the opening or major extension of a settlement, lots were taken out of the leases a few at a time. It was often the situation that these scattered parcels of land could not be operated profitably unless the undersized trees were cut. Whether by permit or not, operators pursued the strategy of cutting undersized lumber as a means of beating settlers to the forest resource.

After settlers were placed on the Crown lands, lumber operators needed all the means at their disposal and more to compete for the wood on settlement lots. Neither the Department of Lands and Mines nor the lumber operators had the resources to detect all of the wholesale cutting that went on in the settlements. To even attempt to account for all of the nibbling that settlers continually engaged in was entirely futile. Indeed, the commitment to enforcement was highly uneven, as Deputy Minister Prince noted on many occasions. "Experience has shown that there are many lots which were approved ten or fifteen years ago which are not resided on and which have been practically abandoned by the applicants", he informed one scaler, "except that they continue to cut their wood and occasionally a few logs without any interference".[85] When the

---

84 Prince to Burchill, 20 September 1924; Burchill to Prince, 30 September 1924, DMOR, box 52, PANB. The Vanderbeck Settlement was subsequently reopened at the urging of Liberal MLA's J.S. Martin and Charles Morrissey; see Morrissey to Prince, 8 September 1924; Martin to Prince, 29 October 1924, DMOR, box 52, PANB. By the beginning of 1926 some of these lots were already being returned to the Burchill's lease. See W.E. McMullen to Burchill, 27 January 1926; Prince to Burchill, 23 April 1926, DMOR, box 54, PANB.

85 Prince to A.J.S. Branch, 26 March 1926, DMOR, box 54, PANB.

deputy minister tried to comfort a disgruntled lumberman in 1927 by telling him, "we are planning at least one annual inspection of every lot approved and perhaps two", he was as much as admitting that the department had little control over the cutting done by settlers on approved lots.[85] Until 1928, when a man was employed specifically for the purpose, inspections were usually carried out only when reports of violations were received by the Fredericton office. Most scalers and forest rangers were too busy with their many other duties or otherwise reluctant to investigate settlements on their own initiative.

"In practice", A.R.M. Lower commented, "how to distinguish between cutting incidental to making a home and cutting for sale for its own sake is a very nice question".[87] At the core of the administrative problems was a recognition, on the one hand, of the need for settlers to cut and sell wood to sustain themselves and, on the other hand, attempts to control their cutting through largely unenforceable regulations. By making some pretence to settlement, which could mean building a small shack to live in while cutting on the lot or clearing an acre or two, settlers could carry on virtually without fear of penalty. Lumber operators could get little satisfaction from the department when settlers were cutting within the designated areas and making some attempt to improve the land. The pattern that this promoted, well outlined by Gloucester County scaler A.J.S. Branch, was familiar throughout the settlement areas in the province. In a discussion of the general inadequacy of enforcement, he noted that many settlers "simply cut what they could from the ten acres and then leave the lot or they would sell their claim to another party who would cut another ten acres". The end result was that "quite naturally the lots get stripped of all the lumber and the Department gets almost nothing".[88] Unless the department was willing to invest the time and manpower to measure off every ten-acre settlement lot, the boundaries could be stretched considerably to include the good timber around the edges.

From the perspective of lumber operators and government officials, the dangers of settlement extended beyond individuals cutting small amounts of wood on their own lots. Applicants sometimes brought in other men to take advantage of the opportunity, in which case the amount of pulpwood cut on individual settlement lots could exceed 200 cords in a year.[89] Cutting on vacant

---

86   Prince to Paul Kingston, 12 December 1927, DMOR, box 59, PANB.

87   Lower, *Settlement and the Forest Frontier*, p. 132.

88   A.J.S. Branch to Prince, 10 April 1926, DMOR, box 54, PANB. Using land concession records and parish registers, Irene Landry found that this was the pattern on the St. Quentin Settlement she studied. Landry, "Saint Quentin et le retour à la terre".

89   An investigation by Michael Fletcher in 1930, for example, revealed that 4,415 cords of pulpwood were cut on 24 lots in the Davidson Settlement in Northumberland County in the period from 1928 to 1930; Fletcher to Prince, 12 March 1930, DMOR, box 63, PANB.

settlement lots and nearby Crown land was another means by which settlers could exploit the forest resource. Trespassing involved some risk, as detection could result in a levy of double stumpage by the Department of Lands and Mines, or sometimes the seizure of wood. However, as a letter from J.L. O'-Brien to the department indicated, the level of surveillance was not often sufficient to deter trespassers:

> For several seasons we have had great difficulty with a license we hold near Blackville. The people living in the vicinity have been nibbling at the land and we cannot catch them with sufficient proof to prosecute. The settlement is not close to the highway nor the Railway and they can work without the outside world knowing just what is going on. The logs we are sure are sold to a M. Schaeffer in Blackville and delivered to his mill after dark. If we do manage to catch them the quantity they have at any one time would not be sufficient to make it worthwhile, and in any event these people have not anything to go after. You can see they are running a pretty safe operation, with everything to gain and nothing to lose.[90]

"The people only look at it as a cute trick or a game of checkers", a Gloucester County forest ranger explained: "If he is not found he wins and if he is caught he pays the stumpage that's all, and gets at it again the first chance".[91] The Department of Lands and Mines was certainly concerned with the amount of trespassing carried on by settlers, but it was ill-equipped to handle the problem. This was demonstrated by Octave King in 1927 when he requested that the vacant lots in his district be put back into the Fraser lease, so that the company "could keep watch over them". "Otherwise", he maintained, "it will take a gatteling [*sic*] gun to keep trespassers away".[92]

Detection and punishment of Labor Act violators was also inhibited by political considerations. New Brunswick law provided for the incarceration of people stealing wood from Crown land, and, although there was some support within the department for sending offenders to prison, it almost never happened. As Prince explained to a frustrated forest ranger, filing criminal charges was "followed largely by private land owners" and was "a course prescribed for the Crown", but the normal practice was "to collect double stumpage and let the trespassers off".[93] Few politicians wanted prosecutions. Crown land administration was conceptualized more as a political than a bureaucratic process in rural New Brunswick. It did not reflect favourably on local officeholders to allow im-

---

90 J.L. O'Brien, 2 July 1926, DMOR, box 34, PANB.

91 P.T. Robichaud to Prince, 30 December 1926, DMOR, box 57, PANB.

92 Octave King to Prince, 10 April 1926, DMOR, box 51, PANB.

93 Prince to P.T. Robichaud, 29 June 1927, DMOR, box 59, PANB.

poverished constituents to be incarcerated for what were considered, at most, petty transgressions of the law.

In fact, local politicians sometimes actively blocked prosecutions. Gloucester County ranger A.J.S. Branch, for example, ran afoul of the local politicians in 1926, when he wanted to measure and mark off all of the ten-acre lots where settlers were residing in his district. "The Peanut Politicians we have in this county objected", he explained to Prince, "and I only measured off a couple of lots".[94] Harvey Malcolm encountered similar problems in Restigouche County. Settlers in his district, he reported to Inspector G.L. Miller, were "only causing alot [sic] of extra work". "The way they stand with politics in connection", he continued, "makes it all the harder".[95] Thus, it was not uncommon for settlers to depend on a measure of protection in their illegal cutting activities from some of the same politicians who helped them get applications approved, and it was incumbent upon field agents to understand the possible consequences of strenuous enforcement of Labor Act regulations in their districts.

Settlers were adept at protecting themselves by employing a number of less overt traditional rural tactics of resistance to authority. The already troublesome job of administering the Labor Act was made more onerous for field agents by the lies, threats, accusations, rumours and intimidation regularly perpetrated against them by settlers.[96] In the course of their dispute with the Ritchie Company, the Mullin brothers employed several common tactics: intimidating the jobber hired by the Ritchies, accusing Holohan of not carrying out his duties, threatening to use political influence, allegedly bribing him, and confronting Inspector Fletcher. The defensive posture assumed by Charles Holohan suggests the seriousness with which these matters were considered. The attitude of the department toward such allegations was expressed by Deputy Minister Prince to Inspector Donald McBeath. "It is unfortunate that such complaints are made from time to time but we are very glad to know that they are without foundation", he told the inspector. "You will understand how difficult it is for the Department to know whether correspondence deserves attention or not. For this reason, we endeavour to treat all alike until we are informed or learn information which guides us differently".[97] McBeath may have been cleared, but Prince

---

94   Branch to Prince, 10 April 1926, DMOR, box 54, PANB.

95   H. Malcolm to G.L. Miller, 3 September 1928, DMOR, box 61, PANB.

96   On the tradition of rural people using such tactics see E.P. Thompson, *Whigs and Hunters: The Origins of the Black Act* (New York, 1975); James Scott, "Everyday Forms of Peasant Resistance", *Journal of Peasant Studies*, 13, 2 (January 1986), pp. 5-36; *Weapons of the Weak: Everyday Forms of Peasant Resistance* (New Haven, 1985); Andrew Turton, "Patrolling the Middle Ground: Methodological Perspectives on Everyday Peasant Resistance", *Journal of Peasant Studies*, 13, 2 (January 1985), pp. 36-48.

97   Prince to McBeath, 14 December 1928, DMOR, box 61, PANB.

also reminded him that his actions were open to scrutiny, both in the field and in Fredericton.

All rangers and scalers who had dealings with settlers had their integrity challenged at one time or another, and the claims made against them, some of which were anonymous, were investigated by the department as a matter of policy. The charges could include dereliction of duty, political involvement, drunkenness and nepotism. A letter charging Northumberland County scaler Joseph Grogan with nepotism is representative of the allegations made by settlers against field agents. "Mr. Hugh S. Daly and another cousin of Mr. Grogan has worked on the Crown Land all his life and never pays any stumpage", charged a man who identified himself as J. Cameron of Chatham. "I think the sooner the Government gets a new Scaler on the job in this section the better". When asked to respond to the charges, Grogan vehemently denied any wrongdoing and further contended that the letter was sent from St. Margaret, a settlement to the southeast of Chatham, by a man named George Cook with whom he had had a scaling dispute the previous year.[98]

It would be difficult to document with any accuracy the overall impact such confrontations, nasty little rumours, anonymous letters and other charges had on the administration of the Labor Act. A confrontation involving Michael Fletcher in Newcastle, however, was one instance in which such tactics can be shown to have had an effect. In the course of deciding whether to reopen the Vanderbeck Settlement in 1924, Inspector Fletcher was instructed to make another assessment. He asked to be excused. Evidently in response to being "approached in Newcastle very strenuously by friends of the applicants", he remarked, "as my recommendations do not meet with the approval of the applicants...I think in all fairness to the applicants and myself that a report should be made by some other person".[99] This particular correspondence suggests with some certainty how field agents could succumb to intimidation or community pressure, and how such pressures could, ultimately, alter the administration of the act. Fletcher had after all reported in May 1923 that "I think it is a mistake to open this land for that purpose....I don't think that any of the applicants will ever homestead in that settlement".[100] Subsequently, the Vanderbeck Settlement was reopened, albeit with the intervention of the local MLAs. Although the impact of specific acts was rarely as tangible as in this instance, constant exposure to petty acts of malice and defiance undoubtedly contributed to the reluctance of field agents to investigate settlements unless given specific instructions.

---

98 J. Cameron to Department of Lands and Mines, 12 January 1925; Prince to Cameron, 15 January 1925, DMOR, box 49; Grogan to Prince, 29 January 1925, DMOR, box 51, PANB.

99 Fletcher to Prince, 27 September 1924, DMOR, box 52, PANB.

100 Fletcher to Prince, 7 May 1923, DMOR, box 52, PANB.

Settlers were aided and encouraged in their illegal cutting by the complicity of buyers. There were literally hundreds of wood buyers in New Brunswick in the 1920s; representatives of lumber and pulp mills, small contractors, general merchants, storekeepers, pulpwood brokers and portable sawmill owners all bought wood from settlers. The pulpwood export market — the largest consumer of wood from settlements — was pyramidal in entrepreneurial structure, with large pulpwood brokers who represented mills in Maine and New York purchasing wood through smaller local buyers. George Kerr of Campbellton, for example, shipped up to 60,000 cords of pulpwood to New York mills each year, buying from 75 smaller pulpwood dealers in Restigouche, Madawaska and Gloucester counties.[101] At the local level, merchant credit exchange relations often united the interests of buyer and seller in moving the wood up the pyramid without interference from the Department of Lands and Mines. Pulpwood was, in a great many instances, the only currency with which settlers could pay their debts, and it was readily accepted by local merchants throughout the province because it could be resold at a higher price.[102] Local dealers and merchants were naturally reluctant to assist field agents in their efforts to sort out illegal cutting activities and assess stumpage. The problems of the department could also be compounded when the wood-buying merchants, such as Gloucester MLA J. André Doucet, also wielded political power.

An even more symbiotic relationship developed with the many portable sawmill owners who set up operations in close proximity to settlements. Portable sawmills both provided a market for settlers and saved the owner the expense of purchasing a stumpage contract.[103] On the Grog Brook settlement, opened in 1928, for example, there were already two portable mills and an application to put another on adjacent Crown land before the end of the first year of its existence. Of the third applicant for a mill licence, Inspector Donald McBeath commented, "he wants to build and no doubt buy his timber from the new farms now being surveyed by E.R. Rutledge, so I would advise not to issue a permit, for we will be tormented to death by their trespassing on the Sydney Lumber Co. rights".[104] The caretaker of the settlement, Hermengilde Boulay, had an interest in one of the mills and was constantly requesting that the department

101 Information on the entrepreneurial structure of the pulpwood export industry is from Dominion Forest Service, Transcripts of the Hearings of the Royal Commission on Pulpwood, 1923-24, RG 39, vol. 593, nos. 4, 5 and 10, NAC; testimony of George Kerr, see RG 39, vol. 593, no. 5, pp. 587-608, NAC.

102 On the merchant credit system see Rosemary Ommer, ed., *Merchant Credit and Labour Strategies in Historical Perspective* (Fredericton, 1990).

103 On the proliferation of portable sawmills in New Brunswick in the 1920s see "Portable Sawmilling in New Brunswick Makes Great Strides", *Canada Lumberman*, 15 January 1928.

104 Donald McBeath to Prince, 14 September 1929, DMOR, box 61, PANB.

extend the settlement. Not surprisingly, the mills soon created difficulties for the department, when illegal cutting became rampant in Grog Brook.[105] As the Ritchie-Mullin dispute showed, even the travelling buyers of lumber and pulp companies, who generally worked on commission, on occasion bought wood indiscriminately from settlers.

An incident in which the department cracked down on a small mill in Gloucester County revealed much about the nature of exchange relations between settlers and merchants and the attitude of buyers who had a vested interest in their wood. In 1927, the A. and R. Loggie Company set up a lath wood mill on the north side of the Big Tracadie River and began receiving wood as payment on credit accounts. The arrangement got the company into trouble in 1928, when the department sent it a stumpage bill for wood cut in trespass by settlers who were not fulfilling the regulations of the Labor Act. A. and R. Loggie proceeded more cautiously in 1929. In February, when it came time to buy lots of wood along the river in anticipation of the spring drive, manager J.E. Dixon began writing to the department on behalf of the poor settlers. The company claimed it wanted very much to help the people, but could not on account of the likelihood that A. and R. Loggie would again be liable for stumpage. "We cannot understand why the Government wishes to keep these people ground down", the manager stated. "We sincerely hope that Hon. Mr. Richards allows these people to cut at least enough to support their families, and if he does", Dixon vowed, "we shall see that the privilege is not abused. We shall limit our buying so that they will cut no more than will buy provisions".[106] The comments of A.J.S. Branch, the forest ranger sent to investigate conditions on the Big Tracadie River, provided an alternative and less charitable view of the motivations of the company and of the nature of paternalist merchant credit relations in rural northern New Brunswick. "I have been on this same river for eleven years now", he reported to Deputy Minister Prince, "and before the A. and R. Loggie Company put their lath mill on the river the A. and R. Loggie were never interested in the well being of the people on the river, their interest ceases where they cannot buy lathwood".[107] In the end the department did waive stumpage for

---

105 From all indications, Hermengilde Boulay was a political appointment who had more interest in promoting sawmilling than in administering the Labor Act. See Prince to Boulay, 7 May, 5 November, 26 November 1927; 20 April, 20 June 1928; Boulay to Prince, 15 November, 8 December 1927, 5 June, 28 June 1928, DMOR, box 58, PANB; Prince to McBeath, 14 December 1928, 23 January, 1 March, 11 March, 11 July, 16 July, 21 August 1929; McBeath to Prince, 9 December, 11 December 1928 (quoted), 19 January, 8 March, 7 August, 14 August 1929, DMOR, box 61, PANB.

106 J.E. Dixon to Prince, 6 February 1929, 11 February 1929, 6 March 1929, DMOR, box 61, PANB.

107 Prince to A.J.S. Branch, 8 February 1929; Branch to Prince, 12 February 1929, DMOR, box 61, PANB.

some of the settlers, but it was the poverty of the people along the river, not the magnanimity of the company, that was the deciding factor.

Deputy Minister T.G. Loggie's opinion that the Labor Act was "perplexing and difficult to administer" and "very unpopular for the person handling it, as he must give offence, no matter how he acts", was undoubtedly shared by all of the scalers and forest rangers who dealt with settlement matters.[108] In the course of carrying out responsibilities, field agents were required to balance the often contradictory pressures placed on them by the department, leaseholders, settlers and politicians. Administering the Labor Act was troublesome for everyone involved, but the amount of conflict faced by scalers and rangers could vary, depending upon how well each individual was able to understand and balance these contradictory pressures. The logistics of Crown land administration in the 1920s, as had always been the case, allowed field agents the autonomy to assert personal sympathies and conceptions of how formal policy should be adapted to the realities of the local environment.[109] The successful field agent was one who could tailor administration in his district in such a way as to hold the confidence, or at least the grudging respect, of both settlers and leaseholders, while maintaining the image of propriety in the eyes of the ministers. In this respect they were not mere ciphers waiting to be pushed in one direction or the other, but active participants in the struggle between settlers and lumbermen for control of the forest resources.

Beyond the possible political ramifications, one of the more difficult aspects of investigating Labor Act violations was that even charging double stumpage for the wood they cut illegally could impose considerable hardship on settler families. There were surely instances in which field agents winked at illegal cutting by settlers. In their correspondence with the ministers, many scalers and forest rangers expressed reluctance to enforce the regulations of the Labor Act due to the poverty of settlers, but it would be impossible to discern how often or when sympathy translated into non-enforcement. P.T. Robichaud of Kent County was one scaler who seemed favourably disposed to turning a blind eye toward Labor Act violations. On more than one occasion he requested that the department deal leniently with settlers caught trespassing. "It would be almost impossible to express the poverty of these settlers by writing", he explained at one point; "a man would have to see for himself".[110] Robichaud's attitude was not lost on R. O'Leary and Sons of Richibucto. With regard to extensive cutting by settlers on their lease, the elder O'Leary remarked, "Mr Robichaud has never

---

108 T.G. Loggie to J.L. O'Brien, 18 February 1921, box 34, DMOR, PANB.

109 On the autonomy of field agents in the 19th century see Graeme Wynn, "Administration in Adversity: The Deputy Surveyors and Control of the New Brunswick Crown Forest Before 1844", *Acadiensis*, VII, 1 (Autumn 1977), pp. 49-65.

110 P.T. Robichaud to Prince, 31 July 1925, DMOR, box 53, PANB.

taken any interest in this item at all". He "seems to have a very sympathetic attitude toward a certain class of poor settlers".[111] The accusations of the O'Learys, which would eventually lead to an investigation of the scaler, were further supported by an anonymous correspondent, who contended that when Robichaud visited settlements he would "go only where they show him an he tell al the peepel 2 an 3 days an sometime on weke before he go to seze them so they can hide them [*sic*]".[112] Arrangements such as the one that Robichaud apparently had with the settlers in his district aided them in their inter-connected struggles for survival and for control of the wood.

At times, field agents were encouraged to revise policy to bring it more in line with, or enhance, the possibilities for enforcement. Deputy Minister Prince was always open to suggestions on how the Labor Act could be better administered, which usually meant controlling the cutting by settlers. The most concerted attempt to impose order on illegal cutting was made by Octave King in Madawaska County. In May 1926, King, with the consent of the department, instituted a system of rebates designed to ensure bona fide settlement. He arranged for the Fraser Company and its buyers in the district to withhold $1.50 per cord from the price paid to settlers for pulpwood. When the settlers had made sufficient progress in clearing land, King would notify the company to forward them the remaining $1.50 per cord; if the settlers failed to make progress, the money was sent to the Department of Lands and Mines as payment for stumpage. "I am doing this with the view of preserving the wood and causing more lots to be settled", the scaler explained, revealing the curious paternalism of his scheme: "Holding back the money is for their own good...otherwise they will get their money, spend it, then it is impossible for them to work on their lots clearing land for the comming [*sic*] summer". In a self-congratulatory letter to the deputy minister written one year later, King proclaimed his rebate programme a success, declaring that it was the "cause of the residence and clearing" and "should have been done years ago". Prince wrote back to "congratulate" King for his innovation, which was "after all in keeping with the spirit of the Act".[113] King seemed to have demonstrated to the department that effective control could be exerted on the settlements and that applicants could be made to follow the regulations of the Labor Act.

In the end there was a not so subtle irony to this initiative. When the scaling returns from the Fraser Company began to arrive in July 1926, Prince called a halt to the experiment. The arrangement may have resulted in more cleared land, but it did nothing to prevent illegal cutting. "It is evident that our administration of the Labor Act is far from perfect", the deputy minister wrote, noting that

111 R. O'Leary to Prince, 17 July 1926, DMOR, box 56, PANB.

112 Anon. to Department of Lands and Mines, 1926, DMOR, box 54, PANB.

113 King to Prince, 9 May 1926, 1 September 1926; Prince to King, 13 May 1927, DMOR, box 55, PANB.

some settlers cut "as high as 125 cords" on their lots, "which it is very unlikely came off the four acres or even within the ten acres". "Consequently", he continued,

> much of the material purchased by the Fraser Companies Ltd. must have been taken outside of the area being cleared and would therefore be subject to double stumpage. It seems to me that the whole matter should be reversed in method and instead of the Fraser Companies Ltd. holding back money the applicant for the lot should not be allowed to cut or sell without a permit signed by our representative....With the large number of unapproved lots in Madawaska County it is almost an impossible task for one man to keep a reasonable check on the cutting. I believe that there is at least 1000 ungranted lots occupied or partially occupied in your county. The holding back by the Fraser Companies Ltd. of the $1.50 has shown the seriousness of the problem.[114]

By 1927, the department had been fully aware of the seriousness of the problem for some time, but was not much closer to a solution. Its inability to control settlement could not have been made more glaringly obvious.

Class, Clientelism and the State

The Labor Act brought together leaseholders, rural workers, politicians, clergy, state, administrators and a host of merchants and forest entrepreneurs in a complex set of interactions. Fundamentally, however, New Brunswick Crown land settlement was a class competition between workers and leaseholders for control of forest resources. On the surface, the struggle was carried on in a practical manner, with each side utilizing the means at hand. Underlying the struggle, however, were competing conceptions of the Crown lands. When Kent County leaseholder Richard O'Leary commented that settlers cutting on land he held under licence "seem to have gotten [sic] into a way of thinking that this particular piece of land is public property, and it takes alot [sic] to convince them to the contrary", he touched upon these competing conceptions of the Crown forest.[115]

Technically, the Crown land was, of course, public property, but as O'Leary's remark suggested, there was some ambiguity among leaseholders in accepting it as a reality. While leaseholders often claimed to be unopposed to bona fide settlement, such claims were usually made as a preface to condemning the Labor Act. In the minds of leaseholders, Labor Act settlement was a violation of the social contract that formed an intrinsic, if unstated, part of the licence agreement. Leaseholders, particularly the older lumbering families, believed that

---

114 Prince to King, 18 July 1927, DMOR, box 55, PANB.

115 R. O'Leary to G.H. Prince, 25 September 1926, DMOR, box 56, PANB.

their efforts as community patrons, providing tax revenue and employment, justified unfettered control over the land they held under licence. The moral indignation with which many leaseholders reminded the government that they had paid ground rent and other fees for decades was, in effect, an assertion of perceived rights. The use of phrases such as "our property" in referring to their licences revealed that, for long-term leaseholders, the distinction between public and private forest land had become blurred.[116]

Within rural New Brunswick communities, there was an alternative understanding regarding Crown resources. The statement by frustrated Labor Act applicant Bert Lyons that "I think it is about time the Department was taking more interest in the working man instead of lumberman who gets whatever they ask for", expressed a widely shared sentiment.[117] This hostility was rooted in an understanding that the public domain, which should have been utilized to promote the general welfare, had been progressively endowed to a few wealthy lumber operators. In corresponding with Deputy Minister Prince in 1925, Donald Gordon of Northumberland County articulated the extent to which dissatisfaction with the administration of the Labor Act was part of a wider critique of state Crown land development policy:

> It looks to me that the Crown Land Office has to do what the banks and lumbermen tell them....I might say here that the lease held by Burchill and the Royal Bank is illegal and therefore they are trespassing on that lot. It seems strange that all of our Crown Land should be held by Banks and Trust Companies to be exploited at the expense of the people of the province[,] but we may be able to make some changes when the next election comes if we can have a plank in the Opposition Party platform calling for a cancelling of all the leases and going back to selling the them by auction and that will give every man a chance.[118]

---

116 On the responsibilities assumed by leaseholders see Bill Parenteau, "Reclaiming the 'People's Heritage': Political Protest and the Administration of Crown Land in New Brunswick, 1930-39", unpublished paper, University of New Brunswick, 1992.

117 Bert Lyons to G.H. Prince, 5 February 1929, DMOR, box 61, PANB.

118 D.S. Gordon to G.H. Prince, 5 May 1925, DMOR, box 51, PANB. Donald Gordon lived in the vicinity of the controversial Curtis Settlement and in 1925 wrote a series of letters criticizing the Department of Lands and Mines for its handling of the Labor Act. He was particulary incensed by the department's tolerance of lumber operators stripping lots during the first year of approval. The comment on the illegality of Burchill/Royal Bank lease referred to a clause in the Crown Land Act which prohibited the holding of leases in trust by financial institutions. The Burchills, like many other leaseholders, were forced to put up their Crown land leases as collateral after the lumber market crash in the early 1920s left them deeply in debt to the banks. However, the clause prohibiting trusts was

The undercurrent of hostility toward Crown resource distribution never coalesced in a direct challenge to existing political structures. Instead, the hegemony of lumber operators over the forest resource base was resisted at a lower level, through such means as using the Labor Act, to gain access to the Crown land. Such means required little or no organization and allowed rural workers to use the existing system to their best advantage. It is important to recognize the alternative conception of proper Crown land use and the difficulties faced by the state in legitimizing unequal resource divisions in order to understand the almost casual manner in which thousands of applicants violated the letter and spirit of the Labor Act.

The process by which rural workers gained access to the Crown lands points to the need for a re-examination of the relationship of political clientelist networks to class-based action.[119] It has been generally accepted that the hierarchical and individualistic nature of patron-client relations inhibits class consciousness, action and organization. Inasmuch as they provided rural people with an avenue in which to pursue certain benefits, thereby linking their interest to those of local Conservative and Liberal party members, clientele networks may well have acted as barriers to the development of established class-based parties and political movements in New Brunswick.[120] However, formal organization constitutes only one element in the spectrum of class action.[121] In

never enforced by the provincial government. See Parenteau, "The Woods Transformed". For contemporary comment on the issue see Notes on Interview between Innis and G.H. Prince, in "Notes on the Maritime Lumber Industry", H.A. Innis Papers, b72-0003, no. 6, pp. 82-5, UTA.

119 Again, a clear distinction needs to be maintained between political patronage and economic patronage, as the leaseholders were certainly important in the clientelist structures of the province but opposed the Labor Act.

120 See Christopher Clapham, "Clientelism and the State", in Christopher Clapham, ed., *Private Patronage and Public Power: Political Clientelism in the Modern State* (New York, 1982); R. Lemarchand and K. Legg, "Political Clientelism and Development: A Preliminary Analysis", *Comparative Politics*, 4 (1979), pp. 149-78; S.J.R. Noel, *Patrons, Clients and Brokers: Ontario Society and Politics, 1791-1896* (Toronto, 1990); R.A. Young, "Reconstruction in New Brunswick".

121 While the patron-client model is a useful tool for understanding the economic and political organization of New Brunswick communities that are dependent on the forest, it is necessary to move beyond the narrow parameters in which pluralist scholars of clientelism have defined class action. The statement by R.A. Young that "clientele networks are based on relationships which are hierarchical, particularistic, and diffuse, and so they inhibit class consciousness and horizontal organization", is typical of the manner in which class is dismissed as a category of analysis based on an article of faith rather than on any attempt to examine the internal dynamics of a particular system. In this regard the pairing of "class consciousness and horizontal organization" is significant, as it reflects

New Brunswick, as elsewhere, rural class relations grew organically out of material conditions of existence and were shaped by available opportunities. Because of public ownership of the most important resource in northern New Brunswick, existing patron-client political networks provided rural workers with their most practical means of addressing inequality in the distribution of resources. A shared conceptualization of Crown land administration as a political process promoted an exchange between rural workers, who desired access to the resource, and officeholders, who used the Labor Act as a means of reproducing a loyal constituency. With respect to the Labor Act, political clientelist networks were an important tool employed in the pursuit of class interests, rather than a rigid structure preventing class action. This is not to suggest that rural workers controlled or were the principal beneficiaries of patron-client relations, either in the political or economic form. It is to suggest, rather, that such political relationships could be an integral, though not necessarily determinant, element in the small and limited class struggles undertaken by rural workers.

A discussion of the Labor Act also demonstrates the need for a closer examination of the contradictions between state policy making and administration. Historians of resource development policy in Canada have generally concentrated on the tip of the iceberg — the point at which the state promotes large structural changes in the division of Crown resources.[122] At the upper level of policy-making, the state often appears as an instrument of the dominant faction of capital, as subordinate entrepreneurial and producing classes do not possess the resources to mount effective political challenges that would change policy at this level. With regard to the transformation of the New Brunswick forest industries in the 1920s, for example, there was little real consideration of opposing interests when the government facilitated the transfer of thousands of square miles of Crown land and the vital water power resources of the province to a few pulp and paper companies.[123] However, there was a much broader set of relationships revolving around the administration of Crown lands that were very different from the more visible processes at the top. Such was the case with the

only a crude attempt to understand the nature and scope of class relations. The argument here is that clientele relations are often class relations, specifically because they are hierarchical, involve unequal exchange and are structured to maintain the position of elites. The desire to gain access to the public resource by rural workers was a conscious act by a specific class and was not made any less conscious because it was pursued within clientelist political structures. Young, "and the people will sink into despair", p. 128. On the reluctance of Marxist scholars to utilize the patron-client model see Peter Flynn, "Class, Clientelism and Coercion: Some Mechanisms of Internal Dependency and Control", *Journal of Commonwealth and Comparative Studies*, 12 (1974), pp. 129-56.

122 See, for example, Nelles, *The Politics of Development*; Martin Robin, *The Rush for Spoils: The Company Province, 1871-1933* (Toronto, 1972).

123 Parenteau, "The Woods Transformed".

Labor Act, a programme that, despite progressive initiatives in the 1920s, defied any formal division of resources or the application of consistent administrative regulations.

The wide divergence between formal statutes and their implementation reflected the limited power of the state in New Brunswick to legitimize and enforce resource divisions constructed at the policy-making level. Thus, at the level of administration, the state reappears not as a monolith defined by its promotion of the interests of a single class faction, but as a social formation being continually reshaped by its own limitations and by pressure exerted from various classes of producers and entrepreneurs. Individually or in small groups, rural workers competed effectively at the administrative level, the point at which they best understood how the state functioned and had the means by which they could gain control of resources. However small and even petty the individual events which made up such competitions, their cumulative impact was significant. Often wielding the "weapons of the weak", rural workers in New Brunswick acted to pursue and defend their interests within a harsh political economy of necessity and subsistence.

Time, Memory and Rural Transformation: Rereading History in the Fiction of Charles Bruce and Ernest Buckler

Erik Kristiansen

The literature of Atlantic Canada is permeated with representations of the historical transformation of the region. Historical change and community transience are central concerns in regional fiction; indeed, they form a common paradigmatic feature of its form and content. It is commonly understood in literary criticism that history, memory and common sense are patterned in our individual and collective navigation of past and present, but criticism too often merely assumes these moorings, noting them as little more than a backdrop to the narrative. If we look beyond this backdrop, we can see how centrally the historical transformation of the Atlantic Canadian countryside figures in the creation of regional novels. In particular, we should note that strands of anti-modernist thought run through regional literature in Atlantic Canada. Writers such as Charles G.D. Roberts, Bliss Carman, Andrew Macphail, Thomas Raddall, Hugh MacLennan, Alistair MacLeod and David Adams Richards have all offered us critical assessments of modernity.

A number of critics simply dismiss this tradition as regional conservatism or imply that it is somehow out of step with contemporary literary concerns. The examples of Charles Bruce and Ernest Buckler, however, suggest that while this perspective is conservative, it is not naive: it is an anti-modernist, sometimes even anti-capitalist, radical conservatism. While often excessively romantic about life in rural Atlantic Canada, these writers do not view their homeland as a rustic utopia cut off from the modern world. They have witnessed modernity's intrusions and lamented its effects. They reject urban modernity and much of what it stands for. Modernity has thrown the world into a state of chaos, driving us forward at an ever-accelerating speed of cultural, technological and social change. At the centre of this revolution is the commodity. The commodification of social life has thrown religion, politics, personal relationships and even our innermost thoughts into the impersonal marketplace. This exploration of the imagined regions of Charles Bruce and Ernest Buckler highlights their anti-modernist critique of the process of capitalist transformation in the Maritimes.

Most of the criticism devoted to Maritime writers has been strongly influenced by the New Criticism. Literary scholars influenced by this movement often silence historical and ideological questions. Literature is seen as a special discipline that must avoid the approaches of philosophy, history, political theory, political economy and other fields. These critics centre on the analysis of literary structures and on a biographical and psychological approach to understanding the motivation of their fictional characters. However, there is a need to combine the examination of the literary and psychological structures of fictional characters with the biographical study of the authors' developing world view and their understanding of the rapidly changing world in which they lived. Focusing on the authors' awareness and articulation of historical, social, cultural and economic issues is an approach that must involve a broad interdisciplinary and intertextual grounding and migrate across the borders of the currently entrenched academic disciplines.[1]

Janice Kulyk Keefer has recently written the first major criticism of Maritime literature. Her work is powerful and sweeping, both in its range and insight, yet it lacks a sustained treatment of Maritime critics of capitalist transformation. Her treatment of Buckler and Bruce stresses the importance of history to both writers, although she takes a very narrow view of history as "times past". It is surprising that Keefer's awareness of class, capitalism and market forces, so effectively used in her analysis of Hugh MacLennan's *Barometer Rising*, is not extended to her analysis of Buckler or Bruce. She argues that Maritime fiction is "overwhelmingly representational...selecting out of the welter of phenomena...those things that have a peculiar resonance for the writer and have been habitually overlooked by the reader". She adds that "Maritime writers would seem to share a confidence foreign to modernist and postmodernist alike, a belief in the reality and significance of the accessible world of human experience common to reader and writer. That which is actual, to hand, and meaningful by virtue of association with established patterns of thought and action...."[2] Keefer seems to be arguing that both Maritime history and our regional literary canon are transparent and perhaps "simple" to under-

---

1 My notion of intertextuality and interdisciplinarity is derived from the work of Mikhail Bakhtin who argues that criticism should move in the "liminal spheres...on the borders of all the aforementioned disciplines, at their junctures and points of intersection". See Mikhail Bakhtin, "The Problem of the Text in Linguistics, Philology, and the Human Sciences", in *Speech Genres and Other Late Essays* (Austin, 1986), quotation at p. 103. I would like to thank Ken MacKinnon, Ian McKay, Scott Milsom, Daniel Samson, Anders Sandberg, Maggy Burns and Maggie Austin for comments and discussions over the course of writing this piece.

2 Keefer, *Under Eastern Eyes: A Critical Reading of Maritime Fiction* (Toronto, 1987), p. 6. Raymond Williams' discussion of realism, while noting its many senses, explains that realist "art or literature is seen as simply one convention among others, a set of formal representations, in a particular medium to which we have become accustomed. The object is not really lifelike but by convention and repetition has been made to appear so". See Raymond Williams, *Keywords: A Vocabulary of Culture and Society* (London, 1983), pp. 257-62.

stand. Of course, there is no obvious reason for this to be true, except in the mind of a critic.

Keefer is clearly arguing that "the intractability of reality" forces all but some recent Maritime readers as well as writers to prefer a representational fiction. This may be a defensible position, although not one she maintains consistently.[3] More problematically, however, Keefer also suggests that the literary critic should accept Maritime realism or transparency as the only approach suitable for the study of our regional literature and history. The only possible explanation for such an anomalous regional fiction would be that Maritimers are isolated and naive in their understanding of their own world. A contrary case is argued here. In this view, while their fictionalized readings of Maritime history may not be quite as accurate as we might now like, Charles Bruce and Ernest Buckler explored the historical complexity of the rural transformation and did so in ways that suggested the emergent "non-transparency" of a society in rapid change.[4]

Bruce and Buckler were both intimately concerned with the transformation of small, face-to-face, pre-modern communities into localities integrated into an impersonal, modernized society. This theme is not confined to Maritime novelists; it was a preoccupation of many 19th- and early-20th-century social theorists. Ferdinand Tonnies' ideal types, *gemeinschaft* and *gesellschaft* (literally, community and society), provided a paradigm for examining differences between small pre-modern societies and modern urban-dominated ones.[5] Such an apparent binary conceptual framework is also present in the work of the English literary and cultural historian Raymond Williams. Distinguishing between the transparency and opacity of social relations within the text, Williams posits that, on this basis, we could set up a contrast between the fiction of the country and the city: "In the city kind, experience and community would be essentially opaque; in the country kind, essentially transparent".[6] He goes on, however, to qualify this distinction: "But a knowable community, within country life as anywhere else, is still a matter of consciousness and of continuing as well as day-to-day experience. In the village as in the city there is division of labour,

---

3   See Keefer's interpretation of Buckler's *The Mountain and the Valley*, in *Under Eastern Eyes*, pp. 224-31.

4   For a critical evaluation of Keefer's approach to history see Erik Kristiansen, "Keefer and the Search for an Ideal Community", *New Maritimes* (September/October 1988), pp. 29-33; and "Crisis of Rural Community", *New Maritimes* (November/December 1988), pp. 29-34.

5   Derek Sayer notes that "past and present" contrasts have characterized 19th- and 20th-century social theorists: Tonnies' *gemeinschaft* and *gesellschaft;* Weber's "traditional" and "rational"; Durkheim's "organic" and "mechanical" solidarities. See his *Capitalism and Modernity: an Excursus on Marx and Weber* (London, 1991), pp. 9-13.

6   Raymond Williams, *The Country and the City* (London, 1985 [1973]), p. 165.

there is the contrast of social position, and then necessarily there are alternative points of view".[7] Williams escapes nostalgic romanticism by recognizing also the social positions of the authors and their historical context. It is "not only the reality of the rural community; it is the observer's position in and towards it; a position which is part of the community being known".[8] Rural communities are transparent not because they are knowable in a simple empiricist manner but because their indigenous observers are grounded in the language and "reality" of their fellow inhabitants' mode of living in and "thinking" the world. What is equally clear, though, is the limited basis for the writer to have a particular insight as a knowing observer.

Community for Williams is a product of a face-to-face society, but the issue is that of whom one comes into social contact with and the basis for that contact. Both for the author and the characters, to be face-to-face is already to belong to a class. Williams distinguishes between the known and the knowable community. The knowable community is "a selected society in a selected point of view". He demonstrates that in the 19th- century English novel, characters of other classes, usually subordinate, generally appear "as a landscape". What we learn about these people, and how we learn about them, comes to us not directly but "only through externally formulated attitudes and ideas". Only where the idiom of the novelist is connected with the idiom of their characters can we see the individual as a "real" character; the other characters, those of a different class and speaking a different language, emerge through the eyes and ears of the characters who speak the author's idiom.[9]

Williams' notion of the "knowable community" is an important one for students of the literary representation of Maritime rural transformation. Many Maritime novels convey representations of the capitalist transformation of the countryside, and this essay focuses on only two significant figures for whom Williams' categories are important.[10] This reading of the novels of Bruce and Buckler demonstrates that the transformation of pre-modern Maritime communities and the emergence of a capitalist modernity are problems that preoccupied these writers and raised for them difficult questions of "realism" and "representation". Rereading these crucial novels reveals the importance of allowing history to enter fictional texts, and to be read from them as well. A knowledge of the historical transformation of the Maritimes can, enrich our un-

---

7   Williams, *The Country and the City*, pp. 166.

8   Williams, *The Country and the City*, p. 165.

9   Williams, *The Country and the City*, pp. 166-9.

10   This research is the first part of a longer project concentrating on the social history of the Atlantic Canadian novel. Douglas Lochhead suggested such an approach to our regional literature in "The Literary Heritage: The Place, The Past, The Prospect", in *Atlantic Provinces Literature Colloquium Papers* (Saint John, 1977), pp. 3-9.

derstanding of both our regional writers and their aesthetic creations, just as their insights can enrich and complicate the findings of social historians.

Charles Bruce and the Uncertainty of Modernity

Charles Bruce's *The Channel Shore* calls attention to the historical transformation of Maritime Canada's countryside and the continuities and discontinuities of our historical experience. Focusing on the distance which separates urban capitalism from the mode of living associated with small Maritime farming and fishing communities, Bruce brings to life the transformation of class and gender relations that accompanied the gradual decline of both subsistence and small commodity production, enabling us to see the far-reaching changes to a mode of work widespread in the rural Maritimes.[11] In his fictitious community of the "Channel Shore", based on the Port Shoreham area of Guysborough County, Nova Scotia, Bruce captures the capitalist transformation of the countryside. It was a movement away from a culture and sense of community suffused with an ideology of kinship relations and a jack-of-all-trades craft mentality to an urban, capitalist society, one he sees as alien to Maritimers.

This historical rupture is situated at the centre of both *The Channel Shore* (1954) and Bruce's later collection of thematically connected short stories, *The Township of Time* (1959), covering the broad period of time from 1786 to 1950. Both *The Channel Shore* and *The Township of Time* tell the story of non-capitalist communities as they are transformed by capitalism.[12] Bruce provides us with a glimpse of the complex interplay between the major centres of capitalist development and a region on the periphery. Indeed, his consciousness of an apparent historical mutation, and his attempt to come to terms with it, is the integrating preoccupation of much of Bruce's writing. Sadly, the depth of his historical insight and the critical edge of his thinking have been largely ignored.

Interpretations of Charles Bruce's *The Channel Shore* have largely ignored the history foregrounded in the novel. John Moss and Andrew Wainwright both note Bruce's historical awareness yet ignore his obvious concern for the histori-

---

11 In this paper, subsistence producer refers not to an ideal type, but to a mixture of subsistence and small commodity production. Small commodity production will refer to limited production for exchange in the marketplace. See Martha MacDonald and M. Patricia Connelly, "Class and Gender in Fishing Communities in Nova Scotia", *Studies in Political Economy*, 30 (Autumn 1989), p. 63.

12 Charles Bruce, *The Channel Shore* (Toronto, 1954). All subsequent references are to the 1954 Macmillan edition. The New Canadian Library edition (1984) and the Formac Press edition (1988) are photo reprints of the original Macmillan edition. *The Township of Time* (Toronto, 1959). The New Canadian Library edition was published in 1986.

cal context of his characters' lives.[13] Similarly, Andrew Seaman argues that *The Channel Shore* "describes a process of social integration",[14] but his lack of interest in the historical context of *The Channel Shore* leads him to neglect the disintegration which the Shore has already experienced. This history, as the novel repeatedly tells us, has always been present, and it forms the context for continual reintegration. Janice Kulyk Keefer argues that the "dominant force" in *The Channel Shore* is the "passage of time and the process of change, both of which, we are made to feel, will ensure the Channel Shore's survival as a living community".[15] Yet Bruce is hardly so optimistic; his conclusion is ambivalent but certainly suggests the community's disintegration may be final. This history of modernity's effects frames the entire story. Such issues as rural/urban polarities, the decline of small commodity production and the expansion of wage labour must certainly have advanced a break with the past and a quest for some sense of continuity. Indeed, it is the movement around discontinuity and the search for continuity and reconciliation with which the novel is most concerned.

Articulating an ambivalence in his dialogue between past and present, Bruce conveys a social vision of an expanded kinship network to confront the inevitable tensions of capitalist modernity. He uses the realist novel to situate the different responses of rural Nova Scotians to these intrusive forces. Because of the open-endedness of his aesthetic vision, Bruce permits a polyphony of voices to engage in a dialogue about an emerging Maritime modernity.[16] He also uses

---

13   John Moss, *"The Double Hook* and *The Channel Shore"*, in Moss, ed., *Patterns of Isolation in English Canadian Fiction* (Toronto, 1974), p. 181; Andrew Wainwright, "Day of Future Past: Time in the Fiction of Charles Bruce", *Studies in Canadian Literature*, 8, 2 (1983), pp. 238-47 and *Charles Bruce, A Literary Biography: World Enough and Time* (Halifax, 1988).

14   Andrew Seaman, "Visions of Fulfilment in Ernest Buckler and Charles Bruce", *Essays on Canadian Writing*, 31 (Summer 1985), p. 159.

15   Keefer, *Under Eastern Eyes*, p. 56.

16   This clearly is not the case in other Maritime novels that deal with rural change. Hugh MacLennan develops a deterministic social philosophy and extends it to include the naturalist form of the novel in *Barometer Rising*. His solution to the dilemma of modernity was a form of nationalism, one with obvious religious overtones, that would resolve the social, economic and cultural dislocations resulting from the expansion of capitalist social relations and the marketplace. The various voices in *Barometer Rising* are submerged in MacLennan's paean to nationalism and his middle-class ideological agenda. MacLennan seems to have suffered no such internal debate and becomes the spokesperson for a particular vision of modernity. *Barometer Rising,* dominated by MacLennan's voice, becomes an example of Bakhtin's monologic novel. These arguments are developed further in Erik Kristiansen, "Time, Memory, and Transformation: Representations of Development in the Nova Scotian Novel", M.A. thesis, St. Mary's University, 1991.

the realist novel to explore the experiences of Maritime women and men who for the last century have struggled in a variety of ways to live in (and come to terms with) the continuing experience of historical transformation.

Bruce was undergoing his own internal debate about the nature of his home, his own lived experience of a variety of voices speaking in his own consciousness. Although he was the product of rural Nova Scotia — Guysborough County was and still is one of the least urbanized parts of Nova Scotia — Bruce lived in large urban areas from the 1920s on: Halifax, Toronto, New York and wartime London, cities divided by class tension, poverty, violence and crime. Such opaque cities, vast hubs in which the individual could easily become isolated and anonymous, Bruce perceived to be the very antithesis of the face-to-face transparent rural community. Such rural areas as the Channel Shore

> gave to the cities bordered with woods and grass
> A few homesick men, walking an alien Street;
> A few women, remembering misty stars
> And the long grumbling sigh of the bay at night.[17]

As one character in *The Channel Shore* puts it with memorable bleakness, in "Halifax you could be alone with...aloneness" (p. 287). There was more here than the nostalgia of the uprooted Maritimer. Bruce's rejection of cities implied a critique of the capitalism they exemplified. This economic critique is foregrounded throughout Bruce's major work, *The Channel Shore*.

Early in *The Channel Shore*, the reader is confronted with a quotation from the first volume of Marx's *Capital*. Stewart Gordon, one of the more "traditional" characters in the novel, puzzling through the intricacies of Marx's political economy, discloses the seriousness of his reading: "This Marx", he remarks in frustration to his daughter. "Trouble is, you have to learn a whole new language. Listen to this":

> 'The two phases, each inverse to the other, that make up the metamorphosis of a commodity constitute a circular movement, a circuit: commodity-form, stripping off of this commodity-form, and return to the commodity-form'.

"Now", Stewart concludes, "I've got to go back and figure out commodity-form again" (p. 29). Stewart Gordon is an avid reader, but it seems unlikely that Bruce introduces Marx simply to reveal Stewart's love of reading. This reference may provide a conceptual key that allows us entrance to a fictionalized

---

17 "Words are Never Enough", in Wainwright, *Charles Bruce*, pp. 70-1. Originally published in 1951, it is also found in Andrew Wainwright and Lesley Choyce, eds., *The Mulgrave Road: Selected Poems of Charles Bruce* (Porters Lake, N.S., 1985), pp. 50-2. Thanks to Ken MacKinnon for this reference.

Ruesdale

Maritime community in economic and cultural transition. The concept of commodity goods or services produced primarily for their exchange value, rather than for their use value, can be used to map a route through *The Channel Shore* and examine the political economy of the community described early in the novel.

The novel is framed throughout by the history of the Shore and of its people. Characters continually invoke the past — their own and that of the Shore — to situate their present. Integral to their history is the recognition that what is valuable in the present is a product of how life was once lived. Alan Marshall, reflecting on what "made up living" on the Shore, points to "haying or the herring-run" (p. 234). Work, how you did it and for whom, is central to how Alan sees value. Similarly, Stan Currie, who has returned to the Shore after years in Toronto, knows how wage labour takes away one's independence: "When you go to a city", he reminds Bill Graham, "you put yourself under a boss. You're back where you were a hundred and fifty years ago" (p. 395). Dependence and wage slavery characterize the city; the essence of the Shore lies in independence. But as the 20th century proceeds, this rural alternative is being eroded. The Shore is no longer capable of supporting people's personal or collective independence. The history of the Shore — a history structured by work — has been overtaken by its urban antithesis.

Beginning in 1919, *The Channel Shore* takes us through the community's major changes over the following 30 years. The economic life of Bruce's Shore is spread over a 30-mile area of his imaginary Copeland County. The community known as The Rocks is the "beginning of down-shore", and thus "began the stretch of shore on which men still gave most of their time to fish — trawling for cod and haddock, netting salmon, and setting their herring-baited pots for lobsters" (p. 34). In the 19th century, from The Rocks to Forester's Pond, fishing dominated the economy, while, up-shore, farming and working in the woods were the centre of a stagnating economic life. But in Currie Head, the central location in *The Channel Shore*, fishing has lost its importance; except for the annual herring run in July, nothing remains of the community's fishing tradition (pp. 15, 61). Few of Currie Head's people are still engaged in fishing, and those who are appear as cultural and economic conservatives, out of step with the time and marching to the echoes of a drummer long since dead.

Describing the historic settlement and use of land and sea around the Shore, the narrator outlines a period of development followed by a prolonged economic depression. The shore was a "frontier" which had freed its settlers from the "bonds of Europe", only "to become a breeding-place for migrants, men and women who were born there, raised there, and who left the Shore in youth for the States and the West". There was, however, a "golden period" when the area had "prospered by the standards of the time...[and] exported products other than its flesh and blood":

It was a harsh prosperity, based on circumstances that were not to last; but while they lasted the Shore overflowed, up its small and crooked water-courses, over the fold in the land, into the standing woods. Younger sons and new settlers chopped out and burned and planted new fields, a mile, two miles and more, from salt water (p. 12-13).

But the golden age did not last long: "most of the back fields had returned to woods", and life along the Shore was now marked by few opportunities for its young. As soon as they were old enough to work for wages, young people left the Shore. A few remained, but the best, we are told, go to Toronto or further west, while others find work in the "Boston States". It is these disruptions, "those small continual migrations" (p. 290), which form part of the Shore's confrontation with modernity and its painful integration into a larger capitalist market.

The central concern of *The Channel Shore* is with development and underdevelopment. Many of the Shore's first inhabitants were Scots, émigrés from the wrenching modernization that was the clearing of the Scottish Highlands. The parallel with the Shore, and with Nova Scotia in general, is obvious. At one point, Alan, the foster son of the central character, Grant Marshall, is reading his school history text:

> *Though not part of the loyalist movement, the Scottish emigration to Nova Scotia belongs roughly to this period. Economic conditions in the Highlands...* (p. 198, original emphasis).

Alan's reading of the text is interrupted by a conversation with his foster father about economic development along the Shore. He then returns to his reading: *"...in the Highlands of Scotland were the principal cause. In 1773 the vanguard arrived..."* (p. 198, original emphasis).

Life was hard for these Scots on the Shore. They wrested a "harsh prosperity" from land and sea which could not endure. Like the natural rhythms of seasons and the tides, their fates were subject to change:

> *Years ago things changed in this part of the country. We got into hard times. It's like a tide, only it's years between the high and low. The tide went out because the nature of things change...Fish got to be business, and the mack'rel scarce...More money for day labour and less for what you could catch or grow. Cheaper to buy than to make...When a man made wages and spent them there was more to show in the house. Boughten carpets, parlour organs...but after a while there wasn't enough work for wages to go 'round. You can't turn the tide, so people had to find what they wanted...* (pp. 352-3, ellipses and italics in original).

The comparison of the economy with the natural movements of the tide is significant. Just as the shoreline and the forests ebb and flow through the tides and settlement, in *The Channel Shore* a transforming economy is experienced as both hostile and "natural" — and it is intrinsically opposed to the needs of a humane community. Bruce seems to be suggesting that societies are held captive by their economic organization and geographic location. The emergence of a commodity culture and of unsatisfied desire reinforces this sense of powerlessness in a changing world. And, ultimately, it comes to undermine Bruce's beloved rural community as well. This perception of an economy as both autonomous and reified establishes the boundaries of Bruce's historical vision. His tidal trope both dramatizes and, to some extent, subverts the deliberate infiltration of history into *The Channel Shore*. The compelling intrusion of memory never diminishes. History, like the all-encompassing and unavoidable movement of the tides, fills every corner of this work. Therein lies its brilliance, but also a significant limitation. An abstract historical determinism weakens this work as a historical novel: we are presented with major economic forces severed from the history of social relations, both along the Shore and the larger world outside, and from the choices and alternatives faced by the people of the past.

Social transformations are part of this tidal change. *The Channel Shore* explores the waning and eventual demise of a variety of non-capitalist extended kinship bonds and their replacement by a new capitalist spirit. Bruce describes an economy composed of a single class of small producers, with varying degrees of status and influence, on its way to becoming a part of a more complex society structured around the existence of a highly differentiated class system. Josie, an elderly woman, remembers the countryside of her past and the roughness of life when she was young in the closing decades of the 19th century:

> "Yes. Rough. Life was a little rough...Y'know, when I was a girl — I used to help father with the fish....When I was fifteen, sixteen....People thought it was a wonderful thing, I s'pose, when kerosene lamps began to get common....Oh, it *was*, too, I guess. But people were independent, years ago. Not much money, but they didn't need it. Caught fish and farmed. Always a market for fish, and all they'd need to live on was the oats and potatoes and pigs and cows you could grow yourself..." (p. 352, ellipses in original).

We could interpret this as simple fondness for better times passed, a romanticization of when life was simpler. But it clearly points to Josie's uncertainty about modernity's "benefits".

In the first third of the novel, Bruce clearly establishes a number of different voices. The narrative shifts perspectives continuously, each time articulating a distinct social world as viewed through a different character and space. This social geography emerges in the various locations that make up the Shore and in the different world views of characters. Other voices advance particular views and establish the material and discursive bases for difference in the text that is the Shore. These scenes set up the associations and differences upon which various social groups on the Shore meet and clash. Fences cut across land marking one social space, while discourses cut through the Shore marking another, closely related, social space. Our question here, then, relates to whether *The Channel Shore* sustains these identifiable discourses over its course or whether it falls into, in Raymond Williams' term, a "particular and private sensibility".[18]

Four fundamentally different voices emerge in *The Channel Shore*. Each of these voices is connected to — but cannot be reduced to — the differentiation of social classes resulting from capitalism in the countryside and its rapid intensification in the international marketplace. One voice accepts rural capitalism as inevitable — necessary if at least some rural traditions are to be preserved. The second voice — one representing both boredom and unsatisfied desire — echoes the urban spokespeople for an emerging consumer culture. A third voice is scathingly critical of urban capitalism. Finally, there is a fragmented fourth voice, unsatisfied with modernity yet unable to situate itself in a rapidly transforming countryside.

James Marshall is the voice epitomising rural conservatism. Marshall can trace his family roots back to the Shore's earliest colonization in the late 18th century. We are informed that the "Marshalls came down from English officials who had followed the first settlers to Nova Scotia when the province was still a colony" (p. 104). James, for instance, always "changed from working-clothes to a suit for the evening" (p. 151). This symbolic gesture is only a surface manifestation of a sensibility that permeates James' mind. James, an ambitious man, emphasizes "hard work and careful figuring and virtue. The Lord helps those who helps themselves — if they serve Him" (p. 57). The Protestant work ethic underlies both James' presence in the world and his attitude to himself.

James has become a central figure in a gradual transformation of the Shore. He harvests his hay with machinery. His machinery shed, unlike a "hundred sheds along the shore" which "rested their sleepers on wooden posts or low walls of loose stone", is based on concrete (p. 93). Buying a vacant farm, a product of past disruptions, to provide "the extra hay he needed for his sheep and cattle", as well as more wooded land, are part and parcel of James' acquisitive and possessive personality. However, Bruce makes it quite clear that James Marshall is not a capitalist. James lacks the dynamism for seeking "venture", one of the central themes of the novel, usually suggesting, alternately, movement (leaving as venture) and progress (economic and social innovation as venture). Venture involves uncertainty, but "James Marshall's life came down as close to the rock of certainty as James could make it" (p. 162). James operates

18 Williams, *The Country and the City*, p. 180.

his family farm with the assistance of his two sons and his nephew Grant. He hires little wage labour except for local boys who pick cultivated strawberries in their spare time (p. 24). Although James is still a small commodity producer, as are the other farmers in the area, his economic status is widely acknowledged, and, in an important sense, his methods and farming practices make him an incipient capitalist farmer.

A sense of boredom with the conservative rural life of the Shore dominates the second voice. We can see this unsatisfied desire most clearly in the characters of Hazel McKee, Anse Gordon and Joe McKee. These characters see only stasis on the Shore and seek release in "venture". It is this search for venture which Stan Currie pursued in Toronto until he saw what he had left on the Shore:

> "That's why I'm back, if you want to know...What could a man do, that had venture in it, and independence? I looked at what I'd got by leaving. Running water and central heat and something — oh, *cultivation*...Well, they seemed to me to be cancelled out by the pulling and hauling, the pressure to say 'yes' when you wanted to say 'No'...*There was venture in coming back*..." (p. 395, emphasis added [ellipses in original]).

Anse Gordon and Hazel McKee personify a vague but powerful urban, individualist restlessness. Their brief affair, which results in the pregnancy on which most of the plot turns, is based not on love but on an aimless, bored hedonism. Anse is an egomaniac in search of conquest and enjoys his notoriety; Hazel is frustrated, bored with the "sameness that for years had eaten at the core of [her] mind" (p. 24). In 1946, Anse Gordon, the community outcast, returns. When Anse decides to repair his father's old fishing boat, quite a stir is caused along the Shore. When asked why he was doing it, Anse replies, "What for? Oh, fun" (p. 318). This coy reply is part of his efforts to maintain his aura of mystery. But, like the *Bluenose II* (the schooner which serves as Nova Scotia's "tourist ambassador"), the boat is really just a replica; it is used only at the summer fair where the young people of the Shore simulate the seafaring tradition that was once central to their ancestors' lives. The building of the replica proceeds not out of a pre-modern reverence for the past but from a shallow appropriation of history as recreation, undertaken by a man with limitless contempt for local culture. Anse, articulating a yearning for change among the Shore's young, thus gives "venture" its shallow therapeutic face.

The problem of "venture" for a settled rural community is focused with particular intensity in chapter 20 of the novel. Grant Marshall is clearing land for his future home with the assistance of young Joe McKee. Grant admires Joe because he "had a mind full of schemes for making money" (p. 161). Grant realizes that "his own life, too, was a blend now of certainties and gambles. In

years past it had been all certainty. Almost all" (p. 162). Rejecting Uncle James'
desire for certainty, Grant saw that "now the moorings were cast off":

> He was afloat on the same sea as Joe. Joe and all the rest of them. It
> seemed to him now that this was what he must have been looking
> forward to, this tingling sense of life half plan and half chance, in the
> days when he had traced his dream of the future here...But — he had
> been dreaming in terms of certainty or something close to it. He had not
> seen the contradiction (p. 162, ellipses in original).

Joe's entrepreneurial restlessness expresses itself in a burst of enthusiasm for the
possibilities for venture on the Shore, advising Grant: "Put in a crew and go
after pulpwood big? You could make a go of it..." (p. 163). Joe, however, plans
to leave the area as soon as he gets a stake: "That's what I want a stake for.
That's all a man can do around here — raise a stake to get somewheres else" (p.
163). While Grant recognizes that Joe and he may be "afloat on the same sea",
he seeks his "stake" on the Shore.

Grant's voice is a complex one, both critical and admiring of capitalist
entrepreneurship. This critical viewpoint approaches an anti-capitalist conservatism rooted in the independence of the small farmer and fisher. To depend on
someone else for wages means a loss of freedom; entrepreneurship, however,
while abstractly admirable as a manifestation of venture, is morally ambivalent
in its social consequences. Grant Marshall, reflecting on the values of his closest
relatives, emphasizes, "But — working for others; it wasn't necessary, except *in
the ordinary way* of exchanging help....Self-sufficient" (p. 133, emphasis added
[ellipses in original]). Another character, Stan Currie, a former professional journalist, speaks most forcefully in our third voice, arguing that it was to rediscover
independence that the Shore was settled in the first place:

> Some got pitched off the land when the lairds began to see more money
> in sheep than people. I'll bet you most of them ended up here because
> they couldn't stand being pushed around. Highlanders, lowlanders,
> Irishmen, Catholics, Protestants, loyalists, all kinds...Only one thing they
> all had. They *will not* take a pushing 'round. Not for ever. They'll stand
> most anything from land and sea. That's all right. Nobody else is telling
> them...
> ...What they did, getting out, was pull off a kind of rebellion. The only
> kind they could. Personal independence...For a while it opened out on
> this Shore...Then steam came, and other things, and it wouldn't work any
> more. A lot went to the States, and west, and some did all right. Then at
> last there was nowhere to go but cities. When you go to a city...unless
> you're good, in a profession or the arts, you put yourself under a boss.
> You're back where you were a hundred and fifty years ago. The sad thing

is, you got there by following the same urge they followed when they rebelled against it... (p. 395, ellipses and emphasis in original).

Stan Currie has returned to the Shore; his perspective is from afar. Richard McKee has never left the Shore and works in his own way finding value in his independence. While he never articulates a critique as clearly as Stan Currie, the distance he keeps from modernity is equally expressive.

Ambivalence characterizes our fourth voice, best seen in the character of Bill Graham. Bill, the son of someone who has left the Shore, lives in Toronto. He has been to Currie Head only once, as a child in 1919, but his history is also woven into the Shore. His happy childhood memories and a festering discontent with both his marriage and life in general prompt his return (pp. 270-3). Bill's father, Andrew, a Toronto-based professor of mathematics, has never returned to the Shore. He believes his son's desire to return to the Shore is based on his "illusion" of the Shore. "It seems odd", Andrew says,

> ...But I think I know what takes you back. Some sort of illusion. It might be kinder to memory....Suppose the illusion lives. Harder, perhaps, to....harder, perhaps, if you see a kind of rough well-being, to reconcile yourself to the nagging regret, the ice of surface living (p. 271, ellipses in original).

Bill can only visit the Shore again; he cannot remain. He "would never live on the Channel Shore. But it was home" (p. 396). He has visited this "home" only twice in his 39 years. For Bill Graham and Stan Currie and surely also for Charles Bruce the venture was in coming back to where they saw "depth" in the "rough well-being" of the Shore as opposed to the "ice of surface living". Yet, no matter how great his discontent with modernity, Bill Graham returns to the urban world of modernity after his therapeutic stay on the Shore.[19]

This ambivalence is also found in the novel's central character, Grant Marshall. But Grant, who has spent most of his life on the Shore, has lived this ambivalence in a different way: his life has been a dialogue with the voices of the Shore. Grant's personality can be seen as a product of a combination of these voices, a critic and a pioneer of "modernity". He firmly admires independence. Yet, Grant and his wife, Renie, "had begun to think about leisurely things: comfortable furniture, hardwood for the fireplace, china and silver for the table" (p. 280). A few years earlier Grant had been worried by the novelty of such comfort:

> There must have been quite a bit of talk about useless gadgets — running water, a furnace, a bathroom. In a region where there was little

---

19   See T.J. Jackson Lears, *No Place of Grace: Antimodernism and the Transformation of American Culture, 1880-1920* (New York, 1981). Lears argues that anti-modernism assumed many forms, one of which was an escape into a therapeutic pastoralism.

essential change except birth and death and moving away, perhaps it *was* odd to contrive something new... (p. 190).

Change, however, involves more than new material possessions. Although Grant is still working close to home, his major economic activities are not centred on the household. Moreover, for his wife Renie, modernity means neither independence nor a "traditional" role in the rural household; she is a "modern" housewife and a good mother, caught between being central in the productive household and independence. Renie is perhaps the most stereotypical modern figure in *The Channel Shore*: the housewife who stands behind her male breadwinner.

How Grant sorts out the strands of his life is centred on his finding a stake on the Shore. He is an ambitious and talented man who adamantly refuses to leave his life on the Shore for "steady" work. Grant combines the clearing and working of a small farm with short periods of work away from the Shore in order to accumulate much-needed cash. Eventually, he hires part-time labourers to cut pulpwood and lumber that he sells for a profit; he then goes on to establish a lumber mill, one of the few distinctly capitalist enterprises along the Shore. Grant's business activities contribute to a far-reaching change in the class organization of the area. Ironically, then, while he is often the most eloquent critic of modernity in the novel, Grant and his foster son, Alan, become part of an emerging local capitalist class.

The critique of wage labour is part of Bruce's dialogue with modernity and clearly foregrounds a passionate voice of resistance to capitalist modernization. Yet he presents the budding capitalist, Grant Marshall, in so favourable a light that any critique of urban capitalism is countered by a voice favouring some rural capitalist development. This dialogue between the opposing voices of development and conservatism appears to be resolved in favour of a conservative rural capitalism: an independent producers' society closer to the perceived economy of the Shore's past. A feeling of ambiguity pervades the closing chapter. One is left with a sense that something irretrievable has been eroded.[20] In the closing lines of the novel, the narrator describes Bill Graham's thoughts about the many people who have left the Shore:

20 In his biography of Bruce, Andrew Wainwright points out that Bruce was a heavy drinker during the time he was working on his unpublished first novel "Currie Head". Wainwright also emphasizes the close links between the fictional life of Stan Currie and Bruce's personal life. Stan eventually returns to the Shore, as does the later Stan Currie of *The Channel Shore* to escape the drudgery of his work as a journalist. Bruce was not happy with either his career as a journalist or with his life in Toronto. In fact, Wainwright suggests that the writing of "Currie Head" was "very much an attempt by [Bruce] to come to terms with who he was (and *is*, at the time of the writing) and where he came from". See Wainwright, *Charles Bruce*, pp. 85-101.

Idly he thought of them. Of their minds turning, sometimes, to the Shore
in waking dreams. Wondering, perhaps, as he would wonder, how long a
time must pass before they saw this land again, and heard its voices.
A long time...
Already it was passing (p. 398).

Value is truly to be found in the Shore, but the source of that value is under pressure, threatened by modernity. Bruce's loss of his childhood home, his search for
a present actuality that could satisfy his desire for historical rootedness, per-
meate both *The Channel Shore* and *The Township of Time*.

For Bruce, fiction and poetry seemed to be "resources of hope", vehicles for
remembering that enabled him to mobilize memory to resolve, on an imagina-
tive level, conflicts and frustrations that seemed irresolvable outside the bounds
of aesthetic imagination. The transformation of his childhood home, together
with his long-term absence from the Maritimes, made him eternally homesick
for a way of life that had disappeared. In contrast with Bruce's nostalgia for the
Maritimes was his life in Toronto, which, although he had been a successful
journalist and administrator for Canadian Press, he regarded himself as part of
the rat race.[21] Because of its ruthless inaccessibility, the passage of time becomes, particularly during periods of intense change, a preoccupation of the
present. *The Channel Shore* is obsessed with time and memory. Phrases such as
"the eternal present", "the timeless land of memory", "the precarious present",
"time in precarious balance" and "the lengthening run of time" suggest that
Bruce was fascinated and, indeed, preoccupied with a deeply rooted sense of
historical transience and estrangement.

Alan, searching the past in a loft above Richard McKee's work shed, grasps
this sense of "permanent" transience:

His hands roved and probed as his eyes explored the chest. A jumble of
worn objects, unrelated to each other, but all linked with some aspect of
life on the Channel Shore. Linked, most of them, with ways of doing
things that had changed and faded and been replaced by tools and
methods of the present. He fingered again the brass-studded palm, and
for a brief moment had a curious vision, a sense of knowing the past,
when wind in the tanned sails of two-masters had been the Shore's
transport, when the road was a track and buggies few and gasoline
unheard of. He felt a little sad, not at any sense of old things lost and

---

21 Bruce's experience of homesickness and his identification of urban modernity as
a rat race is found especially well-developed in one of his long poems which expresses this sentiment in a particularly virulent form, *The Flowing Summer*
(Toronto, 1947). Bruce's nostalgia for the lost home of his childhood is found
interconnected with his rat-race conception of modernity in Wainwright's biography. See *Charles Bruce*, pp. 95, 212, 213, 221 and 238.

gone, but at the realization that the present things, the tools they now worked with, the lumber truck, the saw-mill they didn't yet possess, would some time go the way of these mouldy tags of living stowed in the workshop loft. But there was revelation in the feeling, and this submerged the brief sadness. When present things were gone, new ones would take their place. For the first time, he was conscious of glimpsing yesterday, today and tomorrow as part of a continuing whole. It put things in balance, and in a kind of abstract way was comforting when you thought of it (p. 243).

Such sentiments, common in Bruce's poetry, are particularly poignant in his long poem *The Flowing Summer*: "The task of living was a chase", wrote Bruce, "that left / No time for living" (p. 2).

Bruce's childhood home, Port Shoreham, became more than an object of nostalgic reverie for him. He used his remembrance of the rural community with its strong kinship ties as a stabilizing influence and ideal in the urban world of routine, alienation and class division. The kinship of blood relations is examined throughout *The Channel Shore*:

There was now a kind of kinship for all others isolated in their aloneness, stricken by circumstance, caught without an answer to the riddle of living. A new sense of the future, of being one among many who must move and change with time (p. 124).

Bruce's understanding of this new type of kinship corresponded to the emergence of a new set of economic arrangements both on the Shore and in Canada as a whole. But his reduction of the complexities and contradictions to kinship issues, even granting his broader conception of kinship, mutes his criticism of capitalist modernity. It is here, that Bruce fails to transcend his nostalgia for time past.

This failure is firmly rooted in the limitations imposed by the author's class position. Distance from home and a long career with Canadian Press may well have blunted the edge of his criticism. Perhaps the diffuse critique of wage labour in the closing pages of *The Channel Shore*, combined with his desire for a new kinship of hope, was as far as he could go in his overt discontent with capitalist modernity. It is important, however, to remember that only two voices — Andrew Graham, a minor character who is given only a few lines in the novel, and Anse Gordon — can be interpreted as advocates of modernity. Both characters are ultimately rejected, although in very different ways. While Bruce lived in modernity, he was not about to celebrate it in his novel.

Bruce never seems to overcome a profound ambivalence toward modernity. We are left with Grant Marshall as a kind of unfulfilled hero, living Bruce's ambivalence but, unlike Bruce, staying on the Shore. Bruce spends the first third of the novel establishing differences in the four voices we have seen. But in the

final pages, if there is a dominant voice, it is the voice of ambivalence and uncertainty; in the end, it is those who can satisfy desire, who can find venture on
the Shore, who dominate the dialogue. We go back to Raymond Williams and
remind ourselves of the limitations of the author's perspective. Capitalist modernization is only in part the penetration of the market from outside; it is also the
internal differentiation of the community in the wake of its failure to keep pace.
The problem is not so much the *emergence* of capitalism as the *failure* of
capitalist development. The "golden age" was based on trade and commerce; it
was not pre-capitalist, though neither was it the capitalist modernity of Halifax
and Toronto. When Josie Gordon recalls the "rough" prosperity of the past, she
recalls not an age of pre-capitalist social relations but the relative prosperity of a
rural community interacting with a broader capitalist market. This "prosperity"
was underpinned by the connection to the land and the support of a household
structure not entirely dependent on wage labour; it is this feature of the past that
survives and which Bruce sees as threatened. These voices represent the residue
of older class positions. The "transparency" of their relations is historical — and
these characters certainly recognize the historicity of their relationships — but it
is limited within these groups. It is not only modernity's failure to support the
Shore that Bruce criticizes, but also modernity itself.

Ernest Buckler: The Agony of Modernity

For Ernest Buckler, the issue is far more clear. Modernity was deeply trou-
bling for Buckler; it formed an irresolvable paradox for his writing. Writing
from his farm in the Annapolis Valley, he saw the countryside as a beleaguered
shelter from the storm of modern industrial capitalist society. For Buckler,
modernity is that ever-in-flux, shifting, moving cultural space of the capitalist
city, where lived experience is shaped by this "unremitting process of rapid
change and its social consequences".[22] It is a world where change is so rapid that
the past becomes quickly alien and we no longer remember how "we" got
"here". The experience of modernity — "the glory of modern energy and
dynamism, the ravages of modern disintegration and nihilism...[an] uncertainty
about what is basic, what is valuable, even what is real" — was the negation of
all that Buckler saw as valuable.[23] Counterpoising the rootedness of country life,
where "you felt like a tree", Buckler describes urban living as like those "air
plants ... with no roots in any basic soil" (p. 136).[24] We can recall Marx's comments on modernity where "all that is solid melts into air" as markedly similar.

---

22   Marshall Berman, *All That is Solid Melts into Air: The Experience of Modernity*
(Harmondsworth, 1982), pp. 87-129, quotation at p. 121.

23   Berman, *All That is Solid Melts into Air*, p. 121.

24   Ernest Buckler, *The Cruelest Month* (Toronto, 1963). All subsequent references
are to this edition.

When we read Buckler's major works we are continually confronted with his scorn for the shallowness and disunity of the city and his yearning love of the country.

Buckler locates modernity in the city, principally in the fragmented culture and psychology of urban people and their distance from themselves and others. In both of his novels, we can see his concern in the critical stance he takes on urban life, but it is important to recognize that he situates his critique as much in the countryside as in the city. He was greatly attached to rural life and spent his youth and much of his later life in the Annapolis Valley. For Buckler, the countryside was a haven from the pressures of modernity. He lived there and celebrated its difference from the world of the modern. It is important to note that much of that celebration dwells on what rural people are *not* as much as on what rural people *are*. His long-time friend and literary admirer, Claude Bissell, remarked that it was "as if Buckler were tying to erect Nova Scotia into a barrier against the modern world he increasingly hated".[25] But he also saw that it too was endangered. Modernity was infiltrating the countryside at every turn; even there he saw modernity's reach enveloping the pre-modern islands he perceived rural communities to be.

Much of his writing is composed of dialogues between past and present and between the country and the city. For Buckler, the penetration of the marketplace into the countryside meant that rural Nova Scotia could no longer be truly rural, and there seemed little hope that these areas would gain any of the advantages of contemporary urban life. In Buckler's three major works — *The Mountain and the Valley* (1952), *The Cruelest Month* (1963) and *Ox Bells and Fireflies* (1968) — we are once again confronted with a conflict between what are perceived as two distinct patterns of culture and modes of production. At the very heart of this economic and cultural revolution is the commodity and the expanding capitalist marketplace. Buckler remained steadfastly devoted to the pre-modern countryside. He was painfully aware of the devastating incursions of the commodity: the reduction of human relationships to market transactions, and the intensification of this whole process of commodification by the culture of tourism. Buckler approaches the problem of rural transformation by examining its effects on small, largely non-capitalist communities, and by celebrating the maintenance of what was not modern. Rural Nova Scotia is always sharply contrasted with the modernity of urban life; the ominous present is seen against the backdrop of an earlier time where modernity's intrusions were much less prevalent. But where Charles Bruce felt some form of resolution might be possible with the modern world, Buckler saw the conflict as incapable of resolution. Indeed, even his cherished homeland would not be spared: "Nova Scotia", he remarked, "is no Shangri-La".[26]

25   Claude Bissell, *Ernest Buckler Remembered* (Toronto, 1989), p. 130.

26   Ernest Buckler, *Nova Scotia: Window on the Sea* (Toronto, 1973), p. 111.

Claude Bissell's fascinating study of Buckler provides important insights into his intellectual formation. Born and raised in the Annapolis Valley, Buckler left in 1926 to take his B.A. at Dalhousie University. In 1930 he completed the requirements for an M.A. in philosophy at the University of Toronto.[27] Buckler, at this time, translated his mature anti-modernist concern for a "classless" society of small producers into a desire for a socialist transformation of existing social arrangements. In an unpublished essay, "Greek and Christian Views of the State", written during his M.A. year, Buckler writes:

> If Christianity may be said to have an economic policy explicit or implicit it might be socialism. The Christian problem regarding riches disappears. The difficulty is not that man is "rich" but that man is "richer than." There is no objection to the goods of the world if they are shared. There is plenty for all and instead of man being rich, in socialism all will be equally poor and the needle's eye will have stretched and the camel shrunk so that a passage is possible. Socialism may seem contrary to the apparent extreme individualism of Christianity but the kingdom of God on earth is really what Kant calls a Kingdom of ends wherein the highest individuality is reconciled with social interdependence and where service is more or less perfect freedom.[28]

While hardly a revolutionary call to arms, this passage is suggestive of Buckler's early disenchantment with the competitiveness of the capitalist modernity he found in Halifax and Toronto. After completing his M.A., Buckler continued to live in Toronto. He worked as an actuary for Manufacturer's Life, which he referred to as the "Manufacturer's Life penitentiary". In 1936, Buckler returned home to West Dalhousie in the Annapolis Valley after apparently suffering a "breakdown in his health".[29] There he sought therapeutic relief from the city, combining farming with writing for the rest of his life.

Buckler's critique and ultimate rejection of modernity is an interpretive option that has been largely forgotten in Maritime literary studies. His affirmation of a "common sense" standing outside the world of the commodity and his passionate advocacy of a rural moral economy with only limited connections to an impersonal marketplace are easily dismissed in a world that is becoming a global shopping centre. Buckler's rural frolics, pie sales, local bartering and voluntary offering of labour linger on in our nostalgic fantasies about a simpler and more "natural" past.[30] When he describes our world of "Shopping Centres"

---

27   Bissell, *Ernest Buckler Remembered.*

28   Quoted in Bissell, *Ernest Buckler Remembered*, pp. 36-7.

29   Bissell, *Ernest Buckler Remembered*, p. 41.

30   See Ian McKay, "Twilight at Peggy's Cove: Towards a Genealogy of 'Maritimicity' in Nova Scotia", *Border/Lines*, 12 (Summer 1988), pp. 28-37.

with their "aisles of marked down goods putting as if an ash on the quick of the crowd-drubbed faces of the people who wander them", it is to reawaken our memory, the memory modernity refuses, of time past: of how shopping centres "sprang up where once were orchards. Television aerials comb the night for dross or screams where once the night kissed righteous muscles with the balm of rest".[31] We might criticize Buckler's romanticized representation of the rural world, but the contrast he poses with our own is dramatic and effective.

Throughout his frequently nostalgic attempts to recreate the past in words, Buckler's aesthetic critique of urban/industrial capitalism finds expression in the lives of fictive Nova Scotians. Sometimes the major character in a novel may, in the words of Frederic Jameson, act "as the vehicle and recording apparatus for a complex new and as yet unnamed feeling about things".[32] David Canaan, the pivotal personality in *The Mountain and the Valley*, is such a character. In Buckler's fictional community of Entremont, David is something of an odd figure, the stereotype of the artist as outsider: intelligent, introverted and profoundly different. Yet the world of rural Entremont so captures David's devotion and aesthetic imagination that he chooses to remain there and make it the centre of his future novels.

In *The Mountain and the Valley*, David Canaan's preoccupation with language is connected with his extreme self-consciousness, and with his isolation from the community in which he has lived all his life: "Inside [David] was nothing but one great white naked eye of self-consciousness, with only its own looking to look at".[33] When David is walking up the mountain road, he muses, "It's perfect here", because at last he is "absolutely alone" (p. 286). David's feeling of isolation, of an intense separateness from Norstead, is present throughout the epilogue. Early in the epilogue David is contrasted with Steve, a local farmer whose "health was in him like a cadence" (p. 282) and who is absolutely lacking self-consciousness: "Steve's half-thoughts made a cadence only slightly louder than the unattended cadence of his flesh" (p. 282). David is not healthy; he has recurring headaches and serious heart problems. Psychologically, David is simply not "together". David is defined by his self-consciousness, his alienation from Entremont, which he nourishes, and his ability to misrepresent himself. (In *Ox Bells and Fireflies* these personality features are all identified with city people). His precocious intellect alienates him from the down-to-earth values of the barely literate farming families who have lived in the community for many generations. David Canaan, notwithstanding the biblical optimism of his name, is the personification of alienation, and Entremont is no Eden. Indeed, it is a world undergoing profound and often disturbing transformation.

31 Buckler, *Nova Scotia: Window on the Sea*, p. 125.

32 Frederic Jameson, "History and Class Consciousness as an Unfinished Project", *Rethinking Marxism* 1, 1 (Spring 1988), p. 54.

33 Ernest Buckler, *The Mountain and the Valley* (Toronto, 1982 [1952]), p. 281. All subsequent references are to this edition.

Buckler's three major works foreground the transformation of the countryside by the gradual infiltration of the culture and commodities of an urban-based industrial capitalism. His Annapolis Valley commenced its transition to modernity in the 19th century. The process gained momentum in the years following the First World War.[34] Describing land surrounding David's family farm, the narrator of *The Mountain and the Valley* tells us how the area had been transformed when "a big American company had bought these farms solely for their timber. The company had no interest in the houses or the fields. The people had moved to town" (p. 253). The Canaans, however, were fortunate; they "didn't sell off the land to make ends meet, as some did" (p. 125). But Joseph, David's father, still had to work occasionally for wages to supplement the meagre income from the farm. Cash was increasingly necessary to operate a small farm in Entremont:

> When Joseph came home from the drive there were ten-dollar bills amongst the one's — but those all went for the country rates, the tote-load of flour and feed, things like that. There was often two hundred dollars upstairs...but that was "cattle money". It might be borrowed from but must be repaid, against the time when Joseph bought another pair (p. 125).

Most of their purchases — a "set of portieres for Martha. A shotgun for Chris. A book for David. The silk dress for Anna" (p. 125) — belie any semblance of an independent rural life.

Buckler bemoans this new world, one which has lost touch with a supposed history:

> Neighbours had changed, as the village had changed. The road was paved now. There were cars and radios. A bus line passed the door. There was a railway line along the river. With this grafting from the outside world, the place itself seemed older; as the old who are not remembered are old (p. 229).

It is not only these obvious manifestations of change, however, that Buckler dislikes; he sees a much more profound change in the people of the Valley. In his memoirs of his childhood, *Ox Bells and Fireflies*, Buckler laments that "the people had lost their wholeness, the valid stamp of the indigenous":

> Their clothes were so accentuate a copy of the clothes outside they proclaimed themselves as copy, except to the wearers. In their speech (freckled with current phrases of jocularity copied from the radio), and

---

34 Margaret Conrad, "Apple Blossom Time in the Annapolis Valley, 1880-1957", *Acadiensis*, IX, 2 (Spring 1980), pp. 14-39.

finally in themselves, they became dilute. They were not transmuted from the imperfect thing into the real, but veined with the shaly [*sic*] amalgam of replica (p. 229).[35]

No longer an independent and resourceful rural folk, they now bore the expressions of a commodified world made for them.

One of Buckler's most common metaphors is the island. Emphasizing separateness, he uses it to suggest both the alienation of modern urban life and the isolation of rural communities from modern society. In the fifth chapter of *Ox Bells and Fireflies*, his most sustained non-fictional critique of the modern world, he describes cities as occupied by masses of isolated individuals, each one an "island". However, in the same work he describes the fictional community of Norstead — the Entremont of *Ox Bells and Fireflies* — which is also an island. This time, however, insularity is employed as a positive metaphor. The communal kinship of this rural world is referred to as "the greenest island of all", and as "island[s] of fraternity". But, for the most part, Buckler uses the island as a metaphor for isolation. Buckler's vision is of reified urban residents, "moving no less blindly than things". With a nightmarish quality, Buckler sees the isolated islands of city dwellers as centres of some sort of cosmic disenchantment. An urban alchemy had transformed the world and left it "stonestruck"; a lifeless human vision had people cut off from any meaningful contact: "There is no brother look in any of it ...". In cities we find only "the flat dead light of drilling is-ness..." In cities people are not only denied kinship with nature and other people, they have also lost any inward experience of kinship with themselves: "You look inside yourself and you see no brother-besiding self there either. Only the chalk-face of dismay..."(p. 83).

Buckler continues his prolonged and despairing preoccupation with modernity, comparing the "effigies" (mannequins) in store windows with the tide of people flowing through the street. He makes it obvious that this dehumanization springs from the social, economic and cultural organization of the modern city. Buckler's imagined origin for commodities is the city of capitalist development. The "effigies" in the shop display "their wax smiles ceaselessly against plate glass. Each face has its window to itself walled up, each with the small world behind it running like clockwork wound up and forgotten" (p. 85). However, we then read, "They jostle each other", and promptly realize that this forgotten world is not the window display surrounding the effigies, but the everyday world of people in city streets. The men and women in the streets are, indeed, effigies of "real" people — unlike the people of Norstead. City people, like the store-window mannequins, are dressed in the prevailing fashions of the time, not thinking but acting on directives. These "headless subjects and predicates" have

---

35 Ernest Buckler, *Ox Bells and Fireflies* (Toronto, 1974 [1968]). All subsequent references are to this edition.

lost control of their fate. Modernity has become their cage. Even faces are commodified: "There are fashions in city faces. Each [face] looks as if it had been
bought off the racks in a shop that stocked only the prevalent masks" (p. 87).

The scene shifts again, back to Norstead, where "eyes drove no bargain with
themselves or with the eyes of anyone else". Buckler "burn[s] with homesickness" for the wholeness of Norstead. "In Norstead", he consolingly tells us, "it
was not like that" (p. 85). The first half of "The Chords and Acres" section
focuses on the distance between the mode of living in Norstead — clearly a
parallel to Entremont in *The Mountain and the Valley* — and the daily routine of
the cities of modernity: "When you walked down the road and talked to each
other you made each other solid as places" (p. 87) Self-identity in Norstead was
"solid"; the self was never "bargained" in the daily life of Buckler's rural community. Buckler selectively remembers his rural childhood:

> Your dialogues with the field chimed below the surface of your mind like
> the tune of health....Even the old were not shunted aside. The sound of
> their lives had been so long a keynote in the family chord that it never
> ceased to resound (pp. 86-7).

For all his fervently anti-modernist celebration of the rural community, Buckler
does insert something of urban modernity into his beloved rural Nova Scotia. In
The Mountain and the Valley, the narrator remarks that people in rural areas
were becoming increasingly involved with urban-produced commodities and
suggests it was a habit few farm families could sustain. In *Ox Bells and
Fireflies*, Buckler observes that rural communities close to large towns and cities
were the first rural regions to experience the transformation to modernity. Indeed, all of the chapter entitled "Like Spaces, Other Cases" is devoted to a rural
community, Claymore, whose inhabitants have taken on the emotional, intellectual and "spiritual" characteristics of Buckler's urban population.

The Cruelest Month retreats somewhat more from an idealized memory and
introduces a "modernized" countryside. This novel can be read, in part, as a sustained and sceptical gaze at modernity and at the culture of tourism generated by
a "modernism of underdevelopment".[36] Buckler never directly explores the
complex reasons for the emergence of a distinctive Maritime modernity. But in
The Cruelest Month we take a number of excursions to the world of urban
modernity. His preoccupation with time past and time present continues as the
social, economic and cultural organization of cities was steadily penetrating further into the countryside. The traditional non-capitalist culture was being
replaced by a new dominant culture associated with the emergent capitalist

---

36 The phrase "modernism of underdevelopment" comes from Marshall Berman,
All That is Solid Melts into Air, pp. 173-286. It refers to an area which has been
penetrated in various ways by the culture of modernity, but has remained
economically underdeveloped.

marketplace. Describing how Paul Creed, the major character in *The Cruelest Month*, came in to possession of a farm which he turned into a tourist inn, the narrator informs us that

> a farmer called Mansfield had owned it then. The Brewster Lumber Mills had made a clean sweep buying up the other farms along the road, but he'd held out for a stiffer price. Then the company had gone bankrupt (p. 10).

The farm Paul bought turned out to be "the last house on the road. The lumber company had promptly demolished the other farms as fire hazards" (p. 11). Where in *Ox Bells and Fireflies* Buckler fondly describes how history was written into local place names — something Bruce also describes — modernity simply and relentlessly bulldozes history, literally wiping it out of existence.[37]

Buckler recognizes throughout the novel the importance of economic underdevelopment and the economic problems faced by rural people. An increasing number of people turn to the possibilities provided by tourism. Tourism performs two functions in Buckler's fiction. It provides an "industry" for the region, where their underdevelopment becomes "quaint" for the sophisticated urban dweller; and it provides a therapeutic retreat for those seeking an escape from modernity. Buckler brings into focus what Ian McKay has referred to as a "culture of consolation", although such a tourist-oriented culture, of course, would not have provided lasting consolation for such a convinced anti-modernist as Buckler.[38]

The Cruelest Month gives us countless people from outside the Maritimes who see the region as a haven for tourists, sports fishermen and hunters. A number of times in the novel, the rural Maritimes are desired for their potential therapeutic value. We learn that Sheila Giorno, another of the main characters and a thoroughly modern woman, is hoping to take her husband for a vacation:

> And all at once she had this rash and fierce wish that she could take him off some place where nothing or no one could ever close in on him again. Some island. Some simple, innocent spot. Just the two of them. Some wide, free, country place. Like Nova Scotia...(p. 52).

Morse Halliday, a visiting American novelist, continues this apology for the therapeutic value of rural life:

> "You drive from Yarmouth to Granfort through disembodied villages, with the man walking from the porch to the well looking like a man in a primitive painting walking from the porch to the well. I've never seen a

---

37 Buckler, *Ox Bells and Fireflies,* see especially the chapter "Memory".

38 Ian McKay, "Twilight at Peggy's Cove: Tourism and the Politics of Culture in a Dependent Canadian Region, 1880-1960", unpublished manuscript, 1987.

place quite like Granfort. It washes you clean of whatever your chronic mood. This is the very soil where settlers from the Old World first set foot on the New. You really feel it....Shell-coloured buildings pocketed in the living green above it still catch the light from another time" (p. 11).

Nova Scotia is perceived as a therapeutic haven, a place to regain the necessary psychological equilibrium that will permit re-entry to a harsh competitive urban world. Apparently, for some people, Nova Scotia *is* a Shangri-La.

For the people of the Valley, however, tourism, Buckler suggests, has meant a kind of collective delusion. Bruce Mansfield provides local commentary on tourist culture. One of the two main characters in the novel who are from the Annapolis Valley, his parents had previously owned the farm prior to its conversion to a tourist inn. When visitors explain to Bruce that they were late arriving at the inn because "they lost time behind a parade of some kind", he explains local tourist culture — the Mayflower Festival — an obvious play on the Apple Blossom Festival - with disgust:

> "They were crowning a fool Mayflower Queen. The Mayflower's our provincial emblem. And the funny thing is that, as a crowd, nobody could see the least thing foolish about it. It's like I say. In groups, we're a mess. But take any one of that group by himself and he'd be all for having a Pied Piper lead the whole fool procession right down to the wharf and into the river" (p. 98).

Buckler's anti-modernism was not to be appeased by trivial moments in which an imaginary "good life" of rural simplicity was temporarily paraded.

The anti-modernist position developed in *The Cruelest Month* is extended well beyond a critique of tourism. Bruce Mansfield, a spokesman for some aspects of Buckler's philosophy, reminisces about a vanished Golden Age:

> "Right here. Working with my hands. I'm right back where I started from. Where I belong."...In the last few days he had really come home. He had breathed again, as if he were standing in a breeze of it, *the spirit of how it used to be here.* When no one was more important than anyone else. No one gaining height by standing on someone else's face. When one man's trouble was everyone's, like the weather...(p. 135, ellipses in original [emphasis added]).

Bruce Mansfield's critique of a class-based society has both anti-modernist and progressive implications; his nostalgia for a simpler egalitarian past suggests that Buckler may not entirely have lost sight of his earlier socialist vision.

There is, however, also an element of a therapeutic modernity in Bruce's romanticized memory of the past. The therapeutic function of the cult of tourism infiltrates Bruce's classless rural haven. The life of rural small producers becomes a <u>form of psychological therapy</u> for the "stressed out" victim of modernity:

> All work but this left its own particular tarnish on your hands. This was the only place you could come back to with whatever little you had left and be able to feel sound and whole again, with no questions asked. It put no poultices on you, but you didn't fester. And while you worked you could lay down your wounds, like your lunch pail, somewhere in the shade beside you and the ground sat by them and took care of them. You must still pick them up again when the work was done; but you found them clean, not clogged with dust and grime. It was the only place where exhaustion made you feel cleaner at night, not dirtier. Because you'd been putting your muscles to the use they were meant for. No other workers felt tired that same clean way (pp. 135-6).

Mansfield's return to the "valley" is a form of therapy similar to that which Buckler himself had sought. Bruce Mansfield, before he returned as a casual labourer at Endlaw, had been training as a doctor in Halifax. At the end of the novel, Mansfield, after receiving the therapy of Endlaw, discovers that he is "whole" enough to return to the city. Unlike Buckler's permanent return to the Valley, Mansfield channels his anti-modern sentiments into a brief therapeutic respite from the rigours of a Halifax medical school — akin to the therapy provided by the culture of tourism.[39]

The apparent cultural unity of Buckler's rural, small and face-to-face community finds a parallel in the unity of the psyche, a wholeness of self fundamentally different than the fragmented self of urban modernity.[40] In Buckler's conception of the pre-modern and transparent rural community which appears in *Ox Bells and Fireflies*, "you can see both yourself defined for everyone and your self reflected out into all things" (p. 84). He contrasts the lack of cultural diversity in pre-modern communities with the cultural pluralism and personal fragmentation found in the cities. Kate Fennison, an "unfulfilled" 40-year-old intellectual from Halifax and one of Buckler's most modern

---

39 Bruce Mansfield's anti-modern sentiments — his return to the rural countryside of his childhood — function to enable him to return to the urban world of modernity. This is similar to the role tourism plays for Sheila Giorno and Morse Halliday in *The Cruelest Month*. It is interesting to note that Buckler also associates "recreational" sex with a therapeutic consciousness. In *The Cruelest Month*, Paul Creed reflects on therapeutic sex: "Casual, therapeutic sex. That kind of sex (and it was abundant hereabouts) had never threatened control of his own boundaries in the least" (p. 59).

40 The apparent homogeneity of Buckler's pre-modern Norstead and Entremont contrasts with the cultural pluralism in Charles Bruce's *The Channel Shore*.

women, provides one of *The Cruelest Month*'s numerous allusions to the fragmented self:

> My self's not continuous, like yours. You've never been alone enough to
> understand that. How, the minute you *are* alone this door inside you
> opens and you see your self standing there, waiting. That's the only self
> I ever see. The minute there's the hum of being with someone else it
> vanishes. That's the only self I can talk about: *to* myself, alone (pp.
> 154-5, emphasis in original).

Kate's understanding of her "self" foregrounds its incapacity to remain present;
it lacks solidity. Again we have this sense of airiness and unreality. It is a self
that seems "unreal" when contrasted with the integrated and wholly present
women of Norstead or Entremont.

We can read *The Cruelest Month* as a dialogue between the "forces" of
modernity thrusting people into apparent isolation and the integrating communal
ethos of the pre-modern community. This sense of community, and the simple
Christian religious beliefs of the people, form a nexus of meaning. This foundation of meaning is, for Buckler, absent in the world's various centres of
modernity. The isolation of the individual and the experience of psychic fragmentation are revealed in a particularly interesting manner in the erotic
relationship between Bruce and Sheila. The narrator describes Bruce's "mysti-
cal" and apparently "redemptive" experience of making love to Sheila as the
"one supreme holiday from self" (p. 194), recalling the therapeutic function of
tourism. The redemptive power of community and church in Buckler's rural
Eden is replaced by a sexual holiday but, as for any tourist, the respite is brief.

Buckler's understanding of modernity, however, is not grounded in either the
home as a "haven in a heartless world", or in sexual experience as psychic
therapy. Nor does this sense of estrangement find its roots in the fragmented
psyche. His is, instead, a much more *social* vision. Community breakdown and
the resulting "confusion" in language form the foundation of Buckler's dilemma.[41]   When Sheila in *The Cruelest Month* uses her urban consciousness to
convince Bruce to give up longing for his rural roots, the narrator tells us that he
"had never seen a face so multilingual in every feature" (p. 212). This line forms
a beautiful contrast with a similar reference in *Ox Bells and Fireflies*. Describing
the faces of the inhabitants of Norstead, Buckler describes "each face" as "writ-

---

41   Buckler's interest in the separation between language and the "reality" which it
suggests is foregrounded in both *The Mountain and the Valley* and *The Cruelest
Month*. In *Ernest Buckler Remembered*, Bissell tells us that Buckler read serious
philosophical works throughout his life (p. vii). It is more than likely that Buckler would have encountered "language philosophy" in his reading, and, perhaps,
even earlier in his graduate work in philosophy.

ten and readable in the same language as its neighbours" (p. 84).[42] Sheila's urban sophistication creates a radical separation between her and Buckler's pre-modern rural woman. Buckler's pessimism is striking here, as we witness their doomed relationship fade. Sheila's metaphorical multilingualism is a part of the fragmentation characteristic of modernity, which, for Buckler, is the inevitable result of the breakdown of pre-modern communities.

Buckler is not glorifying the outsider. David is an example of the fragmented self that is completely alien to Buckler's conception of the ideal personality. David's psychological "dis-ease" and modern sensibility are, in the epilogue to *The Mountain and the Valley*, related to his language crisis and, indeed, to a crisis in aesthetic realism. David, in one way or another, is preoccupied with the inability of language to represent reliably a complex ("swarming") reality to the mind. David resembles an urban intellectual more than a rural farmer. He discovers that "shape and colour reached out to him like voices" (pp. 286-7). He then realizes that there "seemed to be a thread of similarity running through the whole world" (p. 287). However, we become rather confused when David makes the leap to, "shape could be like a sound; a feeling like a shape; a smell like a shadow of a touch" (p. 287). And finally his "senses seemed to run together" (p. 287). Objects outside of David's consciousness project voices which will be processed by his mind. David seems to be experiencing "voices" as representations of reality. These voices, however, "swarm" (pp. 291, 296). The "voices" of past and present fragment and become infinite in number (p. 292). Can language, David repeatedly asks, represent them "exactly"? Even with the most careful use of language, memory cannot represent the past. When the epilogue is finished, we are left with the impression that language can never adequately recapture memory or even experiences that are thought to be grounded in the present.

We must counterpoise this modernist malaise of memory with how Buckler understands rural people's knowledge of their own historicity. Buckler appears to be suggesting that David represents a changing sensibility that becomes increasingly common as modernity disrupts the rural countryside. As the known ways of pre-modern rural communities confronted these changes, they became

---

42 For an alternative interpretation of language and self-consciousness in *The Mountain and the Valley* see Gerald Noonan, "Egoism and Style in *The Mountain and the Valley*", in *Atlantic Provinces Literature Colloquium Papers*, pp. 68-78. Although Noonan is aware that language is foregrounded in the novel, he misses its connection with the philosophy of language. He sees Buckler's concentration on language as an aesthetic flaw. My thanks to Ken MacKinnon for pointing out this article to me. Andrew Wainwright and Janice Kulyk Keefer also explore the significance of language in The Mountain and the Valley. See Wainwright's "Fern Hill Revisited: Isolation and Death in *The Mountain and the Valley*", *Studies in Canadian Literature*, 7, 1 (1982), pp. 63-89; and Keefer, *Under Eastern Eyes*, pp. 224-31.

unsuitable for life in a society dominated by a marketplace and capitalist commodities. Both linguistic and aesthetic realism as a way of knowing and experiencing the world became highly uncertain. To suggest, as others have, that David's problems are a product only of his alienation from the community and the loss of his sister Anna is in effect to leave David's alienation as only some form of existential angst and to miss the social and historical complexity of Buckler's vision.

The Cruelest Month develops this idea of the crisis of meaning in a modernist babel of tongues. "Progress", Buckler asserts elsewhere, is the "advance spy of Babel and steel, [and] has already begun to infiltrate and infest the land...".[43] The modernist plurality of voices is, in Buckler's social theory, a symptom of decay. This crisis in both language and meaning is foregrounded in *The Cruelest Month*, which can be read as a critique and rejection of writing — an ironic position for a professional writer to assume, but one very much related to Buckler's hatred of modernity. Buckler identifies the widespread and specialized use of writing with a period of historical development in which the organic and transparent rural community of face-to-face relationships had been displaced by the social relations and cultural forms of modernity, set in motion by an impersonal market. This transformation was most developed in Buckler's dreaded cities, that is, in the very centre of modern mass society. On the one hand, writing is connected with the fragmented self, alienation, a competitive impersonality, social inequality and entrenched hierarchies. On the other hand, we have speech, which is related to the small rural community, the immediate presence of other people, authenticity, integrated personalities, community solidarity, and social equality (pp. 97-8).

In *The Cruelest Month*, Morse Halliday, a published novelist who is in the creative doldrums, describes writing in rather bizarre ways. He refers to writing as a criminal act, something that left a "sour taste" in his mouth, and compares it to vomiting, and to masturbation,[44] the ultimate act of isolation. Morse questions the very act of writing, especially writing which imagines itself to be realistic: "What hope in hell did you have of trapping thoughts and feelings in a net as coarse as words?...Can't you see? One man, one little hen scratch. It's so impossibly hopeless" (p. 149). Morse Halliday, like David Canaan in *The Mountain and the Valley*, rejects the possibility of writing being faithful to the

---

43   Buckler, *Nova Scotia: Window on the Sea*, p. 125.

44   Jacques Derrida's reading of Rousseau sees a close connection between his analysis of writing in *On the Origin of Language* and his comments on masturbation in his *Confessions*. Derrida understands Rousseau to mean that they are both "supplements", in that both deal with representations of reality, or images, rather than reality itself. For Rousseau, however, speech directly encounters reality just as hetero-eroticism directly encounters another human body. See Jacques Derrida, *Of Grammatology* (Baltimore, 1976), pp. 144-57, 165-7.

complexity of either past or "present" reality. Paul Creed also rejects writing's ability to capture the complexity of life, going so far as to destroy his notebooks and a sketch for a novel because "lines themselves were merely the pencil drawings of thoughts with their eyes left out". He realizes they "brought back no shadow of the moment of which they had been the sole content at the time he had set them down" (p. 273). Paul, however, carries his criticism of writing further than either David Canaan or Morse Halliday. Paul rejects his modern world of language; he targets books in general as well as sophisticated speech, both associated by Buckler with an encroaching modernity:

> He didn't want books. He didn't want talk. The talk he'd been used to. That was forever on its toes, twisting and interlocking knowledgeable allusion; that was forever a tiring octave higher than the key speech is written in, as if it were always talk to be overheard, like the talk in books. He had a sudden disrelish — almost to loathing — for books and that kind of talk (p. 294).

It is not difficult to connect Paul's thoughts with Bruce Mansfield's nostalgia for a lost Promised Land, which was a vision of a time when "there were no specialized and worldly knowledges to put one man ahead of the other...[when] life then had no long, complicated words in it at all" (p. 267).

Reading Buckler, we must be attentive to the continuous dialogue between the social, spatial and historical relations of moderns and pre-moderns, the exchanges between his islands of rural culture and the larger world of modernity. It is not a simple vision. But the outcome, for Buckler, seems certain. The ending of *The Cruelest Month* is no more optimistic than the epilogue to *The Mountain and the Valley*. Paul's housekeeper, Letty Spence, is the voice of pre-modern culture. Letty, however, has been thoroughly exposed to the world of modernity — a road that, for Buckler, always leads away from Eden. Letty is barely literate and her speech is uncomplicated, still containing the older dialect of the region. At the end of the novel, Letty decides to impress Paul by learning to speak the "proper" way, the way tourists speak. Modernity has once again extended its parameters. Buckler offers the reader a vision of reality that questions fundamental assumptions, usually seen as common sense, about modernity. Unfortunately, Buckler's version of historical truth is all too easily dismissed by both modern and post-modern intellectuals who have, all too frequently, lost a sense of the historical grounding of memory and tend to see the past as an earlier and outdated dialect of the present.

Conclusion

In his classic essay, "Wolf in the Snow", Warren Tallman writes: "History has had and continues to have her say....When the impact of accomplished history imposes distinctions upon that actuality, sensibility must adjust itself to the distortions. The story of these adjustments is, I think, the most significant feature of North American fiction in our time".[45] Although the New Critics frequently pay homage to history, their actual critical practice *subverts* a significant historical engagement with the text. A critical methodology emerging from such an extreme version of the New Criticism implies an underlying assumption that the aesthetic text must be isolated from its connection with the world in which it was both created and read. What is, so remarkable about Tallman's historical awareness is his conceptual inability to put into practice such an emphatic claim.

Tallman views David Canaan's growing isolation and alienation as a failure to develop nourishing personal relationships. David is odd man out. When *The Mountain and the Valley* joins epilogue with prologue, David's only surviving relationship in Entremont is with his grandmother Ellen. Tallman's analysis is limited because the various strands of David's artistic sensibility, which also must be viewed as a product of his social world, have been separated from the larger historical fabric. It is not surprising that Tallman also fails to explore the historical foundations of Buckler's aesthetic sensibility. Tallman's New Critical approach, which treats David as an historically isolated individual, also validates the isolated aesthetic text. It is important, however, to keep in mind that the aesthetic text is not the only historical construction present in literary studies. Both the principles for reading and critiquing literature, as well as the institutional mode of production of these interpretive strategies, are historically constituted.

My own reading of Bruce and Buckler has been informed by the conviction that historical experience and the expression of diverse subjectivities are deeply connected. Literary approaches to fictive individuals must be broadened to include an examination of the "history" that exists within any work of art. Many Maritime novelists and poets conveyed their visions of historical transformation and economic development in their aesthetic productions. Exploring such diverse reactions to the emergence of a Maritime modernity could do much to enhance the understanding of our regional literature. Indeed it could be the first stage in exploring the possibility of a social history of Maritime culture. A complex understanding of the capitalist transformation of the Maritime countryside requires an exploration of the ways this epochal event was represented and reimagined, sometimes confusedly and sometimes brilliantly, by those who told the region's story in fictional form.

---

45   Warren Tallman, "Wolf in the Snow", *Canadian Literature*, 5 (Summer 1960), pp. 7-20; and *Canadian Literature*, 6 (Autumn 1960), pp. 41-8. Tallman's essay is also available in Gregory M. Cook, ed., *Ernest Buckler* (Toronto, 1972), pp. 55-79.

Afterword:
Capitalism and Modernization
in the Atlantic Canada Countryside

Daniel Samson

In putting together this collection we have attempted to write against the grain of the major narrative line of regional historiography. These essays are elements — parts taken from larger studies, slices cut from larger realities — they are neither aimed at synthesis nor presumed to be representative of complete understandings. Here I would like to pursue what introducing these new elements might mean. If these essays suggest the limitations of too narrow an interpretation of the "rural", they also stand against a deep-seated tendency to dismiss the value of rural work. And if, as suggested in the introduction, the urban-industrial framework that has dominated Atlantic Canadian historiography has produced a "two worlds" understanding of the region's past, then we should pause to consider what a different historiography might look like. The assumptions of modernization and transitions, in both their Marxist and liberal guises, have produced a historiography which "makes sense" — but much less so when we focus on elements which lay on that history's margins. These new elements are not anomalies. They are of the same world, but its people did not experience them in the same way. These remaining pages, then, explore further the dominant paradigms, and bring out something of our common critiques. Finally, I also wish to suggest how we might recast regional historiography to incorporate an understanding of the differences and similarities represented by the countryside.

Throughout the 19th and early 20th centuries, most workers and their work remained only partly incorporated within the spheres of urban-industrial society.[1] Rural people's lives continued to incorporate other practices; the

---

1   See, for example, Shirley Tillotson, "The Operators Along the Coast: A Case Study of the Link Between Gender, Skilled Labour and Social Power, 1900-1930", *Acadiensis*, XX, 1 (Autumn 1990), pp. 72-88; Allen Seager, "Minto, New Brunswick: A Case Study in Class Relations Between the Wars", *Labour/Le Travailleur*, 5 (Spring 1980), pp. 81-132; and Sean Cadigan, "Battle Harbour in Transition: Merchants, Fishermen, and the State in the Struggle for Relief in a Labrador Community during the 1930s", *Labour/Le Travailleur*, 26 (Fall 1990), pp. 125-50. Also suggestive here is the work of Kris Inwood and John Chamard which describes the relatively greater importance of small-scale artisanal, and heavily rural, production in the Maritimes as compared with Ontario. See Kris Inwood and John Chamard, "Regional Industrial Growth during

regulation of their lives could still revolve around periodic waged work and the maintenance of some independence from a capitalist labour market. Their work experiences may not have been strictly local, but the social relations which conditioned their entry into the labour market were. So long as complete dependence on wage labour could be deferred, so long as local politics and markets could provide what industrial society only *might*, and so long as something of a material and cultural distance remained between those rural locations and the nearby industrial centres, so, too, would liberal modernity form only one aspect of their lives. We can see something of this in Bill Parenteau's contribution to this collection, which outlines the localized basis of class politics in New Brunswick in the 1920s. The ability of Labor Act settlers to wrest minor concessions from local politicians and timber operators illuminated the limitations under which the state and capital acted. Although policy was directed towards limiting the abuse of what was supposed to be a farm settlement programme, the reality was that the settlers were more interested in cutting wood, and patron-client politics facilitated the continuation of this "abuse". These concessions were granted in offices in the provincial capital, but they came out of pressures directed locally, through the influence of individuals or communities. It was a cost that administrators and politicians accepted to secure a loyal constituency and their own hold on power.

Part of the analysis of these stories takes us to the importance of community as a conceptual tool. As Parenteau argues, underlying the complexities of this story were differing conceptions of Crown land; for the lumbermen it was "our property", but for the rural poor it was land to be used for the public benefit. It was the rural poor's ability to mobilize these shared notions within their own communities that created the local political pressures. Yet their support was by no means uniform, and different conceptions of the people's "rights" were contentious. "Community" is an imprecise and often misleading term. While often used only to identify a particular location, it usually signifies much more.[2] Community understandings underpin other studies in this collection. Daniel Samson and Steven Maynard both point to associational groups as communities or point to normative standards as being related to local understandings. Yet, one of their central concerns is to highlight the cleavages and points of conflict which cut

the 1890s: The Case of the Missing Artisans", *Acadiensis*, XVI, 1 (Autumn 1986), pp. 101-17. I wish to acknowledge the very helpful comments and support of Alison Forrest, Anders Sandberg and Ian McKay. Each of the contributors to this volume also read and commented on this essay before publication. Although some points of disagreement remain, I thank them for drawing my attention to a number of problems with the first version of this essay.

2   A useful short-hand route into the historical usage of community is Raymond Williams' discussion in his *Keywords: A Vocabulary of Culture and Society* (London, 1983), pp. 75-6. See also his important discussion in *The Country and the City* (London, 1973), especially pp. 165-81.

across groups of people — households, villages, occupations — in different ways. An event such as the 1909 coal strike in Inverness, pitting miners against miners, reminds us of the dangers of turning associations into "communities". And, as Rusty Bittermann's essay makes clear, Atlantic Canadians moved in and out of different work situations all over the region, suggesting the many ways communities were continuously formed and dissolved. Community becomes a spatial and social referent which looks very clear from afar, but which becomes more complex on close examination. This was the dilemma, as Erik Kristiansen argues, for Charles Bruce and Ernest Buckler, who each only partly overcame the distance between the communities they described and the realities on which they were based. Our dilemma is how to apply the insights that have been made at the local level without losing sight of the fact that the people whose lives we study were not necessarily limited to the bounds — and bonds — which our community studies tend to impose on them.

A more compelling explanation for the persistence of the local basis of power in the region lies in a better integration of the categories we have employed to analyse economy and society. How do we explain the ability of poor, rural workers to frustrate the most far-reaching plans of "modernizing" bureaucrats and other actors in the modern state? Or their ability to "bargain" with distant, powerful capitalists? We must begin by re-framing the analysis to include the connections between capital, the state and rural communities. Political historians, following the activities of the state at its institutional level, have detailed the growth of an activist state in the 19th and early 20th centuries where formal government assumed greater and more centralized functions.[3] Labour and working-class historians, looking to the centres of industry, have described the emergence of an industrial capitalist society in the region, one with very clear parallels to developments throughout North America. Indeed, the ingredients which make up a view of the transition to industrial capitalism — industries, technological change, urbanization, capital consolidation, a working class — come together best in the region's labour history, and this work is perhaps most responsible for our view of how that transition occurred. Yet there is

---

3   On the modern state in the region see Ernest R. Forbes, *The Maritime Rights Movement, 1919-1927: A Study in Canadian Regionalism* (Kingston and Montreal, 1979); Ian McKay, "Tartanism Triumphant: The Construction of Scottishness in Nova Scotia, 1933-1954", *Acadiensis*, XXI, 2 (Spring 1992), pp. 5-47; Rosemarie Langhout, "Developing Nova Scotia: Railways and Public Accounts, 1848-1867", *Acadiensis*, XIV, 2 (Spring 1985), pp. 3-28; Peter Neary, *Newfoundland in the North Atlantic World* (Kingston and Montreal, 1988); and Jim Kenny, "'We must speculate to accumulate': Mineral Development and the Limits of State Intervention, New Brunswick, 1952-60", forthcoming, *Acadiensis*, XXIII, 2 (Spring 1994). For a more sceptical account, see Graeme Wynn, "Ideology, Society, and State in the Maritime Colonies of British North America, 1840-1860", in Allan Greer and Ian Radforth, eds., *Colonial Leviathan: State Formation in Mid-Nineteenth Century Canada* (Toronto, 1992), pp. 284-328.

often a questionable insularity to the spatial and social locations assumed within these studies. While noting the importance of rural society, the dispersed enclaves of production and the larger movements associated with out-migration, we find ourselves looking for more ways of carving this into manageable units of analysis instead of searching for the connections. We focus on communities, industries or sectors of the economy with very little recognition of the simple fact that, while separable, they were in many ways interconnected.

To illustrate this point, I want to turn briefly to Graeme Wynn's *Timber Colony*, which illustrates some of the benefits to be found in such a more integrated view, as well as some of the pitfalls which might still lie ahead. Wynn's work stands as one of the key books on the development of economy and society in Atlantic Canada. Most importantly, for our purposes, it follows this story with a broadly rural focus: illuminating the close ties between the timber trade and agriculture, revising an earlier view of their injurious effects on economic prosperity and development, and bringing into sharp relief the many and complex social, ecological, political, technological and economic facets of the story.[4] Conditions in New Brunswick in the early 19th century compelled many, if not most, settlers to work simultaneously their land, the timber trade and the merchant's ledger. By mid-century, we have seen the transformation of a society where the aspirations of a "yeomanly independence" were overtaken by the realities of dependence on large timber merchants and the effective proletarianization of many of the rural poor — a series of changes, Wynn suggests, very much like the classical pattern of the Industrial Revolution in Britain.

Yet some of the essays in this volume suggest more continuity than Wynn's argument might allow. Looking at the early 19th century, one end of what Wynn refers to as an "age of transition", we have Rusty Bittermann's essay which suggests that the era of the "independent yeoman" may be more a reflection of historians' assumptions than a historical reality, at least as a general case. Moreover, by situating the forces which compelled rural people in seek wage labour *within* the countryside, we might reassess the role of the timber trade in producing those conditions which Wynn labels "proletarian". To the extent that these people were even analogous to proletarians, the farm economy surely played as important a role here. At the other end — indeed, 70 years later — we have Bill Parenteau's description of New Brunswick settlers in the 1920s which depicts a society where, for the rural poor, life had not changed that much since the mid-19th century. Labor Act settlers were not acting in the same context as settlers had a century earlier.[5] But however new the context, in terms of making

---

4   Graeme Wynn, *Timber Colony: A Historical Geography of Early Nineteenth Century New Brunswick* (Toronto, 1980). For some sense of Wynn's achievement, compare his account with that of A.R.M. Lower, *Great Britain's Woodyard: British America and the Timber Trade, 1763-1867* (Montreal, 1973).

5   Bill Parenteau, "The Woods Transformed: The Emergence of the Pulp and Paper Industry in New Brunswick, 1918-1931", *Acadiensis*, XXII, 1 (Autumn 1992), pp. 5-43.

a living within this "political economy of necessity", the techniques employed were not that much different. These rural workers drew on their past experiences — including their ability to work the land, their knowledge of woods work and available resources, and the local powers of patron-client relations — to limit the hand of the state and capital, and to maintain some independence from a market which continued to hold little promise for them. The point of concern here is not so much with the idea of transition as it is with the assumption of change such an idea brings with it, and where we choose to locate its determinants. It may have been, for example, that the 19th-century cycle of debt, (sub)subsistence rural production and seasonal employment was as important to the long-term reproduction of the social formation as any "modernizing" trends in the economy were in transforming it.[6]

We need to better our understanding of the differentially constituted relationships both within and between such sectors. The agricultural economy itself — and, moreover, the farm households which comprised it — played a decisive role in determining where and on what terms a farm household entered the networks of exchange as buyers or sellers of goods or labour. Very often entering rural markets meant exchange within the farm economy, but equally often it drew rural people into these other sectors. And, once people entered these relationships, rural exchange networks brought together landless labourers, poor farmers, surplus-producing farmers, country merchants, timber barons and sometimes international capital in a single, though differentiated and complex, economy. Cash earned by poor farmers in the timber trade often found its way back to the surplus-producing farmer via the country merchant; and capital accumulated by surplus-producing farms often found its way into investment in the timber trade (in a sawmill, in shipbuilding or in hiring someone to cut timber). If we are to understand even these particular economies, we need to expand how we conceptualize the rural and its central place in the region's social formation. Locating rural households within such a more broadly understood countryside draws our attention to a world whose apparent "backwardness" should not allow us to miss its dynamism.

Establishing a framework for understanding transitions demands that we attend not only to the technical manifestations of change but also to their material effects and possibilities. Capitalist development required the creation of a class of wage labourers, but this was not the only precondition. In Newfoundland, for example, social differentiation and a nascent capitalist fishery were underway in the late 18th and early 19th centuries. But, as generations of Newfoundlanders

---

6   This is in keeping with suggestions made in Eric Sager and Gerald Panting, *Maritime Capital: The Shipping Industry in Atlantic Canada, 1820-1914* (Kingston and Montreal, 1990). See also Ian McKay, "The crisis of dependent development: class conflict in the Nova Scotia coalfields, 1872-1876", in G.S. Kealey, ed., *Class, Gender, and Region: Essays in Canadian Historical Sociology* (St. John's, 1988), pp. 9-48.

have witnessed, industrial capitalism's development was weak, even by the standards of a chronically underdeveloped region. Sean Cadigan's contribution to this volume demonstrates that the failure of capitalist development cannot be explained by pointing to simple obstacles to change; a number of factors posed barriers to further development, highlighting the context within which these class processes unfolded. The particular variant of capitalist development in Newfoundland must be seen minimally as a product of the combined effects of fishing households' resistance to change and merchants' success in employing domestic production, and not, as some have argued, as the outcome of active merchant resistance to diversification or as the consequence of the powerlessness of fishing households. The limitations of international markets and local resources blocked capitalism's progress as much as did merchant hegemony. As Cadigan has argued elsewhere, those who reduce social relations to the nature of the resource (the staple) and those who underestimate the importance of the resource in "narrow[ing] the channels" in which class development occurred, equally over-simplify social relations and treat any social geography as if it were 19th-century Great Britain.

Rural people's activities bring out continuities in rural life which at many turns undercut the notion of a simple movement to modernity. If there was a central characteristic of the Atlantic Region throughout the 19th and early 20th centuries, it was the unevenness of its social formation. Attempts to tidy up this unevenness by reducing social and economic diversity to one clear narrative of modernization can be actively misleading. A critical history of an area where the "expected" outcome of industrial capitalism did not generally occur must demonstrate and explain that difference, not force it further onto the margins. These essays critique some common assumptions about rural society in the region. Drawn from different locations in different time periods, they take us in quite different directions: to the role of the law (not, as many have assumed, always working in the interests of Newfoundland merchants), to the role of the state (not an autonomous realm), to the role of gendered conflicts over resources within the rural household (not the egalitarian shelter), to the importance of wage labour in maintaining that hold on independence (not deriving their independence solely from the land), to the integration of agrarian labour requirements with those of industry (not mutually exclusive) and to the breadth and power of anti-modern assumptions even within the region's middle class (not out-of-step romantics but situated firmly within the modernist tradition).

More broadly, these studies also remind us of the various ways the development of capitalism — within the region and beyond — undercut and encouraged, and altered and maintained, various aspects of social life in Atlantic Canada. Drawing on their backgrounds for the resources available to them, many rural people articulated and lived conceptions of resources and society which were often completely at odds with the liberal ideologies taking hold over the 19th and early 20th centuries. Whether collectively determining use-rights to open-access resources, exchanging goods and labour between households, demanding more equitable work arrangements for seasonal employment in rural industries, or assuming the legitimacy of their claim to the forest resources, they addressed differently the issues of their day and often forced their way on to the political agenda of their social superiors. Wielding only the "weapons of the weak", they challenged that power, relying not so much on their mass strength as on their ability to withdraw to the relative security of the land. When set against an urban-industrial view, they suggest a variety of histories operating under logics which defy unilinear assumptions about the modernization of the countryside, simple cultural presuppositions about conservative or powerless peasant-farmers and fishers, and arguments based on "the needs of capital".[7] What we see in examining rural workers is not the mere contestation of dominant ideology and practice but broad-scale and very often successful resistance to the uncertainties of dependence on the market. For all the bridges that existed between rural and urban worlds, and for all the variation we can see *within* the countryside, we must remember that rural society was still something apart.

At the same time, we must not simply presume difference. In recognizing what was distinct within rural communities we risk reinventing "the folk", of turning rural dwellers into a variety of "primitive", pre-capitalist peasants. These studies force us to consider many rural people's acceptance, indeed their encouragement, of aspects of the emerging liberal and market cultures. In studying the history of Atlantic Canada, we have no need to explain the origins of capitalism; it came with European settlement. What we do need to understand is capitalism's particular forms and its reach, and how it came to form such a central aspect of rural people's everyday lives. Although they probably did not perceive their actions in these terms, evidence of rural people's role in the creation of markets emerged in their marketing and payment forms, the desire for consumer items, the negotiation and litigation of wages, and the simple requirement for cash. Counterpoising the market versus custom is clearly at odds with evidence which places people's patterns of production and consumption in both realms.[8] It is at these hybrid locations that we can describe the dynamic processes of both social reproduction and change. Establishing such poles draws our

---

7   See, for example, Gerald Sider, *Culture and Class in Anthropology and History: A Newfoundland Illustration* (Cambridge, 1986); and James R. Sacouman, "Semi-Proletarianization and Rural Underdevelopment in the Maritimes", *Canadian Review of Sociology and Anthropology*, 17 (1980), pp. 232-45.

8   See Stuart Hall, "Notes on Deconstructing the 'Popular'", in Raphael Samuel, ed., *People's History and Socialist Theory* (London, 1981), pp. 227-39; and Douglas Haynes and Gyan Prakash, eds., *Contesting Power: Resistance and Everyday Social Relations in South Asia* (Berkeley, 1992). See also Patrick Joyce, ed., *The Historical Meanings of Work* (Cambridge, 1987); and James A. Jaffe, *The Struggle for Market Power: Industrial Relations in the British Coal Industry, 1800-1840* (Cambridge, 1991).

attention to potentially important distinctions; uncritically leaving them in place as underpinnings for our stories risks returning the countryside to the margins of our history.

Existing theoretical approaches have both helped and hindered our analysis. Our view is too often limited to the structural, and largely economic, bases of the decisions which shaped rural lives; we interpret culture from those structural bases, but understanding the cultural bases which shaped those decisions is not yet within our grasp.[9] As Ian McKay has observed of Atlantic Canadian studies, sociologists have viewed this history from afar and effectively described the region's past as one without people, while richly detailed labour histories, describing regional communities in the light of more advanced capitalist societies, have "failed to register, let alone account for, the distinctiveness" of the region.[10] Certainly, part of that distinctiveness lay in the centrality of the countryside. Indeed, given the importance of the rural economy and its role in the formation of capital and class, we might argue that the development of Atlantic Canadian capitalism was fundamentally a rural story. The problem, though, is not theory but how we employ it. Only by employing theory creatively — theory which does not subsume difference and denies the either/or categorical imperatives of external/internal factors, class/pre-class, market/non-market, capitalist/pre-capitalist or the primary determinations of class or gender or ethnicity — can we begin to usefully describe (and account for) the distinctive history of the Atlantic Region. If we continue to mould regional history to the supposed universal categories of the development of capitalism, and if we continue to employ the language of that narrative (which describes distinctive-

---

9   Outside of Newfoundland, there is not a particularly strong ethnographic tradition in Atlantic Canadian studies. See, however, Gary Burrill, *Away: Maritimers in Massachusetts, Ontario, and Alberta: An Oral History of Leaving Home* (Kingston and Montreal, 1992). On Newfoundland see Gerald L. Pocius, *A Place to Belong: community order and everyday space in Calvert, Newfoundland* (Kingston and Montreal, 1991). Pocius situates such an analysis more historically in his "The House that Poor-Jack Built: Architectural Stages in the Newfoundland Fishery", in Larry McCann, ed., *The Sea and Culture of Atlantic Canada* (Sackville, 1992), pp. 63-105. See also Sider, *Culture and Class*; Georgina MacNab-de Vries and Pieter J. de Vries, *"They farmed among other things..." : Three Cape Breton Case Studies* (Sydney, 1984); and Gail R. Pool, "Anthropological Uses of History and Culture", *Acadiensis*, XVIII, 1 (Autumn 1988), pp. 226-37.

10   McKay, "The crisis of dependent development", pp. 11-13. See also Michael Clow, "Politics and uneven capitalist development: The Maritime challenge to Canadian political economy", *Studies in Political Economy*, 13 (Spring 1984), pp. 117-40. On similar issues within Quebec historiography see Catherine Des-Barats, "Agriculture within the Seigneurial Regime of Eighteenth-Century Canada: Some Thoughts on the Recent Literature", *Canadian Historical Review*, LXXIII, 1 (1992), pp. 1-29.

ness only in terms of what it is not — *pre*-capitalist, *ir*rational peasant-farmers, *un*free labour, *non*-market), then we will have registered only aberrations from a norm, an otherness which marks only some kind of failure.

One of the most striking features, however, was that rural people maintained their attachment to the land or returned (or desired to return) to the land. Some, perhaps like Anse Gordon in Charles Bruce's *The Channel Shore*, returned for very particular reasons, ones which are probably best left in the hands of novelists. Some returned because they had few other options. Others did not return, but carried those aspirations and practices to the city. Yet the strength of that vision — of maintaining the independence of a soil- or sea-based livelihood, or of straddling different economies — buttressed that society for some time. All of these essays, though in very different ways, have located something of that dream in their studies, even when its contradictions are apparent to us now. What strikes us, for example, in Neil MacNeil's memories of turn-of-the-century Cape Breton — when every man "got his livelihood from nature and did not have to work for any other man or thank any one but God for it"[11] — is how the land held the possibility of independence for these people.

Yet, as Rusty Bittermann argues in his contribution, we need to tease out the mythologized elements of the story and understand their location within rural societies. Here, we need to emphasize both the dream and its limitations. For many, striving for independence meant a complex series of arrangements, not all of which were compatible with the dream. Both Bittermann and Maynard, for all their differences in emphasis, return to the land and its importance as a basis for continuing a soil-based livelihood and a certain independence, whatever its limitations and however it was maintained. Moreover, they also demonstrate that the land and the social practices which revolved around the land, while directed at maintaining the household's place, may have undercut the desired outcome. Surely many of the peripatetic miners at Inverness, as well as many who had lost their place on the land, worked to keep that possibility of holding complete dependence on wage labour at a distance. For some, in the short term, the strategy probably succeeded, but the result may have been very different in the long term. Similarly, Newfoundland fishers struggled for independence, but in an economy so heavily influenced by foreign demand for a single staple that struggle was very often futile.[12] For the Labor Act settlers in New Brunswick, the bases for that vision had changed. Few seriously sought to engage in agricul-

---

11 Neil MacNeil, *The Highland Heart in Nova Scotia* (Toronto, 1969 [New York, 1948]), p. 52.

12 David Alexander notes that between 1884 and 1891, male employment in the fisheries fell from 60,000 to 37,000, a 38 per cent drop in only seven years. Such precarious opportunities for maintaining household independence, while not always so extreme, must surely remind us not only of the structural impediments to independence, but also whom our sources allow us to see. David Alexander, "Newfoundland's Traditional Economy and Development to 1934",

ture for their livelihood; they knew very well the limited possibilities for farming on those lots. Yet the possibility of achieving security and independence remained rooted on the land. These were people who understood the rhetoric of "the people's land" as more than a euphemism for the state's control of access to resources. Understanding that dream of some form of propertied independence holds a key to representing the history of rural peoples. And, as Bittermann observes, it will help us to grasp the importance of the "transformation of the dream" since then — one of the truly fundamental differences between rural life in the 19th-century and in late-20th-century society.

Yet, equally important here is that many were giving up the land, or at least slowly severing their relationship with it. If within the countryside there is indeed a "world we have lost", then we need to more fundamentally reconsider its basis on the land. Most of our examinations of the countryside, including most of these essays, have borrowed heavily from the conceptual terms of the social relations of the town. These are important, undoubtedly, but on their own may be inadequate. The relationship between people and the land is also a social relation, one which conditioned — and was conditioned by — other social relations; we need to reassess what access to land and resources meant to rural people not only in terms of material fulfilment but how they understood the world and their place in it. As Carolyn Merchant has demonstrated for New England, the real "revolution" in the 18th and 19th centuries was as much about changes in the land and people's relationship with the land as it was a transformation in the realm of "economy". Her work is an important critique of where we have sought to locate change.[13] Settlers brought with them a desire for independence, and North America provided the location and the possibility of finding it.[14] Individually and collectively, they drew on older cultural practices, while also creating new ones; the land allowed a particular form of independence, but was itself an object of history. We should re-examine what access to the resources of the land and the sea meant to these people, why some struggled to maintain that access, and why, whether willingly or not, many gave it up.

---

in James Hiller and Peter Neary, eds., *Newfoundland in the Nineteenth and Twentieth Centuries: essays in interpretation* (Toronto, 1980), p. 23.

13 Carolyn Merchant, *Ecological Revolutions: Nature, Science, and Gender in New England* (Chapel Hill, 1989).

14 Such a point demands a full discussion of the forced marginalization — and in the case of Newfoundland, the extinction — of the original peoples who inhabited North America before European colonization. In this region, that process was rather less a story of conquest than it was one of gradual usurpation, although for the Beothuk of Newfoundland the process mattered little. Nevertheless, a fuller examination of the settlement process in Atlantic Canada, as elsewhere, must better come to terms with the dislocation and cultural conquest of its first peoples as part of that process.

Most of our analysis of this issue stems from questions based on the abilities of households to produce: How circumscribed were the choices available to rural dwellers?[15] Wealth and poverty were as much a part of rural life as seed and bait, but what should we conclude about the importance of social stratification? Had, for some, the land become merely a cushion to the labour market, rather than the other way around? If so, had the land lost something, or were there attractions elsewhere? Did rural Atlantic Canadians experience a "consumer revolution"[16] which devalued household production and made wage labour a reasonable alternative? How central was land — or more specifically, property — to rural people's aspirations for independence? Surely part of the answer to these questions must go beyond measurable indices of wealth and production.[17] It is here, at the intersection of culture (or, to borrow Merchant's terminology, "cosmology"), markets, demography, environment and colonization, that we find the possibility for independence on the land (as well as the severe restraints) and the world views which were equally a part of rural society. It is also here that we can begin to refocus our understanding of the connections between capital, the state and rural communities.

In redirecting our attention toward the countryside, we necessarily move further away from plotting the history of dramatic change and toward the quotidian and the commonplace. We do not, however, move toward the simple and the static. The countryside seldom allows historians the luxury of great moments of insurrection which, for example, has sometimes dominated the study of working-class history. More often lacking rebellions or spectacular strikes, rural society might seem to operate at a slower, quieter pace. Yet these studies suggest a much more dynamic countryside than the one historians most often imagine. Indeed, as Erik Kristiansen's essay reminds us, the assumptions which shape the narrator's gaze — of pastoralism, simplicity, otherness — are powerful forces in shaping what we describe. We want to find in these people's lives either the "roots" of our times or some form of golden age when life was simpler and bet-

15 Rusty Bittermann, Robert MacKinnon and Graeme Wynn, "Of Inequality and Interdependence in the Nova Scotian Countryside, 1850-70", *Canadian Historical Review*, LXXIV, 1 (March 1993), pp. 1-43; and T.W. Acheson, "New Brunswick Agriculture at the End of the Colonial Era: A Reassessment", in Kris Inwood, ed., *Farm, Factory and Fortune: New Studies in the Economic History of the Maritime Provinces* (Fredericton, 1993), pp. 37-60.

16 See Carol Shammas, *The Pre-Industrial Consumer in England and America* (New York, 1990). Shammas does not use the term to describe her own work. I take the term from the debate and reviews which have ensued.

17 Recent work by Kris Inwood and Phyllis Wagg emphasizes the influence of rising incomes in the move from homespun to purchased cloth, although they too acknowledge that more may be said in terms of *"mentalité"*. See Kris Inwood and Phyllis Wagg, "The Survival of Handloom Weaving in Canada Circa 1870", *Journal of Economic History*, 53, 2 (June 1993), especially pp. 352-3.

ter. Armed with documents, we believe ourselves to be insulated from the problems Charles Bruce and Ernest Buckler grappled with. Working with our limited views, we are often fooled by the *image* of rural society; we see people on the land as just that: people on the land — that is, part of the landscape, timeless, steeped in tradition, and as unchanged as life could possibly be.

Two fundamental issues emerge: first, a recognition that the country, like the town, was many-sided; it did not always and in every way determine rural people's activities in some common and essential manner. Second, once we have recognized that the countryside, too, has a history, we must re-examine our interpretation of rural people's actions. Most particularly, we need to re-examine the social locations of those who people our stories. As social historians, when we look to the countryside our typical points of identification and categorization are much less clear, as are the aims and strategies of the participants. The challenge here is precisely how to "make sense" of what those categories refuse. In recent rural historiography, this has most often been a case of posing a precapitalist countryside versus a modernizing (and, by extension, presumably urban) world.[18] But, the essays in this collection demonstrate, getting ourselves bogged down in such a binary debate seems fruitless. So, too, does discussing "*the* transformation of the countryside", a framework which carries with it a necessary modernization where differences reflect only variations over time and place. In Atlantic Canada, we can describe "modern" capitalist agriculture as early as the late 18th century, and we can locate "everyday forms of peasant resistance" in the 1920s.[19] Such variation reflects more than local colour or interpretive differences; it reflects the material and discursive bases of a world positioned for change on a number of fronts, but where the outcome was by no means clear. There was no single countryside, no single essential type of country "folk"; it was, as Charles Bruce writes, "made up of people" — real ones, not the peasant dreams of urban historians nor the mythological progenitors of neoconservative capitalism.

Capitalism did transform the countryside — it built and destroyed communities, made and shattered dreams — but behind *it* were people making history, although, of course, not strictly under conditions of their own choice. Too much energy has been expended on demonstrating how those conditions determined what people believed. Many did resist capitalism's incursions into their way of life, their sense of dignity and fairness, and their ability to maintain some form of independence. Yet the meaning of that resistance may be misleading. Whether understood from the vantage point of the unpropertied, the poor

---

18 See Alan Kulikoff's recent summary of the debate in his *The Agrarian Origins of American Capitalism* (Charlottesville, Va., 1992), pp. 13-33. See also Winnifred Barr Rothenberg, *From Market Places to Market Society: The Transformation of Rural Massachusetts, 1750-1850* (Chicago, 1992).

19 James C. Scott, *Weapons of the Weak: Everyday Forms of Peasant Resistance* (New Haven, 1985).

smallholder or the improvement-minded farmer, the most central concern was the maintenance of the household, and more especially the patrimony.[20] In the formation of markets for goods and labour, some people responded to its possibilities by buying labour and selling goods, others by selling their labour; however they responded, whatever particular strategy a household employed, markets influenced the available options. We need to remain aware of the variety of options and responses — avoiding the knee-jerk responses involved in describing this as either resistance or market orientation — and begin to explore the contexts of that world. Even within households, market participation could express very different meanings. Men's and women's interests were sometimes different, and often quite contradictory.[21] For most women, work in their own home meant their labour was unwaged and undervalued, a reminder that one person's independence was often based on another's dependence. Surely, too, we need to examine critically how gender influenced not only the material bases of independence but also its discursive position. Reciprocal networks of exchange and kinship, as Steven Maynard's essay suggests, may have been as much rooted in gendered differences as they were shared features of communities.[22] The axes upon which we could list such variables are virtually endless. But this complexity is not just of detail, it is also of history — it is of what we have chosen to emphasize as important. Far from being unchanging, the countryside does have a history. Far from being simple, the countryside was vastly complex. Here, indeed, is the stuff of rural history: of recognizing the variable bases and possibilities which existed within what we once thought whole.

Wage labour and the land, the town and the country, and the farm and the factory seem to have been linked much more closely than we have imagined. From the perspective of the farm, wage labour and the utilization of markets for goods and labour were vital. Conversely, many industries relied heavily on that labour. Daniel Samson's description of the mines at Inverness demonstrates the

20 For a remarkably clear analysis of the family-centredness of "economic culture" in early American studies, one which emphasizes the tensions inherent within the unity of familial endeavour, see Daniel Vickers, "Competence and Competition: Economic Culture in Early America", *William and Mary Quarterly*, XLVII, 1 (January 1990), pp. 1-29.

21 See Tillotson, "The Operators Along the Coast"; Miriam Wright, "'The Smile of Modernity': The State and the Modernization of the Atlantic Canadian Fishery", M.A. Thesis, Queen's University, 1990; and Marilyn Porter, "She was Skipper of the Shore Crew: Notes on the Sexual Division of Labour in the Newfoundland Fishery", *Labour/Le Travail*, 15 (Spring 1985), pp. 105-23.

22 See also Jeanne Boydston, *Home and Work: Housework, Wages, and the Ideology of Labor in the Early Republic* (New York, 1990); and Nancy Grey Osterud, "Gender and the Transition to Capitalism in Rural America", *Agricultural History*, 67, 2 (Spring 1993), pp. 14-29.

importance of rural workers to that town's industries, and, while only a single case study, it suggests that the heavily seasonal labour demands of coal mining throughout the provincial industry were met by rural workers; more than a "problem" on the supply side of the labour market, their actions forced the hands of capital, the state and their urban co-workers. In their much broader study, Sager and Panting have described the integration of labour demands in the shipbuilding industry and the needs of petty producers in the countryside. The decline of the region's largest and most widespread secondary industry in the late 19th century must have represented the loss of a central underpinning to the rural economy and undoubtedly contributed to the dispossession of rural smallholders.[23] Yet, as important as coal mining and shipbuilding were to this region, these are only isolated industries.

We must begin to appreciate how widespread and essential this kind of labour market was to the region and how that has shaped its past. Coal mining, shipping and shipbuilding, the timber trade, the fisheries and many factories relied upon a steady supply of workers from the countryside,[24] a fact which underscores not only the complexity of the social formation but also the problems inherent in examining these people only once our sources locate them at particular worksites. Because the essays in this collection are, for the most part, only partial examinations, they can carry such an argument only so far. But together they suggest that periodizing Atlantic Canadian historiography around a transition from mercantilism to locally based competitive capitalism and then to monopoly capitalism and underdevelopment, with a parallel rural historiography, glides too easily over the continuous and central place of most of its people, across numerous economic sectors, to at least 1930. Rather, we need to rethink fundamentally how we have compartmentalized the region's social formation. In so far as these essays can demonstrate the ways rural people organized their working lives, they suggest that carving up their lives — and

---

23   Sager and Panting, *Maritime Capital*, especially pp. 192-6.

24   See, for example, Margaret E. McCallum, "Separate Spheres: the Organization of Work in a Confectionary Factory: Ganong Bros., St. Stephen, New Brunswick", *Labour/Le Travail*, 24 (Fall 1989), pp. 69-90; D.A. Muise, "The Industrial Context of Inequality: Female Participation in Nova Scotia's Paid Labour Force, 1871-1921", *Acadiensis*, XX, 2 (Spring 1991), pp. 3-31; L. Anders Sandberg, "Dependent development, labour and the Trenton Steel Works, Nova Scotia, C. 1900-1943", *Labour/Le Travail*, 28 (Fall 1991), pp. 127-62; Ginette Lafleur, "L'industrialisation et le travail rémunéré des femmes, Moncton, 1881-91", in Daniel Hickey, ed., *Moncton, 1871-1929: Changements socio-économiques dans une ville ferroviare* (Moncton, 1990), pp. 63-88; and Daniel Samson, "Family Formation in Mine and Farm Households: Pictou County, Nova Scotia, 1860-1880", paper presented at the meeting of the Canadian Historical Association, Charlottetown, June 1992.

missing the connections that they made everyday — is to misunderstand both the economy and people's place in it.

In the 1870s, Elizabeth and John Fraser, farmers at McLellan's Brook in Pictou County, Nova Scotia, regularly corresponded with Elizabeth's brother Archibald McDermid, now farming in Minnesota.[25] Describing recent events in the community and the family, both John and Elizabeth wrote of major life-events — births, deaths and marriages — as well as the general welfare of friends and relatives. John's greatest attention, however, was to economic matters. He asked his brother-in-law about market prices for farm goods in Minnesota, then detailed prices for his own crops and other farm products — what the local tanneries were paying for leather and the demand for timber at the mines and shipyards. He also discussed the local labour market; jobs were in short supply and wages had fallen, the coal mines were not hiring as much as they had a few years past, and there were only two ships being built in the area. The Frasers were not marginal backland farmers. They were producing for the market; selling their produce in the local shipbuilding and coal- mining towns, their hides to the tanners and their timber wherever they could. Yet, even for these "market-oriented" farmers, the local labour market was part of their economic life. Moreover, it also had important repercussions for their family — the lack of jobs meant their eldest son would not marry, while another son sought work in the United States; their daughter moved to the town of New Glasgow to work as a domestic, leaving Elizabeth with only the youngest daughter to help at home. Their cousins had given up the land and also moved to New Glasgow; but they had no work and were living "poor as rats" in a single room.

Such letters are a rich source for understanding the social worlds of rather ordinary 19th-century rural households; here, however, I wish only to note the breadth of forces which conditioned their well-being. For this household, "farm" issues were important, but apparently their lives were also affected by the demand for coal in the eastern United States and for ships in the English market. What is most striking about these letters is not the variety we see but the seamlessness which they felt no need to remark upon. Life and work, the farm and wage labour, were part of a package, one that extended beyond the farm to the mines and shipping enclaves across the region and for their children to Massachusetts and California. When we can see something more than a middling farm household or occupational pluralism in the lives of the Frasers, then we may begin to understand one of the most important social and economic settings of life in the 19th and early 20th centuries.

It was only with the near-complete collapse of the regional economy in the 1920s and 1930s that the economic bases of rural society were fundamentally

25 Public Archives of Nova Scotia, no. 27, vol. 93, MG 100. The collection contains nine letters written between 1868 and 1877. Most of this information comes from letters dated 23 February 1875 and 17 December 1875.

altered. And it is only to the extent of people's ultimate dependence on such forces that we can view such a movement as inevitable. That collapse reached far into the countryside. But to understand that reach we need to know much more about developments within rural society — as something integrated with, not merely articulated by, other aspects of economy and society. If we are to build a more comprehensive and illuminating historiography of the countryside, then we must attend to the many structures of rural life and the manifestations of power from the household to the state. Such issues reassert the importance for a more broadly conceived, socially situated household, in a world where the rules were changing and constraints were being removed, but where older patterns persisted. An understanding of the range of household strategies employed would suggest important bases for an understanding of the historically patterned strategies and the broader features of society — expressions of a varied and complex social geography.

There are many important issues outside the range of these essays: the effective marginalization of peoples of colour (very much a rural story), the regional features of the gendered division of labour, demography and household formation, environmental issues including land use and the resource base on which these economies emerged, and the ideologies formed within these conditions. Some of these histories have been recounted, but always in isolation and seldom with a view to exploring the connections to wider political and social contexts. It is not paradoxical that to write this history we need to shift our focus to the "unprogressive" margins of the narrative — that is, to what lies outside its logic — where we can see its limitations. What is paradoxical is that many continue to explore the countryside with the same assumptions they bring to the city, while also presuming that rural society was homogeneous and lay wholly apart. We must recognize the activities of rural people and their positions within the historically specific logics of social and economic development in Atlantic Canada over the past two hundred years. Capitalist development was significantly predicated upon the utilization of a largely rural work force, a work force composed of people who variously resisted and encouraged its demands. The countryside and its people belong at the centre of any history of economy and society in Atlantic Canada.

CONTRIBUTORS

Rusty Bittermann used to be a farm-based occupational pluralist. He has published numerous articles on 19th-century Maritime rural life and will soon publish a monograph on the Escheat movement on Prince Edward Island.

Sean T. Cadigan currently has a two-year contract to teach Canadian economic history at the Memorial University of Newfoundland. In addition, he is pursuing research for a social and economic history of St. John's, Newfoundland from 1775 to 1855.

Erik Kristiansen studied literature and social history at Dalhousie and Saint Mary's Universities in Halifax, as well as at the University of Illinois. He currently teaches English and Cultural Studies, while also serving as an Associate Editor for *New Maritimes*.

Steven Maynard has taught courses on working-class and social history at Queen's University. He has published articles on class and masculinity in *Labour/Le Travail* and *Acadiensis*. Currently he is completing a Ph.D. dissertation on the history of sexuality in turn-of-the-century Ontario.

Bill Parenteau recently completed a thesis on the political economy of the New Brunswick forest industries, with particular emphasis on the transition from a sawmilling to a pulp and paper economy in the early 20th century. His work has appeared in *Forest and Conservation History* and *Trouble in the Woods: Forest Policy and Social Conflict in Nova Scotia and New Brunswick*.

Daniel Samson is currently finishing a doctoral thesis at Queen's University on rural industries in northern Nova Scotia before 1879. When not writing, he teaches Atlantic Canadian history and grows very unimpressive "giant" pumpkins.